PREFACE

To the Most Reverend and Right Hon. R.A.K. Runcie MC, DD, the Lord Archbishop of Canterbury:

Your Grace,

We were appointed in July 1983 with the following terms of reference:

> 'To examine the strengths, insights, problems and needs of the Church's life and mission in Urban Priority Areas* and, as a result, to reflect on the challenge which God may be making to Church and Nation: and to make recommendations to appropriate bodies.' (*'The term Urban Priority Areas is used to include inner city districts and many large Corporation estates and other areas of social deprivation'.)

We must first record with sorrow the death of our colleague Sir Wilfred Burns in January 1984. He made a significant contribution to the work of the Commission in its early months.

We were not established as an ecumenical body as such, although two of us are not Anglicans. We have however paid close attention to the ecumenical dimension to the Church of England's ministry in the cities, and have received full co-operation in our work from the Roman Catholic Church, the Free Churches, the British Council of Churches, and from independent Black-led Churches.

We have held 17 Commission meetings, 5 of them residential weekends. In these meetings, we have attempted to address the total picture – the religious and secular dimensions – of contemporary urban life. We undertook much of our work in Sub-Groups, each of which examined particular issues. This meant that individual members of the Commission have concentrated more on some subjects than others. Seventy Sub-Group meetings were held in the course of our work.

Our investigations have been greatly helped by the large number of written submissions we have received in evidence. Those who submitted written evidence to us are listed in Appendix F. We thank them.

iii

We also undertook a series of visits as a Commission to particular areas in our major cities designated by the Department of the Environment for particular assistance from the Government's Urban Programme. During the course of 1984 we spent five weekends in the Dioceses of Liverpool, Newcastle and Durham, the Stepney Area of London, Birmingham, Lichfield and Coventry, and Manchester. On each of these visits, we held open public meetings (usually in about five or six scattered locations) to listen carefully to the views of local residents, Church people and others. Sub-Groups of the Commission have also paid visits to other towns and cities to pursue particular issues. A full list of the places we visited is at Appendix G.

We wish to thank those who assisted us in our work: in particular Canon John Atherton, Mr Michael Eastman, Prebendary John Gladwin, Mr Graham Howes, Canon Eric James and Mr John Chilvers (who was seconded from the Bank of England to assist us on financial and staffing matters).

Our thanks are also due to Dr Hugh McLeod and Mr Roy McCloughry who prepared context papers for the Commission, to Dr Grace Davie who undertook research work for us on the nature of belief in the urban priority areas, to Mr Gordon Heald and Mrs Rachel Rhodes of Social Surveys (Gallup Poll) Ltd for their help in mounting a survey of clergy, and to Dr Janet Birkett who took on the task of cataloguing the Commission's papers. We are particularly grateful to Miss Nikki Stacey for undertaking the formidable task of typing our report with cheerful competence. We also owe thanks to those dioceses who made comprehensive arrangements for our field visits with thoroughness and generosity.

We owe a particular debt of gratitude to our Secretary, Mr John Pearson, who was seconded to us for two years from the Department of the Environment. His contribution to the Commission's work has been beyond praise. His tireless work, his meticulous drafting and his understanding of the issues have all been of the highest order.

Our greatest debt is to the people we met in the urban priority areas, who gave us their time, hospitality and honest opinions. We hope that this report, and the action taken on it by the Church of England and other bodies, will do them justice.

We welcome Your Grace's appointment of the Reverend Patrick Dearnley as 'Archbishop's Officer for the Urban Priority Areas', to follow up our findings within the Church of England, and with other denominations and appropriate secular bodies.

Our Report is unanimous.

30th September 1985

MEMBERS OF THE COMMISSION

Sir Richard O'Brien (*Chairman*)

The Right Reverend David Sheppard
(Bishop of Liverpool)

The Right Reverend Wilfred Wood
(Bishop of Croydon)

The Reverend Alan Billings
(Vicar of St Mary's, Walkley, Sheffield and Deputy Leader,
Sheffield City Council)

David Booth
(Executive Director, BICC plc)

John Burn
(Headmaster of Longbenton High School, North Tyneside)

The Reverend Andrew Hake
(Social Development Officer, Borough of Thamesdown)

Professor A.H. Halsey
(Director of Barnett House and Fellow of Nuffield College,
Oxford)

The Reverend Dr Anthony Harvey
(Canon of Westminster)

Ron Keating
(Assistant General Secretary, National Union of Public
Employees)

Ruth McCurry
(Teacher in Hackney; Clergy wife)

Professor R.E. Pahl
(Research Professor in Sociology, University of Kent at
Canterbury)

Professor John F. Pickering
(Professor of Industrial Economics, University of Manchester
Institute of Science and Technology)

Robina Rafferty
  (Assistant Director, Catholic Housing Aid Society)
The Reverend Mano Rumalshah
  (Priest-in-charge, St George's, Southall)
Linbert Spencer
  (Chief Executive, Project Fullemploy)
Mary Sugden
  (Principal, National Institute for Social Work)
The Reverend Barry Thorley
  (Vicar of St Matthew's, Brixton)

Resource Bodies and Advisers
The Boards and Councils of the General Synod
  (represented by the Reverend Prebendary John Gladwin)
Christian Action
  (represented by the Reverend Canon Eric James)
The Evangelical Coalition for Urban Mission
  (represented by Michael Eastman)
The William Temple Foundation
  (represented by the Reverend Canon John Atherton)
John Chilvers
Graham Howes

Secretary
J.N. Pearson

CONTENTS

ix

PART IV CONCLUSION AND SUMMARY OF RECOMMENDATIONS

APPENDICES

INTRODUCTION

A serious situation has developed in the major cities of this country. This was recognised in the 1977 White Paper, 'Policy for the Inner Cities', and has been re-affirmed by senior ministers of successive governments. A number of central government measures has been taken in response. But the 1981 Census, and other official published statistics, show clearly that even if such measures are still being maintained or have not been reduced they have had little effect: things have worsened rather than improved since 1977. All the signs are that, by a vicious circle of causes and effects, the decline of the quality of life in what have been designated as 'Urban Priority Areas' is continuing, as the collapse of the West Midlands' industrial base clearly illustrates.

This is not a new situation: there have been other occasions in the last two hundred years when urban poverty has presented an acute challenge to society. But the recent dramatic reduction and redistribution of employment in the manufacturing industries around which so many of our great cities were built, and the decentralization of the new and growing industries to smaller towns and even rural areas, have speeded the process of decay in parts of once-flourishing industrial cities to an unprecedented degree. This observation does not depend on any particular theoretical or political stance. The social, political and economic factors can be described and analysed in many different ways; different sets of indicators can be used to identify poverty and deprivation. But whatever method or framework is used to establish and to present the facts, the same message of acute human misery is received.

It was in the light of the apparent gravity of this situation that the Archbishop of Canterbury in 1983 set up his Commission on Urban Priority Areas (henceforward UPAs). Our primary task was to report on the Church in these areas, which is undoubtedly having to meet challenges and difficulties, and to respond to social changes (such as the arrival in our cities of large numbers of adherents of other faiths), that are unprecedented in the history of the Church of England. But our Terms of Reference also authorized us to make our own independent enquiry into the social and economic conditions which characterize the areas in which these churches are set. The Church does not have particular competence or a distinguished record in proposing social reforms; but the Church of England has a presence in all the UPAs, and a responsibility to bring their needs to the attention of the nation. If our Report has a distinctive stance, it arises from our determination to investigate the urban situation by bringing to bear upon it those basic Christian principles of justice and compassion which we believe we share with the great majority of the people of Britain.

We decided at the outset that we must spend some time in the UPAs to see for ourselves the human reality behind the official statistics. In the course of a series of visits we saw something of the physical conditions under which people in the UPAs are living, and we listened to their own accounts and experiences at open public meetings and in smaller invited groups. We also spent many hours with representatives of local government, the police, social workers, the various caring agencies and the local churches themselves.

We have to report that we have been deeply disturbed by what we have seen and heard. We have been confronted with the human consequences of unemployment, which in some urban areas may be over 50 per cent of the labour force, and which occasionally reaches a level as high as 80 per cent – consequences which may be compounded by the effects of racial discrimination. We have seen physical decay, whether of Victorian terraced housing or of inferior system-built blocks of flats, which has in places created an environment so degrading that some people have set fire to their own homes rather than be condemned to living in them indefinitely. Social disintegration has reached a point in some areas that shop windows are boarded up, cars cannot be left on the street, residents are afraid either to go out themselves or to ask others in, and there is a pervading sense of powerlessness and despair.

Our own observations and the official statistics tell the same story. Clearly these are symptoms of something seriously wrong in our cities. Physical appearances, and the response of those affected, may vary greatly from place to place; but the underlying factors are the same: unemployment, decayed housing, sub-standard educational and medical provision, and social disintegration.

How are these conditions best communicated and understood? They may be described, quite simply, as *poverty* – 'We have three problems', a Councillor in the North-East told us: 'poverty, poverty and poverty'. Of course this is not poverty, as it is experienced in parts of the Third

World; people in Britain are not actually starving. But many residents of UPAs are deprived of what the rest of society regard as the essential minimum for a decent life; they live next door to, but have little chance to participate in a relatively affluent society; by any standards theirs is a wretched condition which none of us would wish to tolerate for ourselves or to see inflicted on others.

Poverty is at the root of *powerlessness*. Poor people in UPAs are at the mercy of fragmented and apparently unresponsive public authorities. They are trapped in housing and in environments over which they have little control. They lack the means and opportunity – which so many of us take for granted – of making choices in their lives.

One way of seeking to understand these phenomena is as signs of an evident and apparently increasing *inequality* in our society. It can of course be said that there will always be inequality, just as there will always be poverty. But there are degrees of inequality, just as there are degrees of poverty. What we have seen exceeds the limits that would be thought acceptable by most of our fellow citizens.

Another possible analysis (which we shall make some use of ourselves) is in terms of *polarization*. It is arguable that rich and poor, suburban and inner city, privileged and deprived, have been becoming more sharply separated from each other for many years, and that the impoverished minority has become increasingly cut off from the main stream of our national life.

In addition, there is undoubtedly a geographical dimension to the problem – conditions are worse overall in the north and the midlands than in the south, worse in the nineteenth century industrial cities than in York, Norwich or Bristol.

None of these methods of analysis is fully adequate; all are simply aids to understanding, to be discarded if they are found wanting. We have not committed ourselves to any of them, though we have found the concept of 'polarization' particularly useful. Indeed, the academic task of analysis may actually be a distraction from the plain message both of published statistics and of personal observation. It is our considered view that the nation is confronted by a *grave and fundamental injustice* in the UPAs. The facts are officially recognised, but the situation continues to deteriorate and requires urgent action. No adequate response is being made by government, nation or Church. There is barely even widespread public discussion. Tackling the varied and multiple problems which are seen so starkly concentrated in the UPAs (though they are also found, sometimes in an acute form, in many other parts of this country) must become a priority for Church and State. In the later part of our Report we shall spell out this conclusion in as much detail as has been permitted by the time and resources at our disposal.

However, we begin by affirming our belief that our cities are still flourishing centres of social, economic, and political life. The danger of drawing attention to their miseries is to invite pessimism about the possibilities for change. On the contrary, we confidently assert that the planned resurgence of the British city is both possible and desirable in the immediate future. Nothing we say in this report should be interpreted as evidence against our firm belief in an urban future of which all citizens may be proud. Happily, we have found grounds for encouragement and hope. We have observed an amazing variety of human responses to conditions of adversity; we have seen courage, resilience and dedicated service; we have encountered local pride and profound human loyalties. The same is true of the Church. Often threatened, often struggling for survival, often alienated from the community it seeks to serve, it is often also intensely alive, proclaiming and witnessing to the Gospel more authentically than in many parts of 'comfortable Britain'.

In obedience to our Terms of Reference it is to this Church that we attend first in our Report. But throughout we address what we have to say primarily to the Church of England as a whole, which, like the rest of the nation, seems to show far too little awareness of the acute situation which has developed at our doorstep. We call on Christians throughout this country to listen to the voices of our neighbours who live in the UPAs, to receive the distinctive contribution that they (not least the black people among them) can make to our common life, and to set an example to the nation by making our support of and solidarity with them a high priority in our policies, our actions and our prayers.

Part I
The Challenge . . .

i   In the first part of our Report, our purpose is to describe the
     urban priority areas. In Chapter 1, we view them primarily from
     a secular standpoint; in Chapter 2 we then consider the
     relationship between the Church of England and the city. This
     second Chapter also contains some major findings from a survey
     of clergy we commissioned, and the results of a separate review
     of denominational patterns and ecumenical co-operation in
     selected areas.

ii   In Chapter 3 we reflect on the implications of the Christian
     Gospel for the challenge of the UPAs. This Chapter provides a
     theological and moral perspective which forms the basis for the
     recommendations contained in Parts II and III of our
     Report.

Chapter 1

URBAN PRIORITY AREAS

'It is difficult to avoid the conclusion that one is living in an area that is being . . . treated with hostility by the rest of society'
(Vicar in Greater Manchester) *

1.1   Urban life increasingly dominates human society. In the century of industrial development from 1831 to 1931 the percentage of the British population living in areas classified as urban rose from 34 to 80, and now stands at 90 per cent. The future of humanity, on the projections of experts, seems to be ever more urban. If past trends continue to the year 2000, Mexico City might have 31 million inhabitants, Sao Paulo 26 million, Tokyo 24 million, and New York 23 million. The population of the world, now rather less than 5 billion, may double to over 10 billion in 2050. By that time the European Community will constitute less than 5 per cent of the world's population. Human multiplication is mostly beyond Europe in the poorer continents of Asia, Latin America, and Africa, and within these areas the cities are growing at twice the general rate.

1.2   For the world as a whole, in quantitative terms, the urban picture is the opposite of decline. The recent history of the traditional city in Britain, however, is largely one of economic, physical and social decay. London in Victorian times was the leading city of the world: but it had fallen to fourth place in the population league by 1975, and will be below twenty-fifth by the end of the century. People and jobs in the 1960s and 1970s have been decentralized to smaller towns and suburbs. Our view of the city in Britain is derived from the official statistics and from listening to the people we have visited in the urban priority areas; areas from which people and wealth depart and in which poverty and powerlessness remain. Fact and opinion are intermingled in all interpretations. We want to distinguish between quality and quantity,

---

* These quotations in the first three Parts of our report are taken from the evidence – written and oral – that we received.

3

assuming that growth or decline of urban populations implies no necessary improvement or deterioration in welfare. But in fact, though there are exceptions and variations, the dominant pattern is one of districts in and around British conurbations and cities where both quantity and quality of life are in decline. These essentially are what we shall define as the urban priority areas (UPAs).

1.3   We intend to try to discern, and even prescribe for, the future. First, however, we are conscious of historical paradox. The city has always both challenged and threatened. Jeremiah called the people of God in exile 'to seek the welfare of the city' even though the reference was to Babylon with all its connotations of evil. The city in human history is synonymous with civilisation: yet now we investigate it as a point of breakdown of Christian society. Civicism is the name of the principle that all citizens have equal rights and duties: yet urban priority areas are a symbol of contemporary inequality.

1.4   The British city has nurtured freedom, opportunity, democratic government and civic pride. Yet, in our search for an objective description of contemporary urban conditions, we are aware of the strong thread of anti-urban sentiment which runs through British cultural history. In her review of the literature of urban sociology, Ruth Glass pointed out that British antipathy to the city was already known to the Romans.[1] By contrast with Continental Europe and even Scotland, English preference for the country seat, as the fount of civility and power, has endured through the centuries. We cannot elaborate these persistent peculiarities here. We must, however, note that there was a re-emphasis of this ancient ambivalence following the rapid growth of towns in the nineteenth century. For example, Charles Dickens, in *Bleak House*, contrasts the outlook of Sir Leicester Dedlock from his Lincolnshire estate with the view of Jo, the young street sweeper from the East End of London. Sir Leicester gazes from the great drawing room 'down the long perspective of stately oaks, rooted for ages in the green ground which has never known ploughshare . . .'. Jo inhabits a dilapidated street 'which has bred a crowd of foul existence that crawls in and out of gaps in walls and boards; and coils itself to sleep, in maggot numbers where the rain drips in; and comes and goes, fetching and carrying fever, and sowing more evil in its every footprint than . . . all the fine gentlemen in office . . . shall set right in five hundred years – though born expressly to do it.'

1.5   Descriptions like this, of human selfishness, loneliness, squalor and depravity are the stock-in-trade of secular accounts of the British industrial city. They invite rural remedies. Utopias and model communities were planned and built by nineteenth-century reformers whose main strategy was to escape the menace of the city. Bournville, Saltaire, and Port Sunlight are monuments to this impulse. Ebenezer Howard, the inventor of the garden city, is its patron, Letchworth and the New Towns its twentieth-century progeny, and the 1984 Liverpool International Garden Festival its most recent baptism.

1.6 The Church of England was adapted for a thousand years to agrarian society. We cannot therefore be surprised to find the Church as a bearer of rural nostalgia. The explosion of the industrial town in the nineteenth century was a difficult challenge to it from the outset, presenting the city to the Church in ambiguous and often lurid light. An urban working class rapidly coming to numerical domination of the nation was as unfamiliar to Church mission as it was threatening to secular authority. Accordingly the British version of Christianity has shared the secular ambivalence: it carries the same tension between the evil temptation of Sodom and Gomorrah and the wholeness of the City of God, between imprisonment in Babylon and the promise of the New Jerusalem. For example, the title of a book by the Reverend Henry Solly, published in 1884, expresses a dilemma of sentiment which has run throughout the subsequent century – *Rehousing of the Industrial Classes: or Village Communities versus Town Rookeries.* For Solly, many people in the inner city were 'debased or spirit-broken, hapless victims of an un-Christian civilisation'.

1.7 Even in the great movements of Christian socialism, municipal reform and university settlements in which Christian action was so powerfully mobilised a hundred years ago, there was an anti-urban, pro-rural, bias. In effect, the aim of Arnold Toynbee, Samuel Barnett and the founders of Toynbee Hall was to link the classes together and provide a kind of resident gentry in the inner city. No-one could have been more aware of Disraeli's two nations than Canon Barnett.[2] Christian action in those days did not seek economic equality, but it did ardently desire social integration. It had behind it a vision of unity: a socialism of character as contrasted with the individualism of selfishness. The mission of Christians to the city in the 1880s is an invitation to us a hundred years later to answer the same challenge of increasing inequality and social disintegration which our predecessors so clearly saw and so vigorously met. They turned resolutely to what Henrietta Barnett called *Practicable Socialism.* Today we seek a new vocabulary and a new mission to express renewed faith in the city.

5

1.8   When the Barnetts arrived at St Jude's in Whitechapel (described by the then Bishop of London as the worst parish in his diocese 'inhabited mainly by a criminal population, and one which has, I fear, been much corrupted by doles'), they found the church unserved by curate, choir or officials. 'It was empty, dirty, and unwarmed. The schools were closed, the schoolrooms all but devoid of furniture, the parish organization nil; no Mothers' Meeting, no Sunday School, no communicants' class, no library, no guilds, no music, no classes, nothing alive. Around this barren empty shell surged the people, here today, gone tomorrow. Thieves and worse, receivers of stolen goods, hawkers, casual dock labourers, every sort of unskilled low-class cadger congregated in the parish. There was an Irish quarter and a Jews' quarter, while whole streets were given over to the hangers-on of a vicious population, people whose conduct was brutal, whose ideal was idleness, whose habits were disgusting, and among whom goodness was laughed at, the honest man and the right-living woman being scorned as impracticable.'[3]

1.9   We quote these descriptions not to announce our own prior commitment to any particular programme of action and certainly not to praise or to blame the adherence of some nineteenth-century Christians to the principles of the Charity Organisation Society. Rather we want to make it clear that contemporary description has to be put into an historical context. As Ruth Glass remarked, for the English 'the town was but a station on the journey to social status symbolised by the country seat. It was not, as in other societies, the home of reason and intellect, a symbol of civic pride, but merely a place of new resources for the impoverished landed upper classes, and one where manufacturers and merchants could make money to buy their ticket of admission into the polite circle of the shires.'[4] While we would also wish to recognise the positive urban enthusiasm as well as the rural rejections of our forebears to an extent which Mrs Glass did not acknowledge, our description below of the movement from the cities which continues in the 1980s is sadly but clearly continuous with the attitudes of the past. We shall argue in the end that these trends add up to a pattern warranting the label of polarization in a new, comprehensive and intractable form.

1.10   With or without reluctance, Britain in the twentieth century has been an urban country. The classic logic of industrial development entails urbanization. Britain followed this logic in the nineteenth century so that by 1900 one-tenth of its territory and over three-quarters of its people were administratively classified as urban. In the same process, the transformation of an agrarian into an industrial society left less than one-tenth of the working population in agriculture – a small minority which has been further reduced to miniscule proportions (3 per cent) in our own time. Indeed this rapid civic evolution has effectively destroyed the traditional separation of town and country. Urban and rural settlements have mingled. Increasing proportions of twentieth-century Britons have become commuters. There has been a vast increase in private transport: in 1904 the number of privately licensed cars and vans was 8,465; even in the late 1940s it was less than two million; now it is over 17 million. The private car and the privately-owned and occupied house are integral to the progressive urban development of Britain in the twentieth century.

1.11   Since the inter-war period, and especially in the 1950s and 1960s, people have been moving away from the industrial conurbations to the smaller towns, suburbs and less densely populated areas. Taking 25 or more people per hectare (625 people per square mile) as an urban density, there were 24 million urban Britons out of 45 million in 1931, and 27 million out of 54 million in 1971. But if 1.5 to 25 persons per hectare denotes a suburban density, then the number of suburbanites rose from 15 million to 21 million in the same period. The trend continued in the 1970s, raising the suburban population from 39 per cent to 43 per cent between 1971 and 1981 at the expense of the densely populated cities.

1.12   Another indication of the transformation from nineteenth-century urbanization to twentieth-century suburbanization is that between 1961 and 1974 the metropolitan counties and Greater London lost 5.4 per cent of their people, while the rest of Great Britain had a population increase of 12.8 per cent. Nevertheless, the seven great conurbations (Tyne and Wear, South Yorkshire, West Yorkshire, Greater Manchester, Merseyside, West Midlands, and Greater London) remain demographically dominant, housing about one-third of the population on less than 3 per cent of the total land area. If not necessarily for ever the city and its discontents are still with us.

1.13   To describe the pattern of urban growth and dispersal is relatively simple. To explain it is far more complicated. Obviously urbanization was closely linked to industrialization. Migration from a rural to an urban economy has been the central force of population movements in the modern age. The Anglo-Saxon countries led it in the nineteenth century, just as they have been leading the counter-trend towards suburbanization in the period since the Second World War. The pull of jobs and opportunities was strong for at least a century-and-a-half. Urban industry attracted more industry. The city became the magnet for human populations all over the industrializing world. These dramatic population movements of the nineteenth century brought with them what came to be called 'the inner city problem'. We have referred to its recognition in Britain a hundred years ago. It was a complex problem of creating the bricks and mortar, the sanitary services, the whole physical basis of an urban civilization for people lacking urban experience and faced with long hours and low pay in an often insecure labour market. Looking back we can now see more clearly the two redeeming features of an otherwise grim urban scene – a buoyant economy and widespread political hope.

1.14 Today the metaphor of the magnet is misleading. To be sure, the city centres remain as a focus for commerce and trade, with many new shopping centres and precincts having been developed in recent years. There are also protected pockets of prosperous material life in parts of the inner cities. And there are city jobs for qualified commuters. But for the most part opportunities for jobs, for housing and for the desired amenities of social services, shopping, schools, and leisure have shifted out of the industrial city. Migration has been selectively reversed, and the inner city is increasingly the territory of those left behind in the scramble for comfortable survival. In part, the reversed movement is the result of deliberate public action. As a nation, we set about clearing slums and redeveloping the old centres of the industrial conurbations with considerable vigour in the 1950s and 1960s. Governments encouraged industrial relocation and population 'overspill'. The New and Expanded Towns were an example of earnest and successful social engineering.

1.15 These developments of public planning and private choice can now be seen to have proceeded successfully until the post-war period ended in the mid-nineteen seventies. Indeed a national conception of advanced industrial or post-industrial Britain had been taking shape. It was an idea of a future which blended the perceived advantages of town and country, a vision of a national spread of people, workplaces, homes and services which synthesised traditional rural nostalgia with the advantages of modern urban amenity. A process of decentralising from the congested central areas of the industrial conurbations would both invigorate the smaller towns and rural areas and also permit some development of the inner city at the preferred lower densities of a

8

society with vastly improved communications. And the patterns of work, life and leisure would be integrated with matching location of houses, jobs, training and leisure facilities.

1.16 There is in the 1980s a rich, attractive, employed and well-housed Britain centred on a broad swathe of fringe areas, suburbs, small towns and villages stretching from Dorset to East Anglia. It is not a simple story of economic decline and physical decay in the inner city. It is a more complex story of mismatch between people, skills, housing and jobs which planning failed to overcome and the economic recessions of the later 1970s exposed and exacerbated. Indeed 'success' in the 1950s and 1960s in some cases bequeathed 'inner city' conditions to outlying council estates surrounded by open fields.

1.17 What are now called urban priority areas are districts of specially disadvantaged character. They are places which suffer from economic decline, physical decay, and social disintegration. These factors interlock and together they describe multiple and relative deprivation. Much statistical labour can accordingly be spent in deciding which places are the most deprived or afflicted. Different authorities produce slightly different lists of the 'worst places': but there is essential accord about the typical UPA – it is an old port or manufacturing area connected to an outmoded staple industrial process. It may be at the centre of a conurbation like Hackney, or it may be spatially displaced from the inner city as a corporation estate on the outskirts, like Kirkby to the east of Liverpool, or Killingworth outside Newcastle. But whatever its unique features, it will exhibit the three kinds of blight – economic, physical, and social – which are essential to the definition. Such is the UPA, constituting a different Britain, whose people are prevented from entering fully into the mainstream of the normal life of the nation.

The Structure of Inequality

1.18 This brief definition captures only a small part of the larger and more detailed picture of places and discussions with people which members of the Commission now carry, in our memories, and in the voluminous files of evidence sent to us from the urban priority areas. We know that in attempting a statistical summary, we lose a great deal of the character of the human experience we are trying to describe and that statistical measurement can easily substitute precision for more complex truth. The conclusions we shall draw are formed above all by our direct experience of the UPAs; and behind the simplifying

9

arithmetic there is always the reality that even so small a territory as a parish is likely to cover more than one unique human settlement.

1.19   These cautions notwithstanding, we can put forward a confident and melancholy generalization – that the UPAs are places of severe and increasing deprivation. Economic decline, physical decay, and social disintegration are the three afflictions which denote the poverty of people and places. They are recognised by government for purposes of policy and resource allocation, in the way shown in Figure 1.1. The marked places are essentially identified by the Department of the Environment using six indicators of deprivation. By 'indicator' we neither assume nor imply any causal relation.

1.20   One of the indicators is ethnicity, and we must remark that the fact that ethnic origins can be used to indicate deprivation seems to us to be a deplorable comment on the society in which we live. The ethnic composition of the British cities and the UPAs is of crucial significance to our report. The high tide of immigration ended in the 1960s, bequeathing to Britain a small minority of people with African, West Indian and Asian antecedents – some four per cent – who are permanent British citizens. But members of these minority ethnic groups are not evenly scattered throughout the land. They are heavily concentrated in some conurbations, in the UPAs, in poorly paid jobs, bad housing and unemployment. They are people who carry a disproportionate share of the burden of adapting to the recent economic recession and industrial reorganisation in Britain.

1.21   The indicators of deprivation used in defining UPAs are:
1.   Unemployment
2.   Old people living alone
3.   Single-parent families
4.   Ethnicity: proportion in households with New Commonwealth or Pakistan-born head
5.   Overcrowding of homes
6.   Homes lacking basic amenities

1.22   The hard core of UPAs which have been designated as the Partnership areas and Programme authorities receive the major share of the government's Urban Programme funding (£224 million out of £338 million in 1984-85). We discuss this aspect of inner city policy in Chapter 8. The technicalities of identification need not concern us here except to note three points. First, our visits to UPAs have made us aware of more than six dimensions of poverty and inequality. Second, more

FIGURE 1.1
LOCATION OF SELECTED URBAN INITIATIVES
(As at November 1984)

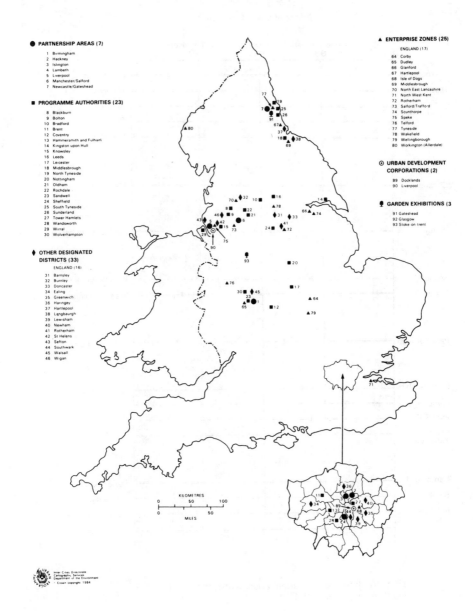

FIGURE 1.2

Some Standardized Mortality Statistics 1981 by District Health Authority

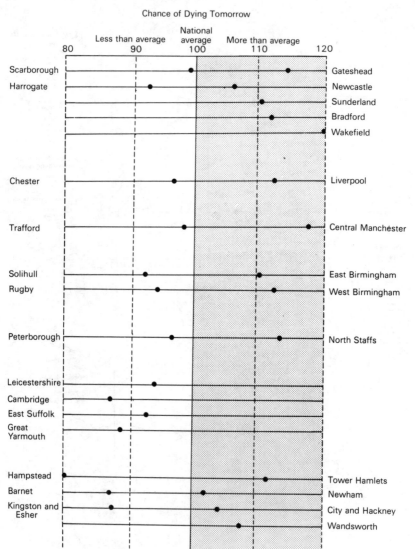

Chance of Dying Tomorrow

Source: OPCS Vital Statistics series, Local Authorities and
Health Authorities, 1981.

elaborate and sophisticated measures have since been developed in studies funded by the Economic and Social Research Council.[5] Third, the inclusion of the fourth and sixth (and perhaps the fifth) indicator may often serve to underestimate the deprivation of peripheral council estates like Killingworth or Kirkby because post-war estates are not usually bereft of the basic amenities of baths and indoor lavatories, and many do not include ethnic minorities.

1.23   The nature of the inequality which burdens the UPAs can be elaborated in many different ways. UPAs shelter disproportionate numbers of vulnerable people – the unemployed, the unskilled, the uneducated, the sick, the old, and the disadvantaged minority ethnic groups. They are places which suffer conspicuously from low income, dependence on state bureaucracies and social security, ill health, crime, family breakdown and homelessness. The sombre statistics of all these conditions provide the details of the map of inequality.

1.24   In other words, there is unequal spatial distribution of opportunities to share in the life which society has to offer. Statistics of mortality (death rates) and morbidity (illness rates) are, quite literally, indicators of life-chances. The UPAs can be shown on such measures to be places where British life is most tenuous and difficult. The pattern is illustrated in Figure 1.2 which shows the stark geography of the likelihood of dying tomorrow. On the right-hand side are UPAs like Gateshead or Tower Hamlets. On the left-hand side are the prosperous suburbs, towns and rural areas around the inner cities. The rates are standardized, meaning that they are adjusted to take account of age and sex. Obviously death rates are higher for older people: they are also higher for men than women because women on average live longer. Standardization allows Gateshead to be compared for mortality with Scarborough taking account of these differences. The comparison is then of standardized mortality rates for adults where 100 is the average for the whole nation, higher numbers represent higher risks of death, lower numbers indicate safer, more protected populations. The pattern is clear: life chances are strongly associated with residence in comfortable 'arcadian' Britain. Thus to describe UPAs is to draw a spatially systematic picture of inequality before the grave. The people of the urban priority areas are less healthy and less well cared for in all respects. Not only do people in the inner cities do badly in relation to national averages; they also fare notably worse than their more immediate neighbours in the outer parts of conurbations and in the regions that surround them. There is a gradient of material advantage running upwards from the UPAs to the fringe areas to which the fortunate are encouraged and aspire to move.

Economic Decline

1.25   Unemployment rates are the obvious monitor of urban economic decline. Figure 1.3 shows unemployment in 1981, but this has increased subsequently. Many inner cities have been losing their working population to middle Britain, in some cases since the 1920s and 1930s, in other cases only markedly since the 1960s. Supply and demand of labour have become unbalanced with the unskilled, unqualified, elderly and disadvantaged left behind in the areas of heaviest unemployment. Moreover the shift from manufacturing to service industry has reduced full-time male employment even if it has created more part-time jobs for women. The movement of people from the inner cities reflected economic decline and a changing occupational structure. It is part of the gradual reduction in numbers of the urban working class which is one of the deep transformations of twentieth century Britain. It is also a consequence of deliberate planning – the clearing of slums, the development of roads and communications, and the provision of inducements to industrial location or re-location away from the traditional urban areas. And it is further amplified by individual search for better houses in pleasanter places with more space and superior amenities elsewhere. Migration is selective. It is the younger men or couples, with more skill, more confidence and higher incomes, who are most likely to move out. It is the old and the poor, the unskilled, the single-parent families, the sick, and the unemployed who have difficulty in finding shelter elsewhere who are especially likely to be found in the UPAs.

1.26   The peripheral council estates are a special case of economic decline. In the 1950s and 1960s they were new centres of hope for those who were moving from inner-city slums and who found work in the expanding suburban factories which were producing cars, clothes, food and consumer durables for the prosperous mass markets of the post-war period. Now they are Britain's 'forgotten areas of deprivation',[6] the displaced fragments of inner-city decline. They typically experience unemployment levels of three times the national average as the suburban factories have contracted or closed. With 30-40 per cent or more unemployed they have become local subsistence economies, utterly dependent on state benefits. Few families have cars and public transport is poor. The estates therefore become cut off from employment opportunities elsewhere, inhabited by workers without

14

FIGURE 1.3
INNER AREAS - 1981

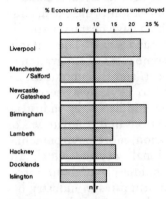

UNEMPLOYMENT

% Economically active persons unemployed

0 5 10 15 20 25 %

Liverpool

Manchester / Salford

Newcastle / Gateshead

Birmingham

Lambeth

Hackney

Docklands

Islington

n|r

The depth of each bar is proportional to the economically active population living in each Inner Area: hence the area of each bar is proportional to the number of people unemployed (i.e. scale of the problem)

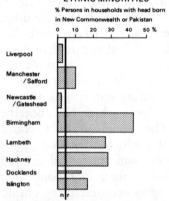

ETHNIC MINORITIES

% Persons in households with head born in New Commonwealth or Pakistan

0 10 20 30 40 50 %

Liverpool

Manchester / Salford

Newcastle / Gateshead

Birmingham

Lambeth

Hackney

Docklands

Islington

n|r

The depth of each bar is proportional to the population living in each Inner Area: hence the area of each bar is proportional to the population in households with the head born in the New Commonwealth or Pakistan.
The 1981 Census recorded only those black and Asian people in families whose head had been born overseas. The proportions do not therefore take into account the descendants of British-born black or Asian people in cities such as Liverpool, whose black population has been established for centuries.

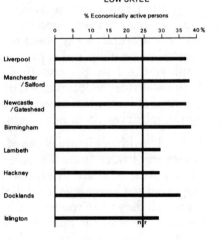

UNEMPLOYMENT 16—19 YEAR OLD MALES

% Economically active 16—19 year old males

0 5 10 15 20 25 30 35 40%

Liverpool

Manchester / Salford

Newcastle / Gateshead

Birmingham

Lambeth

Hackney

Docklands

Islington

n|r

LOW SKILL

% Economically active persons

0 5 10 15 20 25 30 35 40%

Liverpool

Manchester / Salford

Newcastle / Gateshead

Birmingham

Lambeth

Hackney

Docklands

Islington

n|r

Note: England and Wales National rate n|r
Source: 1981 Census

1981 CENSUS
Inner Cities Directorate
Cartographic Services
Department of the Environment
© Crown copyright 1983

15

jobs and with too little money even to generate an informal economy of home maintenance and local services.

1.27 The loss of manufacturing jobs from the major cities was particularly dramatic during the 1960s: 50 per cent in Greater London since 1960, 40 per cent in the other main conurbations. And the decline has been concentrated in the central areas which have characteristically lost jobs at a higher rate than the conurbations as a whole. The lost jobs are a result in some cases of plant closure, in some cases of emigration to other sites. With developments in transport and communications, manufacturing enterprises are no longer tied to the railway terminals and the docks which had rooted them in the middle of the industrial cities. They are more able to choose their locations in the new towns or other sites which offer more space for expansion, more environmental amenities, and more cultural and professional services which are attractive to their increasingly skilled and middle-class labour force. The drop in manufacturing employment opportunities in industry has been mitigated in some cases by an increase in the service industries and commerce.

1.28 An excellent report on employment trends by Stephen Fothergill and his associates stresses two factors. 'The first is the decline in the number of workers per unit of factory floorspace. This appears to result from the increasing capital intensity of production' leading to 'large job losses on existing factory floorspace in all areas. The second national economic trend is the increase in industry's demand for floorspace. Most of this increase – and the jobs that go with it – occurs in small towns and rural areas' because, it is argued, 'there are physical constraints on industrial expansion in cities. Thus cities' manufacturing employment falls because they get little new factory building to compensate for job losses on existing floorspace, whereas in small towns and rural areas the loss of jobs on existing floorspace is more than offset by the jobs created in new factories and factory extensions.'[7]

1.29 The urban picture is one of decline and the new white-collar jobs attract employees from the outer rings rather than the people of the central areas who are disproportionately unskilled or, in many cases, employed at a lower level of skill than that which they once deployed or for which they were trained. Like those of the outer estates, figures for the inner areas of the industrial conurbations show rates of unemployment in some cases nearly three times the national average. The Scarman enquiry into the Brixton riots of 1981, for instance, reported an estimate of 55 per cent of black youths under nineteen unemployed compared with a national rate for that age group of under 20 per cent.[8]

1.30   As the Brixton figures for black young people suggest, unemployment is correlated with the characteristics of the workforce, particularly age, colour and skill (Figure 1.3). Younger people are especially vulnerable in Lambeth and in other areas where the demand for labour is falling. National legislation and union pressure tend to mean that existing jobs are protected so that new entrants to the labour market, and those who change jobs, suffer most from the declining opportunities for work. Young people who are black are further disadvantaged in the search for jobs through racial discrimination.

1.31   The characteristics of people looking for work are, of course, only part of the explanation of unemployment. The main cause is the lack of jobs. We will cite more recent figures in Chapter 9, but even in the early 1970s a survey of eighteen-year olds in one district of Merseyside, carried out in the course of the Liverpool inner area study, showed a higher proportion of boys unemployed and a lower proportion entering jobs with apprentice training than in Liverpool as a whole or, more markedly, than in the north-west region. Demand for apprenticeships far exceeds the supply; a couple of local firms received between fifty and one hundred applications for each apprenticeship place offered in 1980.[9] Unemployment, as elsewhere, was concentrated among the least skilled. Fewer of the young unemployed had stayed at school beyond the statutory leaving age, fewer had passed examinations, and fewer had any further education than had those in work. Black youths were especially likely to be unemployed, and nearly half of all those out of work had fathers who were themselves unemployed, living away from home, or dead.

1.32   Further analysis of the significance of lack of skill among workers and the loss of low-skilled jobs reveals nearly 40 per cent or unemployment among the low skilled in the inner areas in Birmingham, Tyneside, Manchester, and Liverpool in 1981 when the national average for the low skilled was 25 per cent, and for all workers under 10 per cent.[10]

1.33   The disappearance of jobs from the inner areas means additional costs in money and time if work is to be found further afield. The Liverpool inner area study showed car ownership to be low; only 18 per cent of men travelling to work by car, compared with 24 per cent in the city as a whole. Eighty-three per cent of the working population worked within the City of Liverpool, and most of those working outside the area had access to a car.[11] The social area analysis in Liverpool distinguished a ring of especially high unemployment immediately around the city centre. This district had a population of 70,000 people living in the inner council estates and the worst rooming houses. Sixty per cent of household heads were semi-skilled or unskilled: unemployment was twice the average for the city and educational achievement far lower.[12]

Physical Decay

1.34   To describe UPAs is to write of squalor and dilapidation. Grey walls, littered streets, boarded-up windows, graffiti, demolition and debris are the drearily standard features of the districts and parishes with which we are concerned.

1.35   One of the most obvious features of the UPAs is their physical dilapidation as measured by housing conditions. Department of the Environment figures based on the 1981 Census for the inner areas of the Partnership authorities and London's Docklands show all of them with far higher than national levels of crowding (shown by the vertical black line) defined as more than one person per room (Figure 1.4). Birmingham was the worst area with 12 per cent of households overcrowded – roughly four times the national rate – but all of the other areas had at least twice the national average. Liverpool, Hackney and Islington suffered most from lack of basic amenities, with nearly 12 per cent of households in this state compared with just over 4 per cent for the country as a whole, but all the other areas except two were far above the average. The dwellings in the inner cities are older than elsewhere. Roughly one-quarter of England's houses were built before 1919, but the proportion in the inner areas ranged from 40 to 60 per cent in 1977.[13]

1.36   The history of the labour market and of public housing policy lies behind these contemporary inequalities. The inner cities of today are the industrial centres of the last century. Nineteenth century industrialisation required rapidly built housing on a large scale to accommodate the workforce. Much of it was sub-standard. The development of public transport permitted the middle classes to begin the move to the suburbs, in search of green space and fresh air, but the city remained the focus for employment. Rich and poor alike rented their accommodation; in 1914 only 10 per cent of the population were home-owners. The inter-war period saw a large council building

FIGURE 1.4
INNER AREAS - 1981

1. OVERCROWDING

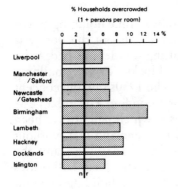

% Households overcrowded
(1 + persons per room)

2. LACKING EXCLUSIVE USE OF BASIC AMENITIES

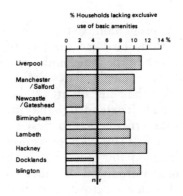

% Households lacking exclusive
use of basic amenities

3. SINGLE PARENT HOUSEHOLDS

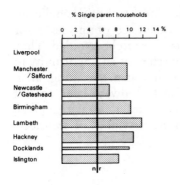

% Single parent households

4. PENSIONERS LIVING ALONE

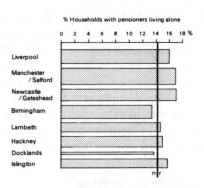

% Households with pensioners living alone

The depth of each bar is proportional to the number of households in each Inner Area: hence the area of each bar is proportional to the number of households — 1. Overcrowded 2. Lacking amenities 3. With single parents. 4. With pensioners living alone (i.e. scale of the problems)

Note: England and Wales National rate n|r
Source: 1981 Census

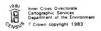

Inner Cities Directorate
Cartographic Services
Department of the Environment
© Crown copyright 1983

programme in industrial cities such as Birmingham and Manchester, and a growth of owner-occupation in the suburbs, particularly in outer London and the Home Counties. In 1945, however, only 25 per cent of the population were owner-occupiers and 10 per cent council tenants. The remainder rented from a private landlord. By 1985 owner occupation had risen to the historically unprecedented level of 63 per cent.

1.37   The programme to repair the results of war-time bombing and to clear the slums changed the face of the inner cities in the post-war period. Much of the nineteenth-century housing was demolished, to be replaced by council estates, often tower blocks. Private building continued in the outer suburbs and beyond. The 1950s saw the concept of the green belt extended to the cities outside London. The great post-war housing crusade was to clear the slums – which had always been overcrowded. If this were to be done, and new demand met, without encroaching on the green belt, urban densities had to rise and the government introduced subsidies whereby grants to local authorities increased with each storey over five, leading to the building of point blocks of up to 22 storeys. Doubts were being raised about the outer estates, which had become single-class communities, and the emphasis moved to 'mixed developments', i.e. mixed housing for a mixed population.

1.38   Though divided as to its social merits, local authorities believed that high building was an inescapable consequence of the need for higher densities if the outer overspill estates were to be avoided. They were welcomed by many, including the Churches, as an opportunity to preserve communities within the inner city rather than 'decanting' them to the outer boundaries. But tenant opinion had always been against them, preferring the traditional urban terrace, preferably with a patch of garden. In Britain 'high-rise' is now almost a symbol of architect-designed and system-built modern slums.

Social Disintegration
1.39   The people of the UPAs are not only typically living on lower incomes in poorer housing than people elsewhere but are also exposed to more difficult social relations. Vandalism is rife. Crime rates, or at least reported crimes, have been rising since mid-century, and bear particularly hard on people living in the districts where poverty and deprivation are concentrated. According to the British Crime Survey, robbery victims are more likely to live in the inner city, and burglary

risk in the inner city is double that of the rest of the conurbation, and five times that of the areas outside the conurbations.

1.40   The UPAs are shown in the Department of the Environment (DoE) analysis of the 1981 Census to have higher than the national proportion of single-parent families and of old persons living alone (Figure 1.4). In answers to our own survey of clergy in 1985, those serving in UPA parishes put greater emphasis than their non-UPA colleagues on the social problems of marriage breakdown, burglary, mugging, rape, violence, vandalism, hostility to the police, and a general frailty of civil order.

1.41   The six DoE indicators of deprivation include three which can reasonably serve as markers of social disintegration. They are the proportion of households which are overcrowded, headed by a single parent or pensioners living alone. The state of the inner cities in these three respects in 1981 is shown in Figure 1.4. In each case, again, the national rate is shown by a heavy vertical line. The UPA inner city districts have overcrowding rates which are typically more than twice the national average, particularly in London and Birmingham. The inner areas have relatively high proportions of pensioners who live alone. As to the proportion of households headed by a single parent, Birmingham, Hackney and Lambeth have twice their share by the norms of the country as a whole.

1.42   A statistical portrait of UPAs thus becomes eventually an elaborate picture of inequality. In the foreground appear the shabby streets, neglected houses and sordid demolition sites of the inner city, in the middle ground the vandalised public spaces of the peripheral estates, while in the background are the green and wooded suburbs of middle Britain. The UPAs lie at the centre of an unequal society, their poverty obscured by the busy shopping precincts of mass consumption, their bare subsistence of dole and supplementary benefit existing alongside material opulence. The statistical detail of the portrait can be turned into a simple bold sketch. The UPAs can be divided between their inner city and peripheral variants and then compared with the most advantaged areas of middle Britain (typically located just beyond the boundaries of the urban agglomerations), with the rest of Britain, including the smaller and the less blighted towns and cities, in between. And the comparison can be made in terms of a composite index of many measures of economic and social advantage and disadvantage[14] of which we have noted six as the DoE indicators.

1.43   The most recent studies of the Economic and Social Research Council offer the materials for such a sketch and it appears in Table 1.1. The measures include things like the proportion of people unemployed (negative), in professional jobs (positive), the infant mortality rate, the proportion of owner-occupiers, car owners and many other manifestations of prosperity or poverty. Column 1 of Table 1.1 shows that there is a gradient of advantage ascending from the UPAs to the fringe areas. For example, compared with the country as a whole, inner Birmingham has an average score on a large range of measures of social advantage which places it down among the five per cent most deprived places in Britain.

TABLE 1.1

Inner City Polarization

Type of Area	(1) Advantage and Deprivation Index	(2) Population Change 1971-81
Metropolitan Inner Cities		
Inner Birmingham	−2.37	−19.3
Inner Manchester	−1.77	−25.53
Peripheral Council Estates		
Knowsley	−1.36	−15.3
Other Old City Centres		
Inner Derby	−1.97	−20.1
Other Old Industrial Urban Areas		
Outer Derby	0.58	+ 7.4
Rest of Greater Manchester	0.67	+ 0.37
Rest of Outer London	1.42	− 9.0
Fringe Areas		
West Midlands South Fringe	1.43	+16.6
Mersey North Fringe	1.22	+17.1
Manchester South Fringe	1.29	+ 5.3
London South Fringe	2.32	− 3.8

Two Nations Recreated?

1.44   We are left in no doubt as to the place of the UPAs in an unequal Britain. But finally we must attempt to discern the direction of movement of British society. Though the quality of life in the inner city improved relatively in the period from the Second World War up to the mid-1970s, the more recent history has been one of growing inequality –in life chances, income, housing, education, public services, and the general level of civic amenity. Moreover, and more alarming, the migration of people and the movement of capital, employment opportunities, private enterprise, and voluntary effort is increasingly away from the UPA districts to the more sylvan and salubrious areas of the South and East, particularly the M4 corridor and the small towns and villages from the South Coast skirting the inner boroughs of the metropolis and stretching out to the eastern seaboard of Essex and Suffolk.

1.45   To discover the movement of these inequalities over time, we can measure the rise or fall of population in the UPAs between 1971 and 1981. This is column 2 of Table 1.1. Column 1 shows the clear gradient of multiple inequality from UPAs to the 'fringe areas'. Column 2 shows that the urban priority areas are losing population. There is a high correlation between population change and the social index. The process is one of deprived people being left in the UPAs as the successful move out to middle Britain. The former have decreasing wealth, health, services, income, investment, and amenity: the latter have rising affluence, opportunity, power and advantage: in one ugly word – polarization.

1.46   The process of polarization is a general one in Britain today. The official statistics published in *Social Trends* show that income disparities, both as between the skilled and the unskilled in employment and among households in the country as a whole, have widened since the mid-1970s. In 1976 the best-off fifth of British households took 44.4 per cent of the total income of the country: that share rose to 47.1 by 1982. The share of the poorest fifth meanwhile dropped from 0.8 per cent to 0.4 per cent. Of course tax and welfare benefit reduced these spectacular inequalities. But even so the movement was still towards greater inequality. The top fifth of households increased their share of post-tax income between 1976 and 1982 from 37.9 per cent to 39.4 per cent and the bottom fifth slipped from 7.4 per cent to 6.9 per cent.[15] In the nation as a whole since the end of the post-war period the rich have got richer and the poor poorer. Similarly, the Oxford studies of occupational mobility show that chances of mobility for men of working-class origin polarized between 1972 and 1983 as the opportunities for upward mobility continued, while the chances of unemployment also rose.[16] Again Chris Hamnett's study of trends in housing tenure concludes that, as between owner-occupation and local authority renting, there has been 'an increasing degree of social polarization.'[17] The analysis by David Eversley and Ian Begg[18] demonstrates that polarization also divides the UPAs from the rest of Britain. It involves a triple process of decision: by individuals competing for advantages in jobs, housing, schools and services: by governments offering mortgage relief and withholding investment from blighted districts; and by enterprises rationally investing where consumer power is greatest and growing.

Conclusion

1.47   We have described the UPAs in secular terms as places of absolute poverty, of the relative poverty which is integral to an unequal society, and of increasing poverty by comparison with national norms and the favoured minority of middle Britain: this has to be termed polarization. We have further described the UPAs in terms of their three essential characteristics of economic decline, physical decay and social disintegration. And finally by putting these attributes into historical perspective we have moved beyond description to the outline of an explanation. We shall take explanation further in our chapters below on Urban Policy (Chapter 8), Poverty, Employment and Work (Chapter 9), and Housing (Chapter 10). From these chapters we shall make particular recommendations. Meanwhile at this point we would emphasise above all that the inner city and the peripheral estate are creatures of the whole society, not simply of their inhabitants. The UPAs are explained effectively only by a recognition that they have emerged out of human decisions, whether through political authority, business management or individual choice. While appreciating the external forces of world-wide recession, currency movements and international markets, we must also insist that there is collective responsibility for the problems of poverty and inequality that we have described.

1.48   Any convincing account of the contemporary poverty of the inner city must recognise the force of both economic and political determinants. It would be wrong to assume that a market economy *necessarily* leads to inequality. The medieval city was in some respects an escape from feudal hierarchy and economic oppression. The ancient city, Athens notwithstanding, was normally a fortress of political (usually regal) power, but the western medieval city was also the cradle of democracy. As the city evolved it became, and in a world-wide perspective remains, the focus of popular aspiration towards a better material and cultural life. Admittedly, the market has intrinsic tendencies towards inequality: unequal property generates classes and thereby makes inequality hereditary. Undemocratic politics may reinforce property power, and democratic politics may, in the name of freedom or efficiency, fail to act as a countervailing force.

1.49   In history the forces leading to greater or lesser inequality have endlessly contended. Our own time has witnessed a more or less crude exaltation of the alleged benign social consequences of individual self-interest and competition. The inner city may justly be seen as the disfigured battleground of this modern phase of an age-old conflict. Its plight warranted a White Paper in 1977. Analysis of the 1981 Census gave no comfort that recognition had led to amelioration. And our evidence is that the decline continues.

1.50   Listening to the men and women in the UPAs and examining statistical evidence, we are reminded that the poor are not confined to the urban priority areas; poverty reflects the structural inequality of the nation and the UPAs reveal it in its most intractable forms. The city remains part magnet to the disadvantaged newcomer, part prison to the unskilled, the disabled, and the dispirited, part spring-board for the ambitious and vigorous who find escape to suburbia, and part protection for enclaves of affluence. The UPA is of our own making. The combination of our private preferences and the ramifications of our political choices are returned to us here as the geographical dimension of an unequal society. The background is sombre but the vision of a nation working and living in a land of garden cities remains as an ideal which could be realized through imaginative and determined collective effort. It is against such a background and such a vision that we turn, in the next chapter, to describe the Church in the urban priority areas.

References

1   R. Glass, 'Urban Sociology, Great Britain', *Current Sociology*, vol. 4, no. 4, 1955

2   Canon S.A. Barnett and Henrietta Barnett, *Practicable Socialism* (first edition 1888, second edition 1894). Third edition, Longmans, 1915. See also A. Briggs and A. Macartney, *Toynbee Hall: The First Hundred Years*, Routledge and Kegan Paul, 1984

3   *Ibid* (1915) p. 109

4   Ruth Glass, *loc. cit.*

5   See V. Hausner (ed) *Changing Cities*, Economic and Social Research Council 1985, and forthcoming volumes

6   Centre for Environmental Studies, *Outer Estates in Britain*, CES Paper 23, 1984

7   S. Fothergill, M. Kitson and S. Monk, *11. Urban Industrial Change*. Department of the Environment and Department of Trade and Industry. HMSO, 1985

8   Home Office, *The Brixton Disorders 10th-12th April 1981*. HMSO 1981. Cmnd. 8427.

9   R. Nabarro, 'The Impact on Workers from the Inner City of Liverpool's

Economic Decline' in A. Evans and D. Evans (eds) *The Inner City*, Heinemann 1980

10   Department of the Environment Analysis of Census Material for the Inner Areas of Partnership Authorities, 1983.

11   R. Nabarro, *loc. cit.*

12   *Ibid.*

13   D. Allnutt and A. Gelardi 'Inner Cities in England', *Social Trends*, 10, HMSO 1979

14   See D. Eversley and I. Begg in ESRC Inner Cities Research Programme – National Studies (forthcoming). This analysis is an improvement on the Department of the Environment assessment. Essentially the method is to collect data at ward level of over 70 indicators of advantage and disadvantage and to standardize them as Z scores. By this means an average Z score can be produced for every territorial grouping over a range of favourable and adverse social indicators. It is a robust and stable score which provides a refined map of inequality. We are indebted particularly to David Eversley for making some of this statistical analysis available to us.

15   *Social Trends*, 15, 1985, Table 5-21

16   J.H. Goldthorpe and C. Payne, *Trends in Inter-generational Mobility* 1972-1983, (forthcoming)

17   C. Hamnett, 'Housing the Two Nations: Socio-Tenurial Polarization in England and Wales 1961-81', *Urban Studies* vol. 43, 1984, pp. 384-405

18   Eversley and Begg, *loc. cit.*

Chapter 2
CHURCH AND CITY

'We still suffer from the effects of what the Church has done to communities, rather than with them.'   (Vicar, West Midlands)

2.1   In the midst of our cities stands the Church of England. It is not the only organised Christian presence in the UPAs. But it has maintained the parish system nationally, and has managed to survive, albeit precariously, the primarily economic pressures which have forced some denominations to withdraw from many inner city areas.

2.2   As we have travelled round the cities of England, we have been struck by the *variety* of Church life there is in the UPAs. In some places we have seen a great emphasis on evangelism and youth work, in others the focus has been on a worshipping community. In some areas, huge barn-like Victorian churches pose perennial problems with heating and maintenance and the ravages of dry-rot; in others, Sunday services are held in the church hall, or a smaller purpose-built church. Everywhere we have been impressed by the dedication of the laity and clergy we have met.

2.3   The Church may be there in the UPAs – but is it seen as relevant? If it made any sense to answer this question in terms of the numbers attending on an average Sunday, the answer would clearly be that it is not. In most of the dozens of UPA churches we have visited, congregations have been small – and in many cases declining (as the population of the area continues to decline).

2.4   Parish clergy come into contact with a range of parishioners through baptisms, marriages and funerals. Despite this, it has to be said clearly that for the vast majority of people in the UPAs the Church of England – perhaps Christianity – is seen as irrelevant. But in this, the inner cities and outer council estates are little different from the rest of Britain. For nationally, membership of the Church of England is in decline, even if not to the extent implied by the fall in electoral roll numbers (from 2½ million in 1970 to 1½ million in 1984).

Historical Perspectives[1]

2.5 The present position has its roots in history. At the middle of the eighteenth century, the great majority of the population were members of the Church of England. However the pattern of Anglican church-going showed marked regional and social differences. Churches and clergy were concentrated in the south and east of the country; in the midlands and north, large and inadequately-endowed parishes meant that many people lived several miles from the church. Even where the majority of the population lived close to the church, it was mainly the poorer people who kept away. Eighteenth century visitation returns are full of comments like the following from the vicar of the Lancashire weaving parish of Radcliffe: 'There are none who profess to disregard religion, but many of the poorer sort are hindered (partly by family concerns, partly by want of decent clothing) from attending the public worship of God on the Lord's day'.

2.6 The Anglican Church had also failed to build enough churches or place enough clergy in newly developing districts in the larger towns, especially those with a mainly labouring population. As early as 1736 in Sheffield and 1751 in Leeds, local clergy were complaining that the lack of churches encouraged the spread of nonconformity and even non-church-going. Until the great programme of Anglican church building got underway in the later 1830s, there was little effective Anglican presence in many of these areas.

2.7 But the Church of England's most enduring 'problem of the city' has been its relationship with the urban working class. Though the cities in general appeared as problem areas for the established Church, it was clearly in working class districts that the problems were most acute. For instance, the 1851 religious census showed that, in the 36 registration districts of London, total Anglican attendances varied from 57 per cent of the population in suburban Hampstead (which was very high, even by rural standards) to 6 per cent in Shoreditch.

2.8 There is some evidence that anti-clericalism among the emerging working class urban dwellers (though not as much as emerged in continental Europe) played a part in this: the clergy were seen in stereotype as well-fed, callous and reactionary. The Church of England was viewed by many as being aligned with the powerful and the privileged. But there also existed a secularist element in the working class, which had an influence out of proportion to its numbers because so many secularists were active in politics or trade unions.

2.9   Less tangible than the rise of the radical political tradition in the city, but possibly even more important, was the development in many industrial communities of a sense of common working class identity, of separation from, and some degree of antagonism towards, other sections of society. Horace Mann, the Anglican barrister who wrote the official report on the 1851 religious census, mentioned the following possible factors as contributing to 'the alienation of the poor from religious institutions':

(i)   the social inequalities within the churches: for instance, the system of hierarchically-arranged rented pews;

(ii)   the fact that class division in society ran so deep that even if there were no such symbols of inequality within the churches, working class people would not wish to worship with members of other classes;

(iii)   the apparent lack of interest on the part of the churches in the material well-being of the poor;

(iv)   suspicion of the clergy because of their middle class character and comfortable life-style;

(v)   the effects of poverty: many working class people lacked time or space for reflection, and were too preoccupied with more immediate problems to give much thought to religion;

(vi)   lack of 'aggressive' missionary activity.

2.10   Mann believed that the clergy were well aware of the Church's weakness in working class areas, and that serious efforts were being made to remedy the situation. In some respects, he was over-optimistic about the progress that was being made; but the second half of the nineteenth century was nonetheless a period of revival for the Church of England. For a variety of reasons the Church of England became much more active in the cities, and its influence grew.

2.11   The third quarter of the nineteenth century was a period of relative prosperity, in which class tensions slackened, fewer people suffered extreme poverty, and the skilled working class enjoyed a marked increase in income. The anti-clericalism of the early nineteenth century was less obvious. Fewer people were so preoccupied with merely keeping alive as to have no interests outside the home, and fewer were discouraged from going to church by a sense of shame about their ragged clothes and inability to rent a pew or contribute to a collection.

2.12 Moreover the clergy were more active, conscientious and committed to their work than they had been 50 years earlier. The Anglo-Catholic Oxford movement in the 1830s and '40s was an important factor, but it was only one of the forces for revival in this period. Equally important was the older Evangelical movement. The influence of F.D. Maurice and the Christian Socialists was also significant.

2.13 There were a number of ways in which the clergy were trying at this time to bridge the gulf that divided them from their working class parishioners: reaching the previously ignorant or indifferent by open-air preaching or systematic visiting from door to door; making church services more attractive; making the church the centre for the whole social life of the parish; identifying themselves with the political concerns of the parishioners, becoming spokesmen for their people. Large teams of curates made it possible for the clergy to maintain personal contact with a high proportion of households, even in urban parishes. Evangelicals and Anglo-Catholics succeeded in establishing some flourishing parishes in working class areas of later Victorian cities. The one point that the well-attended churches had in common was that they all had big programmes of weekday activities, and used large teams of lay volunteers.

2.14 The degree to which clergy were able to identify themselves with their parishioners, and to involve themselves in many aspects of the life of the local community, made a big difference. It was perhaps the biggest barrier that the nineteenth century city clergy had to overcome. For some of them the way of life of the urban poor was simply repulsive. The Rector of Bethnal Green reported to his Bishop in 1862 that the greater part of his parish consisted of 'radicals, infidels and persons who are to all good works reprobate'. Four years earlier, the vicar of another Bethnal Green parish had written: 'my position is productive of what I might venture to call mental torture'.

2.15 If the relative success of the Church of England in the late Victorian period among the poorer working class had much to do with a changing of attitudes, it also involved the dispensing of various forms of charity and social services. Through boxing clubs, saving schemes, sewing circles, debating societies, mothers' meetings and so on, the Church was to some degree in touch with a wide section of the population. But it was very vulnerable to the effects of the growth of the welfare state and of the leisure industry in the early twentieth century. The decline of churches as social centres may offer the best explanation for the serious decline in membership and attendance that set in in the early twentieth century.

2.16   Yet there never really was a 'golden age' for the Church of England in the city. If the touchstone of success is the number of communicants or regular church-goers, then all the efforts by the clergy to attract the working class had relatively little effect. The 1902-03 census of church attendance in London gave a clear indication of the close association between the social status of a district and the level of Anglican church-going. Adult attendance at Anglican services averaged 4 per cent in the poorest working class districts, 5 per cent in average working class districts, 7 per cent in upper working class districts, 9 per cent in lower middle class, 11 per cent in middle class districts, 18 per cent in wealthy suburban districts, and 22 per cent in wealthy West End districts. (These percentages are not directly comparable with those for 1851, cited earlier, which included Sunday school children.) Although most cities had a few conspicuously flourishing working class parishes, the hundreds who attended these churches were few if set beside the thousands who stayed away.

2.17   The measure of Church 'success' is an elusive concept. Numbers of people attending worship are easy to obtain, and often this is the only available evidence of commitment. If people matter, then numbers of people matter. But the Church must beware of using numerical attendance as a sole criterion. A more biblical criterion of faithfulness is required and Church historians cannot avoid judgments requiring sensitive spiritual discernment, if lessons are to be drawn from the past.

2.18   Yet it is clear that the Church of England has traditionally been mainly middle class in character: it never attained the kind of pervasive influence, transcending the boundaries of class, that was achieved by Catholicism in Ireland or nonconformity in Wales. Equally, as it moved into the twentieth century, it carried with it a clerical paternalistic legacy; of a male-dominated Church in which the clergy held the power.

2.19   During the present century, and especially since 1945, there has been a marked decline in the number of middle class people who are active church members. Secularization – the process whereby religious thinking, practice and insitutions lose social significance – has now

31

permeated *all* sections of society. The explanations for this are varied, complex and contentious. They include the dominance of an ostensibly scientific and rational approach to life, the diminished role of Christian education in schools, the pre-empting of much hitherto Church-based pastoral care by the Welfare State, the 'privatizing' of what was hitherto primarily communal in social life, and the rise of car ownership and 'the weekend' as established secular cults. In some inner city areas, the post-war flight of many middle class church-goers to suburbia and beyond may have reinforced these wider trends, while in others re-colonization (or 'gentrification') by the same group has yet to revitalise many local congregations. At the same time, Anglican congregations continue to be much larger in middle class than in working class areas. In particular, people in semi-skilled and unskilled manual jobs are seriously under-represented in Anglican congregations, while those in professional and managerial jobs are strongly over-represented. In this respect the situation is much the same as it was a hundred years ago, though both middle-class and working-class church-going have declined during that time.

2.20   One factor in the situation is a recurrent theme of Church history: where deep divisions in culture and language exist between different sections of society, a clergy drawn mainly from one section (in the case of England, the middle class) is likely to have serious difficulties in communicating with members of other social groups. In a society where class divisions run so deeply, any institution which attempts to identify itself simultaneously with both the privileged and the deprived faces a task that is so formidable that it will tend to side with one or the other.

Urban Ministry Today: A Survey of Clergy

2.21   Against this background, we have attempted to discover, through the eyes of the clergy, how the Church's ministry is being exercised in UPAs today. Because of the great variety of Church presence, any 'pen pictures' we might have drawn would have been either over-general or over-specific. Consequently, to gain a systematic view of ministry in the UPAs, we commissioned a survey of a random sample of 400 parish clergy, which was carried out for us by Gallup. We regret that it was not possible for us to mount a similar survey of lay people.

2.22   The clergy were surveyed in February and March 1985 by means of a one hour personal interview. Of those interviewed, 189 lived in UPA parishes located in the dioceses of London, Southwark,

Birmingham, Lichfield, Coventry, Ripon, Sheffield, Bradford, Manchester, Liverpool, Newcastle, and Durham. Another 213 clergy were drawn from a cross-section of town and country parishes in all other dioceses (except Sodor and Man), and from non-UPA parishes in the twelve listed 'urban area' dioceses. For convenience we refer to this group as the non-UPA sample though it will include a certain number of UPA parishes in the other 30 dioceses. Similarly the UPA sample (derived with diocesan help using criteria similar to the identification process described in Chapter 5) includes a few clergy who did not see themselves as in a deprived area. Where such exceptions significantly affect comparisons between the two groups, they have been excluded and figures quoted for parishes whose status as either UPA or non-UPA was not in any doubt.

2.23   Only stipendiary parochial clergy were included in the survey. The sample was constructed in such a way as to produce a number that would be representative of the totals of incumbents, priests-in-charge, team vicars and assistant curates in each diocese.

2.24   A fuller report of the findings of the survey will, we hope, be published separately. We draw on the results, however, at various points throughout our report. Here we wish to record some key findings about the state of the Church of England in the UPAs today.

2.25   The first is that, for the Church of England nationally, the average adult church attendance in each 'parish'[2] on a Sunday is 119, representing 1.4 per cent of an average parish population of 8,410. In UPA parishes the equivalent figures are an average of 90 adults attending out of a parish population of 10,560 (0.85 per cent). The proportion of the congregation living outside the parish was observed to be much lower in the country (10-15 per cent) than in the suburbs (25 per cent) and cities (40 per cent) though not than on council estates (15 per cent).

2.26   Church attendance per parish in absolute numbers is highest in the suburbs and small towns; but in relation to population it is highest in rural villages and lowest in council estates and inner city residential areas. However, irrespective of location, churches where the clergy classified themselves as 'evangelical' have higher Sunday attendances by either standard than those which describe themselves as 'high church' or 'middle of the road'.

2.27   The survey found that the UPA parishes tended to be much more polarized in terms of whether they were high church or low church compared with non-UPA parishes. For example 38 per cent of all UPA clergy declared themselves 'high church' compared with only 23 per cent in non-UPA parishes. Likewise 32 per cent of UPA clergy declared themselves 'low church/evangelical' compared with 21 per cent in non-UPAs. Far fewer clergy in the UPAs (28 per cent) declared themselves 'middle of the road' compared with elsewhere (51 per cent).

2.28   Clergymen were also asked to assess which denominations within their local area had growing support, which declining support, and which were remaining the same. Most clergy, whether in UPAs or not, seemed optimistic about their own Churches – over half thought that their own Church had a growing support and at least another quarter thought that it was remaining the same.

2.29   Within the UPAs the fastest-growing Churches were seen to be the 'Independent, predominantly black Churches': about one-in-three of clergy reported such Churches in their locality with growing support. A similar proportion of clergy in the UPAs noted that adherents of other faiths formed an increasing proportion of the population in their areas.

2.30   Despite the relatively optimistic view taken by clergy of the support for their own Church, their estimates of church attendance indicate that for every one person who goes to an Anglican church on a Sunday in a UPA parish there are 99 who do not. The clergy were asked what they thought were the three most important things which put people off coming to church in their area these days. 'Ignorance about the Church or Christianity' and 'perception of the Church as irrelevant in their lives' were the two main responses to this open-ended question. The main ways in which adults and teenagers had been brought into the congregation in the last two years were overwhelmingly said to be 'personal contacts', and this was stressed more in UPAs than elsewhere; also important in the UPAs were visiting, baptisms and the occasion of bereavement. (In this connection the survey showed that UPA clergy conduct many more funeral services than non-UPA clergy, primarily in crematoria.) Another important way, especially in non-UPAs, was for parents to come in, or be brought back, to the Church through their children.

2.31   What sort of people made up the congregation? The survey revealed that, in general, most clergy perceived their congregation to be predominantly 'middle class', whereas the social class of the people living in their parish was much more mixed. The church officers and

Parochial Church Council (PCC) members were rated even more 'middle class' than the congregation. Not surprisingly, however, there were large differences between UPA and non-UPA parishes.

FIGURE 2.1

Perceived Social Class of People in Parish, Congregation and P.C.C. in UPA and non-UPA Parishes

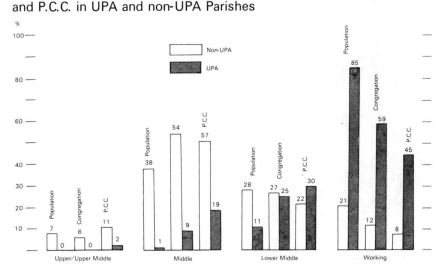

Source: Clergy Survey

2.32   Figure 2.1 shows that in the UPAs, 12 per cent of the people living in the parish were perceived to be 'lower middle class' or above, compared with 85 per cent who were seen to be 'working class'. The middle classes were, however, over-represented in UPA congregations, compared with working class people, and even more so on the PCC. In the non-UPA parishes, 73 per cent of parishioners were perceived as being 'lower middle class or above' and only 21 per cent were rated as 'working class'. Again, however, middle class over-representation and working class under-representation in the congregation and on the PCC were evident.

2.33   Clergy were also asked whether they served in a parish where more than 5 per cent of the population could be classified as being 'non-white'. Just over half the UPA parishes were claimed to fall within this category, compared with only 7 per cent in the non-UPA sample. The 51 per cent of UPA parishes (94 in absolute numbers) with significant minority ethnic communities were then asked details of the ethnic mix of their congregation and PCC. The results are in Figure 2.2.

FIGURE 2.2

Ethnic Mix of U.P.A. Parishes with More than Five per cent Non-white Population

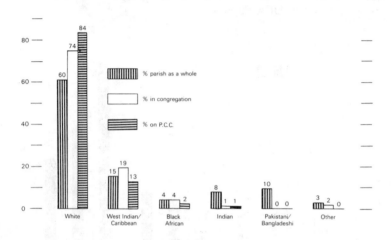

Source: Clergy Survey

2.34 It is noteworthy that those of West Indian/Caribbean origin were seen as accounting for about 15 per cent of the population in these parishes and about 19 per cent of the congregation, but only 13 per cent of PCC members.

2.35 The survey also examined the age structure of congregations, and the split between men and women. The results supported existing data which suggest that congregations are on average far older than the population of the parish, and that the churches in all areas are particularly failing to attract 18-24 year olds. The survey showed that on average 37 per cent of congregations were men and 63 per cent were women. There was no significant difference between UPA and non-UPA parishes.

2.36 The survey provides evidence that people who belong to a Church in a UPA tend to have a relatively high level of commitment in terms of attendance. The ratio of usual Sunday attendance to electoral roll membership is proportionately higher in UPAs than elsewhere. Equally, the number of Easter communicants in the UPAs is not substantially different from the number of usual Sunday attenders. In other areas, a large number of people on the electoral roll attend Easter communion, but are usually absent from Sunday services during the rest of the year. Expressed differently, there tends to be a smaller 'fringe' to UPA church membership.

2.37   A high degree of commitment among UPA church members is apparent in the level of financial giving. Not only is average direct giving per electoral roll member higher in 'urban area' dioceses (£46 p.a. in 1983) than in other dioceses (£38 p.a.) – with the gap between them widening in the past ten years – but our survey suggests that, within dioceses, it is actually higher in UPA parishes than others. Average giving as reported by UPA clergy in the survey amounted to £57 a year per electoral roll member, compared with £52 reported by other clergy. If these absolute levels of giving could be related to incomes, the contrast would be much greater.

2.38   Clergy were asked to assess a range of social problems in their local area on a scale of one to ten, where one indicates 'not a great problem' and ten indicates 'a great problem'. (Hence the higher the rating the greater the problem.) The survey revealed that those in the UPAs rated social problems much higher than those in the non-UPAs, with the only exception being public transport. The problems are listed below in descending order of their perceived seriousness in the country as a whole.

TABLE 2.1

	National Picture	UPA Parishes	Non-UPA Parishes
Incidence of marriage breakdown and other family problems	5.8	7.5	5.5
Quality/price of public transport	5.4	4.1	5.6
Number of elderly people	5.2	6.5	4.9
Adequacy of amenities	4.9	6.5	4.6
Burglaries	4.8	8.0	4.3
Vandalism	4.4	7.5	3.7
Level of unemployment	4.4	8.2	3.4
Quality of welfare provisions	3.7	5.9	3.2
Health among the local residents	3.2	5.7	2.7
Quality of housing	3.1	6.2	2.3
Mugging, rape and other violent attacks	2.6	5.9	2.0
Relations with police	2.4	4.9	1.8
Relation with public employees	2.4	4.5	1.9
Race and community relations	1.9	4.1	1.4

2.39   Two clear conclusions emerge from these results: first, that most of the problems were judged to be much more serious in the UPAs than elsewhere: twice as serious in relation to burglaries, vandalism, unemployment, welfare provision, health, quality of housing, violent attacks, relations with the police and with other public employees, and race and community relations. Second, however, it was the incidence of marriage breakdown and other family problems that was seen, nationally, as the most serious problem. In the UPAs, its seriousness as a problem was only exceeded by the level of burglaries and the level of unemployment. Of the problems listed, race and community relations were seen as the least serious in the UPAs as well as in other areas. Non-UPA clergy, in a later question, acknowledged that the main difference between ministering in a deprived urban area and ministering elsewhere was the marked social problems of the urban areas. In this view they were supported by the UPA clergy themselves.

2.40   It was a noticeable feature of the survey responses that clergy reported a level of job satisfaction that was very high compared with those found in other 'white collar' occupations. And despite the serious view they took of the social problems in their parish, clergy in the UPAs were more satisfied with ministering in their particular type of parish than those in non-UPA ministry. This is perhaps the most striking finding of the survey. The UPA clergy liked working where they did, despite registering greater dissatisfaction with their housing and environmental conditions, with friendships they had made in the parish, with their leisure opportunities and with the adequacy of their Church's involvement within the community. When asked where they would like to move to next, more than half the UPA clergy who expressed a preference hoped to remain in that sort of area. Most clergy working in other areas favoured a small or middle-sized town or village for their next move; however, asked specifically whether they would seriously consider accepting an offer of a position in an area of urban deprivation, half of them said they would.

2.41   The clergy, whether in UPAs or elsewhere, see their own most important Church-backed activities, other than worship, as visiting the sick and the bereaved, Bible study and house groups, and general parochial visiting. Such differences as there are appear to be a greater frequency of involvement by the clergy in the UPAs in youth work, prayer meetings, counselling and training. And in terms of work not sponsored by the Church there is a greater involvement in community work among the clergy in the UPAs.

2.42   Regular ecumenical co-operation – at least quarterly – was reported by two-thirds of the clergy interviewed. There was no markedly different level of ecumenical activity in UPAs compared with the non-UPAs. The pattern of co-operation however seems to vary. Co-operation with Methodists is reported by more than half the clergy, in all areas. Shared worship is more common in the UPAs – with both Roman Catholic and Free Churches – but Bible study and house group co-operation seems more common in the non-UPAs. The sharing of churches and joint prayer meetings are reported by nearly 20 per cent of clergy, mainly with Methodists. Co-operation in respect of schools, office facilities, and parish magazines is more rare.

Other Churches
2.43   We have heard repeated representations about the importance of ecumenical partnership in the UPAs. Two typical comments are:

'my belief in the need for local ecumenism has been greatly strengthened'

(a priest in East London)

'we do not think it is sensible in the inner city not to work in ecumenical partnership'

(a priest on Tyneside)

Nevertheless on our visits we found practical commitment to ecumenical collaboration very patchy, and understandably so, as it can call for resources of energy over and above denominational work which itself makes such heavy demands in UPAs.

2.44   We set out to understand how other denominations approach the mission of the Church in the UPAs. We have talked to non-Anglican clergy and laity during our visits to the UPAs, and we have held meetings with national representatives of each of the main denominations, and of the independent Black-led Churches. We have also noted the work of the city missions.

2.45   Among the other denominations, the Methodist Church is the most centralized in its organisation. Money flows to and from the centre, alongside the assumption that – as far as possible – individual circuits should be self-supporting. The Methodist 'Mission Alongside the Poor' campaign is an attempt to focus attention on areas in which poverty exists, and to promote changed priorities. Smaller churches in the inner city, often struggling with large nineteenth-century buildings to manage, have not found it easy to cope. Nevertheless, there are real and tangible signs of hope, and energies and faith are being channelled in new directions. Although they have little finance, they are able to pay for stipendiary ministry with the aid of grants paid from Methodist Home Mission sources. They are often part of circuits which are like a geographical wedge from suburbs to city centre. In such cases, the main work, life, and power of the circuit is concentrated in the suburbs, but in the case of London (geographically much larger) mission circuits are limited to the inner city areas. However, despite a programme of closure of churches in the cities, the Methodist Church still has 362 inner city Churches with 31,682 members, and 331 council estate churches with 17,474 members.

2.46   The Baptist Union is a voluntary union of independent Baptist local churches, each with the tradition of evangelism and mission. The local church is competent to make all the decisions about mission – including the appointment of a minister. Responsibility for mission is, however, wider than the purely local: there are county level associations in which individual churches do together what can best be done together. The Baptist Church has adopted advisory strategies at association level for mission in urban priority areas. A number of ecumenical projects in UPAs are supported as a result, and £41,000 is raised nationally for the purpose.

2.47   The United Reformed Church has, since its foundation 13 years ago, developed a more centralized financial system. There are two main funds: a Maintenance of the Ministry Fund, for which congregations are assessed and out of which ministers are paid. This includes an increase in subsidy to UPA and other Churches in financial difficulties. There is also a unified appeal for all non-ministerial expenses, much of which is used to help the Church overseas, and from which £20,000 is distributed to new urban projects. As regards staffing, each district is allocated a certain number of ministers only, and the district must consider where to place these. A missionary strategy has been developed and at least some districts which contain UPAs have put back staff into areas of recent withdrawal.

2.48   The Roman Catholic Church in England and Wales is largely organized by dioceses, with the minimum of national organisation and finance. Funds are not on the whole transferred between dioceses, but within a diocese different parishes may help each other financially. Training, buildings, and deployment of clergy are also dealt with on a diocesan basis. The numbers of clergy and religious deployed in UPAs is probably proportionately higher than the average for the country. Clergy are normally ordained to serve the diocese from which they come; unless they are appointed to a national post they remain in that diocese throughout their ministry.

2.49   In contrast with the Church of England and the mainstream Protestant denominations, the Roman Catholic Church has a strong numerical base in the UPAs. Its English history after the industrial revolution is quite different, because of the influence from the mid-19th century onwards of large migrations from Ireland to many English cities. For many of these migrants from Ireland (where the ruling class was mainly English and Protestant) Roman Catholicism seemed to be in tune with Irish nationalism, and to be marked by a pastoral presence among the poor (unlike some other European countries, where national and/or social revolutions had resulted in the Roman Catholic Church appearing as an obstacle to national or social aspirations, and as an institution which was not identified with the interests of the poor). For the Irish immigrants to England, therefore, the Roman Catholic Church, with its quota of Irish priests, was the natural focal point for communities in poor housing and with poor job security in an urban environment, and facing in addition the threat of loss of cultural identity. As Roman Catholics gradually felt themselves becoming accepted in the wider community, 'secularization' took its toll and religious practice declined. Irish migration, however, was a process continuing at various levels over more than a century. The lapsation from practice was therefore masked by a periodical reinforcement of the Irish community – a reinforcement which is now largely in decline.

2.50   The present state of the Roman Catholic Church in the UPAs is not however explained solely by the Irish dimension, and in the last two decades factors other than assimilation have played their part in affecting the level of religious practice. Yet in most English cities today there are likely to be many Roman Catholic worshippers; the numbers at Mass on a Sunday may not differ substantially from those in more affluent areas. Where people have moved out from strong communities in the inner city to more modern outer housing estates, the Roman Catholic community is sometimes less cohesive, and fewer practise their religion. In our East London visit Bishop Guazzelli said that there were large congregations, which were not communities. He said the task was to break them down into several smaller groups – a collection of communities – by developing lay leadership.

2.51   The Salvation Army has ministered in its own distinctive way to many of the very poorest, who have been largely ignored by other

Churches. This work continues through 155 Social Service Centres (including residential homes and hostels) and 32 Goodwill centres in inner city areas. In the Salvation Army, social work is run separately from the development of the life of congregations. As far as major cities are concerned, it would be true to say that their congregations, like those of the other main Free Churches, now mainly come from the suburbs.

2.52   The majority of black Christians live in the urban priority areas. Most are of West Indian origin, many of them have been born in Britain, and they rightly regard themselves as legally and socially British. There are also smaller numbers of African and Asian Christians, although the majority of people in Britain with an Asian background belong to other faiths such as Islam, Hinduism, Buddhism or Sikhism.

2.53   There are a large number of Black-led Churches in Britain today: most are of Afro-West Indian origin but there are smaller groups of African and Asian Churches. The term 'Black-led' (which has been widely accepted, but which Bishop Malachi Ramsay, of the Shiloh Church of Christ, objects to as 'degrading and lacking in respect') emphasises positively that leadership is exercised by men and women whose ethnic background is seen as the main distinguishing factor. Yet none of these Churches excludes white members; indeed there is a determination to avoid the racial discrimination which some black people have felt in some white-led Churches. Nor are there necessarily any doctrinal differences from white-led Churches, though there are differences in emphasis and style.

2.54   The rise of the Black-led Churches has been dramatic. For example, membership of the New Testament Church of God in England doubled between 1966 and 1970 from ten to twenty thousand, and is now about 30,000. The annual average growth rate for these Churches is 5 per cent. It is important to note that many black people are members of historic British Churches and are gradually assuming positions of leadership within them. But whereas in the West Indies membership of the historic Churches was the norm, in England this situation has been reversed: the majority go to Black-led Churches.

2.55   What are the main reasons for this? The industrialization and secularization of British society are important but not crucial. Rather, there is a great deal of evidence that black people felt themselves unwelcome in the English Churches just as in many other parts of

English society. Some Churches already established in the West Indies with American rather than British connections, like the New Testament Church of God and the Wesleyan Holiness Church, sent missionaries from the West Indies to lead and direct their people in England. Many black Christians found in the Black-led Churches the things they needed most: immediate acceptance and pastoral care, participation on equal terms, solidarity with their fellow-Christians, and opportunities for their cultural and spiritual development.

2.56   The picture is of an increasing number of growing and developing Black-led Churches – at present over 160 denominations involving perhaps 100,000 people in about 2,500 congregations. Denominations are constitutionally independent of one another. Some are formed out of splits; many are growing vigorously and by church-planting are multiplying their congregations. The Black-led Churches have also been linking themselves together in a number of networks such as the International Ministerial Council of Great Britain, the Afro-West Indian United Council of Churches, the Council of African and Allied Churches, the Black Pastors' Conference, and the West Indian Evangelical Alliance, as well as through the Conference for Christian Partnership set up jointly by African and Afro-West Indian Churches and the British Council of Churches.

2.57   Services are characterized by greater length and warmth than is found in those of the historic Churches, and sometimes by speaking in tongues. The attitude to the Bible is conservative. There is increasing concern for the social and political implications of the Gospel as well as for the salvation of individuals, and there has been a growth of a self-help movement that fills the gap left by statutory services unable or unwilling to care for the needs of black people. For the most part ministers, both men and women, have to earn their own living and carry out their preaching and pastoral work in their spare time.

The Christian Presence in UPAs – An Illustrative Comparison

2.58   We mounted a separate small-scale survey in addition to our major clergy survey. We asked three dioceses to assemble information to provide an impression of denominational patterns and ecumenical co-operation in a number of inner and outer areas. In Manchester, the inner city area was Beswick, Ardwick, and Clayton, the outer area Wythenshawe. In Southwark, the inner city area was North Lambeth, and the outer area Thamesmead. In Liverpool, the inner city area was Toxteth and the outer area was Skelmersdale.

2.59   The general findings were as follows. There is numerical decline in church membership in the mainstream denominations, but it is neither universal nor inevitable. Roman Catholic membership is generally larger than that of the other Churches together. Ecumenical involvement seems to depend more on the attitudes of clergy and church leaders than the type of area. However, ecumenical co-operation seems confined to the established Churches, and does not in practice involve many Black-led Churches. The training of lay people seems crucial; otherwise there will be a split between the social action of the clergy and their care of a dependent congregation. The key people are lay members who are capable of being active in the community and who encourage and support others who are so involved. For example, when it comes to the ways in which lay members of the Thamesmead Christian Community participate in the affairs of the town, the list is endless. There are approximately 1,200 members of the Thamesmead Christian Community and only a part of their involvement is recognised as being undertaken on behalf of the Church.

2.60   Although there are some common factors in the cases we have examined, there are limits to how far generalizations can be made. A contrast between one inner area and an outer area may be of interest to illustrate the diversities.

2.61   Skelmersdale brings together a new town, with a large population who have moved out from Liverpool, with an old mining and agricultural community in Lancashire. Church membership in the old Lancashire parts is very strong. It is much smaller in the new town areas. Taking Skelmersdale as a whole, church attendance is relatively high. On 17 February 1985 there were 3,000 church attenders out of a population of 42,000. About half of these were Roman Catholic: 1,500 at Mass out of a Roman Catholic population of 10,000.

2.62   The four purely Anglican, Methodist or URC Churches seem conventional in outlook with a desire to convert and build up the individual Christian and church fellowship, though not without a concern for unemployment which in recent years has clearly devastated the town. Between these Churches, there is a fair level of ecumenical involvement. There is a striking difference, however, in the style of the Skelmersdale Ecumenical Centre (Church of England, Baptist, URC, Methodist) with three full-time clergy and a lot of trained voluntary talent. Its premises are used for a wide range of community activities, and its ministers and members are clearly involved in many social, pastoral, and political concerns. The actual Sunday attendance at the

Centre (122) is not as large as two of the Anglican Churches in old Skelmersdale, but comparable with the Anglican Church in a similar part of the new town (Digmoor).

2.63   Five or six independent Churches were reported to us, none very big, though the Assemblies of God was reported to have grown considerably in recent times.

2.64   By contrast, in part of Toxteth (with a population of 45,000) there is a great variety of religious bodies. We were astonished to be told that there are 9 Anglican Churches, 9 Roman Catholic Churches and a community of sisters, 2 Methodist Churches, 5 Baptist Churches, 8 Evangelical Free Churches, 5 Black-led Churches, and 9 other Christian congregations, plus gatherings of each of the main other faiths; total 59. For the most part numbers attending Protestant Churches are small (fewer than 50). Roman Catholic parishes have thousands listed. Local priests say that attendances at Mass on a normal Sunday are much smaller.

2.65   Several Anglican Churches had a high proportion of unemployed people, and professional/clerical workers, but not of employed manual workers. In several mainstream Protestant, including Anglican, Churches there was reported to be a tension between the needs of the community, e.g. for employment and provision for youth, and the pastoral needs of the congregation which was typically elderly and preponderantly female. There was little evidence of sustained ecumenical activity.

2.66   Mainstream Protestant Churches in Toxteth tended to be ageing, drawing a declining membership from the immediate locality, and finding in some cases their members moving away. The Black-led Churches, and the non-denominational Chapels varied between local and wider membership. There are two Independent Baptist Churches which have congregations of some hundreds. A substantial proportion of these travel to worship from quite different areas.

2.67   We cannot claim that the examples we have cited of the Christian presence in inner and outer areas are 'typical', but we believe that they are indicative.

Conclusion

2.68   In this chapter, we have recorded some of our findings about, and impressions of, the Christian presence in our cities. We have attempted to show that the Church of England has never enjoyed a golden age in urban Britain. We shall address more detailed aspects of the Church of England's contemporary ministry and mission in the UPAs in Part II of our report. But first we view the challenge of the urban priority areas from a theological standpoint.

References

1   We are grateful to Dr Hugh McLeod, Department of Theology, Birmingham University, for providing us with a context paper on which we have drawn.

2   The term 'parish' here relates to the one or more parishes for which each respondent had responsibility (e.g. including pluralities). Population figures are based on the clergy's estimates, which in many dioceses are liable to err on the high side by an even greater margin than any overestimation of attendance.

Chapter 3

THEOLOGICAL PRIORITIES

'The Church seems to offer very little to people in the inner city, but surely Christianity has a lot to say?'

(Advice Worker in London)

What Is the Place of Theology in Our Argument?

3.1   The teaching of Jesus makes many demands on us. Some of them may seem difficult to meet in the social and economic conditions of today, and theological reflection may be required to show their continuing relevance. Others, however, are of such simplicity and directness that theology may seem to have little, if anything, to add to them. Jesus' call to show compassion on those in need is one of these: it finds an immediate response in the hearts of Christians (and not only Christians). No 'theology' is required to drive it home.

3.2   Accordingly, when St Paul argued that the churches he had founded should 'remember the poor' (Gal. 2.10) he did not need to mount a theological case to show that this was their duty. Only when certain congregations were slow to respond did he resort to arguments that would stimulate their generosity (2 Cor. 8-9). The example of the Good Samaritan creates an imperative. It is impossible to be a Christian without responding, in some way or other, to the neighbour who is in need. The Church has a long tradition of encouraging and channelling this response through charitable giving, support of welfare work among the poor, promotion of foreign missions and (most recently) 'Christian Aid' for poverty, hunger and homelessness overseas. Throughout its history it has acknowledged its obligation to 'remember the poor'.

3.3   In this country we are confronted by an acute form of relative poverty – officially recognized as 'multiple deprivation' – that is particularly concentrated in the urban priority areas, and that is caused to a great extent by circumstances beyond the control of those who are affected by it. There is a clear Christian duty to respond to this situation

47

and 'remember the poor' in our UPAs. But it can hardly be said that the Church is yet making this a high priority. The Church (like the nation) appears for the most part to be pursuing its concerns and managing its life as if these patches of acute need did not exist. There is a sense in which no further 'theology' is required. The Commission has had the opportunity of observing a concentration of human suffering at our doorstep, of which the great majority of Church members (like the majority of our fellow-citizens) appear to be unaware. It should be sufficient to sound the alert: there is a clear demand on us all to come to the aid of those who have fallen so far behind the relative prosperity enjoyed by the rest of us.

3.4   But what sort of aid? It is here that we enter an inescapable theological debate. The question at issue is whether the acknowledged Christian duty to 'remember the poor' should be confined to personal charity, service and evangelism directed towards individuals, or whether it can legitimately take the form of social and political action aimed at altering the circumstances which appear to cause poverty and distress. We shall argue that these are false alternatives: a Christian is committed to a form of action which embraces both.

To Whom Is the Gospel Addressed?

3.5   The evidence of the gospels makes it clear that Jesus' proclamation of the Kingdom of God had from the start profound social and political implications. It was to be embodied in a community in which the normal priorities of wealth, power, position and respectability would be overturned. Yet it must always be remembered that this proclamation took place in the context of an intensely personal concern for individuals, families and local communities. Only a tendentious reading of the gospels can suggest that Jesus was primarily a social reformer, let alone a violent revolutionary. Whatever the implications for society as a whole (and these indeed have been profound) the characteristic sphere of Jesus' ministry was that of personal relationships and individual responses.

3.6   This personal dimension of the gospel is one that we must never lose sight of. Jesus was deeply concerned for the potential of every individual to become a true child of his heavenly father, and proclaimed the infinite worth of one sinner who repents. The Church has consistently followed him in stressing the inalienable dignity and worth of every individual, and the absolute equality of all before God (a matter of the greatest contemporary relevance, given the racial prejudice still manifest in many parts of our society and even at times within the Church itself). Never was this emphasis more necessary than it is now. The techniques of modern government depend upon the identification of socio-economic groups of anonymous individuals; the social·sciences attempt to predict human behaviour according to patterns that are derived from the observation of collectivities. Even the services from which the most personal attention might be expected – health and welfare – often reduce their clients to the status of 'cases' or 'applicants' with little concern for the ways in which individuals in the same situation may differ from one another There is of course a positive side to this: the administration of justice and the provision of certain social benefits demand an impartial and even-handed approach. But this can also conceal an insidious trend towards impersonality, in the face of which the Church has the full authority of the gospel to protect the God-given dignity of every individual and to bring people a message of repentance, forgiveness and personal transformation that is addressed to the heart and mind of each one of us.

3.7 Yet while many members of the Church of England have generally found it more congenial to express their discipleship by helping individual victims of misfortune or oppression, fewer are willing to rectify injustices in the structures of society. There is a number of reasons for this preference for 'ambulance work'. No-one minds being cast in the role of protector and helper of the weak and powerless: there is no threat here to one's superior position and one's power of free decision. But to be a protagonist of social change may involve challenging those in power and risking the loss of one's own power. Helping a victim or sufferer seldom involves conflict; working for structural change can hardly avoid it. Direct personal assistance to an individual may seem relatively straightforward, uncontroversial and rewarding; involvement in social issues implies choosing between complicated alternatives and accepting compromises which seem remote from any moral position. From the nineteenth century onwards, a distinguished line of Anglican theologians has wrestled with the ambiguities of social action; but most of us still feel a lack of confidence in these grey areas. We have little tradition of initiating conflict and coping with it creatively. We are not at home in the tough, secular milieu of social and political activism.

3.8 It is therefore important that we should give due weight to the other side of an argument in which our natural preferences and inclinations are so deeply engaged. In the first place, the history of

Christianity shows that the very notion of a 'private' religion, without social and political implications, is a relatively modern one. In the early centuries, if Christians had been concerned only with personal salvation and piety, they might well have been able to keep their heads down (as did adherents of the mystery religions, for example) and avoid exposing themselves to persecution. But in fact they saw the appeal to divine authority by the Emperor as something which their faith forced them to challenge; and many paid for this with their lives. In the Middle Ages, it was taken for granted that the whole of political and economic life was an appropriate sphere for the concern and influence of the Church. It was only with the individualistic humanism of the Renaissance, and subsequently with the Cartesian distinction between the thinking soul and the web of material and social phenomena which surround it, that it became possible, and eventually popular, to think of religion as essentially a matter of the relationship between an individual and God, without regard to the society in which that individual is set. We must not oversimplify. Religion had been a deeply personal and private matter long before Descartes. But the separation of religious faith and practice from the rest of life, and the compartmentalization of religion within a fundamentally secular understanding of the world, is made possible only by a dualistic approach to the human person. Such an approach has been popular in the West only since the Enlightenment and may already be obsolete. It is only in this relatively brief period that the question could have arisen of a gospel which was not concerned for society as much as for the individual.

3.9   What is the situation now? Philosophy has moved far beyond Descartes and has finally exorcised 'the ghost in the machine': few philosophers now allow for a separate component, or 'soul', with which religion can be uniquely concerned, and modern philosophy encourages us to return to the idiom of the Bible, according to which God, addresses our whole person along with the social relationships amid which we live. Modern social sciences insist that no analysis of the human person is adequate which does not take into account the influence upon that person of language, culture and social conditions. Christians claim to be entrusted with a divinely revealed understanding of human nature; but they have no excuse for continuing to express this in terms of a once fashionable Cartesian analysis while most philosophers and psychologists have moved on. The suggestion that religion is an entirely personal matter of the relationship of an individual with God should now be as unacceptable as the belief that knowledge is an entirely personal matter of the relationship of an individual with the environment.

3.10   Christian belief in life after death is properly expressed in terms of the Resurrection of the Body: the Greek concept of an immortal soul has never been able to give adequate expression to it. But even in this life the Cartesian model, according to which religion is of concern only to our inmost being or soul and does not touch the material and social conditions under which we live, hardly does justice to the facts. It is possible to adopt such a view when one is fit and comfortable. But suppose one is ill, or starving? Every hospital chaplain knows that a sick person is conscious of one overriding problem – illness. There is no inner self which can be detached in order to attend to religious matters: religion is meaningless to the patient unless it is related to the condition of his or her body. The same impossibility of identifying a 'soul' independent of material circumstances has always been obvious to missionaries working among people who are starving or deprived of the basic conditions of life: ministry to them cannot be divorced from concern for their material needs. And the same, according to our own observation and to the testimony of many who have given evidence to us, is true of UPAs. We have seen areas where unemployment, poor housing and the threat of criminal violence have reached such proportions that they are like a disease: they so dominate people's thinking and feeling that no presentation of the gospel is possible which does not relate to these material deprivations. In these circumstances, everything tells against the notion that there is a 'soul', quite independent of social and economic conditions, to which an entirely personal gospel may be addressed.

The Tradition of Christian Social Thought

3.11   It is against the background of the excessive individualism of much Christian thinking in the nineteenth century that we must place Marx's perception that evil is to be found, not just in the human heart, but in the very structures of economic and social relationships. This perception is also found to a notable degree in the Old Testament (from which, in fact, Marx may have derived it), where there is explicit recognition of the inevitable tendency of the rich to get richer and the poor to get poorer unless some constraint is imposed to limit the freedom of individuals to profit without restraint from a market economy. Most ancient societies were aware of this tendency, and some actually took measures to curb it – Solon's legislation for the cancellation of debts in sixth-century Athens is a case in point. But the Old Testament is unique in attempting to impose a number of controls upon society to check the inevitable increase of social and economic inequalities. Slaves were to be manumitted after a set period; debts were to be remitted every seventh year; the administration of justice must safeguard those with least property and rights; a portion of all agricultural produce must be reserved for the poor; usury was forbidden within the society.

3.12 It is true that there appears to be little explicit continuation of this tradition in the New Testament. This may be due to the fact that in the time of Christ the land was under foreign occupation and it was no longer possible to put any of these economic measures into effect. But there is no reason to doubt that the principle of the periodic adjustment of social inequalities lived on, and was part of the inspiration for that radical reversal of social priorities which is expressed in the Magnificat, the Beatitudes and elsewhere (particularly in Luke's gospel): in the coming new age the poor are to be exalted and the rich are to be brought low. That God has an interest in the ordering of society is thus a conviction which runs right through the Bible and on into a long line of Christian social theorists from St Augustine to the present day. Moreover the New Testament adds its own values to those offered by the Old, values which could be expected to characterize any social order that conformed to the will of God. Jesus' teaching on the Kingdom reveals a pattern of human relationships which can be fully realized only in the new age but which can be at least partially experienced in the present; and other values, such as freely-given mutual service, care for the weak, and the overcoming of racial and social barriers, are so prominent in the Epistles that they can claim a place in any Christian social thinking. The elaboration of these elements into an actual system of social and political life has occupied the minds of English Christians from Thomas More to the Christian socialists of the nineteenth and twentieth centuries.

3.13 No single blueprint has emerged. The prophetic call for justice, with its concern for the rights of the weak and the poor, is heard again and again; but there is no generally agreed manifesto for a Christian social order. Yet this long tradition of Christian social thinking, if it does not offer an immediate alternative to the present political and economic system, has nevertheless kept alive the fundamental Christian conviction that even in this fallen world there are possibilities for a better ordering of society. In particular, we must continue to ask insistent questions about modern slogans which tend to establish themselves as self-evident maxims. It is often said, for example, that the first priority for our economic system is 'the creation of wealth'. There are of course good grounds for this, in that the survival of any industrialised country depends on the maximum use of resources for the production of goods. But there are important provisos. The creation of wealth must always go hand in hand with just distribution. The product must have some intrinsic value, and its production must have due regard to social and ecological consequences. There is a long Christian tradition, reaching back to the Old Testament prophets, and supported by influential schools of economic and political thought, which firmly rejects the amassing of wealth unless it is justly obtained and fairly distributed. If these provisos are not insisted upon, the creation of wealth cannot be allowed to go unchallenged as a first priority for national policy.

3.14   A similar case is presented by the frequently heard proposition that 'industry must become more efficient'. In the full sense of the word 'efficient' – which is a measure, not just of profitability, but of the general excellence of the product or service and general working conditions – this proposition is indisputable. But today the word is often used with the more restricted meaning of employing the minimum number of people in pursuit of lower unit costs and higher profitability. Now of course this is a condition of the survival of any industry in today's highly competitive market: management has a duty to take full advantage of labour-saving technology and to reduce any inherited surplus in the work-force; only so can an industry offer its employees and shareholders a secure prospect for the future. But this is not 'efficiency' as it has been understood by a large part of the business community. The efficiency of industry can be regarded as a top priority only if the necessary provisos of quality, safety, reliability, etc are observed. Moreover the benefits of automation and 'cost efficiency' are liable to accrue to an ever-decreasing number of people. A disproportionate part of the real cost of the 'slimming' of British industry may be borne by those who are made redundant – or, still more seriously, by young people whose prospects of employment are steadily diminishing. The concern for social justice and for the protection of the weak which pervades the Old Testament, and the repeated New Testament call to 'share one another's burdens', authorize us to challenge the slogan of 'efficiency' unless active steps are taken to prevent a disproportionate share of the social cost of modernization being borne by the low paid and unemployed.

3.15   But may not this be only a temporary problem? Under sensible management, and given favourable world conditions of trade and international order, may not the productive base of the British economy grow so fast that the reduced workforce in existing industries will be offset by the emergence of new ones? We argue elsewhere that this is too simple a view. Under present policies unemployment seems likely to remain at around its present level, if it does not increase still further, for many years to come. It follows that we have not only to pursue a more just distribution of the benefits of technology; we have to alter our attitudes to work itself. It is often said that we are all the inheritors (or the victims) of the 'Protestant Work Ethic', implying that men (and now women) are accorded respect only if their lives show evidence of hard and productive work. Certainly our culture presupposes a close connection between employment and status. (There is a distinction, as we shall argue in Chapter 9, between employment and 'work'.) Social position follows types of employment or profession; long working hours are rewarded by extra pay or promotion; personal respect is gained by the ability to 'hold down a job'; one of the first questions asked of a stranger is 'What do you do?'. There is none of this in the Bible or in early Christian tradition. Certainly there is condemnation of idleness: none may unilaterally contract out of the work which is necessary for any society to sustain itself. But, beyond this, work is never seen as a means of gaining wealth or status. On the one hand it is a necessary feature of our fallen human condition; on the other it is an opportunity for partnership with the Creator in making the world a place of justice, plenty and peace. In the course of our visits we have seen tragic examples of the destruction of people's self-respect through loss of a job. We must not only press for the creation of more employment and for a more equitable distribution of available work; we must also work for a real change in public attitudes. Individuals must be judged, not by their ability to find gainful employment in an increasingly competitive labour market, but by what they are in themselves and by the contribution they can make to the common good. Practical thinking along these lines is already well advanced in Christian and other bodies. We need more of it in the Church; we need also a recognition of its importance in statements of public policy.

3.16   These challenges addressed to widely accepted maxims arise not from a clearly defined Christian social and political philosophy but from the existence in Scripture of a different paradigm of social and economic relationships. This shows, at the very least, that there is no inevitability (as many economists would readily admit) in the working of alleged economic 'laws', and that the slogans and maxims of modern industrial practice and economic policy are as much open to moral scrutiny as they have ever been in the past. But underlying all this is a profound unease which a Christian is bound to feel about the moral and spiritual effects of the modern consumer economy, depending as it does on the continual stimulation of all attainable desires. Not only does it come perilously close actually to encouraging the sin of covetousness (which St Paul (Col. 3.5) identified with the fundamental human tendency towards idolatry); it also increases the sense of alienation and powerlessness of those (now numbered in millions rather than thousands) whose income is too low for them to be able ever to respond to the allurements of media advertisements and shop windows. Christians can hardly be expected to propose a realistic alternative to the entire economic system; but there is ample precedent in the Christian tradition for exposing the system we have to moral judgement.

3.17   Three matters in particular have struck us as deserving this kind of scrutiny:

(i)   We need to be vigilant that taxation should always serve its primary purpose of enabling those who have an adequate or more than adequate income to create amenities which are to the advantage of all. The recent discussion of the rating system, for instance, has shown too little concern for it as a means by which the local community can not only provide services for the use of all but can make adequate provision for those least able to help themselves.

(ii)   The high incidence of unemployment and other forms of deprivation obliges the State to provide compensating 'benefits' to those who do not share the relative affluence of the rest. But it is not easy for state benefits to be given to individuals without affronting their human dignity. It is successfully accomplished in the case of non-means tested entitlements such as child benefit, and old age pensions; but when more detailed enquiries into circumstances have to be made it demands the services of well-trained, patient and sympathetic civil servants. The administrative economies introduced by the DHSS in the face of the ever-growing number of claimants produce situations of acute personal humiliation. The large number of benefits not taken up by those entitled to them, and the degrading conditions (which we have seen for ourselves) under which benefits have to be claimed in many DHSS offices, testify to the failure of our society to find an acceptable solution to one of the more inhumane consequences of our free market economy.

(iii)   There is a strong Christian tradition which encourages individuals to live simply themselves and to apply the residue of their income to the good of others. This found expression in the life-style of many Victorian industrialists, whose standard of living was relatively austere and who used their surplus wealth to endow schools and other public utilities. Many people are outstandingly generous today; but it must be said that a society which requires for its prosperity the encouragement of personal acquisition and the maximum consumption of material goods may be one which gives insufficient encouragement to restraint and self-denial. Not that there is less instinctive altruism than there was: there is an amazing response, for example to disaster appeals and to calls for voluntary blood donors. But in a highly competitive and consumer-oriented society the chance to elicit and encourage such motivation is rarely seen, and a concern for social justice, and a human and compassionate response to the plight of the disadvantaged, has become harder to elicit. This is as true within the Church as in the country at large. Christians have a responsibility to give a lead in this respect; but when they do so they run counter to the prevailing ethos of society. Ultimately it is only an absolute commitment to our solidarity one with another, a recognition of the importance of all forms of collective action for the common good, and a passionate concern for the rights and well-being of those least able to help themselves, which can redress the balance of the excessive individualism which has crept into both public and private life today.

3.18   Comment of this kind requires no further justification; it is a legitimate expression of the Church's proper concern for a just and compassionate social order. Again and again in the history of the Church an encounter with the suffering and deprivation being endured by their fellow citizens has impelled church men and women to resort to political action. There are notable examples in the nineteenth century of church leaders, drawn from widely differing traditions of churchmanship, being so shocked by the social conditions of the time that they worked energetically for change.[1] The visits we have made on this Commission have given us the same experience and elicited the same response. Large numbers of people suffering 'multiple deprivation' as a result of factors outside their control present a spectacle of misery which forces us to ask how we – the Church, the nation – can come to their aid. The issue is a practical one of how Christian compassion and a Christian concern for justice can appropriately find expression in such circumstances – and this is not only a matter for Christians. We have met dedicated people working in the inner cities who belong to no church but whose concern and commitment put many church members to shame. This impulse to help those in need is so close to the heart of any authentic response to the gospel that Christians should be particularly sensitive to trends or policies which make this help more difficult to give. Our society prides itself on being compassionate; and all political parties would wish to appear to be making it more so. But if the policies of any government can be shown to be making the plight of some classes of citizens actually worse, and if moreover the resources available to those who seek to alleviate this plight are being reduced, it is a clear duty for the Church to sound a warning that our society may be losing the 'compassionate' character which is still desired by the majority of its members.

Intermediate Action

3.19   Social comment of this kind is a legitimate option for the Church, and proceeds from a long tradition of Christian social concern. Yet we cannot discharge our responsibility merely by political exhortation or even by political action. The working of economic and social processes depends ultimately upon securing the willing co-operation of people. It is the neglect of this crucial human factor which we have seen to be responsible for some of the worst social conditions in our cities today; and this has led us, throughout our Report, to lay great emphasis on forms of action and service which are intermediate between personal ministry to individuals and political action directed towards society as a whole. These are forms of action which promote *community*.

3.20   Here we find ourselves in company with many secular agencies (the police, the probation service, the social services and countless voluntary organizations) which have begun to address themselves to 'community work' or 'community development' of various kinds. The word 'community' needs to be used with care. It may denote a value which is central to some of the most creative social work which is being done in inner cities today; equally it can be a euphemism for inadequate social provision (as when mentally ill or mentally handicapped people are discharged from long-stay hospitals allegedly to 'care in the community'). Sociologists differ widely over its definition, or even over the validity of the concept; 'community workers' themselves employ different methods and pursue different aims. Yet some 'sense of community' remains a value which is generally agreed to be desirable. The idea of a vertical 'street' in a high-rise block of flats has often turned out to be a failure because it is inimical to the kind of 'community spirit' which may develop in a street of terraced houses. The closure of a school on a housing estate, even if the children can then be better provided for elsewhere, is felt to be a serious loss to the 'community' in that it removes a natural focus of local association in an area already suffering from a scarcity of social amenities. However difficult to define, the word 'community' has been justly called a 'warmly persuasive word',[2] usually referring to a value that is found in the social relationships of a particular locality, and a means by which people can recover confidence, dignity and some degree of influence over the conditions under which they are forced to live.

3.21   This growing interest in a 'community' approach to social and pastoral problems must be a matter of concern to the Church. The Church is itself a particular kind of community of which the distinguishing features are clearly stated by St Paul. It is, first, essentially local. It is constituted by people in a certain town or area, who meet together regularly, bear one another's burdens, suffer one another's pain and participate in a common celebration. Every individual matters, conscientious scruples are respected, each person's gift is given full opportunity to be exercised, so long as it serves the over-riding principle of 'building up' the community as a whole. But this local Church should never be inward-looking. It is part of a wider community, a universal Church with which it maintains contact through its ministers and to parts of which it may be called on to give practical or spiritual help. It is through such a 'community' that Christians seek to give expression to the spiritual gifts, the mutual love and care, and the self-sacrificial service to one's neighbour and to all one's fellow human beings which lie at the heart of any serious response to the challenge of Jesus.

3.22   This is not mere theory. Again and again, by the grace of God, Christians have known and experienced this *koinonia* as a reality. When they do so, their shared dedication to a life of worship, prayer and service becomes a powerful testimony to their faith, and can make a significant contribution to the life of those around them. It is true, of course, that the Church has failed to present to the world a spectacle of Christian 'community' at least as often as it has succeeded; moreover in many inner city areas the Church has too small a presence to be able to impinge significantly on the 'community spirit' of the neighbourhood. Yet this Christian pattern of personal relationships within a community authorises the Church both to support and to challenge the principles which govern community work in Britain today. It can support them, in that the Christian doctrine of humanity presupposes that we exist in a network of personal and social relationships in which the God-given potential of each one of us is developed, and that we have a deep-rooted solidarity with all other human beings which finds expression in mutual service, sacrificial self-giving and love. Any form of social work which enhances the dignity, the mutual respect and the opportunities for personal growth and fulfilment available to every individual through involvement in some form of 'community' can be enthusiastically welcomed by Christians and can offer an important field for active Christian service and co-operation. But at the same time the Church has to be ready to challenge any understanding of community which neglects the needs of its weaker members, which is concerned with individuals' rights and material possessions at the expense of the common good, or which is indifferent to the interests of those who happen to be outside. A Christian community is one that is open to, and responsible for, the whole of the society in which it is set, and proclaims its care for the weak, its solidarity with all, and its values which lie beyond the mere satisfaction of material needs.

3.23 By its history and its ethos the Church of England is uniquely placed to make a significant contribution in this field of 'community work'. Its parish system, however attenuated by social mobility and shifting centres of population, still lays on every priest and congregation a responsibility for the locality in which they live and offers an immediate sphere for Christian compassion, concern and solidarity with others: and it has a traditional pastoral concern for those who do not normally attend church but like to avail themselves of it at certain times. Involvement in 'community work' may often be a valuable and appropriate means by which the Church may perform this service to the neighbourhood; but it will always do so in the light of its own inherited understanding of a God-given 'community', and its own vision of the ultimate realization of God's Kingdom in a form of human society.

3.24 There is one feature of English society today which gives particular urgency to this Christian contribution. In our section on Youth we emphasise the profound sense of *alienation* experienced by young people today. This experience is not confined to the young. Whole sections of our society, and particularly many of those who live in UPAs, feel estranged from their neighbours, from social institutions and indeed from the rest of the country. They have lost their dignity, their self-respect and all sense of hope for a better future.

3.25 This sense of alienation provides a social context in which the preaching of the gospel becomes urgent and relevant. Those who are alienated can identify with the forsakenness of Christ on the cross, and may the more easily come to believe that this same Christ now assures us of direct access to God and eternal life with him if, stripped of our own power, status and pretensions we come to him in penitence, faith and love. But this gospel is also one which must be witnessed to by the corporate life of the Church. It is only when the Church itself is sensed to be a community in which all alienation caused by age, gender, race and class is decisively overcome that its mission can begin to be authentic among the millions who feel themselves alienated, not only from the Church, but from society as a whole. The challenge this presents to the Church of England in many aspects of its life and organisation will be spelled out later in our Report. But it is a challenge also to give this corporate, or 'community', aspect of our Christian understanding a high place among our theological priorities.

The Gospel and Other Faiths

3.26   This emphasis on 'community' may also help us to come to terms with an important and often conspicuous feature of UPAs in Britain today: the presence of adherents of other faiths. Their arrival in this country has presented the members of Christian churches with theological problems which they have not yet been able to resolve. Does the truth of the Christian gospel exclude all other truth and oblige us to preach against other faiths and seek to convert all their adherents? Or are all religions simply aspects of the one truth, and can we all live and work together, learning from each other in our quest for knowledge of and obedience to the one God whom we all worship in our different ways and idioms? Are not all our churches and households of faith made up of different strands of dogma, experience and practice, sometimes already in tension with each other, so that in other religions we shall find similar tensions and fruitful avenues of common self-understanding? These are hard theological questions, and the Church of England has not yet been able to reach a common mind on them. But a recent study by the Board for Mission and Unity[3] probably represents a growing consensus in the Church of England (as in missionary societies abroad) that confrontation is no longer an appropriate stance for Christians to adopt in the face of the evident dedication, spirituality and search for truth evinced by so many members of other faiths. It recommends a more open approach, while ascribing ultimate authority to the claims of Jesus Christ.

3.27   The realities of life in UPAs force us to take these questions seriously. The great majority of all adherents of other faiths in this country are of Asian origin, most of whom are from the Indian sub-continent. They form, not just a religious, but an ethnic community. Their legitimate concern to practise their religion, and to preserve their religious and cultural identity, is not separable from their right to decent housing, employment, education and social provision. These are the concerns of all social and educational work in the community which is committed to respecting the gifts, the potential and the dignity of all. Christians, we have argued, are called by the basic postulates of their faith to participate in such work. It follows that they cannot withdraw from multi-faith areas (for instance, on the grounds that witness, worship and ministry there are no longer viable or economically justifiable); they must maintain their presence there, even as Christ was present among people who rejected his claims; they must respect the religion of their fellow citizens as much as they respect their persons, while faithfully witnessing to the truth and primacy of the Christian revelation.

3.28   There are places where Christian service to the community may take the form of helping others to maintain their religious and cultural heritage in freedom and dignity. Many Christians have found that such service, though apparently incompatible with traditional styles of evangelism, in fact represents a faithful and sometimes compelling witness to Christ. For Christ came to serve amid the complex realities of his own time and is still glorified by the service of those who take seriously the religious quest and the religious inheritance of those around them.[4] This task may require a generous approach to the use of church resources, in the ways in which we shall suggest in Chapter 7. We have been told that it is the withholding of these resources which has often been most resented and has robbed the Church of credibility in the eyes of members of other faiths. It is the offering of them which is often the most eloquent and valuable gift we can make. But it need not be all giving. Our responsibility for the community is one that we also share with other religious bodies. As we seek to exercise it together we grow in mutual understanding and respect; and when people of different faiths find opportunities for practical collaboration and mutual discussion they begin to discover for themselves the riches of our shared humanity and the solidarity created by our common quest for God.

The Challenge to Theology

3.29   We believe, then, that there are sound theological reasons (some more apparent today than in the past), as well as solid support in many strands of the Christian (and indeed Anglican) tradition, for the Church to show its care and compassion for our disadvantaged neighbour *both* by personal ministry to individuals *and* by social comment and action; and we have drawn attention to the importance of a kind of intermediate area (often represented by a form of 'community work') embracing the two. But we must be careful not to assume that it is the wealthier and more powerful members of the Church who are always the givers, and the deprived residents of our inner cities who are always the receivers. Poverty may greatly diminish human dignity; but dignity is not necessarily restored merely by the promotion of material standards and values. There is no reason to think that the gospel is more authentically lived out in 'comfortable Britain'. On the contrary, we have again and again found evidence of a vitality and generosity in Church life in deprived areas which is a challenge to more affluent congregations. Our task as a Church is by no means only to show concern for the victims of oppressive social conditions; it is also to find ways of discerning and receiving the gifts of those who have worked out a genuine Christian discipleship under circumstances of 'multiple deprivation'. The failure of the Church today is not just a failure to respond to need; it is – perhaps still more – a failure to attend to the voices, the experience and the spiritual riches of the 'poor' in its midst.

3.30   But how is this to be done? The challenge is one which raises questions about the nature of theology itself. In the West, theology since the early centuries has been understood as a deductive science. Christian truth is conceived as a system, derived both from divine revelation and human reason, and growth in understanding is aided by historical and philosophical disciplines. One consequence of this is that 'progress' in the Christian faith, and hence status in the Christian community, has tended to be seen as a consequence of academic study. The Catechism was traditionally something to be 'learnt'. Confirmation presupposed the ability to answer the Bishop's questions on doctrine rather than evidence of habits of prayer and practical charity, and the building up of a Christian community was promoted primarily by education and study. All this has greatly favoured the life of the Church among people of above average literacy and intellectual ability; it has accorded well with the education, the reading habits and the social conventions of the upper and middle classes. But it has always been an obstacle to nurturing the Church in a working class environment. In particular, it has profoundly affected the church's expectations of its ordained ministers, who are still selected and examined more searchingly on their intellectual knowledge and abilities than on their pastoral gifts and personal sanctity. This is undoubtedly one of the factors which has inhibited the growth of indigenous ministries and congregations in working class areas.

3.31 Must theology always have this deductive and academic character? Certainly there can be no doubt of the value of critical study of the scriptures and of rigorous theological thinking, or of the important role played in the Church by well-trained theologians. Our search for the truth about God demands full use of our powers of reason. But truths which are really important to us are not conveyed and received only through sets of logically related propositions, and there is no obvious necessity to give this kind of thinking priority over other means of communication which God may use to stir our imagination and bend our will to his purpose. The vitality of other forms of theological expression in churches in the Third World, and indeed in certain congregations in our own cities, forces us to ask whether theology must always have such an academic character if it is to be authentic. In fact, there are signs within academic theology itself that a more flexible approach may be possible. 'Narrative Theology', sociology of knowledge, and new techniques of literary criticism such as structuralism, all now find a place in official theological studies, and all represent something of a protest against the deductive procedures of traditional Western theology.[5]

3.32 An important challenge to traditional theological thinking is presented by Liberation Theology. This starts from the observation (which would be taken for granted in the sociology of knowledge but has only recently been taken account of by the churches) that the agenda and the priorities for theology have always been set, even if unconsciously, by those who have practised it – that is, those who are relatively well educated and secure. In doctrine there has been a preoccupation with intellectual consistency which has presupposed certain academic disciplines. In ethics, the questions asked have assumed a freedom of action and decision fully possessed only by the upper strata of society. In spirituality, the classic manuals assume a relatively leisured life. There has of course been a long and honourable tradition of Christian service to and ministry among the poor. But for the most part Christian theology has been created by those relatively well provided with leisure, freedom of action and material well-being. As a result, it has not much concerned itself with the perceptions and the witness of those who do not have these advantages.

3.33 In Latin America the prevailing conditions of extreme social and economic oppression have posed a challenge to these traditional theological priorities. Liberation Theology has proposed a method and a set of priorities which reflect the concerns, not of the oppressors but of the oppressed, not of the rich but of the poor. In this context, theological reasoning has seemed relevant, and in a certain sense 'true', only if it results in a determination and a strategy to liberate the poor from this oppression.

3.34 It is often said, and doubtless rightly, that conditions in Western Europe are not such that this kind of political 'liberation' could ever be a comparable theological priority. Liberation Theology is a development that has grown out of political and economic conditions radically different from our own. Yet it represents a challenge to us to look again at our own theological priorities. It has already contributed to the emergence of a new emphasis in official Roman Catholic theology on 'the preferential option for the poor'. In Britain today, it forces us to ask what it is (in the way of inherited attitudes and priorities) that may actually be preventing people from responding freely to that power which (we believe) is capable of transforming both their individual lives and the society in which they live. Some of us have our freedom of thought and action curtailed by the slogans which dominate public policy or commercial advertising, others by the degrading lack of amenities and opportunities that afflicts our Urban Priority Areas. To all of us, the example of Liberation Theology opens up the possibility that new priorities, as well as new methods, can restore to us a theology that is truly relevant to the needs and aspirations of people today.

3.35 But we do not see these new understandings of theology as the concern only of professional theologians. In Latin America a vigorous Church life has emerged in what are called 'base communities'. These conduct their own form of theological reflection which is not determined by the traditional academic and catechetical patterns of Church teaching but which has proved its validity in nourishing and enlarging an authentic Christian witness, spirituality and mission. Again, this precise form of Church life is not necessarily appropriate to the different social and cultural conditions of Western Europe. But are there not signs that, in UPAs as elsewhere in this country, small groups of people are beginning to follow their own style of theological reflection and to deepen their Christian understanding in ways that spring naturally from their own culture and abilities? May such groups not have a contribution to make to the theological thinking of the wider Church? May we not expect to see in UPAs the emergence of a theology which would provide an authentic basis for a Christian critique of contemporary society?

3.36 Such a theology would start, not from a conventional academic syllabus of Christian knowledge or biblical study, but from the personal experience, the modes of perception and the daily concerns of local people themselves – priorities which might well be different from those of people of a more intellectual background. It would give prominence to the narrative character of much of the Bible: it would stress, for example, the drama of the passion and crucifixion rather than any intellectual formulation of the Doctrine of the Atonement. It would take seriously the power and promise of the gospel to transform men and women, not only in their personal beliefs and moral conduct, but in the whole patterns of their social relationships. Such a theology should not be pursued in isolation from the rest of the Church; indeed, it would require the expert and sensitive collaboration of scholars and educators. We have argued that it has a legitimate place in the total theological scene, and that there are signs of such an approach being taken seriously by theologians. It is time for the Church to recognize that the priorities for theological study and education need not always be set by the prescriptions of a traditional academic syllabus and to give every encouragement to the growth of theologies that are authentic expressions of local cultures.

Responses to the Challenge
3.37 We must emphasize again that none of this must be thought of as a flight from reason. It is rather a recognition that theology is a more varied and flexible activity than has traditionally been thought, and that abstract intellectual formulation does not necessarily have absolute primacy in the understanding and communication of the Christian faith. Others may be 'theologians' (as indeed the Church has always known) than those who subject themselves to the traditional academic disciplines. This has three consequences in particular which are of importance to us:

3.38 (i) *Evangelism and Christian Education in UPAs.* Christian preaching and teaching can no longer rely on a conscious and shared inheritance of Christian concepts and language. But nor does it take place in a religious vacuum. In obedience to our Terms of Reference, we have commissioned a review[6] of the methods and results of sociological surveys of 'common', 'folk' or 'implicit' religion in Britain today. This has alerted us to the immense variety of religious beliefs which exist in different regions and among different types and classes of people, to the dangers of generalization from such intricate evidence and to the difficulty even of agreeing upon what counts as religious. Yet all agree on a fact that was established by empirical investigation over thirty years ago and has been confirmed by subsequent research: that the British people are by a great majority a *believing* people, to the extent that some 70 per cent of the population claim belief in God or in some sort of supernatural being. But the moment one goes on to ask, What sort of God? wide variations occur, often related to locality, age, class, education and personal experiences, and not always compatible even when held by the same individual. Belief in a God who offers help and consolation to all who pray to him sincerely is found alongside belief in a God who shows rigorous justice in punishing moral offences. Fatalistic superstitions about broken mirrors may be allied with a sense of freedom and responsibility for shaping one's own destiny ('you make the bed you lie on'). These beliefs, though they testify to a strong substratum of religion in British society, go along with widespread rejection of institutional religion, and are for the most part far removed from the official teaching of the Church, often verging on sheer superstition. Moreover, with the weakening of the Church's influence on education (which is an important means of transmitting any form of belief from one generation to the next), and the ever-increasing impact of the media (which are nourished by, but also have an effect on, popular religion), it appears that these beliefs are moving steadily further away from the faith of the Church.

3.39   In these circumstances it can be argued that the most urgent task facing the Church is that of nurturing this common belief in God towards an authentic Christian faith. But the same evidence which suggests this priority also shows the need for great flexibility in tackling it. In some parts of England, and in many suburban or country parishes, those who hold such beliefs may be found as occasional attenders of church services and may be influenced by the traditional worship and ministry of the Church. In working class areas, by contrast, there is often a strong resistance to any form of organised meeting or regular commitment, and common belief will be found almost invariably outside the Church. Any attempt to build upon it will then have to be informal, spasmodic and expressed in totally non-technical and highly accessible language. We should be free to question whether the objective should always be a faith that is grasped and expressed in a form that derives from educated and relatively well-to-do circles in the Church. Our evidence suggests that it is the consistently middle-class presentation of the gospel and style of church life which creates a gulf between it and most working class people. A Church which has only a single highly intellectual style of doctrinal formulation and which orders even its most contemporary forms of worship by reference to a closely printed book of over a thousand pages can never hope to bridge the gulf which separates it from ordinary people. We must recognize that theological correctness – that is, the authentic Christian faith towards which common belief must be nurtured – can be expressed and achieved in a variety of styles and idioms – by imaginative story-telling, for example, as much as by expositions of doctrine. This may at last open the way to a truly indigenous Church in the UPAs.

3.40 (ii) *Ministerial Selection And Training.* The main obstacle to the development of truly 'local' or 'indigenous' ministries has been the apparent necessity to ensure that all ordained ministers should reach an agreed standard of academic achievement. Even when this is relaxed in certain cases the ministers concerned are left with a sense of inferiority if their training has not fitted them to 'compete' with their fellow-clergy who have received the conventional academic training. Students, for their part, feel themselves to be under pressure to achieve a certain level of professional competence – which means (in effect) an academic standard. Once again we must emphasise that there is no question here of a flight from theology. The Church requires competent theologians as much as it ever did, and must continue to make provision for their recruitment and training. The question being asked here is about the importance given to academic criteria in church life generally and in ministerial training in particular. If we are now being able to see not just the possibility but the necessity of presenting and receiving the Christian faith in forms other than that of a doctrinal package, we may be able to begin to take seriously schemes for accrediting ordained ministers on other than academic criteria. There is evidence from other Churches that means can be established for testing the pastoral and personal gifts of ordinands through the co-operation of panels of lay people.[7] As a result, criteria are established which are seen to be objective; and (most significantly) achievement in this area begins to be seen by the Church at large as being at least as important as academic competence. Candidates whose gifts are other than academic, and for whom a traditional theological course would be inappropriate, are respected for their achievement of excellence in other aspects of ministry. Yet there are few signs in the Church of England of a relaxation of uniform academic standards in the training of the clergy; and we have been far too slow in establishing any generally recognized requirements to take their place.

3.41 (iii) *The Ecumenical Scene.* Inter-church relationships have been dominated (some would say blocked) by an over-riding concern for

'Faith and Order'. The presupposition has been that unity between the churches can come only when there is agreement in doctrine and ecclesiastical organization. So long as doctrinal consistency had the supreme place as a the criterion for Christian truth, it was not surprising that this seemed a precondition of unity. Yet remarkable diversity has been tolerated, even within one church or communion, in styles of worship or conduct (note the tolerance, through most of church history, of total disagreement among Christians over the fundamental issue of pacifism). Today's climate allows for a greater diversity also in doctrinal matters[8]: unity may be conceived of as an agreement on the limits of diversity over a much wider field. This could give a new dimension, and new hope, to ecumenical co-operation.

3.42   In this chapter we have been concerned to make the following points:

(1)   It requires no theological argument to show that the misery, indignity and despair which we have encountered in the cities of England demand a response from all members of the Church (as they already receive from other sensitive observers). It should be sufficient to alert the Christian conscience to the plight of so many of our fellow citizens.

(2)   Theology can however throw some light on the question of how this concern may be expressed. We have found in the tradition of the church, and indeed of the Church of England itself, abundant precedent both for stressing the need for personal repentance and renewal in the light of the gospel and for actively promoting the social conditions under which that personal transformation may lead to the transformation of society. Indeed, such is the incarnational or 'embodied' character of our religion that we cannot seriously envisage a Christian concern which leaves out of account the physical and social conditions under which people actually live.

(3)   This Christian concern may properly take the form of working for and with our 'neighbour in community'. There is good theological reason to support (and sometimes also to criticize) much of the 'community work' which is being developed by other caring agencies. The Christian understanding of 'community' also provides a framework within which to approach our relationship with people of other faiths and to offer a real alternative to that sense of alienation which now affects so many people in UPAs.

(4)   Along with factors which have been constant in English society for many years – such as the existence of poverty itself, or the failure

of the Church to reach the working classes – we observe some new factors also: the emergence of a new form of economic determinism in public policy, the presence of other religions in our midst, a new readiness among the Christian denominations to work together. We have suggested that there has also been a significant change in the theological climate, and that new initiatives from those involved in urban ministry must be seriously attended to. They represent an authentic challenge to the priorities traditionally taken for granted in the theology and teaching of the Church.

Theology in UPAs

3.43   But we may well be asked: Have we no more to say? Can we not offer a 'theology of the city' which will serve as a guide and inspiration to those who work in Urban Priority Areas?

3.44   This question may be prompted, in part, by that very understanding of theology which we have been calling into question. If theology were always a matter of deduction, drawing upon general principles in order to answer specific questions, then it might be reasonable to expect that we would offer a Christian 'model' of the city which could be applied to the UPAs of Britain today. But theology has always arisen from and reacted to new situations. Doctrine is formulated, not in the abstract, but to settle questions already in dispute; theological commissions are set up, not to create systems, but to respond to particular issues. So it has been in our own work. There may be certain factors common to the crisis which have overtaken our cities. But we have noticed again and again that the response made by different communities to these factors shows amazing variety. It would be highly misleading if we were to propose a 'theology of the city' that claimed to be appropriate to such a wide variety of situations. An authentic theology can arise only as a response to each particular circumstance. We have been offered many such 'theologies' or 'models' in the evidence submitted to us. These are immensely heartening; they demonstrate the vitality of our theological tradition under new circumstances and offer hope and encouragement to those working amid them. It is certainly not for us to sit in judgement over them or to seek to replace them by our own. We see our task more as that of indicating the scope and the constraints within which such theologies can be explored and tested in the Church of today, and to give every possible encouragement to those who are working out their own 'model' or 'theology' in the particular circumstances of their own ministry and vocation.

3.45   We may however conclude by stating certain convictions which we believe to be central to the Christian faith and which have been greatly strengthened in us in the course of our work and observation. We believe that God, though infinitely transcendent, is also to be found, despite all appearances, in the apparent waste lands of our inner cities and housing estates; that men and women are created to glorify God in and through his creation and to serve their fellow human beings in the power of his love; that, even if material values must always be subordinate, salvation involves, not indifference to, but a proper stewardship of, material things; that the city is not to be shunned as a concentration of evil but enjoyed as a unique opportunity for human community; that the justice of God, as revealed in Scripture, is a standard by which all human institutions must be judged; that society, in our fallen world, cannot be purged of its imperfections by careful planning, maintenance and repair (necessary though these are) but requires redemption through suffering and self-giving undertaken in solidarity with Christ; that the gospel, when faithfully proclaimed in word and deed, effects a transformation of individual lives, of families and of communities, and that the Church has a responsibility at all these levels; that St Paul's injunction, 'to be subject to one another'. (Eph. 5.21) implies finding means, both personally and in the institutions of Church and state, to receive the gifts and attend to the voices of our ethnic minority communities; that the Holy Spirit is at work in the churches of our cities as he is elsewhere; that the hope given to us in the resurrection of our Lord Jesus Christ can never be quenched.

References

1   E.g. Wilberforce, Manning, Samuel Barnett. Newman wrote, 'In truth, the Church was framed for the express purpose of interfering or (as irreligious men would say) meddling with the world' (*Arians of the Fourth Century*, III.2).

2   Raymond Williams, *Keywords* (1976).

3   *Towards a Theology for Inter-Faith Dialogue*, GS 625 (1984).

4   Cf David Brown, *A new Threshold, Guidelines for the Churches* (BCC 1976).

5   Cf *Believing in the Church* (Doctrine Commission, 1981) pp 30-33.

6   'The Nature of Belief in the Inner City' by Dr Grace Davie (prepared for the Commission – we hope it will be published).

7   E.g. the Northern College of the United Reformed Church; *Readiness for Ordained Ministry Project* (Province of Western Australia)

8   See the recent study by Yves Congar, *Diversity and Communion* (1982, ET 1984); Stephen Sykes, *The Identity of Christianity* (1984).

Part II
. . . to the Church

i In this part of our Report, we address the Church of England.

ii In a rider to our terms of reference, we were asked particularly to gather information; to evaluate and commend effective forms of mission and ministry; to identify necessary developments and training in a rapidly changing society; and to recognize barriers to effective working at national and diocesan level. Most importantly, we were called on to listen carefully to the voice of Church people and others in the urban priority areas.

iii During the last two years we have attempted to fulfil these aims. The Chapters that follow contain our findings.

iv In Chapter 4 – an introductory chapter – we set out our vision of the kind of Church that is required in the UPAs, and suggest the directions in which the Church of England must move. We set out in detail our recommendations for organisational changes in Chapter 5. In Chapters 6 and 7 we consider respectively the people of the Church and its material resources, and make further recommendations.

Chapter 4

WHAT KIND OF CHURCH?

'How is the Church to take part in the history that the Spirit is making in our cities now?'   (Diocese of Birmingham)

Introduction

4.1   The Church of England in UPAs has presented to us a varied picture. For the most part it is one of faithful presence. There have also been many examples of powerful witness, of the Gospel being lived out in UPA Churches in terms of changed lives and changed communities, and of a Church life which must not be underestimated in terms of its contribution to the Church of England's ministry and mission. Yet unless there is considerable reform this contribution will be progressively weakened, and in places the survival of the Church itself may be threatened.

4.2   Although we were encouraged by the positive view of UPA ministry taken by respondents to our Clergy Survey, we have to report that many people we spoke to claimed that unless the Church of England acts quickly and decisively it will cease to exist in any effective form in many UPAs. We were reminded by others that this warning was not a new one, and that the parochial system has a remarkable capacity for ensuring survival against the odds.

4.3   Our proposals in this Part of our report reflect our argument in Chapter 3 that the Christian Church has a clear obligation to 'remember the poor'. We consequently consider that it is a priority calling to the Church of England to attend to the greatest concentrations of poverty. These are to be found in the UPAs.

4.4   We indicate in this Chapter the broad directions in which we believe the Church should move in the UPAs. Here, and in later chapters, there may be important lessons for the Church in serving other areas as well. We do not have a key to open all doors. What we try to offer in the following paragraphs is 'a clear vision of a possible and achievable future in a world where God is clearly at work'.[1]

4.5   If the Church of England as an institution is committed to staying and growing in UPAs, then much of our evidence suggests that it will have to change. It is faced not only with the general decline of organised Christianity in England but also with the particular pressures associated with the UPAs themselves. The growing crisis in our UPAs is reflected in the life of the Church within them. It can be seen in the lack of local leadership, the never-ending struggles with money and buildings, and the powerlessness associated with being divorced from the centres of power. And there is the fact, as we have already stressed, that historically the Church of England has failed to reach or to keep the urban working-classes. Submission upon submission to us has said that the Church of England's organisation and ministry have been so completely middle-class that working-class expressions of religion have not been encouraged.

4.6   In the face of this situation some people may advocate that 'more of the same' is required: that Church life can be maintained and preserved through traditional ways of teaching, worship, organisation, membership and leadership. In the light of the evidence submitted to us, however, our collective view is that a different approach is needed. We believe that Churches in the UPAs have to become *local, outward-looking*, and *participating* Churches; they must also have a clear *ecumenical* bias. We explain what we mean below.

A Local Church

4.7   G.K. Chesterton said: 'For anything to be real it must be local'. The evidence we received strongly suggests that the UPA Church must become fully local, in the sense of having a firm commitment to the local people and to the places where they live, work and associate.

4.8   This commitment to what is local does not mean we always support the small against the large, the congregational at the expense of the catholic; nor is it a substitute for regional or national action.

4.9   It is, rather, a commitment to *community*. We have commented in Chapter 3 on the pitfalls which surround the use of this word. Yet our evidence has emphasised that the Church must recognise the primary importance of relating to each *neighbourhood* and estate, and to the groups, networks and associations to be found there. This may mean moving towards neighbourhood church or worship centres, and house groups; but is not to be confused with the concept of 'base communities' in deprived areas.[2] The neighbourhood, we believe, is crucial to the growth of the local urban Church, though small neighbourhood groupings should join together in worship and other ways as part of the larger Church of the parish.

4.10   This emphasis also implies that the UPA Church must be sensitive·to the *local cultures and life-styles* in its leadership, worship and manner of operating. Localities can contain a number of cultures and the Christian Gospel is always more than these local cultures. It has something to give to them and to receive from them.

4.11   For example, it has been made clear to us that the Church's committee structures, agendas, and longer-term planning are often approached in ways which make it much less likely that local people in UPAs will take part. Many have argued for more informal and dynamic forms of taking decisions – for example relying more on parish meetings than PCCs – with a real commitment to involve local people more in the Church's government at all levels. A number of submissions to us have recommended the adoption of 'self-denying ordinances' by people already in positions of leadership to make space for and encourage leadership from the local people.

4.12   Commitment to what is local should also be clear in the patterns of worship, music, presentation of the Gospel, and, indeed, in theology. The Church of England in the UPAs must avoid reflecting an inherited middle-class culture, and draw on the gifts to be found in its neighbourhood.

An Outward-Looking Church
4.13   An effective UPA Church will not just be a local Church in the sense of reflecting local cultures and people in its membership, leadership, and styles of working. It will also be a Church which takes seriously the local realities of life as an integral part of its mission to UPAs and the whole of society. It will look outwards because God sends us out into the world. The alienation between Church of England and the majority of working-class people must cause us all to be greatly disturbed. Faced with such a situation the Church cannot persist in the way of self-preservation and that 'institutional self-interest' which so often preoccupies it. It has to move from the policies of maintenance to the outward-looking policies of mission. And most of the evidence we have received suggests that this can only be achieved by taking seriously the realities of life in the UPAs.

4.14   We see the commitment of the outward-looking UPA Church to its locality as an essential part of its mission, evangelism and service.

One Evangelical organisation declared that without such a commitment and involvement there would be 'no hope for the Church'.[3] This commitment must be seen first in theological terms: the Church must be aware that its locality is the first place in which God is to be both encountered and served. Such a stance demands attentiveness to the individual and social realities of local life and a readiness to share in and interpret them in the light of the Gospel. The Church must be able to reflect on local life in worship and prayer and *bring together* God's revelation as presented in the Scriptures and in the pattern of local life. In so doing, we believe the Church will come to respect the depth of faith, and perceive the work of God, within the UPAs. As Fr Austin Smith told us, 'Don't ask what the Church can do for the inner city; ask what the inner city can do for the Church'.

4.15   Our view of mission therefore recognizes that God is at work in society – which means that Christians are called to 'work together with God where Holy Desires, Good Counsels and Just Works are struggling for birth or growth'.[4] A Church which only 'parallels' society – which exists alongside it but is separate – needs to become a Church which is involved in that society. The outward-looking Church should identify what its members are doing in and for the local UPAs, whether in their full-time work or as volunteers, and should recognise this work as part of its mission, and give its members the fullest support in their work.

4.16   The mission of the outward-looking Church must also include giving time willingly to baptisms, weddings and funerals, including visiting and preparation for these 'occasional offices'. It can be very costly, when people seem to 'use' the Church when they want it, with little thought of deeper commitment. Clergy may feel caught in the tension between the view of the Church as a group of committed Christians and our vision of an outward-looking Church available to serve people's needs, meeting them if necessary at the level of their folk religion. There may be no easy escape from these pressures, yet there are great opportunities for the Church to serve people when they are most open to God – even if there have to be many more stepping stones before they might consider becoming full members of the Church.

4.17   Mission can equally be developed through community centres, and other places where people meet, and a variety of other kinds of project which place the Church at the service of the area in which it is located. Mission should include a ministry to the institutions which shape the lives of people in the UPAs, and an involvement in the processes of political life.

4.18   Such an understanding of mission is compatible with different traditions and perspectives, whether they emphasise personal conversion or the sacramental presence of God, or whether they regard social outreach as 'pre-evangelism' or evangelism. It also involves a clear commitment to promoting Church growth, provided that means a growth in the number of people who worship and act together within – and not divorced from – the local UPA.

4.19   The way of mission we are proposing needs great patience and persistence. It will require careful work over a number of years. It will affect the national Church, dioceses and local churches. We set out in the following chapters our more detailed suggestions for action. We also warmly commend the approach set out by the General Synod's Board for Mission and Unity in their publication *Mission Audit*.[5] We recognise that some dioceses may wish to designate particular localities in the dioceses as 'mission areas'. However, our clergy survey indicated that although in the UPAs 99 per cent of adults do not attend Anglican worship on an average Sunday, the national figure, including rural and suburban areas, is 98 per cent. The difference is hardly significant. The commitment of the whole Church must be to mission in every part of the country.

A Participating Church
4.20   We have come to the conclusion that a local mission-centred Church must be a participating Church. It will participate by *collaborating* with the best expressions of local life and by *contributing* to the transformation of life in UPAs through God's sustaining power and purpose. By sharing in the life of God in the world more fully, the UPA Church can become a more responsive and confident Church.

4.21   We have been aware of what is often nowadays called the plural nature of our society and Church, and by its complexity. Many of our urban areas have not just one culture, but many. The complexity of life in our UPAs demands that different spheres of knowledge, experience and skills are brought together, and developed; for example by the Church sharing its buildings and human skills with local groups.

4.22   For the Church in UPAs to move in this direction will mean it will have to develop, above all, the skill of *listening*. We have been urged repeatedly to recognise that a prerequisite for building more effective

Churches in UPAs is a willingness on the part of Anglicans to listen to other local Christians, and other local people.

4.23   For the Church of England to listen more should lead on to the development of collaborative ways of working that will include ministry being shared between laity and clergy; teams of varied skills and functions working together; Churches working with other Churches across parish boundaries, areas and deaneries; and Diocesan Boards and Councils working together with the UPA Churches.

4.24   One of the chief examples of collaboration will be partnership with other denominations. It has been said to us so often and so simply in different UPAs: 'It is madness for us to work separately here'. We strongly affirm the importance of the ecumenical factor in the local, outward-looking and participating Church in the UPAs.

4.25   Ecumenical partnership is a central part of the Christian response to God. Sectarian church life contradicts the calling of the Church to be universal, crossing all boundaries of race and class. Faced with the challenge of UPA life we must do together what can in conscience be done together.

4.26   The differences between the Christian traditions today are not something simply to be ironed away or lost in the search for a lowest common Christian denominator. If, as we argue, one of the primary tasks of the Church is to give attention to and interpret the experience of local life, it should benefit from the variety of local (including ecclesiastical) traditions which provide a richness of experience and language. The skilful use of all these traditions with their own strengths is a challenge facing the Churches in coming together, staying together and working together. We would stress that ecumenical initiatives should not be restricted to the older established Churches: the Black-led Churches will have an important place in any truly ecumenical work in many UPAs.

4.27   The forms ecumenical involvement can take will vary. Despite a growth in formal Local Ecumenical Projects (LEPs) nationally in recent years, there are still comparatively few LEPs in inner city areas. More are likely to be found in post-war housing estates or in New Towns where, perhaps, there is no history of sectarian church life. In LEPs, several ministers can interchange, sometimes one minister can act on behalf of several denominations, there can be shared ministry and shared buildings. Church leaders need to show that they have a positive policy for such sharing of ministry. We are of course aware that interchange of ministry has limitations; yet we have for example seen in UPAs much interchange between Anglicans and Roman Catholics, in social action, pastoral care and services of the Word.

4.28   In some areas it would be unrealistic to talk of entering into a formal LEP in one great leap forward. Informal partnership often brings clergy and congregations into new relationships of trust in which resources are shared with good effect. In several UPAs, lay people from different Churches have joined in sponsoring local projects of various kinds (for example, under the Youth Training Scheme). Partnership in community service of this kind can bring together individual Christians of all denominations. This can lead on sometimes to the sharing of denominational finances for work mutually judged to be necessary.

4.29   Ecumenical partnership is important for ministry with those institutions and structures which shape the UPAs. This is particularly so with chaplaincies in hospitals, prisons, industry and schools. (We were very concerned to hear examples of black church leaders being excluded from chaplaincies because they are not members of the Free Church Federal Council or the BCC.)

4.30   We would encourage the adoption of Local Covenants and codes of good ecumenical practice: these should include the principle of renouncing the take-over approach; there should be a commitment always to begin any ecumenical partnership by asking: How can we do this together?, and not to begin and only then consult other denominations.

4.31   There are bound to be resistances to greater ecumenical co-operation. If Christians see mission as simply keeping their congregational numbers up, rather than being a sign of God's reconciling purpose for the community as a whole, there is the danger that ecumenical commitments will only be fitted in after their own Church demands have been met. It is important for Church leaders to promote good relationships between individual ministers, and try to ensure that the subsequent appointments help to build on progress that has been made. In some UPAs, Church leaders may be inclined to appoint ministers who have considerable drive and strength, on the grounds that they are the only kind who are likely to survive. We need strong clergy in our UPAs, but those who have learned the importance of collaborative ministry.

4.32   Church leaders also need to give a very firm lead to overcome the inertia, insecurity and prejudice amongst local congregations. They will need to sit down together and look systematically at UPAs, in order to encourage and enable local Churches and clergy to work things out for themselves.

4.33   Ecumenical co-operation can only come out of relationships of trust between people. Careful consultation between interested parties is an essential preliminary to good partnership. The temptation to 'go it alone' is particularly strong in deprived UPAs. There will be complexities to be faced: agreements for shared buildings for instance (though there are by now hundreds of successful examples). A trusting ecumenical partnership inevitably takes time and energy, and a high level of sustained commitment. That is part of its cost. We are clear however that for the Christians in the UPAs to act, speak and share life together as far as possible is part of their common mission. It must not be treated as optional.

4.34   In the following three chapters we set out our proposals for action to develop the Churches in the UPAs in the directions we have set out here. We readily admit that it will not be easy, but it is our conviction that to let matters go on as they are will be a recipe for the continued alienation between the Church of England and the people who live in the urban priority areas.

References
1   Address by the Archbishop of Canterbury, Newcastle, 9 March 1985

2   Base communities (comunidades de base, or local, grassroots communities) within the Roman Catholic Church, especially in Latin America, can take many forms, but common to them all is that they are gatherings of the poorest and most oppressed, organised into small groups with deep mutual sharing, and rooted in the neighbourhood, whether rural or urban. Their primary focus is a shared Bible study, using Scripture to reflect on current social issues in the locality and their experience as a community. The members do not recognize any separation between religion and daily life; they translate their faith into concrete poltical action. They are usually lay led, though sometimes facilitated initially by a priest or religious. They are deeply committed to the Catholic Church, with a vision of the Church which emphasises collective responsibility and fellowship rather than an authoritarian model. Worship and the sacraments are related to the needs and the experience of individuals and of the community. The concept of base communities is not directly transferable to the British context. In Latin America base churches are peasant and pre-industrial, not concerned with upward social mobility, and have little reliance on outside professionals. It is important to distinguish these essentially working-class communities from the 300 or more UK 'basic communities' analysed by David Clark in *The Liberation of the Church*. The latter are largely a middle-class phenomenon. Where they exist in UPAs they are usually of incomers. This is also true of the few branches of some of the newer House Church networks which are beginning to appear in UPAs.

3   Submission from Careforce
4   Submission from the Church in Society Committee of the Board for Mission and Social Responsibility, Diocese of Liverpool
5   *Mission Audit* CIO Publishing, 1984

Chapter 5

ORGANISING THE CHURCH

'We're far too busy to have a strategy.' (Vicar to new curate in East London)

5.1 This Chapter contains our recommendations for organisational changes in the Church of England to enable the development of genuinely local, outward-looking and participating Churches in the UPAs. Our proposals are based on the evidence we have received, and have been developed in the light of our consultations with dioceses and appropriate national church bodies.

Identifying UPA Parishes

5.2 The first need is for dioceses, in consultation with appropriate national bodies, to implement an effective system for identifying and designating UPA parishes. If, in addition to being used for diocesan and local strategies, the system is to facilitate national UPA policies, including the allocation of resources between dioceses, it will have to be as nationally consistent as possible, which in turn points to a need for maximum objectivity

5.3 The only national indicators of deprivation that are readily accessible and capable of being related to individual parishes are those we have referred to in Chapter 1, produced by the Department of the Environment (DoE) from 1981 Census data. Even these are limited to the 46 Partnership areas, Programme authorities and other designated districts under the Inner Urban Areas Act 1978. However they do cover the most serious areas of widespread deprivation in the country. The composite measures identify census enumeration districts whose levels of deprivation are among the worst 10 per cent in the country, based on a single index into which six indicators of deprivation are combined using standardized score techniques (z-scores). The basic census statistics used relate to levels of unemployment (with double weighting), overcrowding, households lacking basic amenities, pensioners living alone, ethnic origin and single parent households. The list has its limitations and is capable of development, but it remains a feasible system for the Church's purposes, subject to the following comments.

5.4   Experience has revealed one of its main limitations to be a tendency to highlight primarily the run-down inner city areas, and a failure to highlight other areas of deprivation where economic, social and housing problems are locally recognised to exist on at least as serious a scale. Typical of these are some of the large local authoritiy housing estates, often on the outskirts of cities, where (as we noted in Chapter 1) some of the selected factors may not apply.

5.5   Bearing this in mind, we undertook a preliminary exercise to identify UPA parishes. We started with those revealed as deprived using the DoE indicators. We call these Group A. The working definition we used was a parish containing at least six enumeration districts assessed by the DoE, on the criteria described above, as among the 10 per cent most deprived in the country; or fewer than six such districts if out of a relatively small total or if the level of deprivation was severe.

5.6   Subsequent discussion with dioceses of the resultant list of UPA parishes we had identified led to a few transfers to or from a 'marginal' category: especially where parishes were on the borderline or where the extent of their mixed nature introduced an element of doubt or anomaly into the assessment. Parishes more appropriately regarded as in a 'City Centre' category, whose ministry to industry or commuters (e.g. in central London) resulted in an anomalous ratio of clergy to residents, were also excluded. However, there was no general attempt to exclude markedly eclectic churches, except in cases that were already on the borderline.

5.7   The identification of other deprived parishes had to depend on the more subjective judgement and local knowledge of the diocese concerned. This second group – which we call Group B – comprises all UPA parishes identified as such by the diocese but which did not rank as 'deprived' under the working definition we adopted or were outside the urban areas covered by the data. In some dioceses they were predominantly outer council estates, and are perhaps typified by them.

5.8   The distribution of UPA parishes identified by our exercise is shown in Table 3 of Appendix B. This suggests that the heaviest concentrations of UPA parishes are in the dioceses of Birmingham and Manchester (over 40 per cent of their parishes), London and Southwark (over one-third), and Liverpool (about one-quarter). We doubt that higher proportions than these are likely to be found in any of the urban area dioceses we did not have time to analyse; nor is the more subjective element in identifying the Group B parishes likely to distort the picture significantly. The incidence of UPA parishes in the other dioceses we analysed is roughly 1 in 6 in Newcastle, Blackburn and Bradford; 1 in 8 in Ripon and Wakefield; and 1 in 15 in Lichfield and Coventry.

5.9   Although this method of identifying UPA parishes has been sufficient to enable us to obtain a broad picture and to draw provisional conclusions, a more comprehensive system will need to be developed for the future. We therefore *recommend* that the Archbishop's Officer to be appointed to follow up our report should oversee the development of such a system, in the light of current studies in Manchester, Blackburn and other dioceses, and in consultation with the Church Commissioners, the Department of the Environment and the Boards of the General Synod. Particular attention should be devoted to finding objective criteria that identify those areas of deprivation which can at present only be recognised subjectively.

Deployment of Clergy

5.10   We mounted a separate exercise to assess how far the Church's staffing strategies took account of the needs of the UPA parishes we identified. Most of our analysis in this Chapter centres on the deployment of clergy, given the importance of the decisions reached nationally, embodied in the Sheffield formula,[1] about the allocation of stipendiary clergy between dioceses. We pursue further the deployment of deaconesses, Church Army workers and licensed lay workers in the next Chapter.

5.11   A broad initial picture of the national deployment of clergy can be obtained by looking at dioceses as a whole and comparing the position in 'urban area dioceses' and elsewhere. Table 1 of Appendix B takes as 'urban area dioceses' the 20 dioceses containing 'designated authorities' under the Inner Urban Areas Act 1978, and lists them in descending order of population per parochial clergy. The fact that they account for 18 of the 22 highest ratios reflects the influence of the factors other than population in the Sheffield formula. It is reassuring to note from Chart 1 in Appendix B that, although the average population per clergy has risen sharply since the early 1970s in all dioceses as clergy numbers have continued to fall (by over 20 per cent), the gap between the urban area dioceses and the rest has continued to narrow, though only slightly. The narrowing gap has resulted from, or been greatly facilitated by, contrasting population movements. Populations of urban area dioceses have tended to decline, or at least to remain static, while those of other dioceses have expanded a great deal in the past 30 years.

5.12   It is perhaps not surprising that we found numbers of baptisms, confirmations, Easter communicants and electoral roll members in urban area dioceses to be smaller in relation to their total population than in other dioceses. However Table 2 of Appendix B shows that if allowance is made for changes in population in the two types of diocese, the average rate of decline since the early 1950s has in each case been lower in the urban group than elsewhere. To what extent this is associated with the narrowing of the gap in clergy/population ratios it is impossible to judge.

(a)   UPAs' Share of Available Clergy within Dioceses
5.13   Dioceses are too big and too diverse to permit more than broad conclusions to be drawn. The Sheffield formula was not designed to be more than a first stage in a fairer allocation of available clergy, i.e. between dioceses. The next stage, between parishes, was for dioceses themselves to determine – though presumably with the expectation that they would follow similar principles, even if the actual formula was not generally applicable below the diocesan level.

5.14   If such principles were indeed followed and the original allocation was fair and realistic enough to permit this, it seems reasonable to expect that, within the kaleidoscope of patterns reflecting the diversity of composition and circumstances of each diocese, there would be scope for similar groups of parishes (in terms of population, land area and church membership) in different dioceses to be staffed at broadly comparable levels. In particular the system should permit broadly comparable clergy/population ratios in UPA parishes in different parts of the country.

5.15   We made an attempt therefore to compare such staffing ratios in the urban priority areas of 12 dioceses. As staffing is based on parishes, this entailed first identifying UPA parishes (as described above) and then relating numbers of clergy to parish populations. The choice of dioceses to study was influenced by the availability of reliable parish population figures (in only three dioceses) or the practicability of estimating them, with local authorities' assistance, in the rest. Existing diocesan estimates for population, where available at all, were inflated by margins ranging typically between 15 per cent and 50 per cent , and often much more – even double or treble!

5.16   This suggests grave questions about the statistical data base in many dioceses. It is difficult to follow fair and rational policies in the distribution of resources, along Sheffield or any other lines, if the basic facts of the local situation are not known. Well-presented statistics are crucial to reform. In recent years the Church Commissioners and Central Board of Finance have set an excellent example in their efforts to unravel and communicate the complex statistical facts of life in the Church as a whole. We *recommend* that dioceses follow this lead, perhaps calling on the skills of laity (retired or otherwise) in their parishes.

5.17   As we have noted, it is for each diocese to decide on the internal distribution of its Sheffield allocation of clergy. Population, where known, will undoubtedly be a factor in this decision, but possibly a less dominant one than in the Sheffield formula. Tables 4 and 5 of Appendix B show the distribution of population and parochial clergy, respectively, in the 12 selected dioceses analysed into three main groups of parishes: identifiable UPA parishes, a neutral group of 'City Centre' and 'Marginal' parishes, and the rest. The UPA parishes are sub-divided between what we have termed Group A and Group B parishes. The residual group can be regarded as broadly 'non-UPA', though in practice it will also contain any UPA parishes in those areas of the selected dioceses which it was not possible to analyse.

5.18   The resulting clergy/population ratios in Table 6 of Appendix B do at least allay any fears that might have existed that UPAs invariably receive *less* than their fair share of clergy. Indeed, where clergy/ population ratios in the UPA and non-UPA parishes of a diocese are reasonably similar, it must imply some measure of positive discrimination in favour of the former, in that any lower scoring on other Sheffield factors (membership, churches and land area) is not carrying full weight against them. This would seem to apply in Southwark, Manchester, Wakefield and perhaps London, and in the Group A parishes of Liverpool and Birmingham.

5.19   It can perhaps be seen more clearly in Chart 2 of Appendix B, which illustrates the variations in staffing ratios in different types of parish either side of the average for each diocese (again set out in descending order of population per clergyman, and with 'Marginal' and 'City Centre' parishes omitted in order to make clearer any emerging contrast). In less densely populated dioceses there will be a stronger pull from extensive rural areas with scattered smaller communities. Thus in

Lichfield, Ripon, Blackburn and Newcastle the average number of people in the care of a UPA clergyman ranges from 25 per cent to 35 per cent higher than in non-UPA parishes. Whether the disparities can be entirely attributed to the application of the same principles as are reflected in the Sheffield formula would be difficult to judge without a great deal more work (on the lines of Table 7 of Appendix B). The disparities in Bradford and Coventry – where the average UPA clergyman has twice as big a population to care for as one in a non-UPA parish – must be beyond anything that Sheffield principles alone could explain.

5.20 There is a clear tendency in some dioceses for Group B UPA parishes to be more poorly staffed than the Group A parishes, notably in Newcastle, Birmingham, Manchester, Liverpool and Wakefield – and to a lesser extent Blackburn. One probable explanation is that the rundown in clergy and amalgamation of parishes in the older inner-city parishes has lagged behind the decline in their populations; whereas the staffing allocation policy, or the build-up towards it, on the newer housing estates has fallen still further short of the needs of the Group B parishes typically to be found there.

(b) Disparity in UPA Staffing Ratios between Dioceses
5.21   If we look at the pattern of staffing ratios in the Group A UPA parishes – i.e. those for which we can be more confident in the consistency of definition in different parts of the country – Chart 3 of Appendix B would suggest that those in the more densely populated dioceses are closely comparable with the diocesan average staffing ratio, and sometimes better. But this means they closely follow the Sheffield pattern: where the Sheffield allocation of clergy is low, UPA staffing levels are poor. If this observation is justified (based on so few dioceses), it might be taken as evidence that Sheffield allocations may not permit equivalent staffing levels in comparable parishes in different dioceses – possibly because the population factor in the formula is not high enough (or the others are too high).

5.22   Disparities in UPA staffing levels may arise not from variations in establishment patterns and policy but from unfilled vacancies. These hinge on the availability of suitable clergy. There are two sides to this: the diocesan perception of the supply, and the attitudes and circumstances of individual clergy.

5.23   The age structure of clergy in a diocese may be a factor. The average age is generally lower in those dioceses whose contraction has been smaller – usually the more urban ones. Similarly there are marked variations between dioceses in the allocation of deacons agreed by the House of Bishops; but here again the pattern has strongly favoured the more urban dioceses. Whether this degree of rejuvenation has been sufficient to meet demand – in particular that for the UPAs – is difficult to judge. Asked whether they had any theory that UPAs were better served by a particular age group of clergy or at a certain stage in their ministry, most dioceses claimed no conscious policy. Some inclined towards younger men, recognising it as 'an exhausting ministry, demanding the height of energy and commitment'; others put more emphasis on maturity. Examination of actual age structures of UPA clergy generally revealed little difference from the respective diocesan norms – which was in line with the general picture emerging from the clergy survey. In some (e.g. Southwark and Coventry) the average was slightly younger, and by as much as five/seven years in Lichfield and Bradford; but none of these was seen as the product of deliberate policy. A number of dioceses cited children's education – particularly at secondary level – as the biggest single factor they faced. This was confirmed in the evidence submitted by the Clergy Appointments Adviser. (As we note in Chapter 6, our survey evidence suggests that concern about children's education is an important, but not decisive, reason for rejecting service in UPAs.)

5.24   However, one diocesan submission to us referred to 'the problem of finding priests who are willing to commit themselves to serving in UPAs'. Another diocese put it more strongly: 'sadly there has been some evidence recently that any attempt at a deployment policy in relation to parishes would be futile. In a couple of parishes in recent months the problem has been to find anyone willing to take on the work'. Yet another wrote: 'on the whole it is a question of getting anybody to go who is willing'. It must be said that this picture of reluctance does not square with the response to the clergy survey of those in non-UPAs, 50 per cent of whom said they would seriously consider accepting a position in an area of urban deprivation: they cannot all be in the wrong dioceses!

(c)   Mitigating or Aggravating Factors
5.25   In terms of *supporting staff*, there are many fewer non-stipendiary ministers (NSMs) [2] and Readers in UPA parishes than non-UPA; but UPA parishes have relatively more deaconesses, Church Army officers and licensed lay workers. Responses to the clergy survey lend weight to the view that the combined total of support from these different sources

is broadly similar in UPAs and non-UPAs. If so, their inclusion will not significantly alter the staffing comparison between the two types of parish.

5.26   Some would argue that, if ecumenical co-operation is the dynamic reality it should be, the adequacy of Anglican staffing levels will be affected by the presence in the area of clergy of *other denominations*, ministering at least to their own flock and sharing responsibility for the overall mission of the Church to the population at large. Unfortunately the degree of ecumenical unity and co-operation that this implies is still more of a vision than a current reality. Moreover practical experience suggests that effective ecumenical partnership requires each Church to participate from strength, certainly not by one Church being absorbed by another.

5.27   We have also given thought to a related issue: whether the presence in the area of large numbers of active adherents of *other faiths* reduces the realistic size of the population for which the clergy effectively exercise pastoral or spiritual care. There is no denying the potential importance of the issue: in the clergy survey, residents of Pakistani/Bangladeshi origin were reckoned to represent more than 10 per cent of the population in over 40 per cent of UPA parishes in the sample (and more than 20 per cent in one-quarter of such parishes). Similarly, residents of Indian origin were thought to represent more than 10 per cent of the population in one-quarter of UPA parishes, but there will doubtless be a considerable overlap between the two. A submission from the Leicester Diocese recognised that, in its clergy deployment policy, 'some account may need to be taken of any significant non-Christian presence'; indeed, it is possible that this factor could be part of the explanation for the high ratios of population to clergy observed in UPA parishes in Bradford and Coventry. The presence of large numbers of people of other faiths will affect the essentially clerical workload (in the form of fewer baptisms, weddings and funerals, for example). But we feel that the overall pressures on clergy and opportunities for ministry and service in this sort of parish will be at least as great as in those of comparable size elsewhere, and it is important that they receive instead specialist support in other forms.

(d) Electoral Roll Members Per Clergy
5.28   Table 7 of Appendix B shows that the pastoral responsibilities of non-UPA clergy, as implied by numbers of members on electoral rolls, are likely to be anything up to double those of UPA clergy, and this will

undoubtedly be seen as a partial justification for any disparity in clergy/ population ratios. It is, of course, the thinking behind the inclusion of an electoral roll factor in the Sheffield formula. It does however raise an important question: to what extent should laity be regarded as an asset rather than a liability in clergy deployment calculations? They should not be regarded simply as numbers to be ministered to. Here are the resources for 'shared ministry'.

5.29   It needs to be noted in passing that some of the variation in electoral roll numbers is less a reflection of church membership than of fiscal considerations. The questionable use of electoral roll membership as a prime factor in assessment of quota has caused parishes in many dioceses to pursue reductions in their electoral rolls to an extent that could be counter-pastoral and with results that, in aggregate, give a false impression of the rate of change in the strength of the Church.

Adequacy of Staffing in UPAs

5.30   Leaving aside the question of relative staffing levels in UPAs and elsewhere, what evidence is there that UPA parishes need, and are crying out for, more clergy? Of the UPA clergy interviewed in the survey, 59 per cent saw their parishes as inadequately staffed. (The comparable figure in non-UPAs was 31 per cent.) Of those UPA clergy who said they were inadequately staffed:

53 per cent (i.e. 31 per cent of all UPA clergy) wanted extra full-time clergy

35 per cent (i.e. 20 per cent of all UPA clergy) wanted secretarial/ office staff

27 per cent (i.e. 16 per cent of all UPA clergy) wanted deaconesses

20 per cent (i.e. 12 per cent of all UPA clergy) wanted lay workers

14 per cent (i.e. 8 per cent of all UPA clergy) wanted part-time clergy

(NB: Percentages in the first column add up to more than 100 per cent, and in the second to more than 59 per cent, because some clergy said they needed more than one type of extra assistance.)

These specific pleas for more staff were supported indirectly by the reference to 'exhaustion' as a problem by 36 per cent of UPA clergy in the sample – compared with 15 per cent non-UPA. Indeed, in our visits to UPAs our impression was of numbers of dedicated clergy who were under very considerable pressure – particularly on some of the big housing estates.

5.31   We believe that the survey information will provide some guidance to the Church and to bodies such as the Advisory Council for the Church's Ministry (ACCM). Yet although 31 per cent of all UPA clergy said they wanted an extra full-time clerical colleague, we would stress that as many or more were looking rather for secretarial help, deaconesses and lay workers.

5.32   We have considered very carefully whether we should argue for a new Sheffield Report, with increased population weighting. But we are well aware that we have been looking at only one side of the equation. Even though the position in the rural areas has been outside our terms of reference, we know that any further reduction in the allocation of clergy to rural dioceses would present very serious problems. Hundreds of villages do not have a resident vicar for the first time for many hundreds of years. Many find themselves grouped with three or four other villages and served by one vicar.

5.33   We do not therefore call for a revision of the Sheffield formula, but commend the evidence we have presented above for further study by the Ministry Co-ordinating Group.

5.34   If in the future there is an increase in numbers of stipendiary clergy, we would argue for a proper share of them for UPAs. For the present our judgement is that a high priority should be given to increased stipendiary lay ministries in UPAs – perhaps community workers or administrators – not necessarily tied to one parish. We hope that the Church Urban Fund we propose might make such ministries possible.

5.35   We *recommend* first, that dioceses review the deployment of their clergy to ensure that UPA parishes receive a fair share and that particular attention should be paid to parishes on large outer estates; and second, that dioceses explore the possibilities of fresh stipendiary lay ministries, not necessarily tied to one parish.

Parish and Deanery
5.36   We now turn to organisational matters at parish level. We cannot of course prescribe here for each local UPA Church: each will face its own particular combination of circumstances. Yet national and diocesan strategies must take account of these local realities.

5.37   We believe that there is a need for UPA Churches to adopt a systematic approach to develop their life and mission. As an aid to this we have prepared a suggested outline for an 'Audit for the Local

Church' for adoption at parish level. We *recommend* its further development and use. Such an audit should not be viewed as another form to be filled in, but a means of enabling local Churches to undertake, in a fairly consistent way, an outward-looking review of the needs of their area and the role of the Church in responding to those needs.

5.38   The audit is set out in full in Appendix A. It is in two parts. The first task is to develop an accurate picture of the parish through the use of maps, statistical data, and the views of the local people. This should be considered alongside information about the church's congregation, activities, buildings and finance. The second part is 'planning for action': first, a careful reflection on how at present the Church engages with the realities of life in its area, and then decisions being reached about priorities for action.

5.39   Such audits at parish level will, we believe, be valuable aids in relation to the recommendations we make in this Report on training, staffing and buildings. They should also be treated as an important part of diocesan applications to the new Church Urban Fund which we propose in Chapter 7.

5.40   Parishes may need assistance in the preparation of these audits, and diocesan staff may need to offer guidelines and general advice. But we see a particularly important role here for deaneries in UPAs.

5.41   Deaneries vary considerably in size and therefore in nature in different areas, and they are often regarded as a mixed blessing. Because however they cover an area wider than the local Church and smaller than the diocese they are more easily able to relate to UPAs which cross parish boundaries. We *recommend* that in urban areas deaneries should have a clear role as units of support and pastoral planning. Teams based on the deanery should include, for example, lay administrators and youth and community workers. The deanery should also play an important part in diocesan planning in relation to staffing, buildings, finance and training, and in helping the pastoral needs of the UPAs to be better understood in the Diocesan Pastoral Committee. All this has important implications for the size of deaneries (which we would prefer to be smaller rather than larger) and for the functions and responsibilities of the area dean (who, in urban areas, should surely cease to be known as the rural dean). The relationship of deanery synods to the process of ecumenical planning remains an unresolved issue which calls for new initiatives.

Developing the Parochial System

5.42   We have been impressed by the commitment, on the part of Church and secular bodies, to the parochial system as a way of ensuring that Christian ministry and mission are maintained in the UPAs. However, we have also received evidence which suggests that the traditional parochial system, although necessary for maintaining an Anglican presence in UPAs, has its limitations, and is in need of reform.

5.43   First, as we have already argued, for the UPA Church to be truly 'local' it must take neighbourhoods far more seriously. By a neighbourhood, we mean that part of a locality which is defined more easily by the people living there than by bodies such as Diocesan Pastoral Committees. People know where their neighbourhood begins and ends – at a main road, a canal, a row of shops. They know all its significant meeting places – Bingo hall, pub, clinic, playground etc. An Anglican parish usually includes a number of neighbourhoods. Yet in some places a neighbourhood may be larger than an existing parish and may cross existing parochial boundaries.

5.44   The recognition of the significance of the neighbourhood for the local Church is very much in the Anglican parochial tradition. Parish boundaries were originally designed to make each parish co-terminous with a virtually self-contained community.

5.45   The importance of neighbourhoods suggests that consideration should be given to:

(i)   the need to revise parochial boundaries to relate more closely to such neighbourhoods (as is already possible under the Pastoral Measure);

(ii)   the development of small neighbourhood-based worship centres. This could lead to 'multi-centre' or 'multi-cellular' strategies for the local Church, reflecting a commitment to a locality and not simply to a congregation;

(iii)   the development of centres, preferably ecumenical, in each neighbourhood (for example in house groups) which reach out in care and concern for the whole life of the neighbourhood and all its people. Small groups for prayer, Bible study, healing, and theological reflection on local issues would be based on them.

5.46   Second, we believe that partnership in ministry is essential in the development of an effective Church in UPAs. We recognize that many clergy prefer to work on their own and in their own parish. There is still a powerful surviving image of the 'slum priest', who, single-handed, in an earlier generation, made his mark on an urban parish. (He may, in fact, have had a number of assistants, clerical and lay; but the *image* of the one-man-band remains.) The problems of teams and groups may also have deterred some from collaborative ministry. They can be badly thought through, and poorly supported or resourced, particularly if they are simply a way of staffing parishes with fewer clergy. They can encourage a new form of clericalism because the laity are excluded. They can be too big and inflexible – giving the impression of a large impersonal health centre.

5.47   Yet despite all that can be said to the contrary, we must express our very clear preference for the various kinds of collaborative ministry. These include collaboration in ministry *within* the local Church, most of all between clergy and laity, but also between different neighbourhood Churches, both informally and in teams or groups; ecumenical collaboration; and collaboration between parochial clergy and clergy engaged in other spheres of ministry.

5.48   We welcome the encouragement given to the further development of collaborative ministries in the Report of the Ministry Co-ordinating Group on Team and Group Ministries.[3] Though we cannot prescribe for every situation, we believe that clergy in the UPAs should be in some kind of team or group. Our evidence suggests that most clergy find teams or groups, whether formal or informal, helpful, particularly in terms of mutual personal and practical support.

5.49   We *recommend* therefore that each parish reviews, preferably annually, what progress has been made in the sharing of ministry between clergy and laity, and in co-operation with neighbouring Churches and with other denominations. (Our proposed audit also refers to this need.) Where formal or informal groups or teams are established, it is important that there should be clear job descriptions, which should be reviewed annually.

5.50   Third, for the parochial system to be made more effective will require a development of varieties of sector ministries: to where people work, are educated, pursue their leisure activities and are treated when sick or infirm. In the UPAs ministry to specific groups – such as young people, the homeless, and drug addicts and their families – may be needed. There will also be a need for ministry to particular institutions – prisons, hospitals, hostels, schools and other educational institutions, and the social services. As well as the need to relate to places of employment, an outward-looking ministry in the UPAs should relate to unemployed people.

5.51　No one parish will have the resources to serve such wide-ranging groups of people or institutions: this underlines the need for collaboration between parishes, ecumenically, and with sector ministers who have responsibility for particular groups or institutions. The development of varieties of ministry can also draw on the skills of the laity and on the help that may be offered by special groups. For example, the contribution of the religious communities to the Church in the UPAs over the last century and more cannot be ignored. Although at present the size of the communities and the age of their members may not seem to offer encouragement, we have seen in a number of UPAs what small groups of Roman Catholic and Anglican religious can achieve. A Community House in a UPA, in close relationship to the local Church, can sustain and support imaginative work in the surrounding area.

5.52　We also welcome the fresh commitment of the Church Army to the UPAs. The skills of Church Army evangelists in working with the local Church on a number of housing estates we have visited, and in non-parochial ministries such as the resettlement of single homeless people, have been impressive. Elsewhere, individuals, families and groups from other areas deciding to live in UPAs at the service of the local Churches, sometimes by 'church planting' or as *ad hoc* communities, can make a welcome contribution to developing a variety of local ministry. They should, however, continually assess whether they are contributing to the development of ministry *by* local people rather than exercising ministry and leadership instead of them.

5.53　For effective local Churches to be fostered, and for the parochial system to be developed, will require the adoption of clear diocesan policies for UPAs. Many dioceses have already taken steps in this direction, and the experience gained needs to be shared systematically. This might be helped by the establishment of UPA co-ordinating officers or committees, working closely with the existing boards and councils, in the urban area dioceses.

The Church and Minority Ethnic Groups

5.54　There are probably fewer than 100 black clergy in the Church of England, and no black staff are employed in senior posts by the Boards and Councils of the General Synod.

5.55   Although our survey indicated that 'race and community relations' was not seen by (mainly white) clergy as a major problem in UPAs, this was not the view expressed by the black people (including black clergy) who gave us evidence. There has been a widespread recognition in the evidence submitted to us that racial discrimination and disadvantage still represent a challenge to be overcome in our society. There were calls for the Church of England to respond, by stressing the importance of compliance with the present laws against direct and indirect racial discrimination. It was also suggested that, at local level, churches should enter into dialogue with minority ethnic groups, and perhaps act as brokers between such groups and, for example, local government.

5.56   The Church of England certainly has an unrivalled network of local organisations uniquely placed to take a strong lead in spelling out the message of racial equality. Yet the Commission for Racial Equality said in their submission to us that members of minority ethnic groups who, for the most part, feel left out of the mainstream of British society, feel equally ignored and relegated to the peripheries of church life. Many black Christians told us that they have felt 'frozen out' of the Church of England by patrician attitudes. Some had left the Church, yet others were still solid Anglicans. We have heard repeated calls for the Church of England to 'make space' for – and so better receive the gifts of – black Christians.

5.57   When we came to consider how the Church of England should respond to this situation, we recognised the primary need for national and diocesan policies to be particularly sensitive to the needs of minority ethnic groups. This is reflected elsewhere in our report where we address issues such as training, church schools, and the sharing and sale of buildings.

5.58   This alone is not enough. There needs to be a clear lead from the centre. We believe that organisational changes must be made at national level to facilitate progress with these and other issues. We believe that the Church must make a clear response not only to racial discrimination and disadvantage, but also to the alienation, hurt and rejection experienced by many black people in relation to the Church of England.

5.59   We have consequently considered whether new advisory or executive bodies should be established by the General Synod and in the dioceses, or new appointments made to existing bodies, to enable the gifts of black people to be better recognised and accepted by the Church, and to create circumstances of equal access for black people to service in all its structures. We have also given some thought as to whether changes are required in the arrangements by which representative bodies (and the General Synod in particular) are constituted.

5.60   We have examined various possibilities in the light of three clear objectives we would wish to see achieved:

(i)   that the issues of racial discrimination and disadvantage are given a clearer and more sustained emphasis in all that the Church says and does;

(ii)   the promotion of a greater awareness of these issues, and associated socio-cultural aspects, throughout the Church;

(iii)   the removal of barriers to the effective participation and leadership of black people at all levels of Church life, particularly in relation to the ordained ministry.

5.61   For these objectives to be met, the important considerations in our judgement are that any structural changes would need to be *effective*, in terms of the process of management and policy implementation, and *accountable* within the Church structures and in relation to the black Anglican constituency.

5.62   We have concluded, and accordingly *recommend*, that the following complementary initiatives should be taken in relation to bodies appointed by the General Synod:

(a)   The work undertaken at present by the Race Relations Field Officer of the General Synod's Board for Social Responsibility (BSR) should be carried forward under a new permanent committee and properly integrated in the Board's structure. This would not require the establishment of a new post, but rather for the Synod to fund the whole (rather than 50 per cent at present) of the BSR's work in this field;

(b)   The appointment of a Selection Secretary with responsibilities for black Anglican vocations to the staff of the Advisory Council for the Church's Ministry, together with the nomination of a senior black clergyman to the ACCM Council by the House of Bishops, to promote the recruitment, training and deployment of black Anglican priests;

(c)   The establishment of a wide-ranging Standing Commission on Black Anglican Concerns which should be established for an initial period (perhaps five years) with a review towards the end of this term leading to a decision on the need for an extension of its life.

5.63   The proposal for developing the role of the BSR would provide a more effective means of education, and the proposed additions to the ACCM Council and staff would be a means of encouraging more effective participation and leadership among black Anglicans. The new Commission, which should include a high proportion of black people among its members (some nominated by the dioceses, others by the Association of Black Clergy), would be charged with taking an oversight of all matters connected with race and the Church. Appropriate reporting lines from the relevant staff members in BSR and ACCM to the Commission should be established.

5.64   The new Commission's brief should not, however, be restricted to the issues arising in the context of the work of the BSR and ACCM. It should also consider matters which fall within the responsibilities of the other General Synod Boards and Councils, as far as they have policy implications for minority ethnic groups. The Commission would certainly need to forge links with the Board of Education (for example, on the issue of church schools in multi-racial areas) and the Board for Mission and Unity (about the Church's mission to minority ethnic groups and the wider question of relations with those of other faiths, particularly the Asian religions).

5.65   Any one of these initiatives on its own would be desirable, but not necessarily sufficient: for example, for the change in ACCM to take place (with or without the change in BSR) in the absence of any wider structural initiative would still leave race compartmentalized and – perhaps damagingly – unaccountable to the black constituency. Equally, if the sole initiative were a new Commission for Black Anglican Concerns, even if appropriately staffed and funded, and with rights of access to meetings and papers of the Boards and Councils of the General Synod, there would be a danger that it would be seen as just one more pressure group.

5.66   In relation to staffing we propose:

(a)   One full-time staff officer based in the General Synod Office on a fixed-term contract, as Secretary of the new Commission;

(b)   A full-time worker in BSR, funded by the Synod and responsible to that Board, but reporting also to the Commission;

(c)   A Selection Secretary in ACCM with responsibilities for black

Anglican vocations, who would be responsible to the ACCM Council (to which a senior black clergyman would be nominated by the House of Bishops) but who would report also to the new Commission.

5.67 We would expect these posts to be filled by black Anglicans. Although it might be unlawful for them to be advertised to be filled by black people *per se*, the relevant job descriptions would need to call for candidates to have a good knowledge of the minority ethnic communities, and the particular concerns of black Anglicans. Lay people would clearly be eligible, as well as suitably qualified clergy.

5.68 We make no specific recommendations about changes in diocesan structures. But we consider that each diocese should review its organisational arrangements and the composition of its boards, councils and committees, to ensure that black Anglicans have a voice in decision-making or advisory processes, and that a concern for racial discrimination and disadvantage is reflected in policies and practices.

5.69 In relation to *representative bodies*, we have concluded that it would be unrealistic for us to bring forward a set of detailed proposals.

5.70 We believe, however, that the under-representation of people from minority ethnic groups in the democratically-elected institutions of the Church and in the secular world demands careful attention. The Church is one among many bodies in which there is a marked under-representation of ethnic minorities in elected bodies in proportion to their numbers. There is no elected black Member of Parliament. Under whatever electoral system, people from minority groups comprising no more than 4 per cent of the nation's population are bound to face great difficulties in securing seats in an elected national assembly.

5.71 Despite the use of the Single Transferable Vote system, of the General Synod's 550 members in 1984/85, only 2 (0.3 per cent) were from minority ethnic groups. Although there are no accurate statistics of the number of black Anglicans on church electoral rolls, the evidence from our clergy survey, together with information from the Diocese of Birmingham, suggests that the present level of PCC and Deanery and Diocesan Synod representation is disproportionately low. Clearly every effort must continue to be made to encourage black Anglicans to put their names forward for election to Church governing bodies at all levels.

5.72 We have also asked ourselves whether the Church should

consider adopting some form of quota system within its electoral arrangements for the General Synod.

5.73 We see no theological reason why present electoral systems should be maintained if they are not serving the needs of the Church. An alternative approach has already been accepted by the Church of England in the elections to the World Council of Churches (WCC). Of the 11 members put forward by the Church of England in what is called the '85 per cent category', seven are elected by General Synod and four appointed by the Presidents and Standing Committee of the Synod. The Synod decided in 1980 that, of the seven to be elected, four must be clergy (with no more than two bishops) and three must be lay people (of whom two must be women). So even before the WCC makes up the balance in the '15 per cent category' (see Appendix C), the principle of a quota system – in relation to laity and women – has been adopted by the Synod in this context.

5.74 There is nothing sacrosanct about present *mechanisms* of democracy; the important thing is for those mechanisms to give an effective franchise and voice to all sections of plural society. We therefore *recommend* that the new Synod to be elected in 1985 should consider how a more appropriate system of representation which pays due regard to minority interests can be implemented for the General Synod elections of 1990.

The Wider Church
5.75 Finally in this Chapter we consider the important question of the relationship between the Church in the UPAs and the rest of the Church of England. On reading this report, members of Churches in other areas may ask 'What does all this mean for us?' and 'What can we do to help?'

5.76 The UPA Church – although it is often resilient, faithful and resourceful – does need the support and understanding of the wider Church. We also believe that the wider Church needs the insights of the UPA Church. The recognition of the Church as the Body of Christ, with each part dependent on the others for the effective working of the whole, is fundamental. The quality of the relationship between the UPA and the wider Church is a supreme test of the life of the whole Body.

5.77 Unless the whole Church can be persuaded to take seriously the challenge and plight of the Church in the UPAs, it will cease to be the Church of the whole people. Yet well-intentioned appeals to the wider Church will not necessarily achieve a greater commitment of the whole Church to the UPAs. The obstacles to effective change are deeply entrenched.

5.78   Many outside the UPAs, for instance, have little or no first-hand experience of living in them. They may have some fear of them, or just 'don't want to know'. As we have suggested, the local world is the real world for most people; and the world seen only from the railway carriage window – even though your own way of life may to a considerable extent depend on that world – is not easy for most people to relate to. Some may blame the UPAs for their problems, though the major problems of the UPAs are rarely created or sustained primarily by the people living in them, and as rarely can be solved by them alone.

5.79   The problems of UPAs are admittedly huge, and it is understandable if people – outside and inside them – feel helpless and frustrated in the face of them, unless they are offered realistic help and support. In addition, some may say that 'Comfortable Britain' is already full of demands. 'We've enough problems of our own' may be a genuine enough reaction.

5.80   Many people in the suburbs and the country have consciously got out of the inner areas or outer estates. 'Climbing out' has been costly. It has meant effort and initiative. They have 'bettered themselves' and achieved.

5.81   'Bettering yourself' is a natural desire; but the desire to 'better yourself' must always for the Christian be coupled with the determination to see that others have the same opportunities. 'Bettering yourself' and therefore 'getting out' are not to be related primarily to getting out of a particular *place*. Many who get out (or who want to, for many cannot) do so not necessarily because they want to get out of that *place*, but because it is the only way they can get out of the *conditions* which obtain in UPAs. People want to get to where there is better employment, better housing, better health facilities, better educational opportunity, more space and fewer effects of criminality – or where these things *seem* to be better. Until the deprivations of the UPAs are removed, people will legitimately want to leave them.

5.82   The long-standing divisions between the UPAs and 'Comfortable Britain' are predominantly between areas of different social class. It is possible to make easy speeches about 'partnership between the UPAs and other areas', as though all vestiges of 'the rich man in his castle; the poor man at his gate' had long since been done away. But secular attitudes to power and class still persist in the Church in subtle and not so subtle ways.

5.83   The Church has often reinforced rather than challenged over-simplified attitudes. 'Clergy shouldn't be sent to "difficult areas" as soon as they're ordained' – which evades the question of appropriate training for different difficulties in the suburbs and the UPAs. 'It must be difficult where you are . . . with so little response' – meaning: 'Here in the suburbs we get a larger congregation' – which may not necessarily indicate a greater response to the Gospel of Christ.

5.84   To respond effectively to the needs of the UPAs requires a motivation – a theology and a spirituality – of 'membership one of another'. We have six suggestions to make as an aid to achieving this end.

5.85   First, we must firmly recognise that the Church is, and has the potential to be even more, a major force for good in our society. The Church as a whole can promote a more sensitive climate of public opinion. In a world and society of competing and conflicting claims, of different classes and races, it is important the Church should teach and demonstrate what 'belonging' to society as a whole can mean, and to provide guidance and example on tolerance, acceptance and altruism in a plural society.

5.86   Second, all Christians should take part in promoting that common good which would benefit the UPAs and their Churches, by public commitment to social welfare and justice, to good education, housing, and health for all. It is important for Christians to show themselves committed as 'members one of another' as citizens, as well as within the structures of the Church.

5.87   Third, all Christians need to make the effort to learn what life is like – and why – in the UPAs. Those who live in the suburbs and work in the UPAs can be a most valuable channel of communication between the two. Thousands of suburban families have at least one member who commutes to the inner city, perhaps to work as a doctor, nurse, teacher or social worker. They can help their families, friends and fellow church members in the suburbs appreciate what is happening in the UPAs, and they should be given an opportunity to do so. They also should be supported by their local Churches and clergy recognising their work as a valid part of their ministry, and not necessarily expecting them to run the Sunday School at home after a week in an inner city school. It is also valuable for those who are working in stressful situations in the UPAs to have some support in the area where they work. Local clergy can often offer this – and can also offer opportunities for those who work in the area, but do not live in it, to broaden their knowledge of local life, and to share their experiences and reflect on them with others who are working in the area.

5.88 Fourth, the Church should encourage agencies such as the religious communities, the Church Army, the missionary societies, and the settlements to develop their ministry in the UPAs, in close collaboration with local Churches, and after careful negotiation with the dioceses and the local Church.

5.89 Fifth, exchanges between UPA Churches and Churches elsewhere can be promoted. If such exchanges are undertaken with careful preparation and for the development of both sets of Churches, we believe they can put a human face on 'membership one of another' and provide real opportunities for mutual learning. Yet we are aware of the dangers of exchanges. As one diocesan report on 'twinning' (a word which we do not believe is appropriate) notes, 'It can bring considerable mutual friendship and understanding. However, it does very little to change the lives and environment of those living in the inner city.' Although we would encourage properly-planned exchanges, we do not regard them as a substitute for making much-needed skills available to UPA Churches, and ensuring the proper representation of UPA people and Churches in Church decision-making.

5.90 Sixth, we have been impressed with the way in which Community Service Volunteers (CSV) has provided opportunities for young people to work full-time in areas like UPAs, and has tried to take the complexities of UPAs seriously. Other ways of introducing young people to life in UPAs are organised, for example, by Careforce, in Root Groups, and through settlements. We encourage Churches to give support to young people who want to learn in this way. We believe schemes of this kind should be developed and strengthened in the Church, to extend the age range of volunteers and to cater for part-time volunteer work as well as full-time, and on as disciplined and regular a basis as the present work of CSV. Volunteers could work with vulnerable homeless people, disabled or elderly people, with young offenders and victims of crime. The range of work could be considerably extended at the suggestion and with the co-operation of UPA parishes. We *recommend* that the appropriate Church voluntary bodies consider this proposal, though we recognise that volunteering schemes need to be mounted sensitively, particularly in places where there are high levels of unemployment.

5.91 Finally, we note that many UPAs (especially those close to central London) are by no means socially monochrome; but many professional people who live in the inner city areas opt out of their local Church and indeed out of any responsibility in their local society. They may feel that their home is in, but not part of, the inner city. For the Christian, we have no doubt that living in the inner city and the UPA should normally mean some considerable commitment to the Church in that locality and to the surrounding society. That commitment needs to be made with much thought, care and sensitivity – and without inhibiting the wider development of local leadership.

Main Recommendations

1.   A national system for designating UPA parishes should be developed (paragraph 5.9).

2.   Dioceses should devote greater attention to the effective collection and presentation of accurate statistics (paragraph 5.16).

3.   The internal distribution of clergy by dioceses should be adjusted where necessary to ensure that UPA parishes receive a fair share, and that particular attention should be paid in this respect to parishes on large outer estates (paragraph 5.35).

4.   Dioceses should explore the possibilities of fresh stipendiary lay ministries, not necessarily tied to one parish (paragraph 5.35).

5.   The 'Audit for the Local Church' which we propose should be further developed, and adopted by local UPA Churches (paragraph 5.37).

6.   In urban areas the deanery should have an important support and pastoral planning function (paragraph 5.41).

7.   Each parish should review, preferably annually, what progress has been made in the sharing of ministry between clergy and laity, and in co-operation between neighbouring Churches, and ecumenically (paragraph 5.49).

8.   Appointments should be made to the Boards and Councils of the General Synod, and a new Commission on Black Anglican Concerns established, to enable the Church to make a more effective response to racial discrimination and disadvantage, and to the alienation

experienced by many black people in relation to the Church of England (paragraph 5.62).

9.   The General Synod should consider how a more appropriate system of representation which pays due regard to minority interests can be implemented for the Synod elections of 1990 (paragraph 5.74).

10.   The appropriate Church voluntary bodies should consider how schemes for voluntary service in UPAs could be extended to widen the age range of those eligible, and to allow for part-time as well as full-time volunteering (paragraph 5.90).

References

1   A formula for the deployment of clergy between dioceses, produced in 1974 by a Working Group under the Bishop of Sheffield; its weightings are 8 points for population, 1 for land area, 3 for electoral roll membership and 3 for numbers of churches.

2.   The term *Non-Stipendiary Minister* encompasses a wide range of ordained ministries and does not attempt to define or limit the nature of the ministerial task – which may be a parish-focused ministry exercised by someone in full-time secular employment or a work-focused ministry. The term simply emphasises that the ministry is unpaid. A *Local Non-Stipendiary Minister* is limited by licence to a particular locality. Both the authority to minister and the training to minister will be appropriate only to that locality.

3   *Team and Group Ministries* – a report by the Ministry Co-ordinating Group. General Synod Paper GS 660, 1985.

Chapter 6
DEVELOPING THE PEOPLE OF GOD

'The Church of England has a culture all of its own. It can't see what inner city people's minds might be'. (Clergyman, Liverpool)

6.1   This Chapter deals with the people of the Church. It contains major sections on the development of the laity and the clergy, and here we also consider worship, and children and young people.

The Development of the Laity

6.2   An emphasis on the laity has been a strong theme to emerge in the written evidence submitted to us, and in our discussions in the UPAs. There was a particular stress on the need for a laity in the UPAs committed to making Christianity take shape in the local culture. We strongly affirm that lay people have an important role in developing the mission of the local UPA church. They can present the Gospel to others in a way that will make them feel 'this is for our sort of people'. Only those who are in, and of, a local area can say how God is speaking there. They can tell each other and the wider Church.

6.3   Yet we have also had evidence that there are many obstacles in the way of developing an effective laity in the UPAs. They include the historical domination of leadership roles by those of other cultures, a concentration on words and books and equating intelligence and vocation with academic ability, a dependence on professionals, and a degree of conservatism among the laity.

6.4   To tackle such obstacles effectively, a 'bottom-up' rather than a 'top-down' approach is required. The structure of local churches should be more related to the tasks they have to undertake, which must be discerned and decided locally. The question is not so much 'How is the Church to be run here?', but rather 'What are God's people called to be and to do here?'. The answer to this question may we hope emerge from the undertaking of an Audit for the local Church, as we have suggested. Such a review may give rise to some disconcerting implications for aspects of church life. It may challenge existing views of the role of the clergy, the patterns and means of worship, the appropriateness of church buildings, and the allocation of resources.

6.5   Perhaps most of all, it may lead to a serious consideration of how local lay leadership can be developed. There was a general recognition in the evidence submitted to us that 'the potential for local leadership is there and it needs to be sought, nurtured and encouraged'.[1] A major emphasis in virtually all the submissions we have received is on the need for lay leadership to be developed systematically. Parishes repeatedly asked for training designed to reflect the experience, skills and cultures of local people.

6.6   A universal Church crosses boundaries between ethnic groups, classes and cultures. At the same time, an authentic mark of the presence of the Church in any particular place is that it should be rooted in the culture and character of that locality. We believe that the Church of England has in general failed to measure up to this objective in the UPAs, and that a major factor in this failure is that there has been no sustained programme for encouraging and developing local Church leadership.

6.7   We will argue later for new approaches to the training of clergy to be adopted. But we consider that this on its own, although necessary, will not be sufficient. For the Church to 'belong' in the UPAs will require the development of a Church leadership which more closely reflects the culture, style and patterns of behaviour of the people of the area. In other words, a 'localness' which is social as well as geographical.

6.8   The Liverpool Diocese's UPA report noted that: 'No Church can be a truly local Church so long as leadership and decision-making is in the hands of people who do not live there'. We would go further than this: not only must local leadership and decision-making be shifted towards those who live in the area, but it must be shifted more to those who belong to the predominant social class or group.

6.9   This should apply throughout the Church. Indeed, it is the case already in many rural and suburban areas. But in the UPAs, even some stipendiary clergy from urban working-class roots have found that their training and the expectations of their calling have, perhaps inevitably, turned them into members of the professional classes. They have become socially and culturally distanced from their origins.

6.10   In considering the question of local Church leadership, we have reflected on the writings of Roland Allen, who served in China from 1895-1903. He argued that the missionary Church of his day brought all the leadership, all the answers, and all the money from outside, making the local Church dependent, and wasting its distinct and God-given gifts. By contrast, he noted, St Paul founded a self-reliant Church; he appointed local leaders after what we would regard as a minimum of training. These understandings have been confirmed by more recent experience in the world-wide Anglican Communion (for example, in the latest report of the Anglican Consultative Council – ACC 6).

6.11   It is right we believe to argue in relation to the New Testament, and to much in subsequent Christian tradition, that we should expect to see Christ build his Church in any community in the world, and to see appropriate local leadership emerge. The experience in Britain and in other advanced industrial societies however is that there are great difficulties in the way of achieving this objective, and that any progress in this direction cannot be made quicly. We must be realistic in our expectations. Yet we believe a new impetus is needed. As a contribution to this impetus we *recommend* that in Dioceses with significant concentrations of UPAs there should be active experiments in Church Leadership Development Programmes.

A Church Leadership Development Programme
6.12   There is much God-given intelligence and ability to be found among local people in Urban Priority Areas. However, the experience of frequently being 'put down' by many teachers, employers, parents and clergy has often led to low expectations which in turn have led to low achievements.

6.13   Christians from UPAs have frequently been overawed by finding themselves in a tiny minority on educational courses run by the Church; often they have either withdrawn or have been absorbed into styles of Church life which have de-skilled them for their own area. It would be a new experience for most Christians from UPAs to find themselves in a Church group where the great majority shared their culture and experience of life in city and town.

6.14   We are aware of the existence of actual or projected experiments in such lay leadership training. The *Step by Step* scheme in the Stepney area of the London Diocese is one such programme. Experiments in Liverpool and Manchester Dioceses are also proposed following on locally-gained experience (for example, with the Evangelical Urban

Training Project, the Newton Heath Project, the Communities-in-Crisis programme, and the Salford Pastoral Plan). Their objectives are to enable existing or potential lay leaders to develop their leadership skills and the experience they already have in lay ministries in Church and community, and preferably in both.

6.15   Our concept of a Church Leadership Development Programme is, in essence, a programme of lay development through a varied series of training programmes. It would be locally-based, yet wider than any one parish. It would be designed locally, and would seek to develop existing skills and introduce members to new ones directly related to local leadership needs. It should be informal in style, and learning- rather than teaching-centred. It would not be taught mainly as separate modules on the Bible, Christian doctrine, and so on; its content should embrace both existing experiences and opportunities in local Church and community life, and the major concerns of Christian ministry and mission. Theological reflection and articulation would be developed in and through these experiences. The Programme should be designed and promoted in such a way as to attract women and members of minority ethnic groups. Although it should seek to challenge those aspects of Church life which are foreign to the cultures of the locality, it should also specifically identify, challenge and alter throughout Church life those practices which favour the continuation of a predominantly white male middle-class leadership.

6.16   The selection of candidates for a Church Leadership Develop- ment Programme would normally be a combination of nomination by PCCs (who will need to understand clearly the purpose of the course) and self-selection. Existing and potential Christian leaders of Church and community-based organisations would need to be encouraged to volunteer.

6.17   We see such a programme as a major priority in supporting the People of God already living in Urban Priority Areas. It should be tested out in selected areas in Dioceses, taking account of the following points. It should:

(a)   promote the development of team leadership within the Church with only one or two of the team being ordained;

(b)   generate candidates for various types of lay ministry (and for Local Non-Stipendiary Ministry, which we consider later);

(c)   help to counter what we regard as mistaken expectations of lay ministries among congregations. (The temptation to expect them to do everything for the congregation should be avoided: in their parochial ministry they should not normally concentrate on taking services and pastoral visiting.);

(d)   avoid narrow congregationalism by ensuring that the selection and training are at a level wider than the individual parish.

6.18   The Church will need to devote greater resources to back this initiative than it currently gives to its adult education and lay training programmes. In addition to internal diocesan resources there are a number of other possibilities which, we believe, should be explored. For example, a number of Church educational charities were originally established to pay for education for the poor. They sometimes find it difficult today to fulfil those requirements in their Trust Deeds. We ask them to consider whether programmes of the kind we suggest, which give a second chance to those who have not achieved well at school, might be a proper object for their support.

6.19   There are also a number of Church Training Colleges in inner city areas which have been closed, and their funds put into trust. Such trust funds too would seem directly relevant to what we propose. Indeed the All Saints Trust in Tottenham is already funding a part-time worker for *Step by Step*.

Non-Clerical Stipendiary Workers

6.20   We have recommended in Chapter 5 that Dioceses should explore the possibility of fresh stipendiary lay ministries.

6.21   As we have visited the UPAs, we have been very aware of the contribution made by women to local life, and yet of the under-valuing and under-utilisation by the Church of the talents and skills they have to offer. Their contribution has a particular significance in UPAs for two reasons. First, because of the key role which they play in a whole multitude of other organisations which have responded to changing social attitudes and family patterns much more readily than the Church; second, they are often the principal carers of the elderly, sick, and vulnerable within the community, and heads of single-parent families.

6.22   The issue of the ordination of women to the priesthood has been put to us in evidence. It is not our place to do more than note that there was an emphasis that this would make a major contribution to ministry in UPAs, and that most of us would agree with this view.

6.23   The Church of England already has 540 Deaconesses and 170

Accredited Lay Workers (including some 260 non-stipendiary), many of them working in UPAs. The number of women in training for these ministries almost doubled between 1980 and 1984. Last year there were 226 in training (including 100 for non-stipendiary ministry), 90 per cent of whom wanted to be Deaconesses. In 1980, women accounted for 10 per cent of the total numbers in training for the ministry sponsored by bishops; by 1984 the perecentage had risen to 17.6 per cent.

6.24   The deployment of Deaconesses and Lay Workers for ministry within UPAs is therefore clearly an increasingly important question. Of the 59 per cent of the clergy in UPAs who in our survey said they wanted additional help, over a quarter wanted a Deaconess; and almost as many wanted an additional Lay Worker for their staff.

6.25   Whereas Deaconesses most often do general parochial work, other Lay Workers (both men and women) are likely to have some more specialist role e.g. youth and community work, industrial mission, education and social work – either receiving training for a specialist role or bringing their qualifications and expertise as a professional worker into their ministry. Accredited Lay Workers, like Deaconesses, have had usually at least two years theological training.

6.26   It is important for the Church to publicise the need for Deaconesses and Lay Workers in UPAs; for dioceses to examine their deployment of Deaconesses in relation to the needs of the UPAs; to offer appropriate training for the work there (present training for the work of Deaconesses and Lay Workers is open to the same criticisms as we make later in this chapter about training for Priests and Deacons) and to make financial and other kinds of support available.

6.27   Although Deaconesses, Readers, and Accredited Lay Workers do not technically share the 'cure of souls', the Pastoral Measure 1983 and the Diocesan Stipends Funds Measure 1953 provide that money in Diocesan Stipends Funds may be applied in providing the income of 'other persons declared by the Bishop to be engaged in the cure of souls within the Diocese'. It has been suggested to us by the Church Commissioners that these 'other persons' – who must be baptised, confirmed, regular communicants and licensed by the Bishop – were intended to include Deaconesses, Readers and Accredited Lay Workers.

6.28   The work of the men and women of the Church Army is a special kind of Accredited Lay Ministry and particularly related – by the Army's Articles – to the people and conditions of UPAs. As we noted in

Chapter 5, we have seen for ourselves some of the work of the Church Army. The variety of its work (with unemployed people, Industrial Chaplaincy, community work, work with broken families, and in race relations), and the support it gives to its workers in UPAs, is of great importance.

6.29   We believe that the work of the 60 Church Army staff present in UPAs is to be very warmly commended and is capable of expansion. The potential of the Church Army thoughtfully to undertake both evangelism and social work is particularly important, as is its wide understanding of the meaning of the proclamation of the Gospel to those who have little contact with the Church.

6.30   Clearly not all the work which a parish or diocese decides to sponsor – social, educational, health, youth or administrative work, for example – will be done by those who will either want, or qualify for, the Bishop's licence. This work may be as important and as necessary as other work, but the financing of it has often in the past proved more difficult. Such work may well qualify for finance from the Church Urban Fund which we propose. Because such work is less evidently associated with more formal institutional Church structures, it may, in fact, have a special effectiveness.

The Promotion of a Local Non-Stipendiary Ministry

6.31   The development of Local Non-Stipendiary Ministry (LNSM) in UPAs can be seen as a symbol of the official Church's support for promotion of local, outward-looking and participating churches. We have already declared our commitment to the development of the laity in general and of lay ministries in particular. This priority is seen in our encouragement of a variety of properly recognised lay ministries, and of a Church Leadership Development Programme. Those seeking a LNSM would normally be required to have gone through such a programme. However, we are also well aware of the central significance of the clergy, who are seen as representative of the official Church. So many people still associate (and even equate) the Church with the ordained ministry. To convert that Church to the importance of recognizing the leadership and gifts of some local people by ordination could therefore be regarded as an important sign of the Church's commitment to promoting a truly local Church at the heart of the wider Church. It is not surprising to us, therefore, that in evidence we have received there has been widespread support for the principle of developing a LNSM.

6.32   Potentially valuable experience has been gained with schemes for Local Non-Stipendiary Ministry both in rural areas (the Lincoln Programme) and urban areas (the Brandon and Bethnal Green Projects). Such schemes have, we believe rightly, had the broad objective of developing 'ministry drawn from, trained in, and intended to be exercised in the same community or sphere'.[2] Those ordained do not enter a new or separate category of ministry. They are ordained to the priesthood of the Church. But the fact that their training and preparation is necessarily much more limited than that received by full-time stipendiary priests or by NSMs means that they cannot be expected to undertake all the responsibilities traditionally assumed by a priest in any part of the Church, but will be licensed to exercise a ministry in a particular local context. From a formal point of view, therefore, LNSM should not be seen as a new or separate category of ministry but rather as a variant within the general concept of the non-stipendiary ministry.[3] But in practice both the training and the preparation for it, and the exercise of it, will be significantly different.

6.33   There has been a continuing debate in the Church of England about the nature of the ordained ministry in general, and of local ministry. We will not attempt here to rehearse all that has been said and written on the subject. We believe however that our concern for local Church leadership to be developed in the UPAs converges with many current trends in the Anglican Communion in the theology and experience of ministry.

6.34   There are three main reasons why the Church of England should develop LNSM in UPAs.

6.35   First, it derives inevitably and naturally from what is meant by a fully local Church which reflects the culture of its area. By this we mean 'an indigenous Church, open to God, to each other, to the neighbourhood, to the world, and to understand the present and potential spirituality' of the area.[4] Such a Church would derive its identity and shape from the people in a particular place working out a way of living faithfully, and would take full account of local cultures as well as geography. We see LNSM as a natural expression of such a commitment.

6.36   Second, LNSM in UPAs would be a strategic part of the task of reconciling the local Church to the local community, particularly in the sense of encouraging a closer identity between the two. This relates to, but is wider than, the need to reduce the alienation between local UPA communities and the Church. Given the marginalisation of UPA people and communities, a more local ministry could be an important prophetic action; an example of sharing power and opportunity.

6.37   Third, LNSM must be seen as part of the recognition by the Church that traditional ways alone will not enable it to meet its responsibility to local Christian communities in UPAs. If traditional ways of selecting, training and developing ordained ministries do not work very well in UPAs, it makes good sense to explore other ways of promoting truly local Churches.

6.38   We have considered the main arguments against LNSMs and believe they do not carry sufficient weight. They include first, that the local emphasis of LNSM contradicts the catholic universality of the ordained ministry. Leaving aside questions about the actual universality of the existing ordained ministry, we believe that ordination by the Bishop, an area-based selection and training which transcends the purely local, and the full participation of the LNSM in the deliberations and life of the diocese, should ensure that 'local' does not lead to congregationalism. Secondly, the fear that LNSM will be seen as second-class depends primarily on the association of ordained ministry completely with the norm of professional ministry. A carefully worked-out selection, training, and development of LNSM, and its full recognition in the life of the Church, should continue the necessary erosion of this traditional and highly questionable association. Lastly, the fear the LNSM would demote the laity would not be confirmed if our suggestions for the selection, training and development of LNSM are placed firmly within the primary task of developing the local Church and therefore the local laity.

What Would LNSMs Do?

6.39   What would be the function of LNSMs in UPAs? Whereas in rural area their main task may be to preserve the 'localness' of the Church by maintaining its worshipping and sacramental life in small village communities, in UPAs their ministry should be a wider one, and include the enabling of the Church to engage with the culture and concerns of the locality. Although LNSMs would of course have a contribution to make to the worship and building-up of the spiritual life of the local Church, they would also have particular opportunities to be involved in local issues affecting the community (perhaps working with caring and other agencies in the locality), and to bring the ministry and mission of the Church to bear on matters where local concern is felt.

One might be appointed as the priest responsible for an estate within the parish, including involvement in community groups, house groups, and pastoral care. Another might be responsible for youth work. Above all the ministry of the LNSM would be that of a priest primarily concerned to promote a local Church, truly indigenous to a UPA, and reflecting its culture and ways of learning in its worship, organisation, and mission.

6.40   The tasks of the LNSM would need to be reflected in the Bishop's licence which would need to include a job definition. It will be necessary to ensure that expectations of, and demands on, the LNSM are not unrealistic, and take into account family and other responsibilities. If the LNSM moved from his or her area, and wished to continue a ministry in a new area with the support of a new Church, the case for a new licence would be considered by the Bishop in the normal way. The LNSM should *always* be a part of a parish team or group which would include stipendiary and non-stipendiary clergy, accredited lay workers and lay leaders. This would ensure continuity, mutual support and accountability.

Criteria for Selection

6.41   For the selection of LNSM we suggest that, in addition to the traditional requirements of a Christian commitment, a true sense of calling, and a personal and spiritual maturity, the following criteria should be adopted.

(a)   Candidates should normally live in a UPA, and be local in the sense of belonging to a local culture (there may be more than one) which is under-represented in the Church's leadership. These local cultures will generally be what has been traditionally described as working-class. Experience of other NSM training programmes suggests that unless such UPA residents are taken seriously, more professional people and people living outside UPAs but worshipping in UPA Churches will have too dominant a role in the proceedings. (We recognise the very positive contribution of the latter groups to the local Church, but they already have a well-established route into the ordained ministry through existing NSM training programmes.)

(b)   Candidates should be well based in a local UPA organisation, either Church-centred or community-centred (or preferably both). It would be helpful if they had leadership experience in such organisations.

(c)   Candidates could be employed or unemployed. To exclude the latter in some communities would be to exclude over half the population.

(d)   Candidates should have a proven record of working in collaborative ways in their involvement with local organisations.

(e)   Candidates should have the full support of their family.

(f)   Candidates should normally be over 30 years old.

(g)   Candidates should have demonstrated an ability to grow in understanding and articulating the faith.

The Selection Procedure

6.42   The procedures for selection of LNSMs should start with the PCC of a local Church considering whether anyone should be nominated to an LNSM selection board. Candidates would not be elected but should have the PCC's support. In most cases, such candidates would already have been taking part in a Church Leadership Development Programme (and the PCC should already have been involved in commending people from the parish for the Church Leadership Development Programme).

6.43   Those nominated would then proceed to a selection board which would be at diocesan level. The board should include an Advisory Council for the Church's Ministry (ACCM) representative from outside the diocese, and representatives from the candidate's Deanery; its membership should be equally balanced between clergy and lay people. The board would then advise the diocesan Bishop, who would make the final decision. A few candidates might already possess the right mixture of training and experience to proceed direct to ordination; but in almost all cases we would envisage ordination following a period of training designed for LNSMs.

LNSM Training

6.44   Formal LNSM training would emerge from a Church Leadership Development Programme. In addition to this 'foundation' training, candidates for the LNSM would need to undertake a complementary training programme to equip them for their particular contribution to local ministries as ordained servants of the Church, including the proclamation of the Gospel and the administration of the Sacraments. Such a programme, we suggest, would need to have the following features.

(i)   It should be area-based, and fieldwork-based, involving project

116

work and the use of placements in carefully selected training parishes in UPAs and other areas, and in UPA community organisations.

(ii)   It should include some residential weekend work on common needs and themes emerging out of project work and placements.

(iii)   It would use modern adult educational skills as developed by organisations working in UPAs.

(iv)   It would be particularly concerned to develop theological reflection and articulation by working theologically on matters which arise out of the experience of ministry in Church and community.

(v)   Assessment would be by a diocesan team, based on attendance, contribution to the programme, placement reports, and project work.

(vi)   Follow-up programmes would be needed to provide further training and support.

6.45   We are aware that the money required to finance such training schemes will be considerable. We believe it wrong in principle that those in training for full-time ministry should be financed by central resources but not those in training for LNSM or other non-stipendiary ministry.

6.46   In the initiation of some ordination and ministerial training courses – and their sustaining – some dioceses have been able to make a considerable financial contribution in addition to their normal contribution to central funds for ordination training. Some of those in employment have been glad to make a personal financial contribution to the cost of their training for non-stipendiary ministry. Such contributions from those in UPAs are likely to be significantly less. Use might be made in these circumstances of the Church Urban Fund which we propose.

6.47   The involvement of national bodies like ACCM would, we hope, provide a means of help to dioceses not only in financing schemes but in facilitating, monitoring, and co-ordinating the programmes. We would encourage the appointment of an ACCM staff member to co-ordinate and monitor such programmes.

Transfer to Full-Time Stipendiary Ministry
6.48   We have noted that LNSM would form part of the non-stipendiary ministry and would not be full-time. Past experience of non-stipendiary ministry in the Church of England, however, suggests that

some LNSMs would be likely to seek transfer to stipendiary ministry.

6.49   At present ACCM has no involvement in the transfer of those already ordained from one style of ministry to another. If transfer takes place during training this is a matter on which the Candidates Committee of ACCM advises the bishop concerned. After ordination, transfer takes place at the discretion of the bishop, and dioceses have developed varying policies in the case of NSMs transferring to stipendiary ministry. Since all the colleges and non-residential courses are recognised for training for stipendiary and non-stipendiary ministry alike, additional training is rarely required.

6.50   It may be the case that some LNSMs possess a sufficient combination of experience and training to proceed straight to full-time ministry. Additional training may, however, be necessary. Financing this at present would be the responsibility of the diocese, since the regulations governing the Central Fund for Ordination Candidates do not permit grants to be made to these already ordained. To prevent widely-varying policies on the transfer of LNSMs to stipendiary ministry, we suggest that the diocesan bishop should consult with ACCM in cases of transfer and that any additional training considered necessary should be financed through a central fund established specifically for this purpose.

The Selection of Areas of Experiment for LNSMs
6.51   Because we have so much to learn about LNSM in UPAs, and because of the shortage of people with the experience and skills to promote it, we suggest that our proposals are tested out and monitored in dioceses selected in consultation with ACCM and the Archbishop's Officer for UPAs.

6.52   Within these dioceses, two or three areas only in UPAs should be chosen for LNSM programmes in the light of progress made with Church Leadership Development Programmes on the lines identified above.

Conclusion
6.53   Despite its importance, the contribution which could be made by the development of Local Non-Stipendiary Ministry to a more effective Church in UPAs must not be over-emphasised. On its own, it will not reverse the alienation of people in UPAs from the Church, nor will it

necessarily increase the numbers of local people attending the Church.

6.54   Nevertheless, we are convinced that developing LNSM in the way we have suggested is central to the task of developing a more effective Church in these areas. The cultural localness which is reflected in Church leadership in the suburbs must similarly be built up in the UPAs.

6.55   We therefore *recommend* that the above proposals relating to the selection, training and funding of LNSMs be tested in dioceses selected in consultation with ACCM and the Archbishop's Officer for UPAs; that the LNSM programme be monitored over a ten-year period, under the national co-ordination of ACCM, with additional funds made available by the national Church; and a report be produced by ACCM for the General Synod.

Clergy Training

6.56   Are the stipendiary clergy adequately trained and prepared for their ministry in UPAs? The evidence we have received, not least from the clergy themselves, is virtually unanimous: they are not. Some would go even further, and report that their training 'has not been simply inappropriate, but in many ways has positively unfitted them for the inner urban ministry to which they find themselves committed'.[5] These are very serious charges to level against colleges and courses which are staffed by gifted and hard-working men and women and which are often regarded with great loyalty and affection by those who have received their training in them. We cannot ignore them. How are we to respond to these charges?

6.57   One possible answer is that it would be unreasonable to expect that any college or course could fully prepare men and women for the problems they will encounter once they begin work, or many years after their ordination training. The purpose of theological education is not now usually seen as that of preparing ordinands for specific forms of ministry. Men and women go out from colleges to widely different spheres of ministry. It is argued that what counts is not whether they have somehow acquired appropriate ministerial skills before ordination, but whether they have 'learnt to learn' whatever ministry they will be called upon to exercise. What matters is whether they have developed habits of reflection and social awareness such that they can draw creatively on their resources of theology and spirituality in the face of new realities and engage in a dialogue with those of other faiths or none.

119

Without these habits, they are liable to grasp at any technique of counselling or social work which comes their way, or else just stumble along trying to apply an inherited stereotype of 'priesthood' or 'ministry'.

6.58 This way of thinking, though taken for granted in much professional and vocational training, is a relative newcomer in theological education. In 1944 the task of theological training was defined as that of preparing a minister who 'must know what the gospel is. He must believe it. He must have studied it in itself in the historical form in which it appeared, in its workings in the Biblical history and the history of the Church, in its relevance to the life of the contemporary world and not least in his own life'.[6]

6.59 This daunting programme was faithfully undertaken by colleges and doggedly persevered with, despite the increasing lack of appropriate educational background possessed by many of their students. They were successful, in so far as the great majority of ordinands were enabled to pass a centrally moderated qualifying examination the General Ordination Examination (GOE) or General Ministerial Examination (GME). The purpose of such an examination was defined as recently as 1983 as 'to test so far as it can the candidates' grasp of the faith they will be authorized to teach and preach'.[7]

6.60 But meanwhile there was a growing realization that in many, if not the majority of, cases this success was illusory. The knowledge so painfully acquired was left behind as soon as the active ministry began; books were sold or left gathering dust on the shelf. Sermons were written from one well-tried commentary, and pastoral methods were learnt by rule of thumb. There are thousands of clergy today whose bookshelves as much as their style of ministry are clear evidence that their theological training has borne little fruit in their life's work. The problem was clearly seen more than fifteen years ago, when the first of a long series of reports and papers[8] was published intended to reform the teaching of theology in such a way that it would become a prime resource of every minister throughout his or her working life.

6.61 Today, there are other factors which again call into question the appropriateness of traditional theological teaching methods. Lay people are learning, not just *about* the Bible, but how to *use* the Bible to reflect on their own experience. Young clergy must have the confidence and skill to help them in this. Working among cultures (ethnic or working-class) and religions that are strange to an ordinand's own background must be prepared for by a serious effort to look at the Christian religion from outside the traditional perspectives of academic theology. The importance of practical criteria for learning and reflection in working class culture (as of *praxis* in Liberation Theology) must be allowed to influence priorities in basic theological training.

6.62 Such thinking has undoubtedly had some influence on the training offered by theological colleges and courses; but there is little evidence that it has greatly affected either the style or the results of training. Indeed, it appears that the method has not yet even spread into Continuing Ministerial Education (CME).[9] Both ordinands and theological colleges for the most part still regard as their highest priority the covering of the syllabus required by the General Ministerial Examination. Two colleges which were specifically invited to experiment with new methods were soon closed for financial reasons, and no systematic effort was made to learn from their experience. The promotion of committed and relevant theological study among the Church's full-time ministers seems as elusive an ideal as ever.

6.63 Meanwhile theological colleges and courses have been under pressure from many quarters to make the training they offer more relevant to modern needs. Education, ecumenism, drug-addiction, psychotherapy . . . the list is endless of the 'units' and 'modules' they have been urged to incorporate in their courses. We acknowledge with admiration the extent to which many of them have found means of incorporating some form of 'urban studies' in their already crowded programmes, from specific courses taught in college to extended placements in urban areas. Without these, many ministers would have been even less well prepared to work in UPA parishes then they are now. But the evidence we have received from theological colleges, from ACCM[10] and from the younger clergy themselves reveals a large number of factors which make such initiatives seem almost doomed from the start. The syllabus is already so crowded that additional 'units' are bound to take second place; staff receive little or no training in handling the theological implications of such work or in monitoring students' progress; students with families often resent and resist placements away from their homes; those on extended placements are often impatient to get back to college in order to be sure of completing the formal work which is required if they are to proceed to ordination; there is unlikely to be space on the timetable for theological reflection on, and evaluation of, their placement.

6.64 These obstacles must be overcome. In the United Reformed

Church[11] and in other parts of the world a systematic form of 'Internship Training' is being developed. In the Church of England, progress might most rapidly be made if there were to be a significant change in the academic requirements imposed on ordinands, and if urban studies and placements could be relieved of the pressures of competing with a formal academic syllabus.

6.65   We still have not mentioned a further very serious criticism which is levelled against residential colleges, and which touches not only the courses of training which they offer but the social and cultural pressures to which the student is exposed. The influence of a college on its students' attitudes and perceptions is incalculable[12] – and indeed this was always their intention. It was precisely by withdrawing students into a closed and highly regulated community that appropriate disciplines of prayer and spirituality could be inculcated.

6.66   But many would now say that this somewhat monastic approach to preparation for the sacred ministry has itself become problematical. Many colleges are less than fully 'residential'. A substantial proportion of their students live out with their families and attend the college only by day; and the pattern of spiritual discipline which is possible under such conditions may turn out to be quite inappropriate to the life of a married priest in a modern vicarage serving a multi-purpose church building on a housing estate.

6.67   All the more serious, then, is the charge that a college may exert social influences on students which will mark them for life. In the Church of England ordinands coming from working class backgrounds become involved in an educational enterprise familiar to professional people but strange to their home environment, and are influenced by social expectations and patterns of behaviour which may distance them from their homes and neighbourhoods. Middle class ordinands, by contrast, become conscious of the artificial isolation of the college from the milieu in which many hope to minister, and may become over-sensitive to the limitations of their own background and experience. Women may find themselves inhibited by a male-dominated professional ethos. The commitment of some colleges to a particular tradition of churchmanship may make students ill-prepared to work alongside clergy and lay people nurtured in other traditions. Even on the level of community living, theological colleges are not always able to develop an ethos which can be admired as an inspiration for Christian fellowship and trust.

6.68   All this amounts to a formidable indictment, and suggests the need for a radical review of the Church of England's provision for the training of its ministers. Such a review is far beyond the scope of this Commission; but the evidence we have received shows that, in urban areas at least, the matter is extremely urgent. We cannot ignore the testimony of so many who are valiantly working in inner city parishes and whose training they themselves believe to have been both inadequate and inappropriate. Our ultimate objective must be nothing less than thorough-going reform. The principles to be followed have been strongly advocated by ACCM and others for the last twenty years, but little perceptible progress has been made. The challenges now placed before the Church in UPAs make it essential to press for change. Meanwhile, certain recent developments in patterns of ministry and ministerial training may suggest a way forward:

i)   *Non-Residential Courses*
6.69   Perhaps the most significant development in ministerial training in recent years has been the growth of non-residential part-time courses. The first of these was the Southwark Ordination Course which began in 1960. There are now sixteen such courses recognized by ACCM, which account for nearly a third of all ordinands in training. At first sight, these courses would appear to escape many of the criticisms levelled at residential theological colleges. Many of them are located in or near major cities. The students continue with their own professional work and are often helped to reflect upon it theologically. A high level of motivation is required to fulfil all the demands of the course at the same time as carrying responsibilities at work and in the family. Since the courses are regional, they are obliged (unlike residential theological colleges) to accept all candidates recommended for training in their geographical area, and for the most part the candidates themselves have no choice between courses. This means that courses are not usually marked by a distinctive churchmanship, and the students have greatly appreciated contact with candidates and staff from traditions other than their own.[13] Above all, the ordinands are never removed from their own social and cultural environment, even though occasional residential periods and parish placements give them some experience of the wider Church.

6.70   On the face of it, then, these courses would appear to offer a more favourable milieu for the training of those who will minister in UPAs. But we have to record that in their present form they do not yet seem ready to do so. Virtually all the students admitted to these courses are drawn from the professional and relatively educated classes. For the most part they do not live in UPAs, and the experience to which their theological education may be related has little to do with UPAs. The course they follow is still dominated by the demands of the GME, and those who have not qualified by this examination are simply students who have been forgiven their failure – their training has been no different from that of others.[14] The testimony of the students themselves, of ACCM inspectors, and of a number of Bishops, strongly criticizes these courses for being 'inflexible' and far too dominated by the narrow requirements of an academic syllabus, taught by conventional and often inappropriate methods.[15]

6.71   Yet the formula itself seems a sound one. We have been very impressed by the evidence submitted by the Aston scheme, and other courses occasionally reveal a willingness to show more flexibility. In Chapter 3 we referred to the growing view that ability to minister to the Church and to communicate the gospel to others may be acquired through types of theological training different from those which are traditionally monitored according to a conventional academic syllabus. We also drew attention to progress which has been made in other parts of the Anglican Communion and in other denominations in establishing ways of testing ministerial gifts and abilities by other than academic criteria. If this thinking were applied to the training offered by non-residential courses it could result in a flexibility that would make them better adapted to the needs of those who will minister in UPAs.

ii)   *Post-Ordination and In-Service Training*

6.72   A second area in which some change has taken place is that of Post Ordination Training and in-service training. For many years attempts have been made to achieve some integration between pre-ordination and post-ordination training, so that a common strategy could be developed that would make best use of both. But this has invariably foundered on the fact that, under present arrangements, ordination makes a decisive break in training. Pre-ordination training is the responsibility of theological colleges and regional courses. Everything after ordination is the responsibility of the dioceses. Inevitably, dioceses differ in the resources they can bring to further training and in the purpose and discipline with which they approach it. Any effective co-ordination by the Church as a whole has seemed hopelessly elusive.

6.73   Yet some proposals for change made in a recent report (*The*

Continuing Education of the Church's Ministers, 1980 – GS Misc 122) appear to have marked a significant step forward, and a subsequent review sponsored by ACCM shows that it has met with a warm response and has led to a substantial increase in resources of both finance and manpower being allocated to CME in many dioceses.[16] This report supported the principle of self-motivated learning, and pleaded for an integrated scheme of further training from the moment of ordination onwards. It proposed that £50 per stipendiary accredited minister per annum (at 1979 prices) should be set aside for in-service training purposes, to be used by individual ministers for their own continuing education after consultation with the appropriate diocesan officer. Our own survey showed a substantial number of priests in UPAs (as elsewhere) seeking help in both spirituality and 'personal growth theologically'.

6.74   The proposed new style of continuing education seems better adapted to meet these needs than the old, which concentrated on providing skills and experience which seldom had much to do with encouraging spiritual and theological growth. In respect to UPAs we would like to see this principle pressed home with greater urgency. In-service training can cover a wide variety of training and retraining, from day-release courses to sabbatical periods. It can also offer an opportunity by which non-UPA clergy may be attracted to UPA work and be prepared for it. We see it as having the greatest potential of any means at present available to us for improving the quality and effectiveness of training for ministry in UPAs, and we *recommend* dioceses to explore its possibilities and to make systematic provision for it in UPAs.

(iii)   *Non-Stipendiary Ministry*
6.75   A third new development is related to the emergence of forms of Local Non-Stipendiary Ministry, on which we have laid great stress. What kind of training is appropriate for part-time ministers who, whether in inner city or rural areas, are put forward by their local congregations and expect to minister in the areas where they live and work? Residential theological colleges are out of the question, for practical as well as other reasons. Regional courses, as we have seen, are for the most part not well adapted to the needs of the candidates, though they could become more so if they were allowed to show more academic flexibility. There is however formal precedent for other forms of training, in that some 10 per cent of existing NSMs have been trained locally under more or less ad hoc arrangements approved by their

diocesan bishop.[17] This is no more than a formal precedent, since the great majority of these were post-retirement candidates. But the principle that dioceses might take direct responsibility for the training of certain classes of ordinands has already been applied in two cases to LNSMs, namely in the Bethnal Green experiment in the early 1970s and in the Brandon Scheme (Diocese of Southwark) which began in 1979.

6.76 Both these schemes were launched after consultation with ACCM, but neither has been officially monitored nor appraised by Church authorities. Both have encountered difficulties, mainly in the areas of the relationship of such a course to an academic syllabus, the integration of the candidates into the ministry of the wider Church, and the criticism to which they were exposed from the Church at large that they were being trained only to be 'second class priests'. A rather different pattern is a lay leadership course now being planned in Liverpool and Manchester. This is a first stage; in the second stage some of those who have taken part will go forward for selection and appropriate training for LNSM (priests and male or female deacons), for Readers and also for Youth and Community Work or as other non-ordained ministers. According to this pattern, groups drawn from one or more local congregations meet regularly together and are helped to reflect on their experience in the light of their Christian faith. They will be expected to explore the theological resources which may be of use to them, and to develop the skills which may help them to minister more effectively in their own situation and to communicate the gospel intelligibly to those among whom they live and work. Out of these groups we may hope to see the emergence of a truly local ministry.

6.77 We strongly welcome these experiments. They offer the only opportunity which we can see under present circumstances of raising up a truly indigenous ministry in UPAs. But we must emphasise that we do not see them being successful on a significant scale unless more resources are allocated to them. In particular:

(1) The task of training and supervising such candidates is a specialised and demanding one. It is not just a case of an 'experienced priest' keeping a fatherly eye on their progress. Tutors and supervisors need to be theologically competent, to have skills in adult education methods, and to be sensitive to the social and cultural environment in which the candidates live. The Church of England already has barely enough theologians to staff university faculties, theological colleges and courses, and colleges of education. It makes

virtually no provision for the training of any of these for the particular teaching responsibilities they exercise in the Church. Tutors for new local training schemes are not waiting in the wings ready to come on when the stage is set. They need to be identified, trained for the task and supported in their work. This cannot and will not happen unless resources are specifically allocated for the purpose. We *recommend* that attention should be given urgently to appropriate training for teachers and supervisors in this and other fields of theological education.

(2) Training of this kind requires not only skilled personnel but physical resources in the form of centres for study, books and visual aids, and appropriate theological teaching material. Urban centres are needed to provide theological and educational resources for all kinds of urban mission and training. In addition, independent organizations could be invited to make their specialised resources available for this vitally important educational work.

(3) It is no longer either practicable or desirable for the Church of England to attempt to fulfil these demands on its own. Such resources as there are are to be found scattered among the denominations. This is an urgent field for ecumenical co-operation. It is also essential that we should learn from the experience of other denominations and countries in involving representatives of local congregations in the training of clergy.[18]

(4) Given the greater variety and flexibility which we hope to see in these patterns of training, it is all the more important that their results should be centrally monitored and evaluated. It is vital that ACCM should be given the resources to do this.

New Initiatives
6.78 These developments all seem to us to have potential for providing training that is more appropriate to ministry in UPAs. We have noted also the initiatives which are being taken to encourage the recruitment of black ministers, many of whom will be working in inner city areas, and we urge that attention should be given to their training and that financial resources be made available to implement proposals for experiment in this area. But all this must be seen in the context of the widely recognized need for more fundamental change in our training institutions. We conclude this section with some recommendations which will inevitably seem controversial, but which we believe to be necessary if we are to shake off the paralysis which appears to have affected the Church's will to bring about change.

6.79   We have found that ACCM continues to promote change and experiment in theological training and is sympathetic to much of our thinking, but that it is severely limited in its ability to introduce reform. It is in essence an *advisory* council. Dioceses and colleges possess a cherished autonomy: ACCM's formal responsibility is limited to ensuring some uniformity of standards and criteria in selection and training.

6.80   Yet ACCM is the only resource which the Church of England has for initiating change and experiment in training for the ministry, and we believe it is quite unrealistic to expect it to do so without either financial resources or power to prescribe courses for individual students. Several colleges or courses[19] which were started in response to ACCM thinking came to an end because they failed to attract sufficient students and received no financial backing from Church funds. ACCM is unable to finance even research into the effectiveness of changes which have been introduced. We *recommend*, therefore, that ACCM should be adequately funded to promote and monitor officially sanctioned experiments in theological training.

6.81   We also believe that there must be new experimental courses aimed at equipping ordinands and clergy in UPAs. These need not be entirely separate from existing colleges or courses: they could form a part – perhaps a year – of existing patterns of training. To be successful, these must be relieved of the necessity to compete with the academic claims of the existing syllabus; and they must also be protected from the consequences of the total freedom enjoyed by most ordinands to choose their own course or college. There is of course a traditional and deeply cherished independence both in candidates, when they come to choose their college, and in colleges, when they come to accept or reject them; and this independence is doubtless a valuable component in a Church which is still enriched by a variety of different traditions and different styles of ministry. But the consequences of this independence for the promoting of new patterns of training can be extremely serious. Allied with the lack of provision of central Church funds for a particular course, it can effectively frustrate a scheme of training which has been officially launched following deliberate ACCM policy. In such cases, total freedom of choice, on the part of both candidates and colleges, is a luxury the Church can no longer afford. Candidates are already directed to the Aston Scheme. We *recommend* that ACCM should be given power, in certain defined cases, to direct candidates to courses of training specifically devised for the type of ministry which they may undertake; and we urge Bishops to endorse its direction in such cases.

6.82   We have argued that non-residential courses could be in a better position to provide training for ministry in UPAs than residential theological colleges, and we *recommend* that their potential should be further developed. We recognize that this is not necessarily much less expensive than residential training[20] (apart from the economy of not having to support ordinands' families). It would be wrong to recommend it on grounds of economy alone, since no expense must be spared to provide adequate staffing for good training.

6.83   On the other hand, we have to face the fact that the encouragement of regional non-residential courses poses a threat to residential colleges. More part-time students means fewer full-time ones, and more empty places in colleges. In the long term this could only be met, either by a substantial increase in the number of ordinands (as might follow, for example, the opening of the priesthood to women) or by the closure of colleges. The experience of enforced closures in the 1970s was an extremely painful one, and any proposal which may involve a further reduction in theological college places (this time for other than purely financial reasons) is certain to encounter powerful and understandable resistance. Nevertheless we find the case for change particularly strong in relation to training for ministry in UPAs, and we believe that the Church's failure to grapple effectively with the problems arising from its entire system of training (in which it invests such massive resources) can no longer be condoned.

Conclusion

6.84   Our evidence has convinced us that the training offered to clergy who will minister in UPAs is not only inadequate but often inappropriate. We have argued that this reflects shortcomings in clergy training generally, and we believe that there is need for far-reaching reform. But in the meantime we have noted trends in the development of regional courses, in the provision of further ministerial training and in experiments in locally-based part-time training which we would strongly encourage.

Clergy Support

6.85   There are particular pressures on clergy and their families – as indeed there are on most families – in UPAs. It is important to realise that clergy share in the problems as well as the strengths of UPAs.

Housing

6.86   Problems with clergy housing are not widespread. Two-thirds of UPA clergy described their vicarage as at least 'good'. Nevertheless nearly one in ten UPA clergy in our survey regarded their housing as a serious problem, almost three times as many as non-UPA clergy. Size, design and running costs were cited as the main concerns. In the face of such pressures which, when added to the others identified in this section, can be cumulatively and highly debilitating, three areas for action emerge:

(i)   There must be a very clear and decisive commitment to clergy and their families living in the vicarage of the UPA Church. We do not believe that alternatives such as living outside the UPA or buying their own homes are acceptable – on either theological or practical grounds; the latter include the cost of a realistic housing allowance, as well as a lack of housing for sale or suitable housing for rent.

(ii)   The design of traditional vicarages can often be very ill-suited to present-day UPA life. Many old large inner-urban parsonages will in any event need to be replaced. There is a clear need for continuing special and sensitive support from the Church Commissioners here. For example, architecture is very important in enabling the vicarage family to relate more easily and securely to its neighbours. The vicarage needs to be designed and sited in relation to neighbouring houses or flats, with its door visible for security reasons and its access in some way communal and friendly. It would be valuable if recommendations along these lines could be included in the next edition of the Church Commissioners' guidelines for architects.

(iii)   There is a strong case for special diocesan support for clergy housing in UPAs. Many UPA vicarages are too large to be supported by the clergy stipend. A system of diocesan/Church Commissioners support is needed to provide help with heating and other maintenance costs (as in Southwark diocese).

Clergy Families

(a)   *Clergy Wives and Children*

6.87   We discovered from the Gallup Survey, from some of those who sent submissions, and from our own experience and enquiries, that the relationship between clergy and their wives is much like that between spouses in general when one partner is involved in a demanding occupation. Some wives' main concern was their own employment; other wives did much more as unpaid voluntary workers assisting their husbands. And there was a variety of other arrangements designed to suit the circumstances of individual households. We note these various alternatives and we see them all as equally valid. We subscribe to the unexceptionable view that the way a clergyman relates to other members of his household is a matter for him personally, and there should be no expectations from us about the particular way clergy wives organise their lives.

6.88   Clergy wives have need of support, as well as their husbands, and because of their situation in being married to the person who gives out pastoral care, often find that there is no-one who feels responsible for giving pastoral care to them. It is important for those responsible to bear this in mind, though the fact that wives' attitudes to their role are very diverse means that they are not willing to be lumped together into a generalized group of 'clergy wives' and enrolled into some kind of support system.

6.89   Many UPA clergy and their wives find it a privilege to bring up their children in a multi-cultural area. This view was expressed by clergy wives whose views were collected specially for the Commission. For some this is an opportunity, for some it is stressful and hard to cope with, for many it is a combination of the two. Language barriers can add to the isolation of clergy wives bringing up children in a predominantly Asian area. It appears, too, that the problems of bringing up children in a different culture arise principally because of the social background of the clergy and their wives. UPA Churches are very rarely ministered to by a priest who belongs to the local culture. It may well be that the middle class social background of the clergy and their wives is the main reason why a large minority of them send their children to private secondary schools. Their preferences are very similar to non-UPA clergy: 38 per cent of non-UPA clergy, and 32 per cent of UPA clergy had sent their children to fee-paying secondary schools.[21] Yet the Gallup survey evidence suggests that the problem of clergy children's schooling is not the most commonly-cited reason for rejecting service in UPAs. Some demythologising needs to be done with regard to clergy families, their children, and education in UPAs. Clergy families have different experiences of local schooling and different educational preferences. Given our commitment to developing truly local Churches we would not support any proposal to give financial support to clergy families for the private education of their children.

(b)   *Single Clergy*
6.90   The proportion of UPA clergy who are single (26 per cent) is twice as high as that of non-UPA clergy; but part of this difference arises

from the relatively high proportion of under 35 year-olds (and hence also of curates) in UPAs.

6.91 Single clergy and single Church workers, many of whom are women, often say they find the inner cities more accepting than the suburbs. They are, however, unable to turn to a spouse for support, and thus can be more isolated. 'Loneliness' was cited as a problem by twice as many single clergy as married. When the Gallup Survey asked clergy 'who, if anyone, give you real support in your ministry?', far and away the highest numbers – 63 per cent of all the UPA clergy and 76 per cent of all the non-UPA clergy – said 'wife and family'.

6.92 Those clergy and Church workers who have no spouse and family lack this major means of support. There are proportionately many more single clergy and Church workers in UPAs than in other areas, and this has implications for pastoral support. Homosexual clergy also need appropriate pastoral support, even though in evidence to us they said that they often prefer to work in UPAs because of the greater degree of acceptance and diversity of life-styles. Support needs to be given to them, not least in their ministry to other homosexuals, who tend to be drawn to the inner cities.

6.93 For both clergy families and single clergy there is a clear need for dioceses or deaneries to ensure that holiday cover is available for UPA clergy, and that vicarages will not be left unoccupied.

Finance

6.94 In general, personal financial problems appear no more widespread among UPA than non-UPA clergy (28 per cent in each case). But this could be partly because the threshold of complaint of UPA clergy is higher, in view of the financial problems so many of their neighbours face. Moreover, if we confine the comparison to married clergy, then the incidence is higher in UPAs than elsewhere (37 per cent compared to 26 per cent). We regard this as disturbing. We know only too well, from ordinary UPA families, the pressures on family life associated with 'living from hand to mouth'. We therefore consider that the following proposals should be given a high priority:

(i) Clergy *expenses* are significant and less likely to be paid in full in UPA (58 per cent) than non-UPA parishes (75 per cent). Clergy can be reluctant to claim legitimate expenses from a poor UPA Church. This is clearly something that must be rectified with diocesan assistance (as happens, for example, in Southwark and Manchester).

(ii)   Clergy *housing costs* have already been referred to under the section on clergy housing; but there is an additional important matter regarding the much greater incidence of burglaries and vandalism in UPAs. One UPA vicarage has been burgled 53 times and cannot get insurance cover. Dioceses should give consideration to assistance with the inevitably higher premiums UPA clergy have to pay simply because of where they live and minister.

Support Systems

6.95   There are great pressures on clergy in UPAs. Clergy exhaustion, or burn-out, appears to be twice as serious a problem in the UPAs as elsewhere; it affects the younger rather than the older clergy, and especially the young married (regardless of whether the wife is working). There is a need to rethink the support systems required to sustain the clergy's contribution to the UPA Church. We have also been convinced of the need for a reappraisal by what we regard as the unacceptably high proportion of UPA clergy (25 per cent) who had not had a 'personal talk' in the last year with someone having direct pastoral responsibility for them.

6.96   We would suggest that the following points are taken into account in such a reappraisal.

1.   *Patterns of support.* The general pattern is much the same for UPAs and non-UPAs. One in six UPA clergy felt strongly enough to say they lacked support from the hierarchy.

2.   *Providers of personal support.* For married clergy, wives and family have already been mentioned as their main source of support. For the single (and widowers), it is clear that personal friends, informal groups (e.g. of neighbouring clergy) and individual parishioners provide the mainstay of support. For the under-35 age group, personal friends are well at the top of the list. (For further details see Appendix D – 'Sources of Support for Clergy')

3.   *Lay assistance.* The perceived contribution of the laity to the overall ministry is remarkable similar in UPA and non-UPA parishes, but it varies markedly with churchmanship in both groups; many more evangelical clergy describe it as 'very important' than other clergy. The lack of lay leadership, and therefore of lay support in a shared ministry – cited by 1 in 4 clergy as one of the main differences between ministering in the UPAs and elsewhere – is felt to be more noticeable on outer council estates (34 per cent) than in the inner city (17 per cent). This experience is confirmed from a different angle:

failure to find others to share leadership and ministry is cited as a problem by 44 per cent of UPA clergy (including 57 per cent of those on council estates) but only 29 per cent of non-UPA clergy.

6.97   In the light of these points, we *recommend* that dioceses and deaneries undertake a reappraisal of the support systems for their UPA clergy, Deaconesses and lay workers. We suggest that the following possibilities be explored as part of such exercises.

(a)   Mutual support groups at deanery or sub-deanery levels, of an informal kind. Such a group could be formed within a parish and congregation.

(b)   Pastoral Care Schemes, such as those already in existence in several dioceses (e.g. London, Southwark and Chichester), which have proved their worth not only in personal support and encouragement for the participating clergy but in their more effective ministry.

(c)   Encouraging properly-constituted relationships between clergy and an outside person; a 'safe place' where clergy can say what is in their heart to someone completely outside their situation and who is not therefore a fellow-minister.

(d)   Regular joint work consultations (as have been started in the Liverpool Diocese): these might need to be conducted by teams of consultants, and should be part of episcopal oversight. They should include the setting of agreed objectives and their monitoring.

(e)   'Burn-out' courses (such as those already offered to social workers by the National Institute for Social Work).

(f)   The support gained through the assessment of a parish using the Audit for the Local Church, and involving the congregation with the priest.

(g)   Specific support – as we argue elsewhere in our report – with administrative and secretarial work, and advice on Church buildings.

6.98   Most importantly, we would stress the need for regular, *at least annual*, discussions between each UPA clergyman and a person with direct pastoral responsibility for him.

Worship

6.99   At the heart of our vision, as it has emerged over the last two years, is a commitment to God and his call, and the faithful response of his Church in the UPAs. We believe that such a Church will be locally-rooted and outward-looking, and that its worship will properly reflect this.

6.100   For the local UPA Church to respond to God by commending his gospel, it must talk people's language, so that they have a chance of hearing and understanding. What is sometimes called the 'incarnational' side of the Christian religion is an indispensable characteristic of a worshipping community. The Church in the UPA has to live in and be part of the local world. The roots of liturgy must be found in the ground of society.

6.101   Worship in the UPAs must emerge out of and reflect local cultures: it will always be the worship of Him who is totally Other and yet is to be found, worshipped and served through the realities of UPA life. The worship of the Church that is part of the UPA will be the worship of a Church that is present in celebration, confession, compassion and judgement.

6.102   To understand worship in this way means that certain aspects of UPA life will necessarily greatly affect the formation of the worshipping life of the UPA Church. The main contribution of the Church to our cities is to be itself, and true to its vocation. It will gather up and inform local life. It must 'accept the positive aspects and validity of working class culture, particularly to build on the strong sense of family and community which is often found, and be prepared to communicate through feeling rather than the mind, through non-verbal communication rather than verbal'.[21] It will be more informal and flexible in its use of urban language, vocabulary, style and content. It will therefore reflect a universality of form with local variations, allowing significant space for worship which is genuinely local, expressed in and through local cultures, and reflecting the local context.

6.103   It will promote a greater *involvement* of the congregations in worship. Some clergy and lay people seem to have the idea that anyone with a Cockney or West Indian accent could not possibly read a lesson or lead the intercessions. Their voices may therefore never be heard throughout the service in the heart of the East End of London, Toxteth or Moss Side.

6.104   It will reflect the concern of local UPA people for things to be more concrete and tangible rather than abstract and theoretical. This finds expression in the use of religious objects like banners designed and

135

made locally, as well as more traditional symbols like crucifixes. Worship and study may therefore lay more emphasis on the history, the story, the narrative. Local UPA people often love to tell the stories of their lives, how God changed them, of problems overcome, and of great events and disasters.

6.105 People should be encouraged to come and go – to come into Church when they want to or need to. Many Churches convey an attitude of spirituality which makes prayer and worship available only to those who turn up in the right place at the right time and go through the correct motions corporately from start to finish.

6.106 The worship offered by the local Churches is also important as a means of evangelism. The stranger who comes into services will make a judgement about Christianity on the basis of what he encounters there. Is the worship lively and participatory? Does it evoke a sense of the presence of God while showing a concern for the real things in people's lives? Much of this will depend on how the local congregation order their services.

6.107 Worship is about good dreams: it needs to hold them alongside what is sometimes a very harsh reality. UPA Christians want a beautiful service, but they may have to go home to domestic violence or a leaking roof. A Church life which has nothing to say about these things simply leaves people feeling inferior. They feel they must hide from the clergy and the local Church their debts, their court cases, their sufferings at the hands of their husbands. Reality must be faced. There must be something to understand about God's will for a wife terrified of her husband, for a husband terrified of his gambling debts, for parents who dread that their son is out beating up Bangladeshis.

6.108 Worship will put the harsh realities in a new light. It may enable people to withdraw for a time from the pressures, but it will be 'withdrawal with intent to return', not evasion.

6.109 Running through all the aspects of UPA life as they need to affect worship is the firm and hopeful recognition of 'the importance of the ordinary'. It is that which is so often missing from Church life and witness in UPAs. It can only be properly accepted by a truly local Church.

6.110 Many submissions included suggestions about books, services and groups. As we noted in Chapter 3 to give people a 1300 page Alternative Service Book is a symptom of the gulf between the Church and ordinary people in the UPAs. We have heard calls for short, functional service booklets or cards, prepared by people who will always ask 'if all the words are really necessary'. The work of re-forming the liturgy has really only just begun for the UPA Church, and we *recommend* that the Liturgical Commission pays close attention to the needs of Churches in the UPAs.

6.111   There has also been a clear plea that the formal liturgies so beloved of the wider Church must be complemented in UPAs by more informal and spontaneous acts of worship and witness. Vivid and concrete manifestations of spirituality have proven track records in many UPAs – like, for example, the Way of the Cross acted out through the streets of the East End, Armley, Euston, Notting Hill, Cardiff and Bradford.

6.112   Worship which encourages informality and spontaneity will not dispense with care and preparation. The local UPA Church will be as concerned with the beauty of worship and its excellence as are often the local schools with their productions.

6.113   We have already affirmed the importance of small groups in the local Church, in its mission and in its worship. Yet they need to be complemented by the glorious occasions and celebrations in the local parish Church.

Children and Young People

6.114   Churches everywhere must seek new ways of passing on the faith to the children and young people growing up in the congregation and the neighbourhood.

6.115   In the UPAs, those who are working at building up traditional activities with the young, such as Sunday schools, Bible classes, youth fellowships, uniformed organisations, choirs and youth clubs, report that they receive very little sustained response. There are exceptions, but by and large attendance is small and irregular. Although the children often appreciate the interest and attention they receive, very few show any committed involvement, or attend regularly for very long. These few tend to be the loners; the vast majority do not respond to the traditional organisations, nor to the materials which national organisations make available.

6.116   There is a need therefore to look at other ways of transmitting the faith in the UPAs. One way to build friendly contact between clergy and children is for clergy to visit schools in the parish. They are usually welcomed by the staff, regardless of whether it is a Church school or not, provided they show themselves sensitive to people of other faiths or none, and regard their visits (and assemblies or lessons) as a way of building friendship, rather than a means of indoctrination.

6.117   A children's Church, for children of members of the congregation, during the Sunday service, can be a success. And a very promising approach being used by the Roman Catholic Church is to *train parents* to bring up their own children in the faith and to prepare them for the sacraments. This can lead to valuable learning by the parents themselves, and the development of a teaching ministry by them, as well as ensuring that the children are taught.

6.118   Children are not willing to be silent spectators of adult worship – and teenagers even less. Where young people do take an active interest in Church it is often because they are in gospel or other choirs, bands or dance groups, which take part in the service. This can lead to a feeling of participation and belonging, and enable their efforts to be appreciated by the older generation. But it is only a first step; pastoral and teaching work needs to be done to enable groups of young people connected with the Church to relate the Christian gospel to their lives and to the life of the area around.

6.119   In the 1980s, the Church of England has been increasingly aware of the need to produce a policy for its work with young people. In 1982 the General Synod debated a document 'Towards a Policy for Work with Young People in the Church of England', and a working group was subsequently set up to pursue its implications. This group has spent some time addressing itself to the situations facing UPA parishes. It has argued that 'Christian youth work has a concern for the nurture of young Christians within the Churches, for listening and responding to the needs of young people in the wider community, and for being a channel between the two'.

6.120   We consider the Church's involvement in youth work as such in Chapter 13. We want to stress here, however, that in UPA parishes young people grow up alongside each other, often with different cultural backgrounds and social experiences. Parishes which recognize this begin to respond to the real needs of youngsters.

6.121   Engaging the interest and abilities of young people, and transmitting the Christian faith to them, is a difficult, but vital, task facing the Church in the UPAs. We have offered some limited comments, and *recommend* that a reassessment of the traditional patterns of the Church's work of nurture in the UPAs is undertaken at parish, deanery, and diocesan level.

Main Recommendations

1.   Dioceses with significant concentrations of UPAs should initiate Church Leadership Development Programmes (paragraph 6.11).

2.   Our proposals for an extension of Local Non-Stipendiary Ministry, including those relating to selection, training and funding should be tested in dioceses, and monitored over a ten-year period (paragraph 6.55).

3.   All dioceses should manifest a commitment to post-ordination training and continued ministerial education in UPAs to the extent at least of regular day-release courses (paragraph 6.74).

4.   Urgent attention should be given to appropriate training for teachers and supervisors in all areas of theological education, particularly those concerned with ministry in UPAs, and to the provision of theological and educational resources in urban centres (paragraph 6.77).

5.   ACCM should be adequately funded to promote and monitor officially sanctioned experiments in theological education (paragraph 6.80).

6.   ACCM should be given power, in certain defined cases, to direct candidates to specific courses of training, and bishops should endorse such direction (paragraph 6.81).

7.   The role of non-residential training courses similar to the Aston scheme should be developed further (paragraph 6.82).

8.   Dioceses and deaneries should undertake a reappraisal of their support systems for UPA clergy (paragraph 6.97).

9.   The Liturgical Commission should pay close attention to the liturgical needs of Churches in the urban priority areas (paragraph 6.110).

10.   A reassessment of the traditional patterns of the Church's work of nurture of young people in UPAs is required at parish, deanery and diocesan level (paragraph 6.121).

References

1   Submission from the Diocese of Bradford

2   Advisory Council for the Church's Ministry, ACCM 1974

3   *Local Ordained Ministry*, ACCM (General Synod paper GS 442) 1980, para. 14

4   Submission from the Urban Ministry Project

5   ibid

6   Final Report of the Archbishop's Commission on Training for the Ministry, 1944

7   *Theological Training*, ACCM, 1983

8   From *Doing Theology Today* (ACCM 1969) to *An Integrating Theology* by Peter Baelz (ACCM Occasional Paper, December 1983)

9   ACCM Briefing Paper, p. 9: 'There is little evidence from the review of the development of Continuing Ministerial Education that very much experience is being developed of theological reflection on pastoral practice and experience. Most continuing ministerial education has concentrated on the development of skills for particular tasks . . .'

10   From the Commission's meeting with ACCM, 9 November 1984

11   Evidence from Northern College (URC), Manchester

12   A point strongly endorsed by the Chairman of ACCM

13   *Non-stipendiary Ministry in the Church of England*, by Mark Hodge (GS 583A) 1983

14   ibid para 97

15   ibid paras 82, 89, 98

16   ACCM review (1984) presented to the House of Bishops, paras 7-9

17   Hodge Report (GS 583A) Table 3.2 and para 15

18   e.g. Northern College (URC); 'Readiness for Ordained Ministry Project' (Province of Western Australia)

19   Lichfield, St Augustine's, Basingstoke

20   'The Financing of Training' (March 1983) GS Misc 175 p 16

21   See the explanatory footnote to Chapter 13

22   Submission from the Diocese of Birmingham

Chapter 7

SUPPORTING A PARTICIPATING CHURCH

'To someone who has had electricity cut off because they cannot pay a bill of £70, it may seem scandalous that churches spend hundreds on perhaps unnecessary improvements to church buildings and furnishings.'
(Advice worker in London)

7.1 We have deliberately left our conclusions on buildings and finance to the end of our proposals for the UPA Church, for the allocation and use of the Church's material resources should serve, not determine, policy. Problems with bricks and mortar and money are however a major concern in many of the parishes we have visited.

Church Buildings

7.2 The question of church buildings in UPAs is serious, complex and intractable.

7.3 Its seriousness was made abundantly clear in our clergy survey: 60 per cent of UPA clergy said they faced problems with their church buildings, half of which were 'serious'. Forty-five per cent thought their church, and 40 per cent their other buildings, inappropriate to their current needs. One in six thought assistance with buildings the single most important form of help that would make their ministry more effective, with another 30 per cent rating it second priority. The problems with UPA churches were seen as size, running costs, state of repair, design and versatility. State of repair was seen as the greatest problem with ancillary buildings.

7.4 The seriousness of the question of church buildings has also been put strongly to us in the course of our visits to UPAs, and through the submissions made to us.

7.5 Although we have seen some imaginative schemes to adapt and improve Church buildings, the following comments from dioceses and deaneries are typical of the general picture we found:

141

'It is now increasingly likely that (the Diocese will) lose fifty (churches) within the next two years . . . It is important to recognise that these churches will disappear *not* as part of planned diocesan reorganisation, but simply as a result of the inability of parishes to meet the high cost of repairs.'

'The church in the inner town, and on the large over-spill estate, can easily be caught in a poverty trap. Its impossible burdens of fabric and finance can kill its missionary morale, and thus the life of the local church gets progressively both weaker and more inward looking.'

'Today urban Christians often are tied to old, expensive, large churches and halls, entirely inappropriate for today's needs . . . a cold, ugly *and* uncomfortable church is a very poor advertisement for God's involvement with His creation.'

7.6   An ancient church building *may* be a blessing. In a UPA it is unlikely to be as ancient a building as is often to be found in rural areas. Most old urban churches are Victorian. Yet they may well be the most ancient building in the vicinity, making an important contribution to the local sense of place and worth.

7.7   The historic building may not only be ancient, but also of some architectural significance – perhaps one of the few works of outstanding aesthetic worth in the neighbourhood, which it would be an act of vandalism to destroy. In many UPAs there is much to be said for keeping a number of such churches of character and distinction that enrich the area – perhaps as the parish church of a major parish served by a team ministry.

7.8   An ancient place of worship also has important psychological associations – not only for those who use it regularly. It will have become 'our church' to many. In an urban area it may seem – and more than seem – a rock in an ocean of change. Its demolition, or even its radical adaptation, often cannot be achieved without real personal pain, and, in the end, bereavement. It may *seem* that when a neighbourhood is being abandoned by so many, the Church too is abandoning it. Local people rarely accept the fact that the population of many inner areas has halved since their churches were built. In some cases the population is no more than one-tenth of what it was then.

7.9   History is rarely an unmixed blessing. It can often mean:
      the decay of a building;
      the movement and change of surrounding population;

change – and most probably decline – in the size of the
congregation;
change in the needs of the congregation – and therefore 'functional
obsolescence'.

7.10   One or more of these factors frequently makes the maintenance
of an historic urban church, in terms of its heating, lighting and repair, a
problem beyond the capacity of a congregation. One historic church
may be a manageable problem; a plethora of Victorian churches in one
area is almost inevitably a major intractable problem. The imposition of
VAT on alterations to unlisted church buildings in addition to VAT on
repairs (whether the church is listed or not) has added a further burden
on those responsible for many UPA churches.

7.11   An unsuitable church can be replaced by a new place of worship
under the powers provided by section 46 of the Pastoral Measure. But
this section can only be invoked where sufficient funds can be released
from the sale of surplus land, or made available from other sources. The
problem of raising the money for the repair, maintenance, or adaptation
or renewal of any historic church in an urban area, where the sense of
community is quite different from that of, say, a rural village, and where
the building is evidently now inappropriate to the people's needs, is
particularly intractable – especially if there is more than one historic
church within a relatively small distance.

7.12   The people of a rural parish, though probably fewer in number
than in an urban parish, are likely to include some who are more
prosperous; the church building is more likely to be more valued by
those who do not regularly attend the church, and supporting an appeal
for the repair of the church is probably a more accepted part of village
life. In contrast, the needs and deprivations of urban areas are apt to
make the request for support of an appeal for a church building an
embarrassment.

7.13   These financial questions raise acutely for many the moral
question of the rightness of spending so great a proportion of church
income, and drawing on funds from other sources, on the repair and
maintenance of a building which is as much a curse as a blessing, in the
midst of surrounding urban deprivation and need. Only if the money
spent on the building is going to make it more effectively serve the
community is that moral argument fully overcome. We set out below
some ways in which this might be achieved.

Sharing and Adaption

(i) *The Sharing of Church Buildings with Other Christians*

7.14   The shape of Church allegiance has changed very considerably in UPAs in the last decades. The predominant Church allegiance in many cities is now Roman Catholic. Places like Thamesmead in the diocese of Southwark have happily pioneered Anglican-Roman Catholic sharing arrangements; but more generally the number of such sharing arrangements in urban areas is still woefully few. We have found sharing agreements to be more frequent in outer UPAs than in inner areas – with new churches in new areas rather than with old churches in old areas. The lack of sharing agreements in older areas needs further careful examination, for it probably says something of considerable significance about ecumenical relations in inner urban areas. The sharing of Anglican churches with Black Pentecostal churches is, of course, more frequent in inner urban areas, where most Black-led Churches are to be found. But rarely is there a real sharing agreement. Too often there are simply landlord/tenant relationships with little attempt at any depth of sharing on either side. Sharing raises inescapable and profound questions of identity, and the older Church can easily be seen as a 'threat' to the younger. Often Black Pentecostal churches have special reasons for being jealous of their identity. We have been told: 'what we really want is our own premises'. Probably they share only a hall, not the church itself. Quite often the condition of the hall which they use as a church may leave much to be desired, and the times they are allowed to use the premises may also seem to discriminate against them. This area of sharing provides considerable opportunities for hurt as well as healing.

7.15   It is important to recognise that any Church represented on the General Council of the British Council of Churches or on the governing body of the Evangelical Alliance or the British Evangelical Council can enter into an agreement for sharing church buildings. The sad fact is that this does not include many of the Black-led Churches. In 1980 the BCC Working Group Report *The Use of Church Property in a Plural Society* tried to come to grips with this question. It would be virtually solved if, for instance, the Afro-West Indian Council of Churches were to be added to the three bodies we have named. It is urgent that the question be faced afresh.

7.16   In the Sharing of Church Buildings Act 1969 and the Pastoral Measure 1983 the powers already exist to allow a very great degree of sharing of both work and buildings. What is not possible is a completely shared ministry in relation to the Eucharist. But where there is a shared building, and the area is one of ecumenical experiment, much can be allowed by the bishop.

7.17   It is clear to us, from the Sharing Agreements that have already been entered into, what can be done if there is the will to do it. We *recommend* the wider adoption of such Agreements.

(ii)   *The Sharing of Churches with other Faiths*
7.18   It has been obvious to us in our visits to UPAs that Christians have far more church buildings than they now need, and that those they have are often far too large for their purposes. Equally obvious has been the fact that people of other faiths are often exceedingly short of places in which to meet and worship. This is not surprising, with 500,000 Hindus and Sikhs, and one million Muslims, living in Britain. There are, in fact, 177,000 members of other faiths of Indian sub-continent origin in the West Midlands; 60,000 in Manchester; 92,000 in Inner London and 36,000 in Ealing. One area bishop of inner London estimates that the Muslim worshippers alone would outnumber all the Christian communicants in his area.

7.19   At present, the holding of an act of corporate worship of another faith is illegal in the properly constituted worship centres of most of the members of the BCC, including those of the Church of England. For various reasons, not least courteous sensitivity towards Christians, most of those of other faiths are likely to be reluctant, except in very exceptional circumstances, to conduct their own corporate worship in Christian churches. Nevertheless there are occasions when requests for use of church buildings may be made. The difficulty is then a theological one as much as a legal one. The theological problems are alluded to in Chapter 3, and it is clear that the Church of England has not yet reached a common mind about them. But theological reflection must always take account of the human consequences of the application of a particular doctrine. If you are in great need of a place to worship and you see the local Christian church closed most days of the week, and, when it is used, having only a small group of worshippers in just the building that could house your congregation, you are almost bound to feel a sense of rejection if there is a refusal to share.

7.20   In these circumstances, we believe that it is all the more important to make clear in other ways that though we are people of differing faiths we are also neighbours. This can be demonstrated through sharing church buildings other than churches themselves. For example the sharing of church halls or school buildings with those of other faiths is something we would wish to encourage.

7.21   It was made clear to the Commission on a number of occasions that many individuals of other faiths when they see a Christian church open go in to say their own private prayers. This chance to welcome individuals of other faiths is also important. We would like to record our gratitude as a Commission for the welcome we have received in temples, gurdwaras and mosques in a number of UPAs.

(iii)   *The Adaptation of Church Buildings for Community Purposes*
7.22   Increasingly, and we believe rightly, church buildings, formerly used only for worship, are being used for multi-purpose activities of benefit to the community at large.

7.23   We have seen a number of examples on our visits of Victorian churches which have been subdivided or adapted to make more flexible use of the total space. Thus the church becomes a church/hall or church/ community centre. Playgroups, facilities for the young and old, and for the unemployed, are thus afforded space within what was formerly simply a 'church'.

7.24   It is important that the Church of England should see that in the sharing of its buildings in this way it has an opportunity to serve the surrounding community – like someone opening the doors of her home. A multiracial playgroup in a church hall may do more for race relations than fifty-two sermons a year on the subject. There is a welcome and encouraging way of sharing, and a discouraging 'take it or leave it' way. The 'business' of sharing needs to be informed by the Gospel.

7.25   The condition of the buildings will speak volumes concerning the attitudes of the host. As the Council for the Care of Churches noted in evidence to us, the funds which are available for the adaptation of churches in UPAs are inadequate, despite the generous assistance which has been given to some schemes under the Urban Programme. Many churches do not meet the criteria established for State Aid for Churches in use. Moreover, there are virtually no designated national resources for aiding the extended use and adaptation of churches.

7.26   For these reasons, we believe that a new Church Urban Fund, which we propose later in this Chapter, should have as one of its main objectives to enable the adaptation and sharing of churches and church buildings in the ways we have suggested.

146

7.27   We hope too that special consideration will be given by the Historic Buildings and Monuments Commission for England to the allocation of grant aid specifically to church buildings in the inner city areas, as far as is consistent with their objectives.

The Control and Care of Church Buildings

7.28   There are two main statutory frameworks within the Church of England which bear on proposals to effect changes to church buildings. The Faculty Jurisdiction legislation is concerned with the adaptation or alteration of churches that are in use and are intended to remain in use. The Pastoral Measure regulates the procedure for dealing with the future of Churches that are no longer required for worship, including those which have been 'declared redundant'.[1]

7.29   There can be little doubt that many clergy and local church members in urban areas find the judicial character of the Faculty Jurisdiction an irksome and rigid system of control of the care of church buildings. Yet again there are others who view it as a well-operated system, readily accessible to people and relatively quick and cheap.

7.30   The debate is a long-running one, to which we have found it difficult to do justice given the time at our disposal. We would note, however, that Churches of all denominations have some legal system of control over their property. Given the kind of church buildings the Church of England possesses (with some 12,000 listed buildings) it is difficult to see how there could be a wholly different system for its urban priority area churches. Second, the Faculty Jurisdiction (together with the Pastoral Measure procedures) fulfils a function which, if churches while in use were *not* exempted from ancient monument and listed buildings controls, would undoubtedly have to be met by some other system of control which might be even more irksome. Third, the present arrangements, acceptable as they are to the State, have enabled considerable State aid towards the maintenance of church buildings to be given – in the knowledge that the Church of England has tried to play its part to care for its heritage of church buildings.

7.31   Some changes are in prospect following the publication of the Report of the Faculty Jurisdiction Commission in 1984.[2] It is difficult at this stage for us to judge how the legislation to emerge in due course will eventually affect urban churches. Nevertheless, we can say that, though we are grateful for the Report of the Faculty Jurisdiction Commission and for the evidence submitted to us by the Council for the Care of Churches, we are not convinced that the Church as a whole has as yet given adequate attention to the specific problem of the care of church buildings in urban priorty areas. The question of what should be done about the often more beautiful and mostly more ancient churches in rural areas has been seen as more important.

7.32   Questions must be raised when a congregation cannot keep its historic church building going – not just in terms of repairs but also running costs. The continuing care of churches in this position needs a greater degree of financial support from dioceses, local authorities and local conservation groups than is available at present. We hope that those responsible will strive to find new ways of responding, and to assist parishes actively where buildings are proving a burden rather than a resource.

7.33   In the end, it may be inevitable that a church may have to be declared redundant, in whole or in part. The closure of a church and the declaration of its redundancy are inevitably traumatic. It is difficult to conceive how in such circumstances the procedures can be anything other than painstaking.

7.34   The generalised accusation has been made to us of 'red tape, bureaucracy and delay' involved in the procedures under the Pastoral Measure. No doubt in particular instances the accusations can be justified. On the other hand, we have been reminded that one person's 'delay' is another person's right to be consulted. If a hierarchical episcopal Church is to be democratic it is difficult to see which of the 'interested parties' could be cut out – the PCC, the incumbent, team vicars, the patron, the local planning authorities, the rural dean, the archdeacon, the Diocesan Advisory Committee for the Care of Churches, the Diocesan Redundant Church Uses Committee, the Diocesan Pastoral Committee, the Registrar and Chancellor, the Church Commissioners, the Bishop?

7.35   Yet the rights of individuals and groups to make their views known must be balanced against the need to avoid undue delay. The Commission has been given several examples of historic urban churches which have been left vacant for what has seemed to the parish an unconscionable time whilst a suitable use and user has been sought. They have consequently suffered the depredations of vandals.

7.36   In these circumstances, it has been argued to us that the only way forward is for the system of control – the Faculty Jurisdiction, the Ecclesiastical Exemption and the Pastoral Measure – to be revised so that it better facilitates the mission of the Church. This might imply the

Church of England having to give up its control over its buildings and accept that where churches cannot be supported by the local congregation the future of the church should be passed into the hands of the local authority, through the service of a Purchase Notice. In this way, it is argued, those who wish to preserve the building as an historical monument would have to foot the bill. This would not only concentrate preservationists' minds, but also increase the pressure on the diocese and the parish faced with the difficult decision of withdrawal and redundancy.

7.37   On the other hand, it has been pointed out to us that the abandonment of Ecclesiastical Exemption would leave the Church of England in a situation where it would become practically impossible to alter the outside of any church that was a listed building, or that if the building were subject to compulsory acquisition by the local authority, it would be open to them to sell it to whom they wished regardless of the views of the Church. We have noted that the General Synod has made it clear to the Church Commissioners that there are some uses that it would find most inappropriate for a redundant Church. A change from the present system could mean the loss of any control over this.

7.38   In our judgement it would be unrealistic for us to recommend any radical revision of the present procedures. It was put to us – and we are forced to agree – that a radical revision would be twenty years too late on the one hand – or perhaps twenty years too early on the other. Yet those who have pressed us to recommend changes in the law are not people who want to see wholesale destruction of church buildings, nor local democratic machinery overridden. They are concerned about congregational life and the mission of the Church becoming enslaved to the maintenance of cold and costly buildings. We share this concern. If those whose prime interest is the conservation of buildings do not recognize the importance of this pastoral dimension, they must not be surprised if, in due course, the Church comes to the view that a radical revision of the present framework is necessary.

7.39   There is scope at present however for some streamlining of the existing procedures to be pursued further. There does seem to be too great a stress on the rights of interested parties and not enough on their responsibilities. In particular, we have much evidence to cause us to question whether the present complex committee structure is geared primarily to helping forward what must surely in most cases be the primary interested party – the local church people. They, far more than other interested parties, must be properly consulted. Yet by the time a church becomes redundant they are sometimes reduced to a small beleaguered band of people – perhaps eclectic – whose vision of the needs of the area as a whole may be blinded by the bereavement occasioned by the loss of their church building. There is a clear need for dioceses to display not simply an administrative but a pastoral approach in these circumstances.

7.40   There can often be long delays in finding a suitable alternative use for a redundant church. We would urge dioceses to speed up the processes, and so reduce the time between the congregation leaving the church and its subsequent long-term use. Where necessary, efforts should be made to find a temporary alternative use for the church in this period. Local housing authorities often find short-life users for buildings which they are eventually to rehabilitate or redevelop: would it not be possible for a similar procedure to be followed with redundant churches? The Redundant Churches Fund understandably concentrates most of its resources on the 'gems' which it takes into its care for preservation in the interests of the Church and the nation; we ask if it might not consider devoting some of its funds to maintain and preserve the fabric of the less glamorous, but still important, churches in the UPAs in this interim period?

7.41   The problems of insurance have also been brought to our attention. Once the congregation has left a church on the chosen date of redundancy, insurance firms withdraw a substantial amount of cover because the church is not in use. It is during this period that it is most vulnerable. Finding a temporary use for the church building during this period, as we suggest should be explored, may be one way round this difficulty, as the more the building is used, the less likely it is to be the object of vandalism.

7.42   We have not been able to explore these suggestions in great depth. There may well be difficulties with them. But we are in no doubt that the difficulties being faced by dioceses with many old urban churches are severe. We urge those with responsibilites here to consider further the suggestions we have made, in the knowledge that there is dissatisfaction with the present situation. We now turn to the subsequent uses to which redundant churches and church buildings might be put.

The Sale of Church Buildings
(i)   *Churches Sold or Leased to other Christian Bodies*
7.43   Over the period 1969-1984, 74 redundant churches have been

appropriated under the Pastoral Measure to use for worship by other Christian bodies. These churches are spread over 29 dioceses and their locations range from inner city to rural. However, 30 are situated in and around London (Diocese of London [16], Southwark [12], and Chelmsford [2]). Other inner city locations are Birmingham [4], Bristol [3], and Manchester [3].

7.44   These redundant churches have been acquired by:

Black-led Churches		22
Roman Catholic Church		18
Orthodox Churches		
Greek	15	
Serbian	3	
Russian	1	
Armenian	1	
Joint Greek/Russian	1	
		21
Elim Pentecostal		6
Others		7
		74

7.45   Fifty-five of these buildings have been sold or let on long leases at a premium. Prices or premiums fall within the following ranges (disposals to Black-led Churches are shown in brackets).

Below £10,000	21	(4)
£10,000–£25,000	11	(4)
£25,001–£50,000	15	(9)
£50,001 and above	8	(1)

7.46   Eighteen have been leased for shorter terms at rents ranging from:

Nominal	8	(1)
Up to £1,000 pa	5	(–)
Up to £2,500 pa	4	(2)
Over £2,500 pa	1	(1)

One redundant church was exchanged for a Seventh Day Adventists' building which became the new parish church.

7.47   This list of redundant churches sold to other Churches speaks for itself. It does not suggest that the Church of England has sold its redundant churches 'derelict and dear'.

(ii)   *Churches Sold or Leased to other Faiths*
7.48   Both from the diocesan submissions and from the representations from minority ethnic groups we have been made aware of the strength of feeling caused by the Church of England's unwillingness to sell redundant churches to other faiths. In many inner city areas land shortage and planning restrictions prevent either new building or conversion of domestic property. The Church of England is *seen* as possessing a resource of which it can no longer make use, but which it prefers to sell to developers rather than permit members of another faith to use it for worship.

7.49   The Church of England has sold only one Church to another faith – St Luke's, Southampton – in August 1983, at a cost of £80,000, to Singh Sabha Gurdwara.

7.50   We would like to have agreed with the 1980 British Council of Churches Working Party Report *The Use of Church Property in a Plural Society* which stated:

> 'It is our conviction that in regard to buildings there is now sufficient printed material, and that the ecumenical situation is now adequately understood, for the Churches to formulate appropriate policies for the multi-racial and multi-faith future which is before us in Britain.'

7.51   But no-one reading the account of the 1983 debate in the General Synod on the subject could reach any other conclusion than that there was no agreement at all on the sale of churches to other faiths: indeed, there was very deep conscientious disagreement. The present position is that the Church Commissioners consider each case on its merits in the light of a wide range of factors, and diocesan and other views.

7.52   Given the continuing theological uncertainty it would be premature for us to make recommendations. We can only record the pain to which the present situation can give rise and the practical consequences which hang upon continuing inter-faith dialogue.

(iii)   *The Sale of Redundant Buildings*
7.53   Where a redundant building is not required by another Christian denomination, and is not a candidate for preservation by some other means, the diocese and ultimately the Church Commissioners have to make choices about the sale of the site. In some cities, the main problem may be to find anyone who will buy it. In other places, particularly in London, the commercial site value may exceed the price that can be

afforded if the site is to be used for community purposes. Where land is most scarce and thus prices highest, organisations such as housing associations will have great difficulty in competing with commercial developers. A large church site may represent the only opportunity of building in that particular neighbourhood. The Church Commissioners, acting in close consultation with the diocese, are then faced with a difficult decision: to realise the full value of the site, in order to make more money available to further the work and mission of the Church throughout the diocese as a whole and beyond, or to accept a lower price in order to allow the needs of the local community to be met.

7.54   The much-publicised case of Holy Trinity Church, Paddington, was brought to our attention. The case raised in an acute form the dilemma we have just set out. What particularly upset the local community groups was what they saw as the impenetrable procedure by which a decision appeared to be reached. They perceived there to be no forum at diocesan level where they could present their case for the site's use.

7.55   Other cases have been brought to our attention where housing associations, seeking to work in co-operation with diocesan authorities and to develop a long-term strategy, have felt that their request for partnership was unwelcome. Their request was not that the diocese should always be prepared to make a financial sacrifice, since in many cases they have been able to offer an open market price, but that they should be notified when potential sites were likely to become vacant so that they could negotiate for funding.

7.56   We were glad to be assured by the Church Commissioners that in the last 15 years some 70 per cent of the new uses found for redundant churches have been ones benefiting the local community. Other denominations are obliged under the charity laws to sell to the highest bidder: the Church of England alone has the discretion, under the Pastoral Measure, to sell to other than the highest bidder. Yet we remain concerned that lack of open debate gives the *impression* that diocesan authorities are not interested in the needs of the local community. We have been told that 'some people have gained the impression from their dealings with the Church in property matters that it finds it too much trouble to take non-financial matters into account'. The conversion of a church building into luxury flats (even though it may be the developer and not the Church which profits) conveys an image to the local community of a rich and perhaps uncaring institution. On the other hand, the real distress of a small congregation in giving up their church may be eased if they feel that their sacrifice has been the neighbourhood's gain.

7.57 We *recommend* that the local parish and the diocese should together assess the needs of the local community and consider openly, in consultation with community organisations, the possible uses of each redundant property before placing it on the open market. In this way, possibilities of combining financial gain for the diocese with benefit for the community may be identified. We recognise that such mutually beneficial arrangements will not always prove to be feasible, and hard choices between competing considerations will still have to be made; but constructive dialogue is more likely to produce a situation where each side understands the other and creative possibilities are more likely to emerge.

7.58 It is clear that adaptation or redevelopment is a very demanding task. It is often regarded – in our opinion understandably – by many clergy as 'not what I was ordained for'. The task clearly requires special skills of management which neither naturally belong to, nor can be expected to be acquired by, some clergy. We believe that it must be clear in every diocese who is the 'UPA Redevelopment Officer'. He may well be the archdeacon – or a group under his authority. The Diocesan Advisory Committee also has an important educational and advice-giving role here, beyond its statutory role of advising on faculty applications. The task of redevelopment calls for financial acumen, but also someone in close touch with local planners, housing and social service departments, and heads of other denominations and other faiths – and a constant awareness of and sensitivity to the Church's priorities. He must assist the incumbent and the parish without wresting all control from the local Church.

7.59 But it is not just at times of crisis that such help is needed. The evidence from churchwardens and parish priests in many UPAs is that one of their primary needs is also for professional help with the day-to-day administration and maintenance of their church fabric. We ask dioceses – and especially the Diocesan Advisory Committees – to respond to this concern. They might consider, for example, the scheme in the Liverpool Diocese for Deanery Building Officers, as a means of ensuring that quinquennial inspection reports are followed by swift action – perhaps undertaken by special deanery maintenance teams. In some cases it may be appropriate to seek the involvement of the Manpower Service Commission's Community Programme, provided that there is proper planning and supervision.

Financing the UPA Church

7.60   We examine here four main factors which bear on the financing of the Church of England in the UPAs. Each is linked to, and dependent on, the others. Taken together, they underline the need for the different parts of the body of the Church to work together in partnership. Without this partnership, and the equitable and effective deployment of the Church's resources in their various forms, the development of an effective local Church in the UPAs will not be encouraged.

Current Giving by Church Members

7.61   There is a sense in which, despite the fundamental importance of current giving for the future of the Church of England, it ought not logically to be placed first. All the evidence suggests, and personal experience confirms, that general levels of giving tend to be more a reflection of perceived needs than of church members' overall potential to give. Thus variations in the perceived financial needs between different parishes, or different dioceses, will be mirrored by variations in the level of giving. The assessment of 'need' will be affected not simply by expenditure commitments and charitable donations but, in the case of parishes, by *diocesan quotas* and, in the case of dioceses, by *historic resources* coming to them through the Church Commissioners. We will address each of these in turn.

7.62   But if current giving is in effect a residual component of Church finance, it is nonetheless vital. The effects of inflation in the past 10 years, together with decisions to raise significantly the real levels of stipends and pensions, have meant that giving by the live Church has had to meet an increasing share of current expenditure, including the cost of stipends. For example, whereas in 1978/79 24 per cent of stipends was financed by current giving, in 1984/85 the proportion had risen to 44 per cent.

7.63   Taken overall, levels of personal giving are low in the Church of England, averaging barely £1 a week per church member. This average obscures wide differences from place to place. Statistical analysis suggests that, while giving per member is higher where employment and income levels are higher, the absolute amount given does not rise to the same extent as income rises.

7.64   Since levels of employment and of incomes are lower in UPAs, it might be thought that levels of giving there would also be low. The statistical evidence, supported by our clergy survey and other evidence we have received, suggests however that (as we noted in Chapter 2)

155

inner city congregations have a relatively high level of commitment in terms of the level of their giving. Although the level of giving per head is higher on average in UPA than in non-UPA Churches, despite disparities in income levels, low overall numbers within the UPA Church mean that its total income may still be insufficient to meet running costs – particularly in council estate Churches, where numbers are small and levels of giving lower than in the UPAs generally.

7.65   The General Synod has called for a standard of giving of 5 per cent of income to and through the Church. This is far from being achieved by church members generally. There is a clear need for general standards of giving to be raised within the Church of England. Indeed, we would go further: the principle of live giving, and the actual trends in church finance suggest that the Church should aspire to, and now deliberately move towards, the ideal of dioceses being broadly self-supporting, with the Church Commissioners using historic resources to provide various levels of assistance in response to need and particular developmental opportunities. The practical effect in the short-term might be little different, if at all, from the present situation; but the psychological effect on the richer dioceses, and the speed of movement towards a more dynamic Church, could be considerable. We believe that the Church should give further consideration to this principle, following on, as it does, the Partners in Mission Report (*To a Rebellious House?*).

The Effects of Diocesan Quota Schemes
7.66   The policies adopted in different dioceses for the financing of stipends and general diocesan expenditure vary widely. In most dioceses, both ministry and general expenditure are covered – separately or together – by quota assessment schemes, no two of which are quite the same. The extent to which 'potential' is taken into account in the assessments seems to vary from not at all (where quota is based entirely on income, staffing etc.) to predominance.

7.67   Moreover, 'potential' is used in two senses: quantitative and qualitative. The former relates to numbers of potential contributors (membership, attendance, population etc.); and this may be direct (e.g. a 'per capita' component) or indirect (with several indicators or a points system). Increasingly, however, 'potential' is being extended to include socio-economic factors, based on type of housing, or the relative prosperity of the area (or of members of the congregation). By this means parishes are graded, usually by mutual assessment, and their

156

numerical strength can be weighted accordingly. It seems that over one-third of the dioceses – most of them urban – use 'potential' in this fuller sense in their assessment of parish quotas.

7.68   The message emerging from our clergy survey is that about one in five UPA parishes, and one in seven non-UPA parishes, had been unable to meet their quota assessment in 1984. Confidentiality of individual responses has prevented analysis to reveal where these failures occurred. So it is difficult to use this as evidence that one method of assessment is better than another or, in particular, is a burden or benefit to UPAs.

7.69   For the pattern of parochial (or diocesan) giving to become closely related to 'potential', demands on parishes must be equitably distributed. Within the diocese, this means quota; between dioceses, it depends on Historic Resources and the Church Commissioners' allocations. Members of richer parishes (or dioceses) are not going to give more just for the sake of it, especially if they see it as merely bolstering reserves – or even to enable the Church to give more to charities etc., when they may feel they could do so just as (or more) effectively themselves.

7.70   Although we can draw no conclusions as to the relative merits of different systems, we are clear that introducing an element of potential to the quota system is of fundamental importance in the concept of 'partnership' between the richer and poorer parishes.

The Equitable Distribution of Historic Resources

7.71   We were grateful to have, as we examined this subject, the very clear analysis contained in the Church Commissioners' report *The Historic Resources of the Church of England* published in 1983. This report – usually referred to as the *Green Paper* – has been the subject of consultation with dioceses while we have been undertaking our work. The Green Paper defines, in its summary, the problem facing the Church of England as being that 'the Church's historic resources are not distributed evenly. This means that some dioceses have to find a much higher proportion of their income than others from the current giving of church members' and that these dioceses are not necessarily the ones in the best position to do so. The Green Paper reveals that in 1982/83, for example, one diocese had to ask its parishes for only 21 per cent of the clergy stipend bill because of its high income from other sources: in another diocese, the parishes had to meet 56 per cent of the stipend bill.

In the light of such inequalities, the Green Paper examines some possible ways forward.

7.72   Later in this Chapter, we call for special measures to be adopted by the national Church to strengthen the Church's presence and witness in the UPAs. But the first step is to ensure that the existing framework of financial support is equitable. The Green Paper clearly demonstrates that it is not. The reason for this is simple: dioceses rich in historic resources do not need in practice to encourage realistic levels of giving by congregations in order to balance their own diocesan budgets. By contrast, those dioceses with relatively little in the way of historic income have to struggle to increase levels of current giving in order to remain financially viable, let alone to develop the Church's mission. As the Green Paper itself notes, 'levels of giving are usually and necessarily in an inverse relation to diocesan income from historic and other sources'.

7.73   Dioceses, as well as parish Churches, must be outward looking: they should not seek to rest comfortably on a financial cushion provided by the generosity of past Christians or by the vagaries of history and population movements. The evidence in the Green Paper suggests that there are many dioceses with relatively high levels of historic income in which current giving forms a lower percentage of 'potential' giving (that is, giving related to the incomes of church members), compared with dioceses with lower levels of historic income. If the money available to each diocese from historic sources were to be more evenly distributed, the consequent demands on church members in different dioceses would be more equitable.

7.74   It would be wrong to even out differences in historic resources without taking into account the scope for increased levels of giving. The Green Paper shows that some dioceses with relatively little in the way of historic resources have the potential to increase levels of giving substantially. So any formula for redistribution should take into account potential giving as well as historic resources.

7.75   The Green Paper also refers to the question of 'historic liabilities' – the claim by some more rural dioceses that they face disproportionate levels of expenditure on repairs to historic churches. It concludes, however, that such claims do not reflect in practice 'unusually high expenditure by parishes on the maintenance of historic churches, but the familiar rural problems of clergy in these dioceses ministering to a relatively large number of small congregations'. The Green Paper notes that urban dioceses facing high 'current liabilities' also have claims to make. These dioceses are 'for example, the run-down and semi-depopulated Inner City areas where much of the continuing resident community may be elderly or unemployed' and are therefore areas where needs are especially great compared with the resources available. Our survey of clergy indicated that one-third of clergy in the UPAs (compared with one-fifth in other areas) said that they were unable to meet their parish's diocesan quota *and* other current expenditure in 1984.

7.76   The Green Paper identifies 20 'urban liability' dioceses, of which 18 have *low* historic resources. (By contrast, of the 20 'historic liability' dioceses identified, 16 have *high* historic resources.) The Green Paper argues therefore that it is unwise to conclude 'that rural liabilities are generally greater than urban liabilities'. Indeed, we have seen for ourselves not only the social needs of the UPAs, but also the enormous financial challenges posed by many large Victorian city churches to which we have referred. In the North-West, particularly, there were serious problems with dry rot in virtually every church we visited.

7.77   If, as we believe, the present distribution of historic resources is inequitable, and there is a need to move to a much fairer basis of resource distribution in the Church of England, how best can that be achieved? We believe that reform should be fundamental. The aim should be not merely the fair distribution of staffing resources but for the capital and income resources behind each clergyman, deaconess, and licensed lay worker in the stipendiary ministry to be equalised. We so *recommend.*

7.78   In relation to current resources we propose that the so-called 'in perpetuity' component of historic resources (totalling some £14 million per annum) should be used as the means to redistribute historic income from the richer to the poorer dioceses. The formula used for redistribution should take into account existing historic income and potential giving. The process could be phased over a period of years, to allow those dioceses from whom monies would be withdrawn to build up their level of current giving to compensate. It might not involve the whole of the £14 million 'in perpetuity' monies: if historic resources behind each stipendiary worker could be equalised by the reallocation of only part of this total, or by the allocation of 'new money' arising from profitable investments and inflation, all well and good.

7.79   In relation to capital resources, imbalances between dioceses are also obvious. We have received evidence that in many urban area dioceses, particularly those in the north of England, relatively little money is realised through the sale of parsonages or redundant churches or church sites. But in some parts of the south of England, for example, such sales can release substantial sums of money. Nationally, the lion's share of diocesan capital receipts comes from the sale of parsonages. However, under the 'Sheffield' formula some dioceses have needed to increase their complement of clergy. These include some of the poorer dioceses, who have not had any parsonage houses to sell for profit. There is no way of transferring surpluses from parsonage house sale proceeds across diocesan boundaries, except by voluntary arrangement. The provision for voluntary transfer is rarely used.

7.80 In response to this situation, we propose first, that capital balances arising from the sales of parsonage houses and redundant churches should be viewed as historic resources, and therefore the income arising from them should be taken into account in the process of redistribution we have proposed above. Second, we suggest that careful consideration should be given to the establishment of a capital receipts pooling scheme on a national basis, so that a proportion of the capital resources released in the richer dioceses, particularly from the sale of parsonage houses, could be redirected to needier dioceses. This redirection could in part be carried out, in appropriate cases, by the Church Commissioners, through the existing scheme of specific capital grants to cover the deficit on replacement of clergy housing in those dioceses where the old houses have a low sale value. Finally, we believe that the Church Commissioners should hesitate before advocating any variation in their policy of applying fixed rates of interest, below market rates on deposits from or loans to dioceses. A change to a market rate would benefit those dioceses which already have the greatest funds, at the expense of monies available to the Commissioners for distribution where apparent needs are greatest. A move towards market rates would therefore – unless special arrangements were made – contribute to, rather than reduce, imbalances.

7.81 If our recommendations were to be adopted, there would of course be no guarantee that extra monies gained by urban area dioceses would actually be spent in the UPA parishes. Dioceses must determine their priorities. But the financial problems faced by UPA clergy, and the developmental opportunities for the Church in the cities, are such that we believe that a bias to the UPAs is needed. There is encouraging evidence that a number of dioceses already give such a bias. Yet it is not unusual for UPA parishes to believe that their existence is threatened because of talk about a parish needing to be 'viable'. Diocesan financial policies should lift this anxiety from parishes which have few resources, but which are clearly needed to serve UPAs. In our survey 69 per cent of UPA clergy said that the financial problems of their parish were 'very serious' or 'quite serious' – half as many again as in other areas. The problem is acute. We *recommend* that dioceses should respond.

The Efficient Management of the Historic Resources of the Church

7.82   We recognise that the primary duty of the Church Commissioners is to the clergy of the Church of England as its living agents. The Commissioners are not empowered to spend as income any of their £1,792 million capital. As they reported to us, this capital must be used 'to generate income, as the principal need of the clergy is for the best current income that is consistent with maintaining the real value of our assets'. This is a fundamental charge on the Commissioners given them by Parliament.

7.83   As a consequence, financial considerations must take priority when investments are made by the Commissioners. Yet it is clearly not the only priority a Church body must have. Regard must always be had to the ethical and social aspects of investments.

7.84   With this in mind, we welcome the Commissioners' investment in UPAs; for example, in the Lancashire & Merseyside Enterprise Fund. In particular, we warmly approve their involvement in UPA economies as active management participants rather than simply as sleeping partners: we hope other financial institutions will follow their example. In the light of experience gained, we would ask the Commissioners to look actively for ways to expand this involvement, and to communicate to the wider Church the progress they make here. As the Commissioners noted in their evidence to us, these developments are important demonstrations of the willingness of financial and other institutions to accept that a prudential view of their duties (and we would add of the very concept of efficiency itself) must include incentives for a better life in our inner cities.

A Church Urban Fund

7.85   We have referred to the need for the historic resources of the Church to be re-allocated on a more equitable basis. But if adequate help is to be directed to those urban area parishes facing acute financial and social problems, some measure of positive discrimination is needed.

7.86 We are enormously encouraged that the Methodist Church has, in its 'Mission Alongside the Poor' initiative, demonstrated its determination to respond to the challenge of the inner cities. The 1983 Methodist Conference decided to launch an appeal to raise £1 million in five years. The criteria established for the use of this money refer to projects in 'inner-city, multi-racial and deprived areas' which, by employing additional personnel, and by other means, will 'build up and extend the worshipping communities . . . and explore new styles of Church life and ways of proclaiming the Christian Gospel appropriate to those areas'.

7.87 In the secular world, the Government has retained an Urban Programme, running at over £300 million per annum, despite imposing cuts in the revenue and capital expenditure by UPA local authorities. As we note later in our report, we believe this sum to be inadequate given the scale of the problem. But it is difficult for the Church of England to criticise the inadequacy of this expenditure, when the Church itself at national level has done little to give explicit priority to the UPAs. The Urban Programme does not provide grants for 'religious activities', but it has helped Church projects which 'address community needs'. Examples include environmental works around church buildings, and the conversion or improvement of church halls for use, in whole or in part, as community centres of one kind or another. There is no sign at present however that the Government are likely to relax their criteria to enable grants to be made for capital (or current) expenditures to support Church activities *as such*.

7.88 The Church of England has no financial mechanism or legal power specifically to target financial assistance to the UPAs. In 1953 the Church Assembly passed a Measure to provide for specific financial help to be given to 'New Housing Areas'. Times have changed: the need now is for special efforts to be made to strengthen the Church in the inner city areas and outer estates. We therefore *recommend* that steps be taken to establish a new 'Church Urban Fund' (CUF).

7.89 We propose the following framework for the new Fund:

(a) *Policy declaration.* The General Synod should affirm that the national Church and the dioceses should give an explicit priority to strengthening the Church's presence, and promoting the Christian witness, in the UPAs in ways which meet local needs and opportunities, which may be innovatory or experimental, and which are, whenever possible, undertaken with ecumenical consultation. Dioceses should first look to their existing resource allocations in the light of this priority.

(b)　*Coverage.* The *implementation* of this national policy should involve *all dioceses.* Priority in terms of *extra financial help from a CUF* should however be given to those dioceses with higher-than-average numbers of UPA parishes (the criteria for which will need to be defined), taking into account the relative wealth of dioceses.

(c)　*Process.* Each diocese, but particularly the 'urban area' dioceses, should:

(i)　prepare a *Diocesan UPA Strategy,* based on

(ii)　analysis of *Census and other data* to determine the number and location of UPA parishes together with the results of *local church audits* undertaken in selected areas at parish or deanery level, to

(iii)　determine the *priorities* for ministry and mission in the UPA parishes and areas, in terms of staff and buildings;

(iv)　consider how far these priorities might be met by *redirection of existing resources* (taking into account the likelihood of, and potential for, increased levels of giving);

(v)　propose a list of projects or schemes which rate as priorities, but which could go ahead only with extra financial assistance. These could either be *capital* (e.g. adaptation of an inappropriate UPA church building) or *current* (e.g. a detached youth worker or secretarial support for a team ministry).

(d)　*Assessment.* Diocesan strategies and project lists would be assessed by a central grant-making authority. We propose that the Church Commissioners should undertake this role. They have most of the necessary expertise, and are seen by the dioceses as independent and fair. Bids for grant would be assessed:

to see if they are in line with national policy guidelines;

to determine relative need (perhaps using census-based criteria);

to ensure that the dioceses were pursuing a strategy reflecting the needs of the UPA parishes;

to apply some form of 'means test' in relation to relative wealth. (The size of the Diocesan Pastoral Account might be the most appropriate factor to take into the reckoning.)

Successful projects would receive grant at a rate of 50 per cent (i.e.

the Dioceses would find half the cost from their own funds or from other sources, and the CUF would provide the other half).

(e) *Duration*. The Fund should be a permanent scheme subject to periodic review. In relation to projects, for *capital* expenditure, the CUF contribution would need to be tied to the project timetable. Some allowance for delays would probably be necessary: this implies a degree of flexibility between financial years. Grants for schemes involving *current* expenditure (particularly on lay personnel not eligible for stipends money) might need to be time-limited, if the CUF were not to become 'silted-up'. We suggest that five years should be the normal period over which an annual grant should be paid. If, at the end of that time, the diocese wished to retain the post (as it had proved its value), continuing costs would be met in full from within the diocese. There should, however, be provision for dioceses to re-apply for a further 5-year grant where, exceptionally, local funding for a successful project to continue could not be found.

(f) *Monitoring and Review*. Some central monitoring of schemes on a regular basis would be desirable, both to ensure that Fund monies were spent on the basis agreed, and to facilitate exchange of information and good practice. In addition, we suggest that a major independent review should be undertaken every ten years to assess whether the criteria for assistance needed to be modified in response to changing circumstances.

7.90 We recommend that the *annual* payments from the Fund (for both capital and current purposes) should total £2 million. We believe this amount to be a realistic aim, even though it does not match up to the scale of the problem.

7.91 Of this sum, at least £1 million should, we suggest, come from monies made available by the Church Commissioners *in addition* to those being redistributed under the Historic Resources exercise; the balance should be found through the establishment of a capital fund of £10 million. This sum would be raised by a 'once-and-for-all' national appeal. The interest on this capital sum would provide up to £1 million per annum for grant-making purposes.

7.92 It would of course take time for a national appeal to be mounted, and the £10 million might not be raised quickly. But in this case, the appeal should not delay the establishment and implementation of a Fund based, to start with, on the £1 million from the Church Commissioners. The dioceses would of course need to find a matching sum for the financing of projects. This means that the total annual expenditure on projects would be up to £4 million (on the successful completion of the national appeal).

7.93   We have stressed the need for projects in UPAs to be supported by the Fund to be innovatory and experimental, ecumenical wherever possible, and to meet local needs and opportunities. We do not consider that the criteria should be more tightly-drawn, at least in the early stages of the Fund's life. We have drawn attention to the opportunities for better use of church buildings in UPAs, and to staffing needs. But we suggest that CUF monies should not be given to pay for clergy stipends. The main priority in relation to staffing is increased financial support for the employment of lay workers.

7.94   We recognise that this proposal will require enabling legislation. We would ask that the General Synod resolve to bring forward the necessary legislation as soon as possible after consultations have been held with the Church Commissioners and the dioceses.

Main Recommendations

1.   Sharing agreements with other denominations should be adopted more widely, as should the informal sharing of church buildings (other than the church itself) with those of other faiths (paragraph 7.17).

2.   In cases of the sale of redundant churches, there should be earlier and more open consultation with community organisations and bodies such as housing associations when future uses are being considered (paragraph 7.57).

3.   The historic resources of the Church should be distributed between dioceses to equalize the capital and income resources behind each clergyman, deaconess and licensed lay worker in the stipendiary ministry. The redistribution formula should take account of potential giving (paragraphs 7.77 to 7.80).

4.   Within dioceses, the acute financial needs of the urban priority area churches require a clear response (paragraph 7.81).

5.   A Church Urban Fund should be established to strengthen the Church's presence and promote the Christian witness in the urban priority areas (paragraph 7.88).

References

1 Summaries of the way in which each of these statutory frameworks operates in practice are to be found in *The Continuing Care of Churches and Cathedrals*, (the report of the Faculty Jurisdiction Commission) paragraphs 31-45; and the Annual Report of the Church Commissioners 1984, pages 25-27

2 *The Continuing Care of Churches and Cathedrals*, CIO, 1984

Part III
... and the Nation

i   We have described the economic and social inequalities of Britain, and the inter-connected deprivations of the UPAs, and have argued from a Christian perspective that we are called on to respond to our neighbours in such a situation. We have made particular recommendations to the Church of England about its mission and ministry. In this Part of our Report we take up the invitation in a rider to our terms of reference to 'articulate questions of public policy' which have arisen from our enquiry. We also consider the Church's role in relation to each of the matters we address.

ii   For Christians, one important touchstone for judging any public policy must be how it affects the poor. This will be our perspective in examining the economic, physical and social conditions of the UPAs.

iii   In the following Chapters, we cover a broad range of issues. Each connects with the others. But we pay particular attention to employment and housing, because in our view it is the lack of decent jobs and decent homes that more than anything else lies at the heart of the problem.

Chapter 8

URBAN POLICY

'It is not charity when the powerful help the poor ... it is justice'
Diocese of Liverpool

8.1   In this chapter we review government policy measures directed to the inner cities and raise questions about the degree to which those policies match up to the needs of the UPAs. As part of this, we examine the effect of national public expenditure policies on local government finance.

Public Policy and the Inner City: A Brief History
8.2   The first – and still most recent – comprehensive Government policy statement is to be found in the 1977 White Paper 'Policy for the Inner Cities'.[1] This drew on the experience of Whitehall initiatives in the 1960s and 1970s, including the Urban Programme (run by the Home Office between 1969 and 1976), the Educational Priority Areas of the Department of Education and Science, and other initiatives or experiments such as the Community Development Projects, area management trials, development work on comprehensive community programmes, and above all the major Inner Area Studies undertaken in the early 1970s.

8.3   It is worth setting out the White Paper's analysis fairly fully, as it seems to us as relevant today as it was nearly a decade ago.

8.4   It started by observing that the inner areas next to the centres of our cities suffered 'in a marked way and to an unacceptable extent' from economic decline, physical decay and adverse social conditions. Although much had been done to improve the conditions of life in the inner part of our cities – people had been rehoused from slums, schools had been built, and there had been improvements in transport – too little attention had been paid to the economic well-being of the inner cities, and to the physical environment which was badly neglected or had been left to decay. Particular stress was placed on the erosion of the inner area economy, and the shortage of private sector investment which might assist economic regeneration.

169

8.5   The White Paper also stressed how widespread the problems were. They were seen to be a feature of many of Britain's older towns. The precise mix of economic, social, and environmental problems varied between cities, however, and it was also noted that deprivation existed in some pre- and post-war council estates, some on the edge of the cities. However, particular emphasis was given to the needs of the inner areas of the big cities because of the scale and intensity of their problems, and the rapidity of rundown in population and employment they had experienced.

8.6   There was a note of irony here. Public policy in the 1950s and 1960s had encouraged the movement of jobs and people out of the older, overcrowded, parts of our cities to the new and expanding towns where there were new job opportunities in modern factories. This policy was successful as far as it went. Economic development stagnated in parts of the inner cities for a variety of reasons. Those skilled workers who had been able to obtain work in the new areas of economic growth had moved out. Those who remained were not perceived to have the necessary skills or education to compete for many of the new jobs which became available in or near the city centres in office or service industries. There was a mismatch between available skills and available jobs. In addition, large-scale slum clearance schemes had broken up communities, and displaced small businesses, contributing further to the loss of jobs and population, and also having consequences for social welfare.

8.7   What all this added up to was, the White Paper argued, a collective or multiple deprivation in some inner areas which affected all the residents, even though individually the majority of people might have satisfactory homes and worthwhile jobs. It arose from a pervasive sense of decay and neglect, through the decline of community spirit, through a low standard of neighbourhood facilities, through a greater exposure to crime and vandalism, and so on.

8.8   The White Paper cautioned that if this decay were allowed to continue unchecked, it would mean leaving large numbers of people to face a future of declining job opportunities, a squalid environment, deteriorating housing and declining public services. Without action being taken to respond to this complex of circumstances, the result would be social bitterness and an increasing sense of alienation. It also argued that it would be wasteful to under-utilize or abandon prematurely so much investment by the community: there would be economic costs in doing nothing.

8.9   The White Paper concluded that the phenomenon of collective deprivation called for inner city deprivation to be tackled on an area basis. There had to be discrimination in favour of the inner areas in the working out of public policies and programmes to:

(a)   strengthen the economies of the inner areas and the prospects of their residents;

(b)   improve the physical fabric of the inner areas and make their environment more attractive;

(c)   alleviate social problems;

(d)   secure a new balance between the inner areas and the rest of the city region in terms of population and jobs.

8.10   To meet these objectives, public policy had to cope with different intensities of deprivation, and variation in the mix of problems. The Labour Government in 1977 decided that resources had to be concentrated on the worst areas if an impact was to be made, and that action needed to be geared to local circumstances.

8.11   Local authorities were seen as the natural agencies to tackle inner area problems. They had wide powers and substantial resources, and were democratically accountable. They had long experience in running local services and, backed by the right degree of resources and by adopting policies sensitive to local needs, they could make the necessary impact in tackling the challenge of regenerating local economies. But local authorities could not do this on their own. There had to be a partnership between them and national government, together with the voluntary sector and the private sector. Only if all worked together for the common good, and to a common end, would durable results be seen.

8.12   So the two essentials for inner city regeneration were seen to be the injection of more public resources, and co-operative and co-ordinated action.

8.13   The White Paper laid great stress – and we believe this was right – on the need to use the main policies and programmes of central and local government to the full in order to tackle the problems of inner areas effectively. These include industrial and manpower policies, financial support to local authorities and the whole range of policies for education, health, personal social services, housing, transport and planning, and a wide range of environmental services and improvements. The key was 'bending' these main policies and programmes to give increased help to the inner areas. The expansion of the size of the Urban

171

Programme – additional financial support to designated areas – was a supplement, to allow innovatory and experimental schemes to be tried out. It was the icing on the cake.

8.14   In the late 1970s, central government achieved a measure of success in 'bending' expenditure programmes – in particular Rate Support Grant and Transport expenditure – to give greater help to inner city local authorities. The size of the Urban Programme (UP), which became the responsibility of the Department of the Environment, was increased from about £30 million in 1977/78 to approaching £100 million in 1978/79. On the basis of the analysis of Census data to determine the levels of deprivation in the cities, Partnerships were established in a number of the most deprived city areas (the present list is Liverpool, Manchester/Salford, Birmingham, Newcastle/Gateshead and the London Boroughs of Hackney, Islington and Lambeth). A further 15 (now 23) Programme Authorities were also selected. Inner Area Programmes were prepared in each of these areas to analyse the problems to be tackled, and to propose how the resources of both main expenditure programmes, and the expanded Urban Programme, should be brought to bear in a concentrated and co-ordinated way.

8.15   More limited levels of financial assistance from the Urban Programme were also made available for other areas. There are now 16 'other Designated Districts', each of which receives an annual allocation of money for economic regeneration projects. Additionally, a proportion of the UP (the so-called 'Traditional Urban Programme') continues to be set aside for other selected districts with local pockets of need, who compete for funding in response to an annual circular.

8.16   Since the coming to power of a Conservative Government in 1979, there has been no departure in policy statements from the 1977 White Paper's emphasis on the need for a central government response to the challenge presented by the inner cities. In June 1983, the then Secretary of State for the Environment (the Rt Hon. Patrick Jenkin) affirmed that:

'Inner city issues are serious enough to demand the attention and concern of senior ministers. I intend to implement the Conservative manifesto commitment which reads "we shall encourage greater opportunity for all those who live in our inner cities, including our ethnic minorities . . . we shall continue to give priority to the areas most in need". That will be my policy and my personal commitment'.[2]

8.17   We were told by Department of the Environment officials that the present Government largely accepted the analysis in the 1977 White Paper. But as a result of their general approach to economic management, and particularly their concern to curtail expenditure by local authorities, they had reduced the emphasis on public expenditure solutions to urban problems, and had given increased priority to securing economic regeneration through the involvement of private investors and the voluntary sector in urban renewal. As part of this approach, a number of Enterprise Zones have been established in designated inner city areas (and elsewhere), offering 'rates holidays' and other incentives to business. Two Urban Development Corporations (UDCs), using the model established for the New Towns, have been set up in the derelict former docklands areas of East London and Merseyside. And there has been a special scheme of financial assistance – Urban Development Grant – to 'lever' private sector capital investment into the inner areas.

8.18   But the shift in the balance of policy to secure the greater involvement of the private sector in particular, has gone side-by-side with major reductions in central financial assistance to UPA local authorities despite resources for the Urban Programme nearly doubling in cash terms between 1979/80 and 1983/84. Local authorities in many UPAs have lost far more in Rate Support Grant than they have gained under the Urban Programme. There has been an overall decline in central government financial support. Although the Urban Programme – the icing – has grown in real terms, the cake – the 'bending' of main policies and programmes – has either shrunk or disappeared altogether. There is one exception: the only main central government expenditure programme to have shown a significant growth in the inner cities in real terms since 1979 is that on the police.

The Situation Today

8.19   In the light of the evidence we have received, and of our visits to the UPAs, we are in no doubt that the governments of the last 10 years have been right in accepting calls such as that of the 1977 White Paper for a positive response to inner city problems. As we have argued in Chapter 1, their problems are indeed of such a severity (or of a 'concentration, scale and intensity', as the White Paper put it) to demand such a response. We agree with the White Paper's analysis, and with the proposals it contained. But the stark fact is that there has been no sustained effort to put those proposals into effect.

8.20   Viewed against the magnitude of the problem, government action has been pragmatic: treating the worst evidence of economic decline and poverty by small scale intervention. If the problem of urban deprivation lies in the fundamental structure of the economy (as we believe it does in large part), the public policy response is clearly open to the charge of being inadequate and superficial.

8.21 Many commentators have argued that the selective approach that has been pursued has, even judged on its own terms, been woefully inadequate, amounting to little more than first-aid treatment for the areas of acute urban deprivation when what is really needed is intensive care. Despite the various initiatives which have been taken, conditions in the Partnership and Programme authority areas have not materially improved for many thousands of people. The inner city riots of 1981, and Lord Scarman's subsequent report on the 'Brixton Disorders', came and went without great policy changes – despite fears that the unchecked decline of physical and social standards in the big cities could not be isolated and might well have wider repercussions (not just relating to law and order, but also the possibility of increasing and more widespread alienation from the present systems of democratic government).

8.22 Although 'it took a riot' to place on the nation's agenda in a stark and unambiguous way the consequences of rapid urban de-industrialisation, the debate on where public policy goes from here has been eclipsed in recent times by the wider debate on the appropriate national economic strategy to deal with the recession.

8.23 In the rest of this chapter, we shall argue that:

(a) the policy response to the UPAs should embrace both area-based approaches and the adoption of policies directed towards reducing social and economic inequalities whenever they exist;

(b) a greater priority should be given by government to the problems of the outer housing estates of many towns and cities, which on many indicators are now in need of urgent attention;

(c) there is a regrettable lack of will on the part of central government to support local government and to devote adequate resources to UPA local authorities in the face of the problems;

(d) a co-ordination of programmes is needed, and the concept of partnership needs to be developed to promote greater participation at local level, to combat the pervasive feelings of powerlessness;

(e) the potential for small businesses to regenerate the UPAs (particularly the outer estates) is limited. Education and skill-training programmes are necessary to increase UPA people's chances of creating and gaining 'new jobs'. Better housing and environmental improvements are needed to encourage growth enterprises to locate in the UPAs; neighbourhood action programmes are also needed;

(f)   finally, not least, what the inner cities need more than anything else is a vote of *confidence*. It must be for the government first and foremost to demonstrate this confidence through a sustained programme of public investment on both current and capital account, as has happened in the docklands areas of the UDCs. In this way it will give greater confidence to the private sector to invest.

People or Places?

8.24   Economic and social inequalities are not confined to the UPAs, and in this sense they are not a place apart. What arguably makes them different is that they are places where extreme forms of poverty and inequality are most easily seen, where those with least power and least control over their own lives are to be found in the greatest concentrations, and where economic and social problems bite to such a degree as to transform the problems of employment, poverty, crime and so on into a qualitatively different situation.

8.25   Some of the characteristics of UPAs can be found in small areas in every town or city in the country. Pockets of deprivation can be found in otherwise affluent areas. In a sense, therefore, 'UPAs' can be found everywhere. But it is in the inner areas and outer estates of our cities that the problems are so acute that special action is called for. It is not simply that they suffer from deprivation and poverty, but – as recent research by the Centre for Environmental Studies has shown[3] – there is a danger of many outer estates, in particular, becoming areas which have a quite different social and economic system, operating almost at a subsistence level, dependent entirely on the public sector, where the opportunities for improvement either through self-help or through outside intervention are minimal.

8.26   In short, the danger is that the degeneration of many such areas has now gone so far that they are in effect 'separate territories' outside the mainstream of our social and economic life. There will always be some inequalities between different areas, but when such inequalities begin to be manifested in the creation of almost two different societies it carries serious implications.

8.27 We have noted that the polarization in Britain today is not so much between 'North and South' (though that is still obvious) as between UPAs and other areas – in the relatively prosperous South as well as in the North.

8.28 This in our view argues for an approach which embraces both:

(i) the adoption of 'people-oriented' policies which promote justice by mitigating inequalities wherever they are found; and

(ii) 'place-oriented', area-based, approaches which concentrate resources to a degree which makes a visible and sustained impact, and so offer new hope.

8.29 Areas are places where things can happen, and can be seen to happen. Resources can also stand a better chance of reaching target groups if there is some focus on areas in which those groups are over-represented. In the absence of area-based approaches, not only would there be a danger of resources being dissipated rather than concentrated to help those most in need, but the *visible* improvements which can change the atmosphere of an area could be slower in coming.

8.30 Although it is with *people* that policy must be concerned, there does need to be a dimension to action that recognizes that *places* are important too. *The concept of neighbourhood is about both people and places.*

Outer Estates

8.31 Our visits to the inner and outer areas of the main conurbations have convinced us that it is now the large housing estates in the inner ring or on the fringes of the cities that present the most pressing urban problem of the mid-1980s.

8.32 Huge impersonal housing estates, many post-war, can be found in all our cities. They are often spoken of as being 'monochrome' – that is, drab, dreary, depressing, with no vitality, colour, or beauty. Many outer estates are nothing less than the architect-designed system-built slums of our post-war era. They suffer from poor design, defects in construction, poor upkeep of public areas, no 'defensible space'; with packs of dogs roaming around, filth in the stairwells, one or two shuttered shops, and main shopping centres a 20-minute expensive bus journey away. Unemployment rates are typically 30-40 per cent, and rising. Bored out-of-work young people turn to vandalism, drugs, and crime – the estate takes the brunt, and the spiral of decline is given a further twist.

176

8.33   The residents of some of these estates are not all 'monochrome', as Tony Parker's book about one estate in South London (*People of Providence*) makes clear. But viewed on a number of indicators – unemployment, crime rates, vandalism, reliance on welfare benefits – the residents of the outer estates are suffering acutely from multiple deprivation. They are trapped by their council housing tenure; transfers out are difficult if not impossible, and incomers are often families with multiple problems for whom the estates are used as dumping grounds.

8.34   The indicators used by the Department of the Environment (DoE) to judge the degree of urban deprivation are not adequate measures of these problems. The DoE's statistical index of deprivation does not take into account factors such as housing defects, low income levels, vandalism, physical or mental illness, high crime rates and other depressing facets of life on the outer estates – and thus understates the problems their residents face.

8.35   There are great difficulties in developing an index using a wider range of nationally-available indicators in a consistent way to reflect more accurately the multiple deprivations of the outer estates. This problem may be overcome in time, but for the present we would ask the DoE in constructing their 'league tables' of deprivation used to judge the degree of need, to take the fullest possible account of the recent research by the Centre for Environmental Studies, and the assessments by UPA local authorities, which point to many outer estates being in greater need of special measures to combat multiple deprivation than the traditional inner city neighbourhoods. We *recommend* that the outer estates be given a greater priority within urban policy initiatives.

Public Resources
8.36   Although public sector finance is a minefield (and in the case of local government finance it seems that more mines are being laid every month) it is one we must try to enter. It lies at the heart of public policy for the UPAs.

8.37   We wish to concentrate on two aspects, Rate Support Grant and the Urban Programme. In each of the urban priority areas we visited, we heard significant criticism about the operation of both.

(i)   *Rate Support Grant*
8.38   Rate Support Grant (RSG) is the contribution made by the Exchequer to local authorities' finances. Its purpose is to transfer part of

the cost of providing local authority services from rates onto the wider and more equitable range of national taxes. Historically, the distribution of RSG between local authorities has followed the principle of equalizing resources in relation to expenditure needs. Authorities with high expenditure needs, but a low rate base, need more financial help from the Exchequer than those with below-average needs, but high rateable values and hence rate revenues.

8.39   RSG is the major source of Government financial assistance to local authorities. It supports expenditure which meets a wide range of local needs. The 1977 White Paper therefore argued that it 'is bound to be the prime source of Government funds for helping in the regeneration of the inner areas'.

8.40   In 1977-78 total RSG support in England (excluding domestic rate relief) was £5.5 billion at current prices. The equivalent total for 1984-85 was £8.17 billion; but had the level of RSG support been maintained in real terms this figure would have been nearly £11 billion. Because of government concern to restrain public expenditure for macro-economic reasons, and an expressed concern for greater local accountability, the national total of RSG support has suffered a 25 per cent cut in real terms since 1977.

8.41   Although between 1977 and 1979 some emphasis was given to channelling greater help to the inner city areas, as a conscious response to the analysis in the White Paper, analysis of the DoE's submission to us shows that in recent years grant to deprived areas has declined in real terms, as Table 8.1 shows:

TABLE 8.1

*Rate Support Grant to Partnership and Programme Authorities
Between 1981-82 and 1984-85*

	1981-82 £ million	1984-85 £ million	Change in Grant	
			Money Terms £ million	Real Terms (DOE deflator) £ million
Partnership authorities	650	606	−44	−143 (−22%)
Programme authorities	1,012	1,056	+44	−127 (−13%)

The Partnership and Programme authorities have not therefore been protected from the national cuts in RSG. As the national total has fallen in real terms, so have the amounts directed to inner city authorities.

Within the reduced levels of RSG provision, the share of available grant going to Programme and Partnership authorities has hardly moved, from 19.9 per cent in 1981-82 to 20.4 per cent in 1984-85. This scarcely reflects a strategy of concentrating government assistance on those areas which need it most.

8.42   There are also inherent structural deficiencies in the distribution mechanism which disadvantage the UPAs. The DoE argued in a paper submitted to the Commission that 'the RSG system is tailored to take account of the differing needs and resources of different areas, whether inner cities or rural shires'. Their paper ignores, however, that:

(i)   The RSG distribution system does not reflect the compounding effects of multiple deprivation identified in the 1977 White Paper;

(ii)   A large element in the assessment of need is school population, and that in most of the UPAs there has been a dramatic fall in school rolls; and

(iii)   The assessment of local authorities' resources is based on rateable values which are 12 years out of date. Consequently, the RSG formula does not reflect the decline in the rateable base of inner city authorities, following a decade of population loss and economic decline.

8.43   This last factor, in particular, seriously distorts the distribution of RSG away from the UPAs, and towards the growth areas of the economy. It accounts for as much as two-thirds of the differences between authorities in terms of the amount they receive. It is seriously lagging behind the reality of the present day.

8.44   Inner city local authorities have in recent years also been castigated as 'high spenders' and 'profligate'. Expenditure targets have been set, and authorities overspending these targets have been penalized by the withdrawal of RSG (by as much as £4 of RSG withdrawn for every £1 'overspent').

8.45   Local authorities have sought to compensate for the reduced levels of RSG support by increasing rates. Although the system of expenditure targets is to be ended, the 'rate-capping' legislation is still available to prevent rate increases. Predictions from the Association of Metropolitan Authorities suggested that expenditure on services by rate-capped urban local authorities might have to be cut on average by 11 per cent in 1985/86. Some authorities may however be able to

179

alleviate their financial position by drawing on reserves. But their reserves are not limitless.

8.46 The Government's own statistics show that the need for expenditure by local government in the UPAs has if anything increased since 1977. According to the DoE's analysis of 1981 Census data,[4] although there has been an improvement overall in the housing conditions of the main conurbations, unemployment – the main economic indicator – has increased markedly in the inner areas compared with elsewhere. Indeed on all the economic, social and housing indicators, the inner areas still suffer from worse problems than their surrounding areas.

8.47 Why then have there been severe cuts in what the 1977 White Paper called the 'prime source of Government funds for helping in the regeneration of the inner areas'?

8.48 The then Secretary of State for the Environment was reported on 19 April 1985 as offering the explanation that:

'The fact that a city is high on the deprivation index, which is justification for the many millions of pounds which are going into the Urban Programme, cannot be a justification for running their own services extravagantly.'[5]

8.49 The reports of the Audit Commission provide sufficient evidence that there is wastefulness and extravagance in the way *some* (not all) urban local authorities meet local needs. Clearly this requires remedying. But we wish to question whether the remedy the Government have adopted is an acceptable one, given its consequences.

8.50 As we have noted, the consequence in practice of reductions in Rate Support Grant has been, in many UPAs, that the local authority has had to make up some of the deficit by increases in the rates.

8.51 In a recent report from the National Audit Office[6] the Comptroller and Auditor General concluded that rate increases since 1981 'can be attributed more to the reduction in the proportion of government grant than to increases in local authority spending'.

8.52 It is no local authority's interest to put up the rates if it can avoid doing so. High rates are a heavy burden for local firms to bear, and may well discourage expansion – or force closure. They place a greater burden on the local economy. Having high needs and high rates is a combination of misfortune that is likely to accelerate economic and social decline.

8.53   But is there an alternative remedy open to the Government rather than by dictating lower rate levels from Whitehall? *Would not increasing the amount of RSG to authorities achieve the same end?* The more the burden is carried by the Exchequer, the less requires to be met from the rates. If government is to be serious about directing resources to the areas in the greatest need, the RSG system remains available as a national mechanism to achieve just that.

8.54   But what about waste and inefficiency? It is a perfectly proper concern that resources should not be wasted, and that expenditure should provide good value for money. However, if waste and inefficiency still remain in local government, the policy of improving management by exerting financial pressure overall has clearly not worked. Yet nothing is proposed in its place. The independent Audit Commission is charged with ensuring financial probity and efficiency in local government. We suggest that efficiency audits carried out by the Audit Commission could be a direct and effective means of ensuring that wasteful expenditure is avoided.

8.55   We therefore *recommend* that the resources devoted to Rate Support Grant be increased in real terms, and within the enhanced total there should be a greater bias to the UPAs in line with the proposals of the 1977 White Paper. There should be a greater use of efficiency audits to tackle wasteful expenditure.

8.56   We have concentrated here on the revenue expenditure of local government. Yet we have also noted that the most severe cuts in the amount of local authority expenditure, dictated by central government, have been on capital. In 1977 local authorities' capital spending was £6.9 billion. By 1983, it had dropped in real terms to £4.6 billion – a cut of 33 per cent.[6]

8.57   As a consequence, as well as dramatic cuts in house building programmes, there have been cutbacks in the repair and maintenance of existing stock – schools, houses, highways – which are laying up serious problems for the future. There is no doubt that the backlog of capital work nationally is substantial and cumulative in that it will cost more to remedy the longer it is left.

(ii)   *The Urban Programme*
8.58   The Government provides special financial assistance to designated local authorities under the Urban Programme (UP). Financial support from the Exchequer is also given to the Urban Development Corporations in London and Liverpool.

8.59   The Government's urban budget in 1984/85 is shown in the Chart below:

FIGURE 8.1

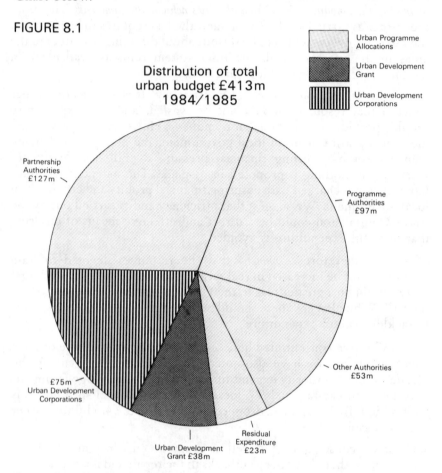

Urban Programme Allocations

Urban Development Grant

Urban Development Corporations

Distribution of total
urban budget £413m
1984/1985

Partnership Authorities £127m

Programme Authorities £97m

£75m Urban Development Corporations

Other Authorities £53m

Urban Development Grant £38m

Residual Expenditure £23m

Source: Department of the Environment

8.60   The UP is seen by government as a means of 'priming the pump' in regenerating the inner cities. As originally conceived, it was seen as a means of enabling innovative schemes to be undertaken by local authorities (and voluntary bodies) supported by grant at a rate of 75 per cent from the Exchequer. Successful schemes which proved valuable would be absorbed by local authorities into their main expenditure programmes – and so release UP monies for further new projects to be undertaken.

8.61   As the Chart shows, the bulk of the money goes to the 7 Partnership and 23 Programme authorities. The schemes supported are those contained in the Inner Area Programmes for the areas concerned. In 1984/85, about 20 per cent of the expenditure went on environmental improvement schemes, 40 per cent on schemes for developing the local economy, and 40 per cent on education, health, social services, and recreational projects. Within the total, 30 per cent went to schemes which involve the voluntary sector.

8.62   The size of the UP has been rising slowly in cash terms over the past 5 years. This growth has now come to an end: total UP expenditure in 1985/86 is now static at £338 million. This standstill in cash terms – a cut in real terms – is resulting in parts of the UP being cut.

8.63   For example, the sum available under the Traditional Urban Programme (TUP) for new projects in 1985/86 has been halved to £7.5 million. It is possible that as many as 35 of the over 100 local authorities who have used the TUP to initiate local projects will be cut out of the programme altogether. The money available for new schemes in the Partnership and Programme authority inner areas is also being reduced.

8.64   We are concerned that potentially valuable new projects will as a consequence not be able to proceed, and that 'time expired' projects, whose 3-year grant has run out, will have to close.

8.65   The Urban Programme is a splendid vehicle for trying out new ways of improving life in the inner cities. In our visits to Partnership and Programme areas up and down the country, we have seen how it has enabled imaginative new schemes to be mounted.

8.66   But we have heard in evidence that

(a)   The funds available under the UP do not match up to the needs in the Partnership and other areas.

The UP has made an important contribution to stemming the tide of urban decline. But there is still a long way to go if *regeneration* is the objective. An expansion of the size of the UP is needed if the objective of regeneration is to be taken seriously. Because the UP is now static, an increasing number of projects is being squeezed out. Rather than being a vehicle for innovation, the UP is now having increasingly to fill the gap caused by cuts in the main expenditure programmes of government.

(b)   The balance of expenditure is too biased towards capital schemes.

We have heard much criticism of the UP's emphasis on capital projects. Capital projects account for two-thirds or more of expenditure in many Partnership and Programme authorities' programmes for 1984-85. This bias towards capital schemes is encouraged by the DoE. But the result can seem, as one Diocese put it to us: 'that things are more important than people when grant aid is sought, and appearance more important than usage'.[8] We suggest that this imbalance needs reviewing.

(c)   The local authority component of UP expenditure is subject to the RSG penalties (the 'holdback arrangements').

(d)   No allowance is made in RSG allocations for the funding of successful UP projects to be transferred to main expenditure programmes, or for the current expenditure consequences of capital expenditure under the UP.

These two criticisms reflect what seems to us to be a serious inconsistency in Government policy. On the one hand, it encourages local authorities to spend money on the Urban Programme; yet on the other, subjects local government's share of the expenditure (with the limited exception of year-on-year increases in net UP expenditure), and continuing expenditure on schemes following expiry of UP grant, to RSG 'holdback' penalties. There have been representations on the question not only from local government, but also from the Association of British Chambers of Commerce. They argue that there should be separate 'disregards' for RSG abatement purposes on 'all expenditure (net of specific grants) on Urban Programme projects . . . and all continuing expenditure in main programmes resulting from the transfer of any project from the Urban Programme'. We endorse this view. With the proposed abolition of targets and 'holdback' in 1986/87, the existing system of disregards will also disappear. Yet there will still be abatement of RSG to local authorities spending above certain limits. We hope that local authorities' share of UP expenditure will not be penalised in this way. We would also argue that there needs to be a greater acknowledgement of the revenue effects of capital schemes. It is no use promoting capital schemes if there is no way of funding their staff.

(e)   There are problems on the expiry of the 3-year grant period if the UP grant is not renewed.

This difficulty is a particular manifestation of the problems noted above. It would not be so serious if the Urban Programme were growing in real terms, or if the RSG system reflected the consequences of initiatives taken within the UP. But the fact that grant for revenue schemes under the UP is normally for 3 years means that, by the second year of the project, uncertainty about its future sets in and voluntary organisations in particular have to spend an increasing amount of time trying to secure continuing finance. UPAs have suffered for too long from 3-year funding; projects have suffered from uncertainty and loss of grant when they are on the point of establishing themselves. We have already recommended that project funding from the proposed Church Urban Fund should be for 5 years. This seems to us a more reasonable period over which a project's funding should be guaranteed. We suggest that consideration is given to applying it to the Urban Programme.

8.67   We have been enormously impressed with the work local authorities and voluntary bodies have undertaken with help from the Urban Programme. It has the great benefit of being flexible, and can be directed at a wide range of local initiatives. In this way it provides a valuable recognition of the diversity between UPAs, and the mix of problems to be addressed within them. We therefore *recommend* that the size of the Urban Programme should be increased, and aspects of its operation reviewed as we have suggested above.

8.68   In conclusion, however, we must question whether the UP – even if given far greater resources – can be relied upon to make more than a marginal impact, when main expenditure programmes (particularly RSG, but also housing investment and other programmes) are being curtailed. Many urban authorities saw their UP allocation for 1984/85 being more than offest by a reduction in RSG. Central government has been giving with one hand, and taking away more with the other. We ask those responsible to reconsider whether this can really be justified.

Promoting Partnership

8.69   The idea of partnership as a guiding principle in urban regeneration is one we welcome. People and organisations working together to similar ends can achieve far more than in isolation.

8.70   Of course, getting people to work in partnership is not easy in practice. There are bound to be tensions and conflicts. We have heard that, for example, some local authorities have had a poor record in co-ordinating joint action; we have heard too that central government departments seem at times to pull in different directions. There are also tensions between local government and Whitehall.

8.71   But it is because the UPAs present challenge on every front of public policy that those responsible have a *duty* to work together. We believe that the 1977 White Paper's stress on joint working was right, and so too was the creation of inner city Partnerships in the most deprived urban areas.

8.72   Partnerships require not only participation, but some give and take on all sides. We have heard in the Partnership Areas that many local authorities feel that central Government has been an unequal partner. The degree of Whitehall participation has certainly varied between Government departments.

8.73   The creation by the Government of City Action Teams (CATs) with the involvement of DoE, the Department of Trade and Industry (DTI), the Department of Employment (DE) and the Manpower Services Commission (MSC), to co-ordinate initiatives better in the Partnership Areas has perhaps come about as a response to those concerns. We welcome this initiative in principle, though we greatly regret that the Department of Education and Science and the DHSS are not directly represented. It is too early to make judgement at this stage as to what effects this initiative will have in practice.

8.74   Partnership also needs to involve bodies other than governmental ones – voluntary bodies, the private sector, tenants' associations and so on. But most importantly it needs to embrace the 'people in the street'. Not only must they feel that positive things are happening; they must feel part of the process. The powerlessness felt by people in the UPAs must be addressed. Local people must have greater opportunities to participate. One means is obviously through wide consultation about plans or proposals which may affect neighbourhoods. In Newcastle, we found that the City Council's Priority Area Teams were promoting this effectively: they also have local budgets which are allocated to groups or schemes in the light of local people's views. 'Community chests' such as these are one valuable way of giving people a greater part in the decision-making process. Another example is the involvement of residents in housing and environmental design and renovation, now being developed through 'community architecture' schemes.

8.75   More generally, there need to be more effective mechanisms to bring public consultation into a wider partnership approach. Public participation is not cheap in terms of time and money. However it can avoid costly mistakes being made, and prove very cost effective in the long-run. Housing departments, planners, education departments and the police are all trying to consult more at a neighbourhood level.

Rightly, in our view, the trend is towards approaches which are 'bottom up' rather than 'top down'.

8.76   We recognize that innovative, participative (and, perhaps, politically sensitive) approaches cannot be implemented everywhere at once. They demand high levels of management skill and sustained commitment – and, we repeat, they can be costly. Nevertheless there is a need for such approaches in the UPAs if the issue of powerlessness is to be taken seriously. We therefore *recommend* that the concept of partnership in the UPAs should be developed by central and local government to promote greater consultation with, and participation by, local people at neighbourhood level.

Encouraging Enterprise
8.77   In retrospect, the development of inner city policy has seen a shift in emphasis from tackling social problems, to physical problems, to economic problems. All three are important. But we would support a major emphasis on economic regeneration. In the next Chapter we consider the economic challenge of the UPAs in more detail. There we argue that we cannot pin too much hope on small business as providing the answer to the economic plight of the inner cities, and more particularly the outer estates. The concept of 'enterprise' has to be a much broader one.

8.78   If we cannot rely on many UPAs being able to pull themselves up by their own economic bootstraps, because the structural depression of local economies has gone too far for reliance on self-employment to be the answer, the real need is for a thriving local economy to be developed which can offer employment.

8.79   This will require three things.

8.80   First, if 'no businessman in his right mind' would invest in certain UPAs, the public sector must provide more employment opportunities and increased income support to those who are at present unemployed. The Economic and Social Research Council's recent findings confirm the importance of public sector employment in the UPAs.

8.81   Second, it remains vital that all those living in the UPAs are given the best possible opportunities in education and skill-training to take advantage of new technology job opportunities.

8.82   Third, the physical environment of the UPAs must be improved to make them good places to live in. We deal with the quality of housing in Chapter 10. We have not attempted to address the wider issues of land-use planning and the design and layout of neighbourhoods in urban areas. But we believe that mounting local environmental improvement schemes in UPAs is important. Not only can such schemes provide a more pleasant and varied physical environment. If implemented as part of labour-intensive programmes, they can help to empower people, and develop local abilities in professional and organisational terms. So we would enter a plea for environmental improvement schemes, involving local people to the maximum extent, being seen as part of strategies for economic regeneration.

8.83   But these initiatives are unlikely to be sufficient to develop or attract sufficient paid employment to the UPAs in the foreseeable future. Imaginative local schemes will also need to be developed.

8.84   We consider that there is a case for greater support, from both the private and the public sectors, for *neighbourhood action schemes* which enable those without jobs to undertake useful work in their neighbourhoods. In some cases this work would be voluntary and unpaid; in others it might start out as, or develop into, a local employment scheme or a small business. The possibilities will vary from area to area, as will the particular opportunities and the skills and abilities available.

8.85   For such schemes to get mounted, a co-ordinated approach at local level is required. It should involve the public, private and voluntary sectors, working in partnership. The key bodies will include employers and unions; local public authorities (including those responsible for housing, health and education); local residents and voluntary organisations (including local churches); and local schools and colleges.

8.86   The initiative for particular local schemes and activities could come from any one of these 'partners', according to local circumstances. But one body will need to take a lead.

8.87   In many cases *local government* can take on this role. The Director of the Local Government Training Board put it to us that:

'there is a willingness on the part of many people in local government to play a part in the search for new approaches, and to break away from conventions, boundaries and practices which have seemingly made it difficult for local services to relate to their customers and communities. Dealing with the public, "networking" and partnership, risk-taking, team-building, and decentralisation are all examples which point in this direction, as is emphasis on policy development in such areas as equal opportunities, economic and employment development, youth and adult training and so on.'

8.88 We saw many of these features in the London Borough of Ealing, where a 'unified community action' initiative has been mounted to bridge the gap between the Town Hall and local neighbourhoods. District or borough authorities in the major conurbations have the advantage of being able to bring a wide range of responsibilities, including education, to bear on the local needs. There is much suspicion and doubt about the effectiveness of local government – in housing estates as well as in Whitehall. We have also noted the low morale among dedicated public servants who are attempting to maintain standards of service in the face of financial and staffing constraints. There are also hopeful signs we have seen: in particular the devolution of local government administration to local area offices, with the various departments working alongside each other, and encouraging residents to participate in responding to local needs.

8.89 Attempts at devolution and decentralisation have been made by a number of UPA local authorities. In others, schemes are in the pipeline. But this approach can run into serious political difficulties and trade union opposition. To implement such schemes effectively will require patient effort and dedication: yet we consider the establishment of neighbourhood offices to be vital if local government is to improve its service delivery to the UPAs.

8.90 The *private sector*, too, can provide leadership. The business world has become increasingly aware of the need to implement corporate social responsibility policies in a flexible and practical way. Many firms now realise that their future ultimately depends on their willingness to help improve the social and economic conditions in the local areas where they operate. There are many ways in which this is finding practical expression; examples include financial support, business advice, and the secondment of managers to voluntary organisations. The benefits to the firm are as real as the benefits to the community. Local enterprise agencies are an excellent example of the way in which key local organisations can be brought together to address economic problems in local districts. There are now over 200 enterprise agencies around the country and we believe their task is nowhere more important than in the UPAs.

8.91   As Business-in-the-Community noted in their submission to us:

> 'There is evidence that significant opportunities can be created over a period through pooling resources, talents, and expertise to stimulate the local economy.'

Impressed as we were by the social responsibility initiatives taken by some large companies and financial institutions we felt that there was a clear need to encourage others to follow their lead. We suggest that Business-in-the-Community should consider promoting some form of national award to recognize achievements in this field. We would also call on the major trade unions to consider how their pensions funds might more actively support social responsibility initiatives by companies in which they invest. Those representing workers' interests need to take a wider view of their responsibilities.

8.92   *Voluntary organisations* can also take a lead in developing local initiatives. Traditionally they have shown a flexibility which enables them to respond quickly to new needs, a capacity for innovation, the ability to operate across bureaucratic boundaries, and a means whereby citizen participation can be enhanced. They have proven management skills in neighbourhood action. The work that the National Association for the Care and Resettlement of Offenders (NACRO) have done in setting up crime prevention schemes on run-down housing estates shows how the voluntary sector, working with local government and others, can encourage residents to help reverse a pattern of decline. Action Resource Centre is an example of a voluntary body with close links with both the business world and local groups. Local voluntary trusts too, like one being developed in South Yorkshire, can provide the means (and the money) to encourage local people to take part in neighbourhood projects.

8.93   The term 'voluntary' can be ambiguous and confusing. We use it in the sense of 'non-statutory' bodies, consisting of people – paid or unpaid – who work together to meet an identified need. Where they employ paid staff, they should not be seen as undertaking this role 'on the cheap'. We reject two extreme views of the voluntary sector's role which are being given currency. First, reliance on 'Voluntarism', in the sense that there should be a massive transfer of responsibility from the State to voluntary bodies, can too easily become simply a cheap option for reducing public expenditure which relies overmuch on the goodwill of unpaid or under-paid workers. We see such an approach as a wholly inadequate response to the needs of our society, and of the UPAs in particular. At the other extreme we cannot accept the view which regards voluntary bodies as standing in the way of a more just society, and seeks their removal from the scene as essential for progress through State initiatives. Cities are complex organisms, and it is foolish to believe that government alone can have the necessary degree of flexibility to respond to this complexity.

8.94　We *recommend* that there should be a new deal between the State and voluntary bodies. At one time it was accepted that voluntary initiatives were useful primarily as pioneering new approaches and, if successful, handing them over to the State to adopt and run. This, we believe, need not always be the case. There is an increasing number of examples where they can and should become a permanent element in the pattern of organisations in a particular area.

8.95　The central element of this 'new deal' would be a recognition by government of the need for long-term continuity and funding for recognised voluntary bodies working alongside the statutory agencies. Even the most successful activities undertaken in the voluntary sector are vulnerable to financial cut-backs; they need a greater assurance of long-term support within a partnership approach. One possibility might be for an additional allocation of Rate Support Grant to local authorities being earmarked for voluntary sector support. However, the State cannot, and should not, be seen as the sole funding agency: in some cases there is still a role for funding from business and from charities.

8.96　Respect for the independence of voluntary organisations must go hand in hand with agreed funding arrangements. Government, both national and local, must accept the value of genuine and open debate and criticism. The line between responsible comment and involvement in party-political opposition may in some circumstances require closer definition. As the National Council for Voluntary Organisations (NCVO) have argued in their evidence to us, 'voluntary bodies need to be clear and firm in their relationships with political parties'. There is some agreement in the evidence we have received that the practice or the letter of current Charity Law is deficient at this point, and needs reviewing. We would support this: it is unrealistic, in our opinion, to expect people to devote energy to conceiving and managing innovatory projects if at the same time they are put under threat that their work will be penalised if they enter into public debate about social values or priorities.

8.97　Whoever takes the lead locally, resources will be needed and there will be resistance to new approaches which will be seen as challenging vested interests. For example, on many council housing estates we have heard time and again that getting minor repairs done quickly – or at all – is a major headache for the residents. The local housing authority has a backlog of repairs, and local residents feel that they should not undertake repairs themselves as it is the council's responsibility as landlord. The result is frustration, anger and anxiety. In this situation, one possible response might be the creation of a special community repair team, of unemployed people with relevant skills from the estate. Management expertise might be offered from local firms; trade unions might agree to co-operate provided the work to be carried out was clearly defined and would not put existing jobs at risk. Those on the community repair team would be paid the rate for the job. Central government could contribute to the costs involved by paying to the local authority in their Block Grant the equivalent of unemployment benefit for every person taken off the unemployment register to work on a repair team.

8.98   We cite this example simply as one illustration of the difficulties inherent in adopting new approaches. Only if all the partners concerned were prepared to make concessions, and to be more flexible, could such an approach (if agreed to be worthwhile) stand a chance of success. However, there are already many schemes in operation which involve the business world, local government, the voluntary sector and higher and further education. A national Commission cannot do justice to the variety of schemes being carried forward at local level: we can only encourage and support such developments.

Confidence
8.99   The future of our inner cities is uncertain. It would be a bold prophet who could claim to know what Toxteth or Brixton or a large outer estate will be like 20 or 50 years from now.

8.100   But one thing can be said with a degree of certainty. It is that the UPAs and the people who live in them need the nation's confidence and support: if we do not give it, the loss will be ours as well as theirs. For if the present pattern of decline continues it will bring wider effects which will touch all our lives.

8.101   We have seen evidence of how confidence can be injected. The two Urban Development Corporations, in the London and Merseyside Docklands, have begun to transform areas of outworn derelict land, and silted-up water, into areas which are beginning to thrive once again.

There are serious reservations, which we share, about the lack of consultation with, and participation by, local people in the work of the UDCs; about the inadequacy of good public rented housing in the London Docklands; and that much of the investment by the private sector is in non-labour-intensive land uses, such as warehousing. Yet the UDCs are without doubt making a visible impact: for example, through the scheme to convert the Albert Dock building in Liverpool – the largest group of Grade 1 listed buildings in the country – into a new multi-purpose centre, including the proposed 'Tate of the North' art gallery; in the achievement of mounting Britain's first International Garden Festival on the banks of the Mersey, turning spoiled wasteland into a magnificent landscaped garden in two years; in the development of new film and television studios and newspaper printing works, and the plans for a new light railway system to open up transport links and improve communications, in London Docklands.

8.102 The single-minded development agency can achieve much in a relatively short time. Our New Towns have proved this: so too have the UDCs. But they have done so primarily because substantial direct financial support from the Exchequer has enabled them to acquire, improve and redevelop the land in their areas. This money, and the degree of central government commitment to the areas, has given the private sector the confidence to invest.

8.103 The UPAs need our confidence. That confidence can be expressed through a major increase in centrally-devoted resources to improve the conditions of life, and encourage private sector investment. It will not be possible to provide substantial extra resources everywhere: there will still have to be a focus on designated areas. Yet it is an inadequate response to say that throwing money at the problem is not the answer. It is *part* of the answer – it is necessary, though not sufficient. The 1977 White Paper recognized this. Its policy proposals have not been tried and found wanting. They have not been tried.

8.104 We have lost a decade. We urge that policy-makers return to the 1977 White Paper and to what it argued was the necessary first step in responding to the inner cities' problems:

'The first essential is a *specific commitment* on the part of central and local government to the *regeneration* of the inner areas. . . both central and local government will be judged by their willingness to *implement new priorities, to make funds available, to change policies,* and *to adapt their organisations.*' (our emphasis)[9]

193

We hope that 1986 will see this commitment relaunched in word and deed, not only in relation to the inner areas but also the outer estates.

Main Recommendations

In this Chapter we have argued for a renewed public policy commitment to the regeneration of the Urban Priority Areas. As part of this, we have recommended that:

1. A greater priority for the outer estates is called for within urban policy initiatives (paragraph 8.35).

2. The resources devoted to Rate Support Grant should be increased in real terms, and within the enhanced total there should be a greater bias to the UPAs. Efficiency audits should be used to tackle wasteful expenditure (paragraph 8.55).

3. The size of the Urban Programme should be increased, and aspects of its operation reviewed (paragraph 8.67).

4. The concept of partnership in the UPAs should be developed by central and local government to promote greater consultation with, and participation by, local people at neighbourhood level (paragraph 8.76).

5. There should be a new deal between government and the voluntary sector, to provide long-term continuity and funding for recognized voluntary bodies working alongside statutory agencies (paragraphs 8.94 and 95).

References
1 HMSO Cmnd 6845 June 1977
2 Department of the Environment Press Notice 245, 17 June 1983
3 *Outer Estates in Britain,* Centre for Environmental Studies Ltd, October 1984
4 *Census Information Note No 3.* Inner City Directorate, DoE
5 Reported in *The Times* 19 April 1985
6 *Operation of the Rate Support Grant System,* National Audit Office April 1985
7 *Capital Expenditure Controls in Local Government in England,* Audit Commission April 1985
8 Submission from the Diocese of Birmingham
9 Cmnd 6845, paragraph 25.

Chapter 9

POVERTY, EMPLOYMENT AND WORK

'Behind the statistics are real people, like the 50 year-old man who cried when offered a place on an MSC scheme because he felt wanted again'
(Black Country Urban Industrial Mission)

9.1   Since the 1977 White Paper on 'Inner City Policy' was published, people in employment in Britain have in general become better off. Real disposable incomes per head have been gradually rising. Price inflation has been successfully moderated. Productivity gains have been made.

9.2   For people in the urban priority areas, however, the economic landscape looks very different. In this Chapter of our report, we examine the growth of poverty and unemployment in the UPAs. We then consider possible responses to the challenge this presents in relation to job creation and income support. Finally we consider how our attitudes to jobs and work might be reassessed. In all this we shall try to reflect the theological stance we have developed in Chapter 3.

Poverty in the UPAs

9.3   We shall concentrate here on the cold statistics of poverty and unemployment, rather than what they can mean in human terms. Poor people in Britain are not of course as poor as those in the Third World. But their poverty is real enough nonetheless. For poverty is a relative, as well as an absolute, concept. It exists, even in a relatively rich western society, if people are denied access to what is generally regarded as a reasonable standard and quality of life in that society.

9.4   Poverty is not only about shortage of money. It is about rights and relationships; about how people are treated and how they regard themselves; about powerlessness, exclusion, and loss of dignity. Yet the lack of an adequate income is at its heart.

9.5   The most recent official figures show that in Great Britain in 1981 over 2.8 million people were living on incomes *below* the Supplementary Benefit level (conventionally taken as the 'poverty line').[1] Over 4.8 million people were dependent on Supplementary Benefit, and so were *on* the 'poverty line'.[2] If we include those living on an income at or less than 140 per cent of the Supplementary Benefit level (the definition of low income used by the DHSS), then in 1981 there were 15 million, or nearly 3 in 10 of the population, living in poverty or on its margins.[3] Families with children outnumber pensioners among those living below the poverty line.[4]

9.6 The indicators of deprivation used by the Government to designate inner city areas for special help (unemployment, pensioners living alone, single-parent families, overcrowding, houses lacking basic amenities, and ethnic minority population) are all indirect measures of poverty. If the ten-yearly Census asked for details of people's income the geographical picture of its extent would be much clearer. But the DoE indicators provide a close enough (though – as we have argued in Chapters 5 and 8 – underestimated) approximation, and they indicate that a *concentration* of poverty is the major characteristic of Britain's UPAs.

9.7 Income support policies are a first step to doing justice to those members of our society who are poorest, and who are most likely to be concentrated in the UPAs.

9.8 Yet in recent years social welfare and taxation policies have tended to benefit the rich at the expense of the poor. Changes in Social Security since 1979 are estimated to have 'saved' more than £8 billion.[5] Total spending has nevertheless risen because the number of people dependent on benefits has risen, partly for demographic reasons (primarily an increase in the number of pensioners), but largely because of the steep rise in unemployment.

9.9 At the same time the burden of tax to those on the highest incomes has fallen substantially, while that on the lower-paid has risen. A married man with two children on average earnings is paying slightly more in tax and national insurance since 1978/79; on five times average earnings he is paying 7 per cent less, and on ten times average earnings 15 per cent less.[6]

9.10 Pay differentials have also widened sharply. In 1978 the lowest-paid 10 per cent of male workers earned 66.7 per cent of the national average wage; by 1984 this had fallen to 61.6 per cent. During the same period the highest-paid 10 per cent saw their average earnings rise from

157.9 per cent to 171.5 per cent of the average wage.[7] *Low pay is also a factor in poverty.* In 1981 of the 9.1 million people under pension age living in low income households in 1981, over 40 per cent were dependent on a full-time wage earner.[8] Almost three and a half million full-time adult workers – two-thirds of them women – had total earnings (including overtime pay) which fell below the £100 a week definition of low pay in April 1983.[9]

9.11   It is the poor who have borne the brunt of the recession, both the unemployed and the working poor. Yet it is the poor who are seen by some as 'social security scroungers', or a burden on the country, preventing economic recovery. This is a cruel example of blaming the victim.

9.12   Much of the rise in welfare spending is a direct consequence of specific government policies. For example, between 1978/79 and 1983/84 central government housing subsidies to council tenants were reduced by 60 per cent. This was a deliberate policy to raise rents, while protecting the poorest through housing benefits. As a direct consequence of this policy, spending on Housing Benefit inevitably rose, and then ironically became a target for cuts. The decision to 'subsidise people rather than bricks and mortar' also resulted in a vast increase in spending on old people in private homes, and homeless people in bed and breakfast accommodation – so again total expenditure was cut, but without alternative provision being made.

The Impact of Unemployment

9.13   It is the steep rise in unemployment in recent years above all else that has significantly increased the number of families living in poverty in Britain today.

9.14   In 1981 just over 2.6 million unemployed people and members of their families were living in poverty or at its margins – *three out of every ten people under pension age.*[10] The Child Poverty Action Group's evidence to us noted that between 1979 and 1981 '*the numbers at or below the poverty line because of unemployment more than trebled*'. With the continuing rise in unemployment since 1981 the position has undoubtedly become considerably worse. Unemployment has become a major cause of poverty in Britain.

9.15   In August 1985 the official figures indicated that there were 3.18 million unemployed workers in the UK,[11] or 13.2 per cent of the workforce. About 1.2 million were under 25 years of age. There were over 1.3 million people who had been out of work for over a year, 800,000 for over 2 years and 500,000 for over 3 years.

9.16   The scale of the problem is widely recognized as a matter for serious *national* concern. However, analysis of 1981 Census data (and more recent information on long-term unemployment) shows that in the inner city Partnership areas:

(i)   total unemployment rates, and unemployment rates in each socio-economic group, are significantly higher than the national average (Table 9.1);

(ii)   there are disproportionately high concentrations of unskilled manual workers, semi-skilled workers, and far fewer employers and managers, than the national average (Table 9.2);

(iii)   the proportion of long-term unemployed is higher than the national average (Figure 9.1, page 200);

(iv)   unemployment among young and older people is very high (Figure 9.2, page 201);

Consequently, a high proportion of people in UPAs have to rely on state income support.

TABLE 9.1 – UNEMPLOYMENT RATES 1981

INNER CITY PARTNERSHIP AREA	A	B	C	D	E	TOTAL
Birmingham	6.5	4.2	17.8	18.3	20.0	21.8
Gateshead	7.7	2.6	17.5	18.4	22.4	16.8
Hackney	5.7	5.9	15.0	12.6	14.5	15.4
Islington	5.5	4.8	13.0	11.2	13.4	12.9
Lambeth	5.6	5.3	14.3	12.0	10.6	14.4
Liverpool	9.3	3.7	19.8	16.9	22.8	22.1
Manchester	8.8	3.4	19.1	17.9	22.5	20.3
Newcastle	4.7	2.5	18.0	21.1	21.7	17.7
Salford	7.1	14.3	21.4	18.9	23.5	20.8
AVERAGE	6.8	5.2	17.3	16.4	19.0	18.0
GB	3.4	2.5	9.8	10.8	14.3	9.4

Key: A   Employers and Managers (SEG 1 & 2)
        B   Professional Workers (SEG 3 & 4)
        C   Skilled Manual Workers (SEG 8 & 9)
        D   Semi Skilled Manual Workers (SEG 10)
        E   Unskilled Manual Workers (SEG 11)

Source: Manpower Services Commission, derived from 1981
        Census of Population

TABLE 9.2 – BROAD OCCUPATIONAL DISTRIBUTION OF EMPLOYMENT 1981

(Numbers in each group as % of total employment)

INNER CITY PARTNERSHIP AREA	A	B	C	D	E
Birmingham	6.4	2.4	23.0	22.0	9.6
Gateshead	6.4	1.7	27.6	16.0	10.4
Hackney	8.3	2.4	17.7	15.7	8.0
Islington	9.1	4.3	15.2	13.1	8.4
Lambeth	8.8	3.5	14.4	11.4	10.7
Liverpool	5.9	1.8	20.8	18.4	12.1
Manchester	6.3	2.1	22.1	18.1	11.1
Newcastle	7.9	3.3	22.4	12.4	11.0
Salford	5.2	1.2	23.6	20.5	13.6
GB	12.3	4.1	19.8	12.1	5.6

Key: A Employers and Managers (SEG 1 & 2)
      B Professional Workers (SEG 3 & 4)
      C Skilled Manual Workers (SEG 8 & 9)
      D Semi Skilled Manual Workers (SEG 10)
      E Unskilled Manual Workers (SEG 11)

Source: Manpower Services Commission, derived from 1981
       Census of Population

9.17   The figures for the Partnership areas are all based on analysis of 1981 Census data, with the exception of those for long-term unemployment which relate to January 1984. The position in the UPAs has inevitably become much worse since then with the rise of unemployment nationally, and these figures also mask the acute concentrations of unemployment and poverty in particular UPA neighbourhoods or on particular estates. For example, the Bidston area of Birkenhead has a 48 per cent male unemployment rate; but within this, there are parts of the Ford estate, which members of the Commission visited, where we had evidence that 80 per cent were out of work. Much the same picture emerged for parts of the Meadowell estates we visited in North Shields. Even in the relatively prosperous South East, apparently low average unemployment rates can hide the serious problems in the UPAs. In the fairly well-to-do London Borough of Bexley, with an average unemployment rate of 7-8 per cent, parts of the Thamesmead estate have 26 per cent male unemployment.[12]

9.18   Some groups of people are being hit particularly hard, especially those who face other difficulties in their lives. Those who suffer ill-health or disability, and younger and older workers, are particularly

FIGURE 9.1

Inner City Partnership Areas: Proportion of unemployed
who were long-term unemployed, January 1984

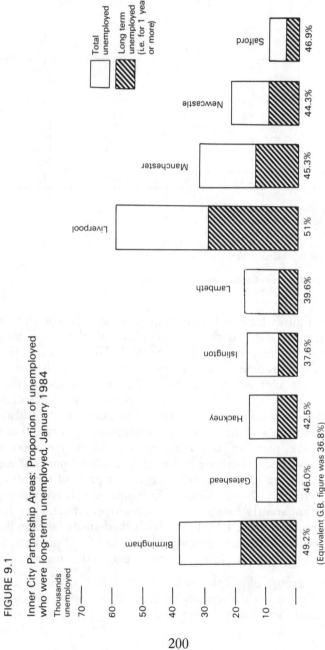

Total unemployed

Long term unemployed (i.e. for 1 year or more)

Thousands unemployed

70
60
50
40
30
20
10

Birmingham 49.2%
Gateshead 46.0%
Hackney 42.5%
Islington 37.6%
Lambeth 39.6%
Liverpool 51%
Manchester 45.3%
Newcastle 44.3%
Salford 46.9%

(Equivalent G.B. figure was 36.8%)

Source: Manpower Services Commission/Dept. of the Environment

200

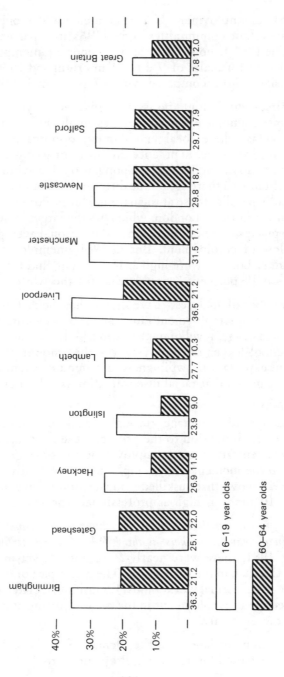

FIGURE 9.2

Inner City Partnership Areas: Unemployment Rates for Young and Older Age Groups, 1981

16–19 year olds

60–64 year olds

Source: Manpower Services Commission, derived from Census of Population 1981

vulnerable to unemployment. Unemployment rates among people from the minority ethnic communities in the UPAs are a particular cause for concern. The 1981 Labour Force Survey reported unemployment rates of 20.6 per cent for males of West Indian origin and 16.9 per cent for those of Asian origin, compared with 9.7 per cent for white males.

9.19   At first sight, it might be assumed that the above average rates of unemployment among ethnic minorities might reflect their concentration in areas where local employment opportunities have been declining for a long time. In practice this does not account for the higher levels of unemployment in the black population. For within each region or metropolitan area there are ethnic differences in unemployment rates which broadly parallel those at the national level. For example levels of unemployment in Inner London, which has the largest concentration of non-white groups, are not much above the national average, despite its sustained loss of employment. But in 1981 unemployment rates for Asians in inner London were high at 15 per cent, and for West Indians higher still at 19 per cent – double that for the white population.

9.20   A number of analyses[13] have shown that the difference between black and white unemployment rates cannot be accounted for in terms of factors such as age, level of qualification, skill, or – in the case of one study of school-leaver unemployment – the amount of job-hunting, employment expectations, willingness to commute or family unemployment. This suggests that racial discrimination is still in evidence in the job market.

9.21   Although disadvantage through racial discrimination adds a disturbing extra dimension to the problem, the main factor associated with the concentration of unemployment in some groups, and the disparities in the incidence of unemployment regionally, is *occupational class*. Table 9.2 shows that unskilled manual workers have unemployment rates up to 10 times as high as professional workers.

9.22   *It is the national decline in the number of manual jobs, and the concentration of manual workers in the UPAs that lies at the heart of the problem.* By 1981, there were nearly 2½ million fewer manual worker jobs in the UK than in the early 1970s. The major part of the decline was in full-time male manual worker jobs (1.8 million), related closely to the absolute decline in employment in the manufacturing and construction sectors of the economy.

9.23   Projections of labour market demand give little hope that this trend will be halted or reversed. Projections to 1990 by Warwick

University's widely respected Institute for Employment Research show a steady decline in manufacturing employment (Appendix E) and an associated steep decline in the number of jobs for manual workers.

9.24   The major source of new jobs in the 1970s was the service sector. Yet projections for the service sector give no cause for great optimism. There was a rapid fall-off in growth in the service sector in the early 1980s, and whilst it is expected to grow substantially during the rest of the decade, this gain is unlikely to be enough to offset the loss of jobs elsewhere in the economy. Moreover, many of these jobs are likely to be taken by women entering the labour market and/or part-time employees. Recent Department of Employment figures show that, between December 1983 and December 1984, 95 per cent of the 200,000 net new jobs taken by women in this period were part-time ones. The net change in male employment in the same period was a loss of 60,000 jobs.[14] It has now been unequivocally demonstrated that employers are preferring to employ part-time labour rather than full-time labour. 'The ability to control the hours of employment through the use of part-time labour represented a more effective method of saving on direct wage costs'.[15] By employing women on a part-time basis (and perhaps at rates of pay lower than would be paid to men) employers may create more jobs and ensure greater flexibility for themselves, but the overall impact on unemployment may be slight. Indeed we are now witnessing a combined growth of employment *and* unemployment, as full-time jobs for men in manufacturing decline and part-time jobs for women in the service sector increase.

9.25   The Government's own public expenditure plans until 1988 (published in January 1985) assume that the number of people unemployed nationally will continue to average 3 million a year, excluding school-leavers. Those same plans propose yet further cuts in public expenditure in real terms on, for example, housing, education and transport, together with further 'manpower savings' in the public sector.

9.26   The majority of people who are in employment are better off in material terms now than they were ten or fifteen years ago. Income from employment has risen from some £30 billion in 1970 to some £170 billion (equivalent to £37 billion in terms of 1970 purchasing power) in 1983. But there is now a sizeable section of our community in Britain which is not sharing in our economic fortunes. If unemployment remains at very high levels nationally, the prospects for many people in the older urban areas of ever having a job look very bleak indeed. All unemployed people (but particularly the long-term unemployed and school-leavers in the UPAs, and a disproportionately high number of minority ethnic group members), are being deprived of the opportunities which the rest of society regards as essential for a decent life.

9.27   Despite the economic history of the urban priority areas, and the way in which structural economic change is affecting them disproportionately, their economic future cannot be examined in isolation. National policies – and attitudes – need to be examined, for their effects on the economic scene in the UPAs are profound.

Is Wealth Creation the Answer?
9.28   Given the enormity of the problem, it would be foolish to suggest that the only way forward would be for Britain as a nation to get poorer. If the national standard of living is to grow, the process of wealth creation must be supported wholeheartedly. The pursuit of efficiency in industry is to follow the biblical insistence on the proper stewardship of resources – providing, that is, such a pursuit does not become a short-sighted and selfish exploitation of human and material resources, and that, as we have stressed in Chapter 3, it is accompanied by the fair distribution of the wealth created. To affirm the importance of wealth creation – as we do – is not enough. Economic policy should be as concerned with the distribution of income and wealth as with its creation. What seems to be lacking at present is an adequate appreciation of the importance of the distributive consequences – for cities and regions, and for groups of people – of national economic policies.

9.29   The responsibilities and burdens placed upon management in promoting economic growth are obviously heavy, and must be appreciated and recognised as such. Business management in today's complex world is a challenging calling for many Christians. Management must, however, respond to changes in the economic scene. Given the increasing competitive pressures in international markets, the requirement for firms to modernise to stay in competition is likely to result in different – and perhaps fewer – jobs in the future. Present trends suggest that these jobs are more likely to be concentrated in the so-called 'sunrise' areas such as the M4 corridor, which have modern factories (with room for expansion at low cost), a pleasant environment, good infrastructure and modern working practices, than in the older urban areas with few of these advantages.

9.30   It is unrealistic to assume that even the skilled and mobile residents of our cities can all 'get on their bikes' and move to the small towns and rural areas which are the focal points of economic growth to get a job – even if there were sufficient jobs (and housing) available for all. Certainly a middle-aged redundant shipyard worker in Gateshead cannot be expected to compete with a young school leaver in the South-East for a new service sector job.

9.31   Although, therefore, continued growth in the economy should be pursued, we cannot ignore the probability that increased competition in manufactures, particularly from our European competitors and the newly industrialised countries, will lead to greater pressures on the UK share of world markets, even if the world economy grows. If British industry is to remain productive and competitive in world markets without a substantial shift to protectionism, an increasing substitution of high technology capital for labour is virtually inevitable. In modern conditions wealth creation tends not to result in job creation.

9.32   Some may argue that the benefits of economic growth will somehow 'trickle down' to unemployed people in the UPAs. We are not convinced by such arguments. We share the view of Business-in-the-Community that 'the principal way businesses can help is to stay in business and secure a healthy economic base . . . But it is fanciful to think that the results will trickle down to deprived areas to make a significant and self-sustaining effect'. Although the size of the national economic cake may grow, there is no automatic mechanism in the market economy for distributing the net increase to those who are not employed.

9.33   Recent history has, on the contrary, seen an increasing divide between rich and poor. As we noted in Chapter 1, analysis in the Government's *Social Trends* shows that in 1982, even after tax and welfare benefits are taken into account, the worst-off fifth of the population received only 6.9 per cent of total income, compared with 7.4 per cent in 1976. In contrast, the best-off fifth increased its share from 37.9 per cent to 39.4 per cent.

9.34   Nor is it correct to assume that most unemployed people are hard at work creating wealth in the informal economy. According to a report published by the *Economist Intelligence Unit*, only 4 per cent of unemployed people get extra money informally. Opportunities for doing extra, informal, work for cash have probably declined in recent years as unemployment has increased. There is a limit to the number of window cleaners or jobbing decorators that any area – certainly one characterized by poverty – can support, and working informally requires more than just time: tools, materials and travel are all expensive. Work for money may be elsewhere but the cost of getting there – or of running a van – kills the possibility of doing it.

9.35   A recent study[16] has shown that full-time employment is the key to participation in *all* forms of work. A process of polarization is occurring here too. Some households have multiple earners and relatively substantial resources of money, time and energy to devote to consumption, self-provisioning and various kinds of unpaid and informal work in and around the home. Once households get on a benign upwards spiral their collective efforts keep them there. But next door to such households may be others where both parents are unemployed, there is no incentive (because of the consequent loss of social security benefit and high marginal 'tax' rate) for one of them to take one of the growing number of part-time jobs, and their young school leavers cannot find work and are increasingly demoralized by the experience of their parents.

9.36   Thus some households are getting richer, and adding to the number of earners as youngsters leave school and are found jobs, and members are busy improving and extending their homes or maintaining their cars. Other households are getting poorer, accumulating more members who are unemployed, and neither own their dwellings nor a car or van. The General Household Survey has indicated that employed male heads of households are nearly twice as likely as unemployed heads of households to have working wives (probably because of the consequent loss of welfare benefits faced by the latter). So the new part-time (and lower-paid) jobs are more likely to go to those households in which there are already one or more earners.

9.37   We are living through a period of structural economic change coupled with relative economic decline. In earlier periods of structural change in the economy (from agriculture through manufacturing to services) the demand for labour in the long term increased. There is no guarantee that history will repeat itself. We share a hope that the new technology, although at first displacing jobs, will create new wealth, and so make a demand for new goods and services which will create jobs in the long term. But the long term seems a long way off, and this hope rests on the assumption that increases in output will outstrip increases in productivity. The current forecasts by Warwick University indicate that with present policies unchanged, the current high levels of unemployment nationally are likely to persist during the remaining years of the present decade, and probably beyond. The shift taking place from labour to capital and from manufacturing to the service sector, is resulting in an increasing polarization, particularly marked in the UPAs, between households that have members in employment and those which do not. The prospects look bleak for the older urban areas, where structural economic changes are giving rise to most acute problems of unemployment. It is on this assumption that we base what follows. Even if, as we hope, economic policies change and these forecasts prove wrong, and the present high levels of unemployment start to fall, there will still be a major problem to be faced in the next 5-10 years – with disproportionately high concentrations of unemployed people in the UPAs.

No Alternative?

9.38   'Unemployment', said Archbishop William Temple in the 1930s, 'is the most hideous of our social evils.' The effects of unemployment in the 1980s have been all too clear to us on our visits to Britain's UPAs. We have been confronted time and time again with the deep human misery – coupled in some cases with resentment, in others with apathy and hopelessness – that is its result. The absence of regular paid work has eroded self-respect. 'Give me back my dignity' was the heartfelt plea from one man – made redundant, and with no prospect of a job – at one of our public meetings in the North-West.

9.39   Unemployment for most people is not a liberating experience. Although unemployed people clearly have more time for leisure pursuits, their financial situation makes it more difficult or impossible for them to indulge in leisure activities. The cheapest form of entertainment available – television – can be a constant and painful reminder of the opportunities of a consumer society that is beyond their reach.

9.40   What has most astonished (and depressed) us has been a widespread feeling among those we have talked to in the UPAs that 'nothing can be done' about unemployment. Not, however, that nothing *should* be done – the feeling is more that the 'social evil' is so widespread and unchanging, the problem so baffling, and the authorities apparently so unresponsive, that hope has been abandoned. We wonder whether some politicians really understand the despair which has become so widespread in many areas of our country.

9.41   We must make it perfectly clear that we believe there is no instant, dogmatic or potent solution to the problem of unemployment. Certainly the Church of England cannot 'solve' the problem of unemployment. It possesses neither the mandate nor the competence to do so. Yet as it is in the position of being the national Church, it has a particular duty to act as the conscience of the nation. It must question all economic philosophies, not least those which, when put into practice, have contributed to the blighting of whole districts, which do not offer the hope of amelioration, and which perpetuate the human misery and despair to which we have referred. The situation requires the Church to question from its own particular standpoint the *morality* of these economic philosophies.

9.42   The party manifestos for the last two General Elections had different emphases. But they all shared the same broad objectives. A united nation with a competitive economy, equality of opportunity, good education, housing, health, and care for the disadvantaged, and a reduction in inflation and unemployment.

9.43   The reality is that many of these objectives held in common are not being attained – indeed, worse than that, are slipping further and further away from our grasp.

9.44   For political parties in Government to achieve the objectives set out in their manifestos requires many difficult judgements to be made, with imperfect tools for analysis. Each government must balance the demands of wealth creation and wealth distribution, of compassion and efficiency, of personal initiative and collective provision.

9.45   The main assumption on which present economic policies are based is that prosperity can be restored if individuals are set free to pursue their own economic salvation. The appeal is to economic self-interest and individualism, and freeing market mechanisms through the removal of 'unnecessary' governmental interference and restrictive trade union practice.

9.46   Individual responsibility and self-reliance are excellent objectives. The nation cannot do without them. But pursuit of them must not damage a collective obligation and provision for those who have no choice, or whose choices are at best forced ones. *We believe that at present too much emphasis is being given to individualism, and not enough to collective obligation.* In the absence of a spirit of collective obligation, or the political will to foster it, there is no guarantee that the pursuit of innumerable individual self-interests will add up to an improvement in the common good.

9.47   No less an advocate of the market economy than Adam Smith accepted in his 'Theory of Moral Sentiments' that economic individualism could not be divorced from moral, religious and social obligations. The complex relationship seen by Smith has been summarized as follows: '(men) could safely be trusted to pursue their own self-interest without undue harm to the community, not only because of the restrictions imposed by the law but also because they were subject to built-in restraint derived from morals, religion, custom, and education'.[17]

9.48   There is always a need, we believe, for an explicit debate about the moral basis for, and implications of, policy decisions taken on 'economic' grounds. Different value systems are implied in much economic analysis and policy, and it is vital for Christians to scrutinize them to see how they match up to their understanding of human relationships and to Christian moral concepts. This view was endorsed by the General Synod in November 1984 when it affirmed that 'the world of economics is not a closed world, and economic values are not self-justifying, but need to be set in the larger context of human values'. We believe that most economists would agree with this.

9.49   So we must not fall into the trap of letting economics suffocate morality by taking decisions for us: economic determinism is an insidious philosophy. The role of economic science is to tell us the likely effects of choices we make on moral grounds.

9.50   If it is by their *outcomes* that macro-economic policies must be judged, we are united in the view that the costs of present policies, with the continuing growth of unemployment, are unacceptable in their effect on whole communities and generations. A degree of hardship may be needed to attain longer-term objectives, but it is unacceptable that the costs of transition should fall hardest on those least able to bear them.

9.51   In the following sections of this Chapter we consider what national measures seem to us to be needed to respond to the poverty and unemployment of the UPAs, in addition to our proposals in relation to government urban policies.

9.52   We do not present a fully-fledged model to replace present macro-economic policies. It would be foolish of us to attempt this. We recognize, too, that there are limits to any government's freedom of action in the face of national and international economic constraints. But we must question whether, at a time when our economy is in transition to an uncertain future, a dogmatic and inflexible macro-economic stance is appropriate. We believe that a more open debate is needed about the type of society present economic policies are shaping. We *recommend* at the Church and its bishops should play a full part in such a debate, for the Christian Gospel sets values in relation to the dignity and worth of each individual, and in relation to human society, against which economic dogma must be judged.

What Might Be Done?

9.53   Debate is important. But it must lead to action. The combination in the UPAs of unsatisfied needs and unused human abilities seems to us as uneconomic as it is illogical and immoral. Given that to cut unemployment to 2 million by the end of this decade, *some 1,200 net new jobs will need to be created every day for the next 5 years,*[18] the challenge is to implement policies which will utilise the human skills and abilities that are available to the maximum extent possible, in the context of a humane and decent treatment for those who cannot find paid work.

9.54   In short, we must use our common wealth, either to provide work for others or to provide an adequate level of income support for those without work. The following sections indicate approaches we believe should be explored by the Church, by Government, and by all those with a concern about the effects of mass unemployment. We would stress that there is no evidence to suggest that action to reduce unemployment levels generally will have any impact on the disproportionate number of minority ethnic people unemployed – unless deliberate efforts are made to this end by the active promotion of more widespread compliance with the law against direct and indirect racial discrimination in employment.

Increasing the Demand for Labour

(i)   *Small Businesses*

9.55   Traditionally, the inner areas of our cities have been places where thousands of new businesses have been started. Many have failed, but many have also grown, and eventually moved out of the city to expand still further. Cities have been good at growing businesses, not at attracting them.

9.56   We welcome the encouragement which the Government is giving to the creation of new business enterprises in the UPAs. Advice, financial packaging and support, and starter units are all needed. The existing means of advice and support in urban areas, such as those run by the Government's Small Firms Service, local Enterprise Agencies, and by local authorities, could be given a new impetus. We have been impressed by the model of the government-sponsored Council for Small Industries in Rural Areas. This body has a proven record in advice and training, and in helping existing small firms to expand and develop. There is no equivalent national body which has a direct focus on urban Britain. We *recommend* that the case for the establishment of a Council for Small Industries in *Urban Areas* is given further consideration, particularly to help small businesses in the UPAs with premises and training.

9.57   But the limitations of relying on small business growth to create new jobs must be recognized. First, small firms are not big employers. Typically, even established small firms have 10-20 employees, and new businesses only 3-5. So for every 1,000 new jobs to be created in this way, perhaps as many as 300 new firms need to be started. Many of these jobs will be precarious ones: existing small firms can fold as frequently as new ones can be created.

9.58   Second, inner city small businesses may also demand types of skill which training or retraining opportunities in the UPAs may not be able to supply.

9.59   Third, successful small businesses depend on the existence of large enterprises to which they can supply goods and services. Major firms can make an important contribution by purchasing locally from the small business sector. But the larger firms are still moving away from the UPAs – or closing their operations in these areas.

9.60   Finally, the potential for the small firms sector to develop in the outer council estates is limited. Suitable premises, finance, and relevant skill training facilities are all likely to be in short supply, or non-existent. There is no thriving neighbourhood economy in which goods and services can be traded. So we cannot rely on the small business sector alone to solve the problem.

(ii)   *Increased Public Expenditure*
9.61   More direct government actions to stimulate the demand for labour in the UPAs will not on its own solve the problem of unemployment. But that does not mean that no action should be taken. Inaction will mean that the unemployment situation will continue to deteriorate.

9.62   First, we share the view of the CBI and TUC and *recommend* that increased *public expenditure on capital investment* is devoted to new infrastructure and housing construction and repair. One of the Victorian values (shared by Liberal and Tory Governments) was a concern to invest for the future, and the inner areas of many of our major cities are still relying on the public assets created a century ago. But they are now, inevitably, decaying and in need of replacement: and nowhere more so than in the UPAs with their severe problems of housing disrepair and collapsing Victorian sewers.

9.63 Additional public expenditure on capital schemes is, given the relatively depressed state of the economy, hardly likely to result in rekindling inflation. And the original provision of sewerage and piped water in our cities could clearly not be termed a 'kindness that kills'. Do we have to wait for the spur of the fear of disease before renewing or repairing our basic infrastructure? As the UPAs have disproportionate concentrations of unemployed manual workers, (and there are some 250,000 unemployed construction workers nationally), the necessary labour is there for expanded programmes of construction and repair. Moreover, skills will be lost in the building and construction trades, unless more investment is forthcoming soon.

9.64 Capital expenditure schemes by their nature require proper planning. They take time to mount. We also *recommend* an increase in *current expenditure – particularly on public services.* Calculations made by Neale and Wilson[19] suggest that more current spending on education and other local government services would have by far the largest impact on jobs. It is also the case that money spent by public authorities increases the demand for private sector goods. Growth in the service sector has been welcomed by government – as long as it is a growth in privately-marketed services. Much public sector service provision has, by contrast, suffered from cuts in expenditure. We find the logic of this very strange. Why should money spent on the National Health Service and on state education be considered unproductive, yet money spent on private clinics and private schools be considered productive? The rationale is simply an accounting one: only *market* transactions (irrespective of their social usefulness) are apparently seen as adding to national wealth. This is a form of special pleading which does not carry conviction to us or to many others.

9.65 There has also been much talk about 'proper jobs'. One implication of this phrase is that only employment which produces marketable goods and services is of economic value. Another view is that only traditional male jobs (e.g. shipbuilding) in particular regions are 'proper'. We do not agree with either of these views. We must confront the implications for society of a belief that the manufacture of rubber ducks for export increases economic welfare, but job-creating public expenditure on environmental improvement or caring for the elderly does not. Equally we must question a romantic nostalgia for the 'real' jobs of yesteryear which ignores the reality of economic change. *We need to return to a common-sense view that what matters is whether expenditure utilises available resources to meet genuine needs, irrespective of whether it is undertaken in the private sector or through government provision.* Where there is no private sector market – as for many public goods, such as roads – it is perfectly proper to view the democratic process of government, locally as well as nationally, as part of the mechanism for resource allocation in the economy.

9.66   Even if it is argued that constraints on public expenditure mean that money for new schemes cannot be made available across the board nationally, we would press for special attention to be paid to the needs of the UPAs. Partly as a result of public expenditure cuts in recent years, and partly because of their concentration of social needs, public services in the UPAs – particularly in education and the social services – are under severe presssure. Shortages of staff and equipment have led to declining standards of service. We have already argued for Rate Support Grant to be increased in the UPAs. The job creation benefits of this would be significant.

9.67   To create new jobs by increasing public expenditure may require tax increases or higher rates of public borrowing. We believe that the present situation may well necessitate such a response. The effects of such increased expenditures would include wider economic benefits through reduced welfare payments, stronger effective demand and a better overall economic and social infrastructure to the benefit of the nation as a whole.

Work Sharing and Overtime
9.68   There are a number of distinct strategies for redistributing work that can be subsumed under the heading of *work sharing.* Each has difficulties:

(a)   The hours that 'full-time' employees work to earn their basic wage can be reduced. This may be done in a number of ways. Existing normal working hours can be compressed into fewer working days per week, month or year. This would not save any basic hours but it would release 'work slots' into which another employee could go. Basic wage rates could be increased as compensation for the loss of

213

overtime hours (though this may have implications for unit labour costs). Alternatively, employees could simply work fewer hours, however these were distributed. They would be unlikely to accept this without commensurate wage increases. Such increases could be paid for out of productivity increases but this arrangement would not necessarily supply more 'work slots' for new employees. Other ways of reducing the number of hours worked throughout the lifetime – by raising the school-leaving age or reducing the age of retirement – raise problems of income support. If, for example, pensions are to be paid to people who retire early, this implies a substantial increase in payments to pension funds and hence reduced real incomes during the income-generating period.

(b)   An alternative approach is to split existing jobs so that each is done by more than one person. This implies that workers doing an existing 'full-time' job would end up doing a 'part-time' job which may not be perceived as a 'proper job'. Unless the whole nation went part-time together, those who first took the plunge would be seriously at a disadvantage in terms of income, pension rights and so forth. Most part-time workers at present are female and low paid. Furthermore, it is typically the low-paid jobs that are easier to share. Insofar as financial rewards are related to greater knowledge, experience, skill or qualities of leadership it may be hard to find the appropriate quantity of 'doubles'. Jobs that require some degree of personal style or political capacity tend to be unsplittable. Having two lavatory attendants instead of one, each working part-time, is probably a quick way to make two households poorer.

(c)   There is a distinction between job sharing and job splitting. In the former case the partners in the job share the same employment rights and benefits. In the latter case neither obtains the employment rights of the original job. Job sharing is more likely to be limited to professionals with high salaries who, towards the end of their careers, can manage comfortably on half their salaries.

9.69   In short, work sharing is not a solution to the employment problems of the UPAs, though it may make a contribution to particular cases.

9.70   As far as *overtime* is concerned, Britain has consistently headed the European league of hours worked and also has the highest overtime rates. It is one of the few countries not to legislate against excessive working hours. Various claims are made about the number of jobs that could be created if overtime work was abolished and the time spent on it redeployed. Despite current levels of unemployment, the proportion of all workers on overtime in manufacturing industry has remained remarkably stable between 1977 and 1983. Indeed the proportion of full-time male manual workers working overtime actually *increased* from 1981 to 1983. At least a quarter of an overtime worker's annual wage comes from overtime work. Indeed were it not for such overtime pay many employees on the basic wages would be below the level for eligibility for Supplementary Benefit. This is a crucial point and its morality must be challenged. Britain is for the most part a *low-wage, long hours economy.* Hence, any policy for reducing overtime must be linked to raising the basic hourly rate (and also output per worker) if workers are not to be substantially impoverished. The output per hour of British workers increased much less rapidly than her European competitors in the 1970s; although in the 1980s the gap has narrowed, Britain is still in a poor position from which to make an attack on overtime.

9.71   Despite the difficulties we have referred to, there are indications based on opinion polls in Britain that if employed people were given the choice they would be prepared to work fewer hours in a collective attempt to reduce unemployment even if that meant lower wage increases (but not, of course, wage cuts). We welcome the concept of 'job bargaining', and hope it will grow; but it must be in the first instance a matter for negotiation between employers and unions.

9.72   Nonetheless, in other countries in Europe more or less stringent controls on overtime have existed for many years. Clearly it can be done. Because of the over-riding importance of increasing employment, we *recommend* that the Government breaks the present conspiracy of silence and encourages public discussion of this issue.

The Manpower Services Commission

9.73   The work of the Manpower Services Commission (MSC) is prominent and influential in the Urban Priority Areas. Its Job Centres handle vacancies and so serve the needs of employers and employees, and they can provide advice on training and other matters to those who need it. The importance of the public employment service to residents in the UPAs cannot be exaggerated and we affirm our strong support for it. Although no detailed figures are available, it is probable that around 30 per cent of vacancies are filled by Job Centres in UPAs.

9.74   Training is one of the main responsibilities of the MSC. The initial training of the young and retraining opportunities for adults are essential to the thriving local economies we would wish to see develop in the UPAs. We welcome the importance now being given by the MSC and the government to adequate retraining opportunities for adults. And we welcome too the proposed introduction by MSC on behalf of the government of a two-year Youth Training Scheme (YTS).

9.75   The introduction of a two-year YTS means that the effective starting age of work for all young people will have become 18 before the end of this decade. This is a development which is long overdue in Britain and is to be warmly welcomed. A two-year period of vocational education and training will provide an introduction to working life needed by the young if they are able to develop themselves and face with confidence the uncertainties of a changing world. Above all, it will give all trainees the opportunity to obtain a vocational qualification. But to be fully effective and generally acceptable two conditions need to be met. First, resources must be sufficient to ensure that places are available and adequate training and further education facilities exist; and second, jobs need to be available for those who pass through the scheme.

9.76   Between July-September 1984, the national 'success' (i.e. full-time employment) rate of YTS was 59 per cent: in all the circumstances, an impressive figure. No separate figures are available for the UPAs, though the MSC figures for 'inner Merseyside' for the same period show a success rate of 39 per cent. The level of youth unemployment for the Partnership areas shown in Figure 9.2 would suggest that the UPAs generally will fare worse than other areas.

9.77   Figures are available for black youngsters leaving the YTS. Again between July-September 1984, only 38 per cent of young people of Afro-Caribbean origin, and 40 per cent of those of Asian origin leaving the YTS went on to full-time employment. There is also evidence that black young people are under-represented on Mode A schemes (which are employer-based).[20] A study by the Commission for Racial Equality[21] of 15 Mode A schemes found that:

there were virtually no black youngsters on them in multi-racial areas;

most black trainees were on schemes in London and the Home Counties;

the black trainees were much less likely to obtain permanent employment with the employer;

black youngsters who applied for YTS places were less likely to be selected than white youngsters;

216

some employers were using methods of recruitment which would result in indirect discrimination.

Persistent complaints were also made to us in regard to equal opportunities and racial discrimination. We had no opportunity to assess how widespread such complaints were; we simply record that they were made to us. We are glad to note however that the CRE's findings are being taken up with the MSC, and a positive response is promised.

9.78   Society will have made a considerable investment in the young people who participate in YTS. Yet there will be only an adequate return on this investment if a high proportion of young find jobs. This demands a comprehensive approach on an inter-agency basis covering:

advice and support;
information and finance;
provision of facilities for leisure, social, and educational activities and voluntary work;
education and training provision;
employment in temporary schemes and in temporary jobs or traineeships;
help to become self-employed.

We believe it to be justified to offer these facilities to YTS trainees in the UPAs and no doubt elsewhere.

9.79   The Community Programme (CP) for the long-term unemployed (including the many young people out of work for more than a year) has been a success, and its expansion recently to 230,000 places is to be welcomed. Yet we have heard criticisms:

the lack of employment opportunities in the UPAs at the end of a 12-month CP placement does lead to great loss of morale;

the training component of most CP projects is still inadequate. There is clearly a limit to what can be achieved in a year, but perhaps more could be done (including life skills training – without a blanket ban on discussion of 'political' issues);

limited eligibility rules, recently introduced, have the effect of excluding from the CP the unwaged who are not in receipt of benefits. This puts an unacceptable limit on who can enrol; women, particularly, suffer here;

many sponsors have complained about over-frequent changes in the MSC's detailed rules and guidelines.

217

We hope that the MSC will consider, and respond to, these criticisms. We *recommend* that changes be made to the eligibility rules, in particular.

9.80 Despite these reservations about the operation of the CP we *recommend* that the scheme should be expanded still further. The Government should offer some form of job guarantee on the Community Programme to those unemployed for a year or more. The promise of a year of useful work might not under the current proposals for income support improve their income, but it would help to give them a continued sense of purpose and allow them to make a contribution to their communities.

9.81 The cost need not be large. Expanding the Community Programme from 230,000 places to about half a million would incur a net extra cost to the Exchequer of about £550-£600 million. This would be a particularly cost-effective way of creating jobs, as a similar sum spent on general tax cuts would, according to the Treasury model, generate only about one-tenth as many.

9.82 The Community Programme can be expanded to the size suggested, with some broadening of the criteria for approving projects. This would mean negotiations between the MSC and the CBI, the TUC, and other interested parties.

9.83 The key issues are how much people get paid, and what they produce. At present CP pays the standard hourly rate for the job, but the MSC's permitted average weekly wage is limited to £63. Even though this means that many people work part-time, places have been easily filled. However, the relatively low pay makes CP more attractive to young single people than to those with families, and we *recommend* some relaxation of pay limits as an incentive for the latter.

9.84 The other question concerns the type of work offered. At present the programme is decentralized and depends on sponsors. This should clearly continue, but there is a need also for special initiatives that would meet social needs. As we have pointed out, the housing stock in the UPAs is in urgent need of rehabilitation; and there is much to be done in the social services. Priority should be given to these areas in expanding the CP as we propose.

9.85 The increase in places would offer a real administrative challenge. A similar challenge was met when the Youth Training Scheme found more than 450,000 places within a year. The guarantee would (as before) be a Government statement of intent, not a legal obligation, and it should be announced now to provide the extra places within the next two years. It would clearly be easier to deliver the guarantee if regular employers also increased their demand for the long-term unemployed. The abolition of the employers' National Insurance contributions for the first two years after such a person has been recruited would encourage this.

Income Support

9.86   Even if the demand for labour in the UPAs were to be increased by measures of the kind we have suggested, the scale of unemployment is such that these would still not solve the problem. High levels of unemployment in UPAs will persist.

9.87   The philosophy of the Beveridge report was based on the expectation of full employment coupled with a system of non-means-tested benefits. National Assistance (which has now become Supplementary Benefit) was a safety net for the few – claimed by 1 person in 33 in 1948. By contrast, in 1983, Supplementary Benefit was claimed by 1 person in 8. Since the Beveridge report, the real value of National Insurance benefits has been eroded, so that now many are worth less than Supplementary Benefit. However, in the present day it is the increase in long-term (in many cases permanent) unemployment – particularly marked in the UPAs – which has transformed the scene.

9.88   We have noted earlier that in August 1985 there were over 1.3 million people who had been out of work for at least a year, 800,000 for over 2 years and 50,000 for over 3 years. Nationally, two out of every five unemployed people have been unemployed for a year or more. In the UPAs, the proportion is much higher. Even in January 1984 (see Figure 9.1) it was between 40-50 per cent, and in Liverpool over half the total number. The position will be much worse now. We believe that society has a special obligation to the long-term unemployed, as they are carrying much of the burden of our economic transition. A lifetime without paid employment faces many who are fit, able and who want jobs. Our collective obligation must be to mitigate the hardships they face.

9.89   The long-term rate of Supplementary Benefit (in 1984-85, £35.70 per week for a single householder; £57.10 per week for a married couple) is not paid to unemployed people after a year on benefit. Instead, a single person receives £28.05 per week and a married couple £45.55 per week. To be faced with long-term unemployment and to be restricted to these rates is to face a particularly cruel economy. The long-term rate recognizes that it is more difficult to survive on benefits after a year, because savings are exhausted and clothes and household goods wear out. It is unjust that unemployed people should be barred from the higher rate.

9.90 The Government have said that the annual cost of paying the long-term rate of Supplementary Benefit to the long-term unemployed would be £480 million[22] and that, *on the ground of cost alone*, any change cannot be justified. We disagree. The cost is equivalent to an additional ½p on the basic rate of income tax. To meet the objective that all citizens should be enabled to share adequately in the life of society, those facing the prospect of long-term unemployment should receive the higher rate of benefit or a similar premium under the proposed new system of income support, and the taxation system should be used to finance this. We so *recommend*.

9.91 We consider that two priorities stand out in addition to more equitable treatment for the long-term unemployed. Our *recommendations* are:

(a) First, that the Government should significantly increase the level of *Child Benefit*. The needs of families with children are particularly pressing, and Child Benefit provides the most effective direct means of meeting these needs. It is a universal benefit, and we are aware that some may argue that it is not targeted at those who are most in need. But it is a crucial means of preventing poverty, and a cost effective way of helping the low-paid. We are dismayed that under present proposals Child Benefit is not to be uprated in line with inflation, let alone increased in real terms.

(b) Second, that the Government should raise the *earnings limits* below which social security claimants are allowed to earn income without losing benefit. People should be provided with an income support 'floor' from which they can, without disincentive, seek work – rather than a benefit provision which forms a 'ceiling' which traps them in their poverty. At present claimants of Supplementary Benefit can earn up to £4 a week before they face benefit withdrawal pound for pound (this 'earnings disregard' has not changed since 1975). Claimants of unemployment benefit can earn up to £2 per day before their benefit starts to be withdrawn. Thus the poverty trap and the unemployment trap are perpetuated. The system which operates in relation to the Manpower Services Commission's Enterprise

Allowance Scheme avoids these pitfalls. Unemployed people can receive £40 a week from the Government for a year to start a new business and enjoy unlimited earnings during that time (so long as they put a minimum of £1,000 into a new employment project). There is no 'clawback' of the weekly allowance. The principle being applied here to the self-employed should apply to those seeking paid employment.

9.92   The need for reform of the current framework for income maintenance is widely recognized. The current system assumes that full employment is the norm; it is complex and difficult to understand; it relies increasingly upon complex and inefficient means-testing, and has the effect of reinforcing the already low self-esteem that many UPA residents suffer. The effects of the Government's recent reviews of Social Security[23] cannot be evaluated until figures for proposed benefit levels are made known. We can however comment on some fundamental principles set out by the Government.

9.93   First, we were glad to note that the proposals for income support envisage an end to effective marginal 'tax' rates of over 100 per cent – one of the worst features of the 'poverty trap'. Yet marginal 'tax' rates of over 90 per cent will still be possible under the proposed income support system (taking Housing Benefit into account). If reducing tax rates is a Government objective, it is surely unacceptable for the poor to face in effect higher tax rates than the rich.

9.94   Second, a flat-rate benefit, as proposed, will produce hardship if there is no discretionary element to help those with multiple disabilities. The present (albeit complicated) system provides additions to benefit as of right; a flat-rate system, although simpler, will mean for example that disabled people will no longer receive supplements for diet, laundry and heating.

9.95   Third, the proposed Social Fund for cases of hardship will offer loans, rather than grants, to claimants. Such an approach might be acceptable for relatively small numbers of claimants, for whom help can be tailored. If, however, a majority of claimants are going to need to depend on it – to 'plead poverty' – then not only are complexity and discretionary anomalies likely to be inevitable (how would the maximum level of assistance be decided in particular cases?), but the result may be to create a nation of poor people in debt.

9.96   We support moves to simplify the present systems of Social Security. But simplification must not be used as a means of worsening

221

the lot of those in poverty. It should rather be part of a move to re-distribute resources towards those in poverty – particularly those without a job.

9.97   Politicians may well ask: do you really believe that those in work would be prepared to make real financial sacrifices to help those who are in poverty – particularly those out of work? We believe that they would – provided that the sacrifice was a *shared one* and *equitably made*. There is a collective concern about poverty and unemployment which has yet to find a means of being translated into action. A survey carried out in 1983, reported in the Government's *Social Trends 1985*, indicated that by a substantial margin (72 to 22 per cent) the public's view was that the gap between those with high incomes and those with small incomes was too large. In the same survey, 32 per cent of people said that more should be spent on health, education and social benefits out of increased taxation. Only 9 per cent wanted cuts in taxation with less spent on health, education and social benefits. The overwhelming preference was for either the present mix of tax and expenditure on social programmes, or if not, for an increase in both tax and expenditures. This was confirmed in November 1984, when a Gallup Poll found that 58 per cent of a nationally-representative sample said they would prefer to see health, education and welfare services extended (even if it meant increases in taxes), and only 12 per cent wanted priority to be given to tax cuts. We are aware that social survey evidence of this kind cannot be conclusive. But it does indicate – and the Church should affirm – that there is a national tradition of collective altruism.

9.98   The experience of poverty is not however simply a matter of how much money is made available. It is also about how it is made available. The way the social security system operates in the UPAs was criticised by a number of those who gave evidence to us. The staff in benefit offices are facing increasing workloads: they are overworked and overstretched. The ratio of Supplementary Benefit office staff to claimants rose from about 1 in 96 in January 1979 to 1 in 128 in January 1983.[24] The greater accessibility of inner city social security offices – coupled with the relatively large number of claimants – leads to a higher proportion of callers. Waiting times are long. An efficient system of appointments is difficult to operate. The offices themselves are often drab and demoralising. The introduction of the Housing Benefit scheme, with its well-documented shortcomings, has compounded the problems of delivering benefits speedily and efficiently. Any system of social security is bound to have its complexities: adequate resources for the efficient and humane distribution of (and advice about) benefits are therefore needed if the dignity of recipients is to be respected.

9.99   The Church in its parishes in the UPAs can play a role here. A particular service it can offer, in conjunction with local authorities and advice agencies, is to help people to make representations about problems they face with claims for benefit; to help with information about rights and entitlements – or point people to specialised agencies who can offer advice; and to give support and encouragement to people to go forward and seek their rights. In 1981 the Government estimated that over £500 million in benefits went unclaimed. Not only would this sum help those entitled to their share of it, but by being spent would help local economies.

9.100   Looking to the future, we believe that a national strategy needs to be developed 'capable of taking the question of poverty into the mainstream of public debate about this country's future'.[25] *Ad hoc* reviews of parts of the social security system are not enough. A much more wide-ranging and longer-term look is needed. We believe that this calls for, and *recommend*, the establishment of a major independent review body with the authority to examine the objectives and mechanisms of the welfare state across a broad canvass.

9.101   The review body would need to investigate what would be a realistic 'poverty line' income which would allow Supplementary Benefit claimants to participate in the life of the community – an assessment of need rather than what can be afforded. The basic question – what are benefits supposed to cover? – has not been answered since the system was introduced in 1948 but has merely been uprated each year (and even in 1948, the levels were based on figures constructed by Beveridge ten years earlier and insufficiently uprated). Since 1948 there has been no attempt to set rates according to some agreed standard of what they should, and could, actually buy. The rates for children, in particular, have never been costed, even by Beveridge, but based on the assumption that whatever the subsistence needs of adults, those of children are less.

9.102   Because of the interrelationship between tax and benefits, the review would also have to include an examination of the effects of the fiscal system (specifically excluded from the 'Fowler Reviews'). If there is a concentration on selective benefits for the worst-off, the result is to push down the living standards of those whose poverty is more marginal. Those in intense poverty tend to be dependent on benefit;

those on the margin are those who are in work but low-paid. As the taxation burden has been shifted towards the low-paid, and the value of Child Benefit has been eroded, the position of the low-paid has worsened. Over 80 per cent of those who claim Family Income Supplement (which tops up low wages) also pay tax. Benefits, pay and taxation form an economic triangle; they must be examined together. The only way to remove the 'poverty trap' is to integrate taxes and benefits in a much more sharply stepped system.

9.103   Some of us take the view that there is merit in further thought being given to a 'basic income' scheme, of the kind canvassed by the Basic Income Research Group. If full employment can no longer be guaranteed, it has been suggested that 'the only fair system would appear to be one in which a basic income was paid to all residents automatically, irrespective of their income from employment'.[26] We would be naive to commend this without recognizing that much work still needs to be done in charting how such a system might be implemented and financed. But we believe there is a pressing need to look at radical alternatives such as this to the present and proposed system of income maintenance. The establishment of a major independent review, as we have suggested, would be the most appropriate way of assessing the various options in an authoritative and comprehensive manner.

Work Not Employment?

9.104   If high levels of unemployment in the UPAs are to persist, as we fear, and even if the position of those without a job is ameliorated by increased income support, a challenge *still* remains. How can people who cannot find employment be enabled to do work which the community will value, and in so doing gain a degree of self-respect and self-esteem?

9.105   If paid employment is not going to be available to all, if there is going to be an increase in part-time employment, if we are to see more women entering the labour market, we must reassess many of our current attitudes to work.

9.106   What constitutes 'work'? We can all understand that there is a distinction between work and paid employment. For example, the housewife and mother (or, less rarely now, the husband undertaking this role) is not paid to do all the various jobs involved in running a home: housework, child rearing, cooking and so on. DIY jobs in the home combine unpaid work and hobby. Equally, much voluntary work is unpaid – but it is work nonetheless. There is a great variety of socially-useful and economically-useful activity undertaken outside the framework of paid employment. Work is, in short, 'doing something useful', for yourself or others.

9.107   It can be argued that there is enough potential status for everyone, because all work carries some status – and there is more than enough work to do. There are difficulties with this approach.

9.108   First, as we have noted earlier in this Chapter, participation in all types of work by an individual is far greater if he or she is in a paid employment. An unemployed person is less likely to be 'doing something useful' around the house, or in voluntary or other groups (though some do).

9.109   Second, for people without traditional paid jobs to view other forms of work as fulfilling, and providing self-esteem, will require not just a change of attitude on their part, but on society's part as well. Society values us by what job we are in and how much we earn; and as society views us, so we tend to view ourselves.

9.110   The Church must affirm that each of us is valued by God, in whose image we are made, for ourselves – and not for what we do. It must continue to explore and interpret human relationships in our changing society. But there is also a need, in a situation where our future understanding of 'work' is uncertain, *for a variety of practical measures to be explored to encourage and enable people to undertake creative and useful activity.*

9.111   Church members can contribute individually, and corporately, to practical initiatives. For example we believe that help should be given to enable more work to be done by unemployed people in and around the home. More 'self-provisioning' is needed – but this may require help with tools and training. We welcome the initiative taken by Church Action with the Unemployed (under its 'launch pad' scheme) to provide small cash grants to enable unemployed people to buy the tools for work of this kind. Schemes of this nature deserve to be supported by local Churches.

9.112   At a local level the Church can also bring its resources to partnership initiatives to create new employment opportunities. In some neighbourhoods, the resources of the Church – people, premises and equipment – are the only ones based locally. Some inner city Churches are already making a contribution in this way – examples being the 'CATS' project in Leeds, and Inter-Church Endeavour in Birmingham. We do not want to paint too rosy a picture – in many UPAs all the Church's energies are taken up with the struggle to survive. Yet we would encourage and *recommend* wider participation in local employment schemes.

9.113 A sustained pastoral response to the needs of long-term unemployed people is also needed. Present Church structures are not well suited to making such a response. On the one hand, industrial mission has developed a deep understanding of the nature of long-term unemployment, its impact on people, and the future of work. Yet industrial chaplains rarely have time and resources for creative counselling of unemployed people (or may not see it as their role), nor do they necessarily have the means of conveying to clergy and congregations their experience of the need for local action. On the other hand, many local congregations are not adequately equipped to react on their own initiative to the complexities of unemployment.

9.114 It was put to us in evidence by Church Action with the Unemployed (CAWTU) that 'no part of the present Church structure finds it easy to accept an unqualified commitment to work on long-term unemployment, with the challenge to attitudes, work patterns, and time allocation that is involved'. There is now a critical need within the Church to build on existing good practice in unemployment initiatives.

9.115 For example, in the Liverpool Diocese, a chaplain with special responsibility for unemployment issues has been appointed with the Liverpool industrial mission. There is an unemployment officer in the Diocese of Sheffield, and the South London Industrial Mission has as one of its team members someone with a special concern for unemployment. We suggest that more appointments of this kind should be considered. We *recommend* that the future development of industrial mission should respond in such ways to the acute and persistent high levels of unemployment in many areas.

9.116 The corrosive effects of endemic unemployment and low pay in the UPAs are a major challenge to the Church and the nation. Those of us – the large majority – lucky enough to have a well-paid job owe it to those who do not to say we do not condone the situation and the inequalities to which it gives rise; we do not consider our relatively fortunate position to be our natural right; that we are part one of another; and that we must continue to strive to develop a society in which the political structures enable all its citizens to share adequately in the economic development of the nation.

Main Recommendations

1. The Church of England should:

(i) continue to question the morality of economic policies in the light of their effects (paragraph 9.52).

(ii) take part in initiatives to engage unemployed people in UPAs in job-creating projects. The use of Church premises for this purpose must be encouraged (paragraph 9.112).

(iii) build on good practice in ministry to unemployed people: Industrial Mission has an important role to play here (paragraph 9.115).

2. The Government should:

(i) give a new impetus to support for small firms in UPAs, perhaps by the establishment of a Council for Small Firms in Urban Areas (paragraph 9.56).

(ii) increase job-creating public expenditure in the UPAs on capital and current account (paragraphs 9.62 and 9.64).

(iii) promote more open public discussion about the current levels of overtime working (paragraph 9.72).

(iv) relax the Community Programme eligibility rules and other constraints, including pay limits, particularly to encourage greater participation by women and unemployed people with families to support (paragraphs 9.79 and 9.83).

(v) expand the Community Programme to provide 500,000 places (paragraph 9.80).

(vi) extend to those unemployed for more than a year eligibility for the long-term rate of Supplementary Benefit, or an equivalent enhanced rate of income support under whatever new arrangements may be introduced (paragraph 9.90).

(vii) increase the present level of Child Benefit as an effective means of assisting, without stigma, families in poverty; and increase the present level of 'earnings disregards' in relation to Unemployment Benefit and Supplementary Benefit to mitigate the effects of the poverty and unemployment traps (paragraph 9.91).

(viii) establish an independent enquiry to undertake a wide ranging review of the inter-relationship between income support, pay and the taxation system (paragraph 9.100).

References

1   *Low Income Families 1981* – DHSS October 1983, Table 2

2   ibid Table 1

3   ibid Tables 1, 2, and 5

4   ibid Table 2

5   Estimate by the House of Commons library. Reported in *The Times*, 8 February 1985

6   Derived from Parliamentary Answers, House of Commons *Hansard*, 13 February 1984 c395–6 and 5 April 1984 c631–2

7   Source: Low Pay Unit

8   *Low Income Families 1981* (op cit) Table 2

9   Source: Low Pay Unit

10   ibid

11   Because the official statistics relate only to those unemployed people entitled to benefit, the actual total lies between this figure and 4 million, depending on which definition is adopted

12   Source: GLC

13   See, for example, S. Field et al *Ethnic Minorities in Britain*, Home Office Research Study No 68, HMSO 1981; R. Richardson *Unemployment and the Inner City – a Study of School Leavers*, DOE/MSC, 1983

14   MSC *Quarterly Report* May 1985

15   Olive Robinson and John Wallace *Part-time employment and sex discrimination legislation in Great Britain*, Department of Employment Research Paper No 43, 1984

16   R.E. Pahl *Divisions of Labour*, Blackwell, 1984

17   A.W. Coates (ed) *The Classical Economists and Economic Policy*, Methuen, 1971

18   See Professor D. Metcalf 'The cheap way to make jobs' in *Management Today* April 1985

19   A.J. Neale and R.A. Wilson: 'Employment' in *Public Expenditure Policy 1984-85*

20   *Ethnic Minorities and the YTS*, University of Bristol, October 1984

21   *Racial Equality and the Youth Training Scheme*, CRE, October 1984

22   House of Lords *Hansard*, 20 June 1984, c287

23   The 'Fowler Reviews': Cmnds 9517 – 9520, HMSO June 1985

24   House of Commons *Hansard*, 30 June 1983 c139

25   Submission from the National Council for Voluntary Organisations

26   ibid

Chapter 10
HOUSING

'People here have to live in a mistake' (Kirkby resident)

Introduction

10.1   Housing has been a dominant theme in the evidence presented to the Commission, both orally in the course of its field visits to the major metropolitan conurbations, and in the written submissions offered by the dioceses and by numerous other organisations and individuals. We have been told, loudly and clearly, that 'housing is a major issue'.

10.2   That this should be so does not surprise us. We have already described in Chapter 1 the part played by bad housing in the physical environment of the urban priority areas. Living conditions are such a basic necessity that they affect well-being in every aspect of life.

10.3   Our society has accepted that every citizen has a right to food, clothing, education and health care, adequate to his or her needs and irrespective of ability to pay. Yet appropriate housing, which is as fundamental to human development as health care and having enough to eat, has never been accepted as a right for all.

10.4   The evidence we have received covers every aspect of housing which will be examined in this Chapter. A common thread running through all the submissions, however, is the stigma which attaches to certain people because of where they live, which contributes to a widely-felt sense of powerlessness and inability to effect change. Similar phrases constantly recur:

'The labelling of the estate by outsiders – particularly those in statutory bodies – as a problem estate (it is still called Bangladesh by many people) does not help, and serves to reinforce the sense of powerlessness which many residents feel.' (Diocese of Carlisle)

'Policemen talk of local residents as "scum". They themselves believe that "we are rubbish". This is a sink estate. Young people know that there is no point in applying for jobs if you live there unless

229

you give a false address.' (Community worker in North Tyneside)
'People go to search for work and don't come back. No-one emigrates to *this* area.' (Unemployed man in Kirkby)

'"Can any good come out of Nazareth?" Many places which are stigmatized pass on that stigma to those who live there . . . and slowly but surely people who have *choice* move from these areas, until the place becomes a collecting point for those who have *no choice.*' (Diocese of Winchester)

10.5   Commission members in their visits to the major cities have seen bad housing of every description, and have been shaken by the experience. The housing we have observed and visited is not identical in every city, though there are common features.

10.6   We do, however, want to stress two important points. First, though the physical conditions of parts of the cities are squalid and depressing, the people who live in them possess worth and talents which are often squandered. They are being denied the opportunity to fulfil their God-given potential. We must all take care not to appear to label them as 'the problem'.

10.7   Second, we wish to endorse the stress placed in much of the evidence on corporate responsibility. For example: 'While the deprivation in Newham is self-evident, we do not believe that deprived areas are the cause of their own deprivation, but that the whole of society, of which the Church is a part, shares the responsibility.'[1] Again and again our evidence underlines the structural causes of the state of our cities, and the link with poverty and powerlessness. What has been clear to us as we have travelled round the cities is the link between bad housing and income. Poor people live in poor housing.

10.8   We believe that a home is more than bricks and mortar, more than a roof over one's head. Decent housing certainly means a place that is dry, warm and in reasonable repair. It also means security, privacy, sufficient space; a place where people can grow, make choices, become more whole people. It also relates to the environment in which the home is located as much as to the conditions inside the front door. Vandalism, graffiti, fear of violence, lack of play space, all affect how people regard their surroundings. How property is managed, as well as its physical condition, is important for it affects how people make decisions. To believe that you have no control over one of the most basic areas of your life is to feel devalued. We will examine how the housing in urban priority areas matches up to these criteria.

Choice and Mobility

10.9   Present government strategy relies heavily on home ownership: 'Our whole housing policy needs to be based on a recognition that we should give every assistance and encouragement to the preferred choice of the people; and that preferred choice is, overwhelmingly, for the pride and independence which go hand in hand with home ownership. We have opened up choice. And choice is at the centre of liberty' (Ian Gow MP, then Minister of Housing, June 1983). But for most low-income city residents, freedom of choice is a cruel deception. What characterises the housing conditions of many people in the UPAs is their lack of choice. Often they never wished to occupy their present home. Frequently they want to move, but know they have no chance. Past experience has led to low expectations. They feel they have no control over their surroundings. As one submission to us noted: 'The first thing which poor people are deprived of is power. That's why they get consigned to the places and the roles which no-one else wants to occupy.'[2]

10.10   In general, the quality of housing in the major metropolitan conurbations is significantly worse than that found in the rest of country. Housing in UPAs cannot be regarded in isolation from wider questions of social, economic and regional policy. The UPAs provide a sharp focus for the consequences of decisions – or lack of them – in other policy areas.

Homelessness

10.11   True choice and mobility require surplus. But in Britain today there is a shortage of good-quality secure homes to rent for those who have no chance to buy. Phrases like 'housing crisis' recur in newspaper headlines; what is less commonly recognised is the hardship which such headlines represent. Millions of people are suffering because they do not have a place which they recognise as a home.

10.12   The official homelessness figures (of those families accepted as homeless under the terms of the Housing (Homeless Persons) Act 1977) provide an indicator of the number of poeple who cannot find accommodation, and confirm the particular pressures on the inner cities.[3] Acceptance of homeless households in England has risen steadily each year, from 53,000 in 1978, the first year of the Act, to 83,000 in 1984. But these figures, dramatic though they are, are totally inadequate as a measure of need. They record merely those limited number of people, mostly elderly or families with dependent children, who are accepted as being in a 'priority category' under the Act. Fewer than half (45 per cent) of those who apply are accepted; and many people outside the priority categories do not bother to apply, knowing that they will not be housed. Local authorities have no duty to provide for those who are deemed to have made themselves homeless 'intentionally', and this is commonly interpreted as covering anyone who leaves accommodation to take up a job elsewhere, even if they have previously been unemployed.

10.13 Even when people are accepted as homeless, shortage of local authority accommodation means that they may have to spend long periods in temporary accommodation, often in dirty, overcrowded and unsafe bed and breakfast hotels. Well over 10,000 families a year[4] are being placed by local authorities in this kind of accommodation, often in a single room. Environmental health officers have found appalling conditions – gross overcrowding, cockroaches, bathrooms without hot water, dangerous fire risks. A large number of the hotels inspected have been classified as unfit for human habitation.

10.14 In November 1984 a Bengali mother and her two young children died in a fire in a hotel full of homeless families. Fire extinguishers were empty and exits blocked. The coroner recorded that 'inadequate fire precautions and means of escape greatly contributed to the deaths'. There is no time limit on the period of temporary accommodation, and in London families are being told that they will have to wait two or three years before they are rehoused. Even then, there is no definition of the quality of permanent housing that must be offered. The easy option for local authorities possessing 'hard to let' (a euphemism for 'hard to live in') stock is to use it for homeless families, generally by means of a policy of 'one offer only'. If that is rejected, the council has no further responsibility. Thus in some local authorities the most vulnerable families are forced to accept the worst stock. This has a double advantage for the authority: it solves a lettings problem and at the same time acts as a deterrent, much like the workhouse under the Poor Laws. Only those who are really 'genuine' and in desperate need will apply, because the conditions are so atrocious that no one would do so if they had any other option.

10.15 It is a mark of the lack of alternatives that despite all these major criticisms the 1977 Act is still regarded as a significant advance. For the first time certain categories of people who are unable to secure housing for themselves can turn to the local authorities. It is unfortunate that the Act came onto the statute book at a time when expenditure on new

232

public housing was being cut back severely (as it still is), so that local authority administrators have been under pressure to interpret it in the most minimal light.

10.16   Single people were largely omitted from the priority groups in the 1977 Act because of lack of resources, but it was envisaged that this exclusion would be temporary. Eight years later, however, their situation has worsened considerably, particularly in the cities. Very few of the households accepted as homeless are single, unless they are old or severely impaired. Single people have no legal right to housing. The building of low-rent housing by local authorities represented an acknowledgement that the private sector would not provide for low-income families; the underlying assumption, however, was that it would provide a sufficiency of accommodation for single people. Consequently, there is very little accommodation for single people, with the exception of the elderly, in most local authority stock, and some local authorities will not even permit single people to register on their waiting lists. The decline in the private rented market has hit single people particularly hard, at a time when their numbers are growing. The 1981 Census showed the population of the inner cities to be in decline; the sole area of growth was that of single person households which are projected to continue to rise significantly.[5] Yet very little provision is being made for their needs.

10.17   In a competition for a scarce resource it is the poor who will lose. An increasing number are forced to resort to cheap lodging houses, or to large institutional hostels which date back to the Victorian period and are due for closure, though replacement has been slow and inadequate. Some sleep rough. The numbers are unknown because no one has a responsibility to record them. Many are 'hidden homeless', continually moving between friends and relatives in search of something permanent.

10.18   Faced with the unwillingness of private landlords to let to anyone who is not employed, many single people have no option but to seek 'board and lodging' – accommodation in commercial hostels or bed and breakfast hotels. The word 'hotel' conjures up images of holidays and luxury living; in fact, as we have seen, these places are usually cramped, insanitary and a fire risk. But because costs to the DHSS are rising, a direct result of the increase in numbers forced into this provision[6] the response has been to place a ceiling on the amount that can be claimed, irrespective of the cost charged. There is no suggestion as to what people should do if they cannot find provision within the limits, as many are now discovering.

10.19   Those under 26 years old are penalised yet further. 'Shock-horror' campaigns in the popular press describing life on the 'Costa del Dole' have suggested that thousands of young people are enjoying an extended holiday in seaside towns at the taxpayer's expense, rather than attempting to look for work. The reality is very different. Most of those in seaside towns have gone there because of the opportunities for casual work; and the DHSS have been unable to produce evidence of widespread abuse. But at the end of April 1985 their residence in board and lodging was restricted to a certain number of weeks (broadly, eight weeks in London, Greater Manchester, Birmingham and Glasgow, and four weeks in the rest of the country, except for seaside towns where the limit was two weeks. A few categories of vulnerable people were exempted from the regulations, as were non-profit-making voluntary hostels). If at the end of that period they had not found permanent accommodation they had to move to another town and repeat the process. They could not claim board and lodging payments in their original town within the next six months, even if they had lived there all their lives. (At the time of writing the imposition of a time limit has been declared unlawful by the High Court, and an appeal is being considered. The Government has declared its intention to seek Parliament's approval to authorising legislation if necessary. Meanwhile, the ceiling on amounts claimed remains.)

10.20   Leaving home is a normal step towards independence. For those who are fortunate enough to go to university it has long been accepted that supervised accommodation in a college or hall of residence should be provided, at least for the first year. Meals and services are provided to bridge the transition between home and total independence, and to give space for decision-making about the future. Trained counsellors are available if required. Yet for an increasing number of those under 26 who are unemployed and dependent on benefits, leaving home would mean being forced to move around the country, unable to remain long enough in any one location to find permanent accommodation or a job. It would be impossible to sign on with a doctor, or to register to vote. The alternative would be the insecurity of moving between friends and relatives, sleeping on sofas and floors, with no permanent home – or, in despair, ending up on the streets. The final irony is that the Government's Review of Social Security declares that because 'most single people under 25 are not householders' they will be eligible for a lower rate of benefit (and Housing Benefit) than over 25s – so that if they should be successful in finding permanent self-contained accommodation they may not be able to afford it.

10.21 Homelessness as defined by law is the most extreme form of housing need. But those with low incomes have such limited choice that their housing is frequently far from satisfactory, whatever tenure they occupy. Throughout England as a whole, 63.5 per cent of the housing is owner-occupied, 25.3 per cent rented from local authorities, 8.7 per cent rented from private landlords and 2.6 per cent from housing associations. Urban development and the drift to the suburbs has resulted in a very different tenure pattern in the cities, with much less owner-occupation and a much higher proportion of rented accommodation, both public and private,[7] as Figure 10.1 shows for Inner London, Birmingham and Manchester in 1982.

FIGURE 10.1

Housing Tenure, 1982

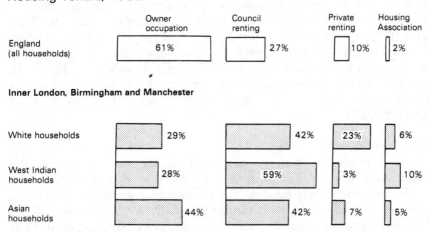

Source: Department of the Environment (Housing and Construction Statistics) and Policy Studies Institute

(a) *Owner-Occupation*
10.22 Owner-occupation is heavily concentrated in the outer suburbs. With the exception of parts of London, inner city owner-occupiers are characteristically on a low-income, often elderly, with a mortgage paid off but little or no money to carry out essential repairs.

Their houses are frequently in a poor physical state, but grants, even where available, make little impact because of the owners' inability to find the requisite percentage contribution (sometimes compounded, in the case of the elderly, by unwillingness to experience the upheaval caused by large-scale renovation). Some would like to move, particularly to be close to sons and daughters who have moved away, but have discovered that the value of their house is insufficient for them to purchase elsewhere.

(b) *Private Rented Sector*

10.23 Although nationally less than one dwelling in ten is currently rented from a private landlord, the vast majority are concentrated in inner city areas where they represent a much higher proportion of the stock. Much of the accommodation provided is poor value, insecure (because of landlords devising ways to circumvent the security of the Rent Acts), of low quality and generally in a bad state of repair, often in multi-occupied houses with shared bathrooms and cooking facilities. The Institute of Environmental Health Officers estimate that 80 per cent of these houses in multiple occupation require some action to be taken under the Housing Acts to remedy unsatisfactory conditions. Well over 100 people die every year in fires in such properties. Except for the luxury end of the market very few people would willingly choose privately rented accommodation; increasingly those who occupy it are (mainly elderly) long-term tenants, immigrant families crowded into one or two rooms, and single people forced there by lack of alternatives.

(c) *Public Rented Housing*

10.24 Intended – with a great deal of success – to break the connection between bad housing and ability to pay, this tenure has never been adequately funded. The result is that supply has never met demand and has had to be rationed, usually by allocation policies bureaucratised into rigid systems of assessing and comparing need. Thus the lack of income that has enabled people to qualify has often resulted in a service that is grudging. Too often council housing has been regarded as 'housing suitable for poor people'. The Poor Law ethic dies hard.

10.25 Social rented housing in the cities varies enormously in standard, from the very desirable to the 'hard to let' and even unfit, from self-contained houses with gardens to flats in concrete slab blocks. What characterises urban development is the skyline; virtually all of the

1960s system-built blocks and towers – and their accompanying problems – are found in the major metropolitan conurbations. Though most of such housing is well-designed internally, the environment is depressing, and frequently frightening: badly-lit corridors, underground walkways, litter, graffiti, and vandalism are all common features.

10.26 In the outer ring estates, the problems of the inner city are compounded by poor and often expensive transport, resulting in a feeling of isolation and loss of contact with relatives (one of the positive features mentioned constantly in North and South Tyneside was the impact of the metro, enabling children living to the north of Newcastle to keep in touch with grandparents in, for example, South Shields). There are no focal points, no buildings with a history ('even the churches are new'). Shopping is bad and worsening as unemployment reduces purchasing power and causes local shops to close down. Many people are dependent on expensive mobile shops which tour the estate.

10.27 What struck us forcibly in every city we visited was the sense of powerlessness experienced by those in the worst housing. Most of them had had no choice at all in the flat or even the area to which they had been allocated; they wished to move but were told the transfer lists were closed. No-one seemed to care.

Who Suffers?

10.28 For many people in the UPAs, choice is minimal at best, and usually non-existent. But two groups, women and black people, are bearing a disproportionate burden.

10.29 Many of the elderly owner-occupiers in decaying terraces are widows, unused to handling housing maintenance and afraid of being swindled by 'cowboy' builders. Their children have moved away from the area and they are unable to join them. They feel deserted and alone.

10.30 Middle-aged single women have been hit hard by the decline in the private rented sector. The mansion blocks which may have been their home for fifteen or twenty years are being bought up by developers and turned into luxury flats or bed and breakfast hotels. Harassment is illegal, yet virtually impossible to prove. Without self-contained accommodation they feel ashamed of their surroundings and cease contact with their acquaintances. Isolated, they are even more vulnerable to pressure. Their average income is two-thirds that of men.

Yet housing association waiting lists are closed and local authorities restrict them even from registering for housing.

10.31   Women's homelessness is on the increase, particularly among young women. Homelessness is however traditionally considered to be largely a male problem, and there is very little emergency or hostel accommodation available for women.

10.32   When families become homeless it is usually women who have to try to look after children in the squalid conditions of bed and breakfast hotels or homeless family accommodation, just as they have to cope with the family in a tower block flat, with nowhere safe for the children to play. Single parents, usually women, get offered the worst accommodation ('they wouldn't be able to manage a garden').

10.33   If women bear a particular burden of bad housing, that of black people is even greater. They experience all the effects of lack of investment in housing suffered by white men and women but are doubly disadvantaged by discrimination because of the colour of their skin. We have noted in Chapter 9 the evidence that black people are discriminated against in employment, so we know that they suffer disproportionately from low income. This fact alone, however, damning though it is, is not sufficient to account for the well-documented disadvantage in housing suffered by black people, whose housing conditions are seen consistently to be worse than those of the white population.[8]

10.34   Racial discrimination in the private rented sector has long been recognised, but in a situation of scarcity is almost impossible to prove. The Race Relations Act of 1968 outlawed overt discrimination; no longer may notices be displayed proclaiming 'No blacks'. But every black person who has tried to find private rented accommodation knows how often the room that is available when they telephone has 'just gone' when they arrive at the house.

10.35   Investigations by the Commission for Racial Equality confirm that despite prohibitive legislation there is still direct discrimination against black people trying to rent or buy in the private sector. In 1980 it was found that two accommodation bureaux which let private flats for landlords had for many years been accepting discriminatory instructions to reject applications from 'blacks', 'coloured tenants', 'Asians', 'immigrants' and 'foreigners'. In the same year a formal investigation into a firm of estate agents found that the particulars of white applicants were kept on white cards and those of black applicants on pink cards.

When vendors specified that they did not wish to sell to black people, only the white cards were produced.[9]

10.36   This kind of discrimination has long been known: and it provides one of the reasons why black people of Afro-Caribbean origin, under-represented in inner city private rented accommodation, are heavily dependent on the public sector. What has taken a long time to be accepted is that although black people gain access to public rented housing, the homes that they are offered are consistently of poorer quality, in system-built or unmodernised flats, and in unpopular areas. In 1971 the all-party Parliamentary Select Committee on Race Relations and Immigration recommended 'as a matter of urgency' that the Department of the Environment start discussions with local authorities on the keeping of records and statistics on ethnic origin and housing in order to find out the extent of discrimination against black people. It took five years for the DoE to respond and then only with a consultation paper suggesting that 'it was up to each local authority to decide whether it wished to keep such records'. Yet each detailed analysis of a local authority's lettings policy, from the GLC's own investigation ten years ago to the recent investigations of Hackney and Liverpool carried out by the Commission for Racial Equality, have confirmed that black people were being allocated the least desirable properties.[10]

10.37   There are many different reasons why this happens, from the working of points schemes and the properties offered to homeless families, to administrative policies that happen to discriminate and the attitudes and assumptions of lettings officers; as we keep reiterating, every area is distinct. But there is no reason to suspect that the authorities which have been monitored are any different from the others. Most urban authorities pride themselves on their colour-blindness; those who oppose monitoring usually do so on the grounds that it is unnecessary, that their authority allocates solely on the basis of need and treats everyone equally. The facts suggest otherwise; and it is only when the facts are collected and analysed that corrective policies can be formulated. All the evidence that we have seen and heard convinces us that ethnic records should be kept, and monitored, by public housing authorities as a step towards eliminating the injustice of discrimination. We so *recommend.*

10.38   In the absence of detailed information of this kind, ignorance breeds prejudice. What has concerned us on our visits is that, far from recognising that black people are allocated the worst accommodation, many white tenants perceive them as 'jumping the queue' and receiving favourable treatment. It is crucial that these feelings are understood, for they are closely linked to the racial harassment which has become a disturbing – and increasing – phenomenon of many urban areas. Misconceptions about black people's access to public services become significantly more important when those services are in short supply. White tenants in East London who cannot get a transfer to a house with a garden, or whose sons and daughters have to move away because they cannot find any accommodation in the area, look for someone to blame, and see the Bengalis. Their attitudes are transmitted to their children, already alienated by fear of unemployment and vulnerable to the arguments of the National Front and British Movement, who take it out on the 'Pakis' – who happen to be physically small. We have heard of families too frightened to leave home without an escort, of physical attacks, of constant smashed windows. Lack of investment in housing, together with the effects of unemployment, is directly related to the increase in racial harassment.

10.39   In saying this we are not in any way minimising the responsibility of housing management officials and of the police, about whom we have heard serious criticism. Both can do much to increase public confidence by swift and sympathetic action. Yet we have heard complaints of councils refusing to take complaints of harassment seriously, alleging that tenants were 'using it as an excuse to get a transfer', and of police slow to arrive on the scene of incidents and unwilling to attribute a racial motive.[11]

The Physical Condition of the Housing Stock

10.40   Many housing problems are invisible to those who are not immediately involved. But what cannot escape the attention of even the most casual observer is that the fabric of our cities is crumbling. The 1981 House Condition Survey found that over 6 per cent of the stock (1.1 million houses) was unfit for human habitation; and more than one house in ten was either unfit, lacking basic amenities or requiring repairs costing more than £7,000 (at 1981 prices). If those homes needing repairs costing more than £2,500 were included, then one quarter of all houses in England were unsatisfactory.

10.41   Once again this is a particular problem for the inner cities since defects are heavily concentrated in the pre-1919 stock, particularly terraced property with a low rateable value, characteristic of inner city housing, much of it privately rented or owned by low-income occupiers. One in six of all the houses in the private rented sector is unfit; and there is a disturbing decline in conditions in the owner-occupied stock. The Survey found that the houses requiring greatest attention were those containing households with the lowest incomes. Most could not afford to take up an improvement or repairs grant.

10.42   Since nearly one-third of the country's housing was built before 1919, and half of these houses require repairs, this gives rise to serious concern. Houses are deteriorating faster than they are being renovated or replaced. At the 1983/84 rate of clearance it would take 1,000 years to replace the existing stock. Yet from June 1984 VAT has been levied on building alterations. This has repercussions for inner city housing associations, frequently important agents of inner city renewal, as well as for individual home owners.

10.43   Concern is not restricted to the older stock. Serious design faults have been discovered in the system-built blocks built to cope with the post-second world war housing shortage. The systems were largely untested and have been found to be subject to water-penetration and consequent dampness. External cladding is falling off high-rise blocks, causing serious anxiety about safety. Heating is often all-electric and heat loss is excessive, resulting in large fuel bills and frequently debt. Sound insulation is inadequate, increasing tension between neighbours.

10.44   The Association of Metropolitan Authorities (AMA) estimates a cost of £5 billion to repair, or in severe cases demolish and replace, non-traditional houses built in the 1940s and 1950s. An equal sum is calculated to be necessary to remedy the defects of the industrialised building of the 1960s and 1970s. Recent independent research on Ronan Point, for example, the tower block in Newham where five people died in a gas explosion in 1968, has shown a severe fire risk and dangerous structural weaknesses. Nine blocks are to be demolished. In addition, the AMA calculates that a further £9 billion is required to repair and upgrade council houses built between 1920 and 1960 by traditional methods. The total repair bill is thus estimated at £19 billion for local authority housing alone. Recently the Audit Commission noted that the construction and repair bill for the total housing stock could be as much as £30-40 billion.

Housing Policy

10.45   Britain is suffering from the lack of a coherent housing policy. The last official estimate of housing need was made eight years ago, in the 1977 Housing Policy Review. The Government has refused to update this, claiming that housing forecasts are unreliable and serve no useful purpose. Owner-occupation, as we have noted, is a clear policy goal; but even on the most optimistic forecast it will never be available to a substantial minority of the population. We now examine each of the main housing tenures, and consider the options for increasing the choices of those on low incomes.

The Private Rented Sector

10.46   The traditional tenure of the single and mobile, the private rented sector has in the past offered ready access to housing for new arrivals in an area, especially those coming to places of high employment to search for work. It also provided for those on lower incomes who could not afford to buy and who had been unable to secure, or were not eligible for, local authority housing. But the sector has been in steady decline for many years. This is commonly attributed to the 1974 Rent Act which is held to have dried up the supply by giving unlimited security to the tenant. In fact the greatest loss of stock followed *decontrol* in the 1957 Rent Act.

10.47   The reason for the decline is largely economic. The private rented sector flourished when building costs and interest rates were low, and building for rent offered a safe and profitable form of investment. The requirements of the landlord and the tenant happened to coincide. Private renting is no longer a commercial proposition. Given high land and building costs, as well as fluctuating interest rates, there is little or no incentive to build to rent, except perhaps at the luxury end of the market, since market rents will be higher than (subsidized) mortgage payments on the same property, and the average tenant could not afford to pay a rent that would give the landlord a competitive return on his capital. Many existing landlords are selling their property to owner-occupiers.[12]

10.48   It is important to remember that, from the first industrial expansion of the cities, there has always been a discrepancy between the provision of good-standard accommodation and ability to pay. Without subsidy there has never been sufficient financial incentive for the private landlord to provide for the poorest, without overcrowding. The Royal Commission on the Housing of the Working Classes in 1884 discovered appalling conditions, the prime cause of which was poverty, 'the relationship borne by the wages they receive to the rents they have to pay'.

242

10.49   To provide landlords with the kind of financial inducement that would compete with rates of return elsewhere would require either a total restructuring of the housing finance system or a substantial increase in payments for income maintenance. The House of Commons Environment Committee, reviewing the private rented sector recently, concluded that rents must at least *double* in order to provide an incentive for landlords to continue investing. At this level of rents those who could afford to pay would normally be better off buying, while those who had no alternative to renting could only afford to pay if subsidized through a staggering increase in public expenditure on some form of housing benefit. Since this seems unlikely, we cannot see a future for the expansion of this tenure.

Owner-Occupation
10.50   Nationally, a steady increase in owner-occupation has been sharply accelerated by the sale of council houses. At the end of 1978 some 56 per cent of houses were owner-occupied; by mid-1985 the figure was over 63 per cent. Owner-occupation is popular because it offers a substantial degree of control over environment and more mobility *within an area* than any other tenure. (The vast discrepancy in house prices between the South of England and elsewhere – the average terraced house bought at the end of 1984 cost £49,910 in Greater London and £15,640 in the East Midlands – makes a move to the South East, in particular, very difficult without assistance from employers.) Owners enjoy the possession of an appreciating asset which is free from Capital Gains Tax.

10.51   Owner-occupation for the majority of those who can afford it offers the maximum choice, determined by ability to pay. Many people are strongly motivated to own the house they occupy, to have the greatest possible control over their surroundings. Certainly, for those who are able to buy, it is a choice which makes good financial sense.

10.52   But owner-occupation will never be available to everyone. The Building Societies Association (in a paper prepared for the Enquiry into British Housing) projects an expansion to 72 per cent of the population by the year 2000. Once the council house sales boom dies down (and it is already tailing off significantly) there will be little opportunity for low income households to become owners; it is possible for existing tenants only because of discounts of up to 60 per cent.

10.53   The most likely area of expansion is the provision of homes for young couples, where both partners are working with below-average incomes and there are no children. Some recent initiatives by public authorities to encourage low-cost ownership, notably shared ownership (where first-time buyers can purchase a share of a house and rent the remainder at a fair rent until they can afford to increase their share of ownership) have helped some young people on the margin of ownership. But overall their impact is limited in inner areas. The same is true of private sector initiatives. Though there is currently a small amount of new private building in the inner city, this is largely accounted for by 'starter homes' for single people and childless couples, most of whom will almost certainly move to the suburbs when they have children.

10.54   It is important here, as so often, to distinguish between London and the other metropolitan areas. In the latter the relatively short distances to the suburbs permit easy commuting. For those who work in Central London and the City, however, travel-to-work times are much greater and fares, particularly from the Home Counties, considerable, and so there is a much greater demand for high-income ownership within the inner city. There are few large sites available for new building in the Greater London area and consequently there is a greater demand for nineteenth-century terraced property. In a few areas there is significant low-income home ownership but as its elderly occupiers die or move they are usually replaced by young professionals. 'Gentrification', though it may reverse the trend of movement to the suburbs, may displace low-income people from formerly rented areas. In Docklands we were told of local young couples, who could otherwise have just afforded to buy, being forced out of the area by the high prices of the new development. Other families were unable to be housed locally because of the lack of funding for public rented housing.

10.55   For many people in the UPAs, low wages and rising unemployment put home ownership beyond their reach. The only chance of housing will be to rent. And increasingly rented housing will be necessary for existing owner-occupiers hit by unemployment. The number of repossessions for mortgage arrears is rising sharply each year. Ten per cent of the families accepted as homeless in the first quarter of 1985 had lost their homes through mortgage arrears; in the first six months 7,400 houses were repossessed by building societies, over twice as many as in 1981. Though the 1985 figure is still small in statistical terms, representing just over 0.1 per cent of the 6.3 million building society mortgages, there has been widespread concern over the rapid increase in the number of people unable to keep up their repayments. Over 50,000 borrowers were more than six months in arrears in mid-1985.

Council House Sales

10.56 Concern about the effects of the sale of council houses has featured largely in the evidence we have received. 'The sale of the century', a central plank of the Government's extension of home ownership, was heralded as breaking up tenure division and creating new mixed communities. But that assumes that all local authority housing is of equal quality and desirability. What has happened is that many couples, who have progressed up the local authority 'ladder' and arrived at the desired goal of the low-rise house with a garden, are being offered a once-in-a-lifetime opportunity – and quite understandably are seizing it. They may well have two incomes coming into the house, and they are offered a discount of up to 60 per cent. They have hit the jackpot.

10.57 As one would expect, it is the best stock that is being sold, almost all houses with gardens. The Right to Buy has had less impact in the cities because a much higher percentage of the stock is flatted, as a result of slum clearance. But having accepted the mistakes of the 1960s development, local councils have returned to building much sought-after terraced housing, sometimes even with tiny gardens. Many of these are now disappearing from local authority stock, whose mix is beginning to be affected by sales.

10.58 We have spoken to numerous young families in barrack blocks who have given up hope of a transfer to a house. One local authority, keen to increase the percentage of home ownership, has even designated all its most desirable estates, together with any individual houses that become vacant, as 'sales only'. They are offered to council tenants, certainly, but if they cannot afford to buy the houses are offered on an open waiting list. The tenants remain on their high-rise estates.

10.59 In order to prevent these estates becoming 'ghettos', poor housing for poor people, as already exist in the large urban centres in the USA, it is important that properties that are sold are replaced with others of equal quality. Sales to existing tenants can fulfil their aspirations and provide a better tenure mix in areas dominated by local authority housing. But polarization will only increase if the estates with houses become owner-occupied, while those families dependent on rented accommodation have no choice but concrete high-rise, and no hope of a future move to a house with a garden.

10.60 We see therefore that those on low incomes in the UPAs have virtually no choice over access to housing. Rising unemployment and low wages put home ownership beyond the reach of most new households. What little accommodation remains in the private rented sector is expensive and of poor quality, and generally unavailable to families with children. The result is a growing polarisation based on tenure and class. Choice is non-existent; public rented housing is increasingly the only option.

Public Rented Housing

10.61 It will be argued by some that public housing has failed: local authority provision has resulted in a product that no-one wants. Certainly there is much to be criticised, particularly in styles of management. We have been told how councillors in the past would regard council housing as 'theirs' to distribute. ('Come to my surgery next week and I'll see you right'.) Just as the Conservative Party since 1918 has seen home ownership as at the same time a 'bulwark against Bolshevism' and a seed-bed of Tory votes, so Labour authorities have seen the provision of housing to their constituents as a cementing of a natural bond. Paternalism has flourished.

10.62 In our visits we have seen much that is bad. We were asked to include the outer area overspill estates in our examination of UPAs, and we have become convinced that some of these estates are more deprived even than some inner areas. But at the same time we have looked behind the 'despair, hopelessness and apathy' referred to so often in evidence to us and seen some of the reasons:

(i) The original concept of 'streets in the sky' was based on an idea of self-contained communities with shops, entertainment, pubs, launderettes and community facilities built into the original design. Constraints on costs dictated by central government meant that these facilities were not provided by the local authority but had to wait for commercial provision. As a result, on many estates it was years before there was even a shop.

(ii) Although the traditional stance of the Labour Party has been to see council housing as open to all who want it, and not just for one particular social class, resources have never been available for there to be sufficient quantity to meet demand. Consequently it has always been allocated on the basis of need, with some kind of points system giving highest priority to low-income families with young children.

This has resulted in very unbalanced communities, in terms of class, income-distribution and ratios of children to adults. Compounded by the effects of long-term unemployment, particularly among young people (low morale, low income, forced to stay at home yet no facilities to occupy them), they are likely to become even less attractive.

(iii) People often did not want to go to particular estates in the first place – or did, regretted it, and wanted to move out. Certainly once an estate gained a bad reputation, only those people with no other choice remained, or accepted a nomination. We have also been told of estates that were already considered slums when they were brand new because they rehoused residents from an old slum area, who brought their notoriety with them.

(iv) Maintenance has been skimped from the beginning, resulting in an atmosphere of neglect. Governments, both national and local, have seen more votes to be won in meeting new construction targets than in cyclical painting.

(v) The maintenance service is seen as very unresponsive. At many public meetings we have attended the poor delivery of repairs has featured high on the list of complaints.

(vi) Tenants have, almost without exception, never been involved at any stage. Tenant opinion for example had always been against the building of high-rise estates. Pre- and post-war surveys show that the overwhelming majority of people who were re-housed in such estates would have preferred a house with a plot of garden.

(vii) 'We make things worse by placing some of the most vulnerable people in some of the most expensive environments created by progress. Those cruel policies are not due merely to administrative ineptitude which could fairly easily be put right. They reflect the powerlessness of the poor . . thus housing authorities reduce the capital costs of their buildings by putting them on cheap, inaccessible land and by installing central heating systems which are as cheap as possible in capital cost. That makes the houses very expensive in transport and fuel costs (which the tenant has to bear). Then they call these neighbourhoods not 'hard to live in' but 'hard to let', or even 'problem estates' – as if their difficulties were somehow the fault of the tenants.'[13]

10.63 But, at the same time, we have seen many signs of hope. Many local authorities, having long since transferred the allocation of housing to professional officers, have now begun to devolve decision-making to a more local level. We have been impressed with the work done by both the Priority Estates Project (PEP) and the NACRO-sponsored Safe Neighbourhoods Unit in regenerating run-down estates. When PEP began in 1979 only three councils throughout the whole of England had full-time, estate-based management offices. By early 1985, 50 councils were operating about 80 projects.

10.64   They have found that the two key elements of success were (i) consulting and involving the tenants from the start and only proceeding with those improvements that were seen as priorities by the tenants, and (ii) the local authority's willingness to set up an office on the estate with officers who were willing to work closely with the residents, and who had authority to make decisions. It was also essential to complete some physical improvements early on in order to build up a belief in the possibility of change, and to overcome apathy and scepticism. There was no point in raising tenants' expectations without a budget to carry out at least some of their priorities.

10.65   Although services such as locally-based repair teams, cleaning and intensive caretaking could be cost-effective, in that they reduced the number of empty properties and thus increased rent income, they were not cheap. At the same time environmental improvements, in some cases involving major capital expenditure, were necessary to upgrade old estates and remedy design faults in 1960s concrete blocks.

10.66   A distinction was made between the inter-war 'cottage estates' on the outskirts of northern towns, which were usually run down because of lack of modernisation, allocation policies and often isolation from the main centre of population; and the modern concrete complexes which were characterised by their confusing lay-out and sense of anonymity, creating a fear of mugging, but which often contained attractive modern and popular flats. The cottage estates were relatively easy to regenerate through good management and capital spending on modernisation of kitchen, bathroom and heating systems because the basic design of the housing was what tenants wanted. The walk-up blocks can be very successfully 'capped' (i.e. the top two storeys removed) and turned into very attractive terraces, as we have seen in Liverpool. The Safe Neighbourhoods Unit has shown how estates can be made more secure by closing off 'bridges', and also how large concrete jungles can be divided into smaller units, with different names and their own staff, so that tenants feel part of a manageable community.

Privatization

10.67 Where small-scale 'hard-to-let' inner city estates have been converted for home ownership, the finished product has been impressive, as we saw in Liverpool. But the design and environmental improvements that have been thought necessary to attract owner-occupiers are the same as those desired by the tenants. Security has been assured, there is 24-hour caretaking, and flats which were once cramped three-bedroomed family accommodation now provide spacious living for single people and childless couples. The lesson of this kind of development is that if money is spent on upgrading and intensive staffing, and people are allowed to occupy the space they feel they require rather than the space they are allocated, then the image of the housing is transformed. But had these features been incorporated originally, the estate might never have become 'hard-to-let' in the first place.

10.68 It is too early to assess the effect of the privatization of a vast outer-area estate such as Cantril Farm/Stockbridge Village in Kirkby. Certainly its image is now beginning to change, because people can see that something is happening. On-site management has greatly improved the repairs and maintenance service. But at the time of writing the scheme has run into financial difficulties, and the tower blocks, which had been intended to be renovated and sold, are now likely to be demolished. Again sharp questions have to be asked about the reason for the estate's original deterioration. The estate manager told us that certain parts of the estate had had no maintenance at all carried out in the 17 years since their completion. He also admitted that people were never transferred off the estate. Their requests would be 'lost', because the estate had such a poor reputation that any unit vacated would take a very long time to fill.

10.69 One of the issues raised by estate privatization is the underlying assumption that 'private is good, public is bad'. Local authorities are not permitted to raise the money to carry out the work themselves; but government assistance is available to the private sector in the form of Urban Development Grant. This cannot be tapped if the local authority is renovating its own property. In order to attract the developer, the estate may have to be sold for less than its historic debt. Less than half Cantril Farm's outstanding debt of £15.1 million was covered by the purchase price; the rest will remain as a charge to the Housing Revenue Account, with no rent income to cover it. Nor is privatization restricted to 'sink estates' which have already been abandoned. Concerned that privatization may be held up by tenants who do not wish to move elsewhere, the Government is currently proposing to abolish council tenants' security of tenure where privatization is intended.

The Voluntary Housing Movement

10.70   Housing associations, which provide accommodation to let at a 'fair rent', are non-profit-making and managed by voluntary committees. Many had their origins in local councils of churches, and church members are still represented on their management. Originally charitably-funded, since 1974 they have received grants from central government through the Housing Corporation and through local authorities, and are totally dependent on this funding for new development. Despite a striving for independence therefore, their financial dependence makes them increasingly subject to central government policy. Nevertheless, though accounting for only 2.6 per cent of the national stock in 1985 they are a signficant force in the inner cities where a relatively small number of associations have played an important part in inner city regeneration. In the cities the majority of their work is in rehabilitation, restoring the older stock. Their role has always been a pioneering one, exploring new initiatives and pointing directions for the future. Much of their work is with housing for elderly people; recently they have been investigating the possibilities of helping elderly owner-occupiers to get repairs done to enable them to stay in their own homes rather than moving into sheltered accommodation. A considerable part of their activity in urban areas is with single people, providing a range of accommodation from small-scale intensively managed hostels for groups needing special care, to independent flats and bedsitters. Because the properties tend to be individual dwellings rather than on estates, housing association homes are sometimes more popular than local authority ones, though cost limits mean that the majority of urban development consists of flats rather than the houses with gardens which most would prefer.

Public Housing – the Way Forward

10.71   In our visits we have looked critically at local authority housing provision. Though not all our impressions have been favourable, we have seen much that is innovative and exciting, and are heartened to discover what can be done. This is one of the most crucial areas of public policy. As owner-occupation is extended, how society treats those who cannot afford to buy – and who have little electoral power when 60 or

70 per cent of the nation are home owners – is an important touchstone.

10.72   There has always been an inner city housing problem, even before the rise in unemployment, in recent years, added a new dimension. Thus policies based on general economic regeneration of the inner cities, though crucially important, will not in themselves necessarily correct their housing problems.

10.73   The great importance of the public housing ideal was that it broke the link between poverty and living conditions. The poor did not have to live in poor housing. But this link is now being re-established. At a time when the decline in private rented accommodation is putting greater pressure on the public sector from those people who cannot afford to buy, public housing has been selected to bear the brunt of the public expenditure cuts. Net capital spending was cut by 44 per cent in volume terms between 1975/76 and 1979/80, and by 52 per cent in cash terms between 1979/80 and 1984/85.[14] The result is that the number of new homes started in the public sector has dropped over the last decade from 174,000 in 1975 to 38,000 in 1984. At the same time there has been a shift in expenditure away from the metropolitan districts and London in favour of the shire districts. The inevitable result is long waiting lists for housing association and local authority homes. For those in poor accommodation this means at best a long wait in unacceptable conditions, at worst the news that there is no hope.

10.74   The scale of the housing problem in UPAs is such that it cannot begin to be contained, let alone reversed, without a net increase in the housing programme financed by public expenditure. A new building repair and renovation programme would, as we suggest in Chapter 9, make economic sense. A programme of investment in building, repair and renovation would give useful work to some of the 250,000 construction workers on the dole, at the same time as giving hope to many in bad housing. If this is not done soon, it will be impossible to expand the industry quickly at a later date. Already almost the only building employers training apprentices are local authorities. The Controller of the Audit Commission warned recently that unless investment in training was significantly increased, traditional building skills would not be available for a major programme: 'We will be back where we started and someone in Whitehall will have a bright idea about something called system building.'[15]

10.75   He also criticised the waste of local authority money on bed and breakfast accommodation. The Chartered Institute of Public Finance and Accountancy (CIPFA) has estimated that the total net cost to local authorities in England and Wales in 1984 of placing families in bed and breakfast was well over £10 million, a rise of 50 per cent on the previous year – and that is merely for the families for which authorities have accepted responsibility. The cost to the DHSS of keeping claimants in ordinary board and lodging accommodation was £380 million in 1984. Yet though it has been estimated that it would be cheaper to provide permanent rented accommodation, none of this money may be spent on investment in construction.

10.76   Numerous organisations, from the Audit Commission to the National Economic Development Council have condemned the inefficiency and waste of the use of construction as an economic regulator. The system of annual allocations makes strategic planning a nonsense; and because it is virtually impossible to control construction spending on a year to year basis there is seesawing between under- and over-spending. A three to five year planning period, with guaranteed budgets, is required for maximum efficiency.

10.77   We can see no alternative to, and *recommend*, an expanded housing programme of new building and improvement to ensure a substantial supply of good quality rented accommodation available to all, including single people.

10.78   We also *recommend* that the 'priority categories' under the Housing (Homeless Persons) Act should be abandoned and the Act extended to cover all who are homeless. Homeless people should not be treated differently from any other applicants; all should have a choice of accommodation, which would have to be of a satisfactory physical standard.

10.79   There should be a recognition that people require different types of accommodation at different stages of their lives, so the choice should include small hostels, shared flats, independent flats and bed sitting rooms, family housing and sheltered housing. Since the family of the future is likely to spend more time and do more work at home, because of increased leisure, early retirement or unemployment, space standards need to be reviewed. Public housing is particularly ungenerous in space for living areas; there is an implicit assumption that all the family members, with the exception of the wife and young children, will be out of the house all day.

10.80   Each authority's stock should include a range of types of accommodation, including well-staffed direct access emergency accommodation. Some accommodation would be furnished, to meet the needs of those who require mobility. (To facilitate geographical mobility, e.g. for employment, there would have to be a small surplus above the level of need. Restrictions on movement between areas would have to be lifted.)

10.81 People should be able to choose what form of housing they wanted to occupy, and the degree of involvement in management. Not all the accommodation would belong to the local authority. Some would be built and managed by housing associations, who have always specialised in small-scale pioneering work. Some would be managed by tenant co-operatives. Residents should be involved in the design process and consulted, seriously, over renovation. Housing co-operatives should be encouraged.

10.82 The emphasis should be on flexible, mixed communities. Tenants would have the right to buy their homes, which would be replaced elsewhere so that there remained a constant stock of attractive rented accommodation to provide mobility. Residents would be able to move between tenures; e.g. some might rent at first, become owner-occupiers, then move back into rented accommodation as old age approached, and they wished to be free of the responsibility for maintenance. Others might choose to remain tenants or members of a co-operative.

10.83 Housing should be tailored to the needs of the residents instead of vice-versa. New building would be small-scale. Like housing associations, local authorities should be able to buy individual houses in a street. They should be able to build or buy large houses for large families.

10.84 The lessons of the past will have to be acted on. Some system-built housing is capable of being renovated; but we have to recognise that there will be some estates whose design faults are so serious that they will never provide accommodation that people will choose to live in, whatever money is spent on them, and these will have to be demolished.

10.85 Housing management will have to become much more responsive. We welcome the moves towards decentralisation of local authority services and *recommend* that this should be extended. All tenants should have access to a neighbourhood office, perhaps responsible to the local management committee, which would provide

253

the base for all local authority services in the area. Management should be at a level which has power to get things done. Staffing should be permanent so that tenants know the people with whom they are dealing. High quality training would be essential. Maintenance and repair should be given a much higher priority (and funding) and should also be locally based so that tenants would get to know those who were carrying out work in their homes. A caretaking service should be provided 24 hours a day. Overall, the general ethos would no longer be 'this is good enough for someone like you – count yourself lucky to have it', but 'you are paying for a service, and have a right to expect it to be delivered to the best of our ability'. The element of choice, flexibility and control which characterizes ownership should be extended to rented housing.

10.86 The proposals we have set out above add up to a major reform of our housing policies. Only in this way, we believe, will the powerlessness that is such a prominent feature of the UPAs be overcome. They add up to an extension of rights. The right to decent, secure housing would take its place beside the right to an adequate education, to appropriate health care, to food and clothing.

10.87 Clearly, it is not going to be possible, even with adequate funding, to achieve all these objectives overnight. It will be necessary in the interim to give additional protection to ensure the health, safety and security of all tenants, particularly those in the private sector where the worst conditions obtain, until there is an adequate stock of secure rented accommodation available to them.

Housing Finance
10.88 How would such a major reform of our housing be funded? We want to stress that our first concern is for those in bad housing conditions. Public spending is about choices. If housing is recognised as a priority, money will be made available for it.

10.89 Nevertheless, we recognise that unless total public spending is increased, the additional resources necessary for public housing must be achieved either by taking them from other expenditure programmes not linked to housing, or by redistribution of existing housing expenditure. A number of the submissions we have received have made references to the funding of housing, and the inequity of distribution between subsidies to owner-occupiers and to council tenants. While investment in public rented housing through local authorities and housing associations has been steadily cut back, the cost of assistance to owner-occupiers through mortgage tax relief, regarded by Inland Revenue as income foregone and thus not subject to public expenditure constraints, has risen without limit.

10.90   In 1985/86 local authorities will be permitted to spend a total of £2.29 billion on housing capital and current expenditure (excluding Housing Benefit). This is cash-limited and therefore subject to restraint. It is also increasingly dependent on asset sales: 43 per cent of gross spending is projected to be financed by the sale of council houses, which reached a peak in 1982 and is now falling off. By contrast the 1985 Public Expenditure White Paper estimates that mortgage tax relief will cost £3.5 billion for 1984/85, an increase of 27 per cent on the previous year.[16] With higher interest rates, the total for 1985/86 is likely to be considerably higher.

10.91   Furthermore, it should be noted that the present system of tax relief is an inefficient method of encouraging owner-occupation, since it gives most help to those who need it least. Tax relief on the interest is available, regardless of income, to anyone who buys a house with a loan from a building society, local authority or bank, up to a ceiling of £30,000. The relief is calculated at the level at which tax is paid, so that the average buyer receives relief at the standard tax rate of 30 per cent. If his income is such as to take him into a higher tax bracket he receives tax relief at that level, up to a maximum of 60 per cent (for incomes of £42,000 or more). So those on high incomes, presumably adequately housed, receive more assistance than those who are struggling to buy their first home. Although tax relief certainly helps the first time buyer, by reducing costs in the early years, it is also available at the same (or higher) level to the existing householder who is 'trading up'. Despite the extension of owner-occupation to many further down the income scale, nearly two-thirds of those benefiting are earning over £10,000 a year, and about half are earning over £12,000. The average relief given for a mortgagor earning £9,000 a year is £430; to one earning £30,000 it is £1,290.

10.92   Crucially, too, mortgage tax relief does not necessarily produce any addition to the housing stock. The Bank of England decided recently to investigate the diversion of mortgage money into other forms of spending and discovered that in 1984 net new loans worth £16.57 billion were made for house purchase, but net private sector spending on housing was only £9.36 billion. £7.21 billion was withdrawn for consumer spending, a figure which the Bank believes to be an underestimate. Between 1982 and 1984 this money, borrowed to fund housing, has added the equivalent of 3.5 per cent to consumer spending.[17]

10.93   One of the many misconceptions about housing finance is that home-owners are self-reliant, buying their houses with no resort to the state, while public sector tenants are the recipients of huge hand-outs. *In fact the reverse is the case.* Because of the imbalance of subsidy, the cost to the community in lost tax revenue of a house built or sold in the private sector is now greater than the long-term cost of providing a home to rent. Council house rents have risen by 150 per cent since 1979/80, with the result that the majority of councils receive no Exchequer subsidy and an increasing number make a *profit* on their housing which is transferred to the general rate fund. Council tenants, whose average income is less than half that of the average mortgagor,[18] not only have to pay service charges to cover the salaries of people like caretakers, cleaners, people to maintain the lifts and the grounds, all of whom would be unnecessary if they lived in terraced housing at street level; some also pay twice (in their rents as well as rates) for services such as estate lighting and cleaning.

10.94   The promotion of home ownership is a deliberate political decision, encouraged directly by central government subsidy and indirectly by withdrawal of subsidy from local authority housing, and the pushing up of rents. The cost of choice for the majority is the absence of choice for the minority who will never afford to buy. As the Shaftesbury Project argues, 'the Right to Buy and growth of owner-occupation are effectively carried on the backs of poor people'.

Relationship Between Fiscal and Income Maintenance Systems
10.95   It is important to understand the facts about housing subsidy because housing problems are so greatly affected by decisions about income maintenance. As we noted in Chapter 9, much of the rise in welfare spending is a direct consequence of other government policies. The Review Teams set up by the Secretary of State for Health and Social Security ('the Fowler Reviews') were specifically instructed to disregard all tax benefits and allowances, including mortgage tax relief. We have commented in Chapter 9 on some of the Government's subsequent proposals. In relation to housing we would want to underline our belief that it is inequitable to disregard mortgage tax relief, which gives most help to those who need it least, while cutting Housing Benefit, which helps those on low incomes. Since no figures have as yet been published, it is impossible at the time of writing for us to say exactly how many people will lose; but it has been estimated that in order to cut £500 million, between 5 and 7 million of the estimated 8.2 million households eligible for Housing Benefit (including 48 per cent of all pensioners)

could be worse off.

10.96   The proposal that every claimant, whatever their income, should pay 20 per cent of their rates in the name of 'local accountability' illustrates the inequities of a simplified flat-rate system. Housing costs, including rates, have always varied considerably across the country, and Beveridge rejected the idea of a flat rate allowance for housing costs because of the hardship it would cause. This was endorsed by the Housing Benefit Review team, whose report is the only one to be published. They believed that there was 'little evidence to suggest that low income households have any real control over their housing costs' and concluded that 'for those on supplementary benefit or equivalent net income it would be unrealistic to suppose that even a small proportion of housing costs could be met at the expense of other personal requirements'. On the Review Team's own figures for *regional averages*, domestic rates nationally vary between £108 and £712. A 20 per cent contribution, financed out of general benefit rates, will hit particularly hard at families in high rate areas and at those with large families.

10.97   We have seen the hardship caused to so many families in badly designed or insulated housing (over which they have no control) who have to pay for fuel out of their standard benefit. People often have to choose between food and heat. A National Consumer Council survey found that one in three of all local authority tenants complained of damp or condensation. Fuel has been used as a mechanism for raising revenue[19]; it is expected that the same will happen with water rates. Since claimants are now to pay their water rates out of their benefit they will not be protected against above-average increases.

10.98   We concluded in Chapter 9 that there is a need for a major independent examination of fiscal policy and income maintenance. Having looked at the acute housing problems of our cities we *recommend* that there should be a similar examination of the whole system of housing finance, including mortgage tax relief, to give most help to those most in need. It is unjust to tell those in bad housing that we cannot afford to do anything for them, that there is no money available to provide them with a home, and at the same time give subsidies to those on the highest income.

The Church's Response
10.99   'The Church of England has had a lengthy history of involvement with housing. Initially concerned with providing temporary

257

shelter for the homeless, it moved to being both a provider of homes for the poorer sections of society and an agitator for reform in the conditions in which the poor were housed.'[20]

10.100   The Church of England's tradition of providing housing for the poor dates back to the medieval almshouses. We have looked at the Church's role in housing associations, many of which originated from the initiative of local councils of churches. Some of the signs of hope that we have seen are found in the innovative projects of these organisations. A recent initiative is the London Churches Resettlement Agency, launched in 1984 jointly by the Bishop of London and Cardinal Hume, to help release the human resources of local congregations who want to provide small-scale housing at a local level for homeless people.

10.101   The Church has been less visible in recent years as 'an agitator for reform'. In the past it has spoken out unequivocally on behalf of the housing needs of the poor. In the early 1930s Bishop Garbett of Southwark told the Convocation of Canterbury that the overcrowded conditions of three and a half million people in England and Wales were 'a practical denial of the belief in the Fatherhood of God'. In 1933 the Archbishops issued a call to all members of the Church of England to join a campaign for the provision of decent housing for everyone, in connection with which Bishop Garbett issued a five-point plan for action, *The Challenge of the Slums*, addressed both to Christians and the Government.

10.102   It took 50 years for there to be another Synod debate on housing, which resulted in the referral by the General Synod of the 1982 report on *Housing and Homelessness* to the dioceses. Most appear not to have given it major consideration.

10.103   The Church of England, through its representation in the House of Lords, certainly plays a part in discussion of housing legislation. During the passage of the 1980 Housing Act, for example, the then Bishop of London played an important role in tabling clauses which attempted to seek protection for single homeless people. The current Bishop of Southwark is following in his predecessor's footsteps, devoting his maiden speech in the House of Lords to housing and speaking frequently during housing debates. But too often debates in the Lords go unreported, and the bishops' voice is unheard outside the Upper Chamber.

10.104   At the present time housing is not an issue of general public concern. Well-housed people's perceptions of the housing problem vary tremendously according to where they live. As we have seen, the majority of the well-housed live in the outer suburbs, well away from and often ignorant of the conditions of the inner areas. Many church members share in this ignorance.

10.105   At local as well as at national level there is a need for information and education, both to raise awareness of the housing situation and to combat the stereotyping attitudes towards those most in need.

10.106   The Church has a responsibility to inform, to speak out to its members. In 1980, for example, the Bishop of London and the Roman Catholic Archbishop of Westminster issued a joint pastoral letter on homelessness in London which was read out in all the churches in their respective dioceses.

10.107   We have argued earlier that there is a need for a redistribution of housing resources, including mortgage tax relief. Successive governments have shied away from tackling this issue for fear of electoral unpopularity. Given the socio-economic composition of Church of England membership it is likely that a large number of its members are receiving this assistance.

10.108   The evidence we received from the Diocese of Coventry was typical of many diocesan responses in calling on the Church to witness to sacrificial sharing: 'The themes of Sharing, Collaboration and Partnership have kept recurring in this résumé. This should be no surprise to the Church which has the Holy Communion as its central act of worship. We share in the Body and Blood of Christ as we remember, give thanks and are given new life by Christ's self-giving love on the cross. But it is the whole Church that is the Body of Christ – the rich and the poor, the strong and the weak. Divided – we may all perish. In partnership – we shall grow in grace'.

10.109   If we truly believe that we are all members of one Body, then we have a responsibility to show that we are prepared to share our personal wealth. We echo the challenge made to its members by the Department for Social Responsibility of the Roman Catholic Bishops' Conference in their recent statement, Housing is a moral issue: 'People are generous enough when they perceive the extent and depth of an emergency. The generosity, in this case, will consist not of a one-off gift, but a resolution to face up to a continuing moral demand. Those of us who have, must be prepared for policies which require sacrifices for those who have not. It is the manifestation of such willingness which will persuade and empower a government to release and divert necessary resources'.

10.110   In addition to the challenge to personal responsibility, the Church of England has a duty to examine the impact of its corporate actions. In Chapter 7 we looked at the issues faced by the Church in the stewardship of its own property; in particular, the likely impact on its witness when local people see a redundant church replaced by luxury flats. But the Church's witness can also be affected by the consequences of the Church Commissioners' holding of residential property as part of their investment portfolio.

10.111   The Church Commissioners control some 4,300 dwellings in London, the majority on three main estates: the luxury, high-rental, Hyde Park Estate, the Maida Vale Estate, and the low-rental Octavia Hill Estates in Walworth and Lambeth.

10.112   We have received evidence which suggests that the Commissioners' holdings in some areas of London, especially the Hyde Park Estate, are so large that they have a significant impact on rents and property prices in the area.

10.113   The Maida Vale Estate is currently making headlines. The Commissioners, having offered the properties for sale to sitting tenants, are now inviting offers for multi-occupied tenanted blocks from housing associations and property investors.

10.114   One of us has visited the Octavia Hill Estates. They provide low-rent housing, responsibly managed. The sense of community among the tenants was encouraging. The Octavia Hill Estates offer a good combination of social benefit and financial return. They make a profit because they have been held for so long that all historic debt has been repaid. The needs of the tenant and those of the landlord happen to coincide. But this may not always be the case.

10.115   For the Church Commissioners a dilemma can arise between their need to sustain a high financial return on their investments in order to provide adequate clergy pensions and to contribute in other ways (e.g. through stipends) to the ministry of the Church on the one hand, and the need for responsible stewardship of resources in the light of the social needs of the area concerned on the other. At a time when values are such that sales will produce a consistently higher return than the rental income available on the same property, there may be particular pressures on the Commissioners to sell to commercial buyers. This may well encourage the local community to conclude that the Church does not seem to care about housing and the needs of local people. The process of 'gentrification' in parts of London suggests that this issue, which is currently of relevance in Maida Vale, may occur elsewhere too.

10.116   The Church Commissioners accept that, for the reasons we outlined in discussing the private rented sector, there is no profit to be made by increasing their holdings of rented housing. Given the potential conflict between financial return and social responsibility in so sensitive a matter as inner city housing, we believe that Church involvement in housing should be developed in the future through non-profit-making housing associations, such as Church Housing, rather than as part of an investment portfolio.

Conclusion

10.117   We have examined the structure of housing in the urban priority areas, looking particularly at how it meets the needs of the poorer members of our society, and have found it totally inadequate. It is clear to us that the present housing situation of the UPAs is quite unacceptable. There are many different visions of what our housing policy should be as well as disagreements about the particular strategies that should be pursued. What is beyond dispute we believe is that a continuing emphasis upon home ownership alone will not solve the housing problems of the UPAs.

10.118   Housing is an expensive commodity; without some form of subsidy or financial help most people cannot afford a decent home. Lack of investment in rented housing hits hardest at the poor, who have no other option. If all are to enjoy decent, secure housing, if everyone is to have somewhere to live that they can truly regard as a home, then subsidies will have to be restructured. Housing in the UPAs is characterised by great inequality, with the poor suffering disproportionately both from substandard housing and from low income. It is this interaction of housing conditions and income that must be faced – and quickly.

10.119   The Report of the Enquiry into British Housing, chaired by the Duke of Edinburgh, was published too late for us to be able to consider its findings in detail. Yet it it clear that its analysis of the physical state of the stock, the need for an expanded rented sector, and the inequity of housing subsidies, particularly mortgage tax relief, is the same as our own. We welcome its stress on an integrated framework for housing policy, and its insistence that housing issues must be considered in a much longer perspective than the life of any government. It has provided a much-needed stimulus for debate.

10.120   We need to begin to rethink housing policy – and we should begin with people rather than political dogma, with the problems and hopes of the people who live in UPAs rather than an ideology of the right, or the left, or compromise. The Church's commitment to the values of the Kingdom is a vision that is rooted in justice for those who suffer; and it is precisely because we have seen so much suffering in the UPAs that we believe that the Church must state firmly and clearly that the present situation is unacceptable. The poor have a right to a home, which does not depend on their ability to pay. This must be the starting-point. Only when this fact is acknowledged can the nation begin to act. And there is no time to lose. Building programmes take time to plan, so it would be some years before an increased investment programme would take effect. The situation we face is urgent.

10.121   The Church at national and at local level has a part to play in this process. As *Housing and Homelessness* reminds us: 'A Church which has as part of its liturgy of initiation a prayer which asks "Grant that their homes may reflect the joy of your eternal kingdom" cannot but be concerned that many people in Britain live in conditions which predispose them towards social disadvantage and which offer little chance of creating an environment in which human life can flourish'. Church members throughout the country have a responsibility to their brothers and sisters to ensure that each of them can enjoy a decent home.

10.122   The time has come for decent secure housing to be accepted as a fundamental right for all. We have set out the directions in which we believe public policy must develop for this objective to be achieved, and have made the following specific recommendations:

Main Recommendations

1.   Ethnic records should be kept and monitored by public housing authorities, as a step towards eliminating direct and indirect discrimination in housing allocations (paragraph 10.37).

2.   An expanded public housing programme of new building and improvement is needed, particularly in the UPAs, to ensure a substantial

supply of good quality rented accommodation for all who need it, including single people. Each local authority's housing stock should include a range of types of accommodation, including direct access to emergency accommodation (paragraph 10.77).

3.   The Housing (Homeless Persons) Act should be extended to cover all who are homeless. Homeless people should be offered a choice of accommodation (paragraph 10.78).

4.   There should be further moves towards the decentralisation of local authority housing services (paragraph 10.85).

5.   A major examination of the whole system of housing finance, including mortgage tax relief, is needed. It should have the objective of providing most help to those most in need (paragraph 10.98).

References

1   Submission from Newham Deanery

2   Submission from Professor David Donnison

3   The rate of acceptance of homeless families per thousand households at the end of 1984 was 1.7 for non-metropolitan districts, 2.7 for metropolitan districts outside London, and 4.8 for London as a whole and 7.2 for Inner London.

4   CIPFA statistics 1983/84: 10,726 households accepted as homeless by councils in England and Wales were placed in bed and breakfast accommodation, at a cost of £8.9 million. These are minimum figures, excluding families in 42 local authority areas which did not send information to CIPFA.

5   Single person households are projected to increase by 41.5 per cent between 1981 and 2001 (Department of the Environment projections)

6   41,000 in 1979, at a cost of £52 million; 108,000 in 1983, at a cost of £277 million; 139,000 in 1984, at a cost of £380 million

7   Figures of tenure by ethnic origin from *Black and White Britain: the Third PSI Survey* 1984

8   e.g. *The Facts of Racial Disadvantage: a National Survey*, David Smith, PEP, 1976; *Black and White Britain: the Third PSI Survey*, Colin Brown, Heinemann, 1984

9   *Report of Two Formal Investigations, (i) Mr G D Midda & D S Services Limited (ii) Allen's Accommodation Bureau*, Commission for Racial Equality, 1980; *Cottrell and Rothon Estate Agents, Report of a Formal Investigation*, CRE, 1980

10   e.g. *Colour and the Allocation of GLC Housing*, John Parker and Keith Dugmore, GLC, 1976; *Stacking the Decks: a study of Race, Inequality and Council Housing in Nottingham*, Alan Simpson, Nottingham CRC, 1981; *Bengalis and GLC Housing Allocation in E.1*, Spitalfields Housing and Planning Rights Service, 1982; *Race and Council Housing in Hackney: Report of a Formal Investigation*, CRE, 1984; *Race and Housing in Liverpool: a Research Report*, CRE, 1984. See also *Public Housing and Racial Minorities*, David Smith and Anne Whalley, PEP, 1975, and *Race and Council Housing in London*, Runnymede Trust, 1975

11 See *Police and People in London, Vol IV, The Police in Action*, David Smith and Jeremy Gray, PSI, 1983.

12 cf Halford Severn of the Freshwater Group, probably London's largest private landlord, quoted in the *Evening Standard* in May 1979: 'The reason we sell is not because of the security of tenure, it's more the level of income and the return on investment. It's purely a question of economics. The value of a vacant flat is much higher than the investment value of a flat when let.'

13 Evidence submitted by Professor David Donnison

14 Source: Public Expenditure White Papers: Cmnd. 7841, Table 2.7; Cmnd. 9428, Table 3.7 (GDP deflators derived from Cmnd. 9428, Chart 1.2.)

15 Speech by Mr John Banham to the Institute of Housing Conference, Summer 1985

16 *The Government's Expenditure Plans 1985-86 to 1987-88*, Cmnd 9428, HM Treasury, January 1985

17 *Bank of England Quarterly Bulletin*, Volume 25 Number 1, March 1985

18 Table 6 of the *Housing Benefit Review*, Cmnd 9520, gives the gross normal weekly household income of local authority tenants as £121.18, and that of owner-occupiers in progress of purchase as £252.73

19 Between 1979 and 1984 retail prices rose by 48 per cent; gas prices rose by 100 per cent, electricity by 72 per cent and solid fuel by 77 per cent (*Newcastle Social Audit*). This hits hardest at the poor whose fuel costs represent a much higher percentage of income (12 per cent for the bottom 20 per cent of the population, compared to 7 per cent of income for the middle 60 per cent and 5 per cent for the top 20 per cent of the population).

20 *Housing and Homelessness*, a Report from the Social Policy Committee of the Board for Social Responsibility of the General Synod of the Church of England, debated by Synod in November 1982.

Chapter 11

HEALTH

'Stress has replaced disease as the problem of the day' (GP in Birmingham)

11.1   None of us is a member of the medical profession, and we have not had the opportunity to undertake a full-scale study of health care in the UPAs. However, during our visits to urban priority areas we were able to meet a number of people involved in community health work; some of us also met representatives of the British Medical Association concerned with general practice, and of the Royal College of General Practitioners. These discussions, along with the evidence taken from recent studies on health in urban areas (especially the Report of the DHSS Working Group on Inequalities in Health),[1] form the basis of this short Chapter of our Report. The fundamental conclusion reached from these sources – and from our own limited observations – is all too depressingly clear and simple: the people who live in urban priority areas are less healthy and less well provided for than people who live in other more prosperous areas.

11.2   Some of the evidence is indirect, in that data refer to social classes rather than to geographical districts. However class differences are a useful indicator of the circumstances of UPA populations which contain disproportionate numbers of people who are unskilled (and thus more likely to be in hazardous occupations) or unemployed, mentally or physically handicapped, or elderly.

Mortality and Morbidity in Urban Priority Areas

11.3   We noted in Chapter 1 that standardized mortality (or death) rates show marked inequalities between the UPAs and 'comfortable Britain'. Social class differences in mortality are most marked in infancy and childhood. DHSS figures published in 1980 show that at birth and during the first month of life, the risk of death in Social Class V is double that in Class I. The mortality rate of infants (1–5) in Social Class

V is five times that of Class I; and in children (1–14 years) it is twice as great.[2]

11.4   Mortality rates are the most commonly-used measure of the ill-health of the community – a reflection of a heavily treatment-oriented health service. However, with increasing emphasis on quality, rather than length, of life, morbidity (or illness) statistics are becoming more widely available. Increasing importance is being attached to the prevention of illness and the promotion of *good health* (defined by the World Health Organisation as 'not simply the absence of disease, but a state of complete physical, mental and social well-being').

11.5   General Household Survey data reveal marked differences between social classes for self-reported illness among adults. In addition to the class differences, there are geographical ones which appear to be linked to atmospheric pollution, and other industrial and environmental risks. Class differences, for accidents among children reflect the heavy commuter or lorry traffic, and lack of protected playing space as well as large families, overcrowding, poverty, a high proportion of mothers working, and the use of unregistered child-minders – all characteristic of inner city areas.

11.6   The effects of high rates of unemployment on health are also becoming recognised. Speaking in October 1984, Kenneth Clarke MP, the then Minister of State for Health, said, 'I've never been under any doubts that our present grave problems of unemployment in this country do indeed add to the health problems of the nation as well, and of course they pose particular problems for people recovering from mental illness and those who work for mentally ill people – professionals, volunteers, friends and relations'. The General Household Survey in 1976 reported that long-standing illness was 40 per cent higher among unemployed men compared with those who were employed, and that long-standing illnesses causing limitation to normal life were 80 per cent higher. Over a longer period, research published in 1974–75 reported a rise in perinatal mortality in Aberdeen during 1968–72, and found an association with low birth weight; the mothers surveyed had had similarly low birth weights, and their mothers had almost all been born during the worst years of the depression (1928–32). So health effects of the current period of high unemployment may continue to emerge over several decades.

11.7   Studies which have allowed for ill-health prior to unemployment, for social class, and for area of residence, show poorer health among the *long-term unemployed* than among the rest of the population. Research carried out in Sheffield[3] shows people unemployed for over three months to have double to four times the chance of minor psychiatric disorder. Still more serious, there is also a clear association between unemployment and suicide and attempted suicide. The Unemployment and Health Study Group believes that there is sufficient evidence that unemployment does in fact damage health.[4]

11.8   Overall, the relationship between social deprivation and health is seen in higher rates of death, illness, admission to psychiatric hospitals, suicides, and accidents, in the UPAs than in the rest of the country.[5]

Health Needs and the Health Service

11.9   At the time of the reorganisation of the Health Service in 1974 it was apparent that resources were not well matched to health needs. Medical resources tended to be most concentrated in the relatively prosperous south and south-east of England. The DHSS Resource Allocation Working Party put forward, in response, the 'RAWP' formula which, with modifications, is still in use. RAWP endeavoured to match health care needs (rather than the demands of the vocal middle classes) with resources.

11.10   It was expected when RAWP was put into effect that it would lead to the greatest growth occurring in the formerly under-provided areas. However, since the late 1970s resources available to the Health Service overall have not kept pace with increasing needs resulting from factors such as the greater numbers of old people, and the increasingly expensive methods of treatment now available. The result has been that the heaviest cuts in spending on health are being concentrated in the areas which are losing resources under the RAWP formula.

11.11   These areas include many UPAs. In the opinion of those who submitted evidence to us, the RAWP formula does not give sufficient weight to multiple deprivation. In Inner London, for example, this is particularly acute because the deprived areas are located within a generally prosperous region, and because of the resource demands of the major teaching hospitals, which serve the wider, more prosperous region as well as the local people. Evidence from Tower Hamlets illustrates the competition for resources between the London Hospitals' regional specialities, and the services for the local community.[6]

11.12   Another problem in the allocation of resources is the high proportion of family doctors who are elderly and who are working in single-handed practices in inner-city areas.[7] These practices may be open for a limited time each week, often without any appointment system. They have restricted lists and a high ratio of health complaints per person. Many UPA residents said to us that they have difficulty in getting on to a doctor's list, and without a telephone and with poor public transport facilities it can be difficult contacting doctors. There are also many problems surrounding the use of agency 'cover' services for GPs.

11.13   The Community Nursing Service also has serious staffing problems. Although the number of funded established posts in the inner urban areas is often higher than in other parts of the country, the nurses tend to be younger, recently-qualified, less likely to be married, and less likely to work part-time. All these characteristics tend to be associated with high rates of mobility. Nearly twice as many Inner London Community Nurses, for example, leave their posts annually compared with those in the Home Counties. Difficult living and working conditions mean that health authorities have severe recruitment problems and are obliged to offer an unusually high proportion of traineeships to attract staff. At the same time, with many General Practitioners working single-handed and unwilling or unable to do much preventive work, responsibility for the immunisation, screening, and surveillance of young children in the highly vulnerable population of Inner London falls to health visitors. Here again, there is an especially high turnover of staff in Inner London. Some districts have to replace over half their health visitors in the course of each year.[8]

11.14   Members of the Commission, when visiting Liverpool, talked with a group of Community Nurses who met together regularly to discuss how best they might approach the problems of their area. They had been involved in a project to reduce infant mortality; and they had also discussed the question of the induction of new nurses who came to work with them, and who needed help in understanding the local situation and coping with specific problems such as the different cultures and languages present. We were impressed with the high standard of the work they were doing, despite shortages of resources, unfilled posts, and new and inexperienced staff.

The Use of Services
11.15   Inequalities in the use of health services are well documented. Although adult consulting rates are rather similar across the social

classes, mortality and morbidity are (as we have noted) higher in Social Class V, so consulting rates are low in relation to need. Children from Social Class I actually go to the doctor more often than children of unskilled manual workers, in spite of the higher incidence of poor health among Class V children. Ante-natal and child welfare clinics are less used by women and infants in Class V, among whom maternal and infant mortality are highest. Poor attendance at clinics tends to be linked with social deprivation. Transport difficulties and lack of creche facilities deter low-income families.

11.16   In these circumstances it is vital that services are developed which increase the accessibility of health services to the people of the area. Community-based health initiatives have a particularly important role in this task. In this connection we should mention the Riverside Child Health Project which some of us visited in Newcastle. This was established in 1979 through the initiative of the Department of Child Health in the University of Newcastle in partnership with the Newcastle Health Authority. The project is staffed by 'a multi-disciplinary team carrying out medical, health visiting and community work in the context of preventative child health services in an inner city area'. It provides basic medical facilities, advice and education in a deprived area where child health needs are unusually high and child health services unusually stretched. The project combines health professionals and community workers as equal partners under one roof, a pattern of interdisciplinary co-operation in child health which the Court Report describes as 'fundamental to good practice'. We were impressed by its work, and applaud the local authority for bringing the medical side into its main line expenditure and for making funds available for the community side until at least 1987. We believe that this is an example that could well be followed elsewhere.

11.17   The multi-ethnic character of many of our inner urban areas adds a further dimension to the question of the adequacy and use of health provision. Minority ethnic families, for example, make relatively little use of ante-natal or child welfare arrangements. Many women are ignorant of the existence of services, or even their right to free health care. Their religion may forbid them to be examined by a male doctor. In the case of some communities, even the fear of encountering unknown males may be sufficient to keep them away.

11.18   Language is a strong barrier to use of services. In some districts a significant proportion of the population cannot speak English, or read either English or their own spoken language. Eighty per cent of Asian out-patients at the Dudley Road Hospital in Birmingham cannot read (including their own language).[9] In Tower Hamlets fifty per cent of births are in the Bengali community. Forty per cent of the Health Visitors' caseload is Bengali families. Yet there are only four full-time interpreters in the Community Health Service and two in the hospital serving a community of up to 30,000 people. In several cities we heard of Asian women with severe gynaecological problems: even when a health visitor called, communication was only possible through the interpreting of a young child, often kept off school for the purpose. We believe that appropriate health care for the minority ethnic population requires much greater resources both of interpreters and of ethnic minority health workers who can gain the trust of the community and explain the services available, how they work and in some cases why they are necessary.

Health and the Environment

11.19   But if progress is to be made in the larger work of promoting healthy living in urban priority areas much more attention will have to be paid to the underlying social, economic, housing, environmental and emotional factors which contribute to ill health. Health care is much more than the treatment of ill-health. Underlying the problem of *disease* is the more fundamental problem of *unease* which has its roots in factors such as anxiety, low personal esteem, broken relationships, and the stress of poverty, deprivation, unemployment and bad housing. It is easy in circumstances such as these for hard-pressed medical staff to try to ameliorate these difficulties by prescribing – particularly tranquillizers – to deal with the symptoms rather than by addressing the causes. Patients too may take refuge in addictive drugs. In the past doctors came to see that the provision of clean water and good sanitary conditions would be a major step forward in tackling disease in areas of gross deprivation. Similarly today to respond effectively to disease and unease will involve tackling their root causes.

11.20   We suggest this must include:

(a)   a sustained and concerted attack on poverty, unemployment and poor housing and environmental conditions as basic to improving the health of urban priority areas;

(b)   new initiatives in communicating with groups for whom traditional methods of health education have not been very successful. A deliberate move to 'health promotion' is needed which would include all Government departments considering the health implications of their policies, and further fiscal and other action designed to promote healthy diet and to reduce the attraction of unhealthy habits (such as dependence on tobacco and alcohol);

(c) the development of neighbourhood projects in which different groups of people can find benefit from support groups designed to meet their particular needs. Handicapped people, the single elderly, single parents, mothers with small children, ex-psychiatric patients and ex-offenders are among a range of groups whose capacity to live with dignity and hope in urban priority areas would be enhanced and developed by the support of such networks.

11.21   The Church needs to promote a broader understanding of the meaning of health. This must be concerned with more than the absence of disease. It must concern the significance of the Biblical concept of 'Shalom' and wholeness: for the care we take for the quality as well as the length of people's lives. This is especially significant for vulnerable groups. The help and encouragement given by the Churches to neighbourhood projects which would benefit the health of such groups would be the immediate practical outworking of such theological concerns.

References

1   *Inequalities in Health* ('The Black Report') DHSS 1980

2   Ibid, citing *Occupation Mortality 1970–72* HMSO, 1978 p.196. See also the report of the House of Commons Social Services Committee, July 1984, which pointed to rates of stillbirth and death in the first week of life being twice as high among unskilled working class families as among professional families.

3   By Professor Peter Watt, Social and Applied Psychology Unit, University of Sheffield.

4   Unemployment and Health Study Group, *Unemployment, Health and Social Policy.* Nuffield Centre for Health Services Study, University of Leeds, 1983.

5   B. Jarman, *A survey of Primary Care in London.* The College of General Practitioners, 1981; London Health Planning Consortium, *Primary Health Care in Inner London,* 1981.

6   Tower Hamlets District Health Authority Agenda paper E, 13 December 1984, *Regional Specialities.*

7   *Primary Health Care in Inner London,* op. cit.

8   Studies such as that of K.J. Bolden, *Inner Cities,* Royal College of General Practitioners, 1981, make similar points concerning the experience of other urban priority areas in Britain.

9   Anthony Bird, *The Search for Health: A Response from the Inner City.* 1981, p.11.

271

Chapter 12

SOCIAL CARE AND COMMUNITY WORK

'The chief characteristic . . . is constant change, movement, instability of population structure, total impermanence'. (Diocese of Birmingham)

Social Care

12.1   Poverty, unemployment, poor housing and social stress in the urban priority areas put severe pressures on families, and can trigger family crises and breakdown. The multiple deprivation of such areas makes it particularly difficult for elderly and handicapped people to maintain their independence. Young children may suffer from stressed family life, and from poor environmental conditions. These and other groups in the UPAs need the support and help of skilled services. In urban priority areas there are heavy burdens on those who offer care: individual carers, the voluntary organisations and, especially, the personal social services.

12.2   A common factor underlying this situation in many UPAs is the lack of traditional *family support* systems in neighbourhoods which have high numbers of single-person households and single-parent families. The tradition dies hard (and perhaps hardest of all in the Church) that all people gain their support through a normal family system. In many UPAs, for a variety of reasons, this is not uniformly so. For example, the UPAs contain many isolated elderly people who have been left behind by families who have moved to the suburbs or country, and young people who have come to the inner city to find work, or excitement, and who may be living in squats or communes. Evidence from the Diocese of Birmingham quotes a description of one such area: 'The chief characteristic . . . is constant change, movement, instability of population structure, total impermanence'. Against this background, many highly dependent elderly people, those suffering from physical and mental handicap, and single and other disadvantaged parents, will be seeking to cope with their problems without a traditional family

272

support system, often in poor housing, with an unattractive and perhaps frightening environment.

12.3   The evidence we received from Age Concern spoke of 'the particular complexities generated by increasing political conflict, the breakdown of traditional employment and living patterns, and the lurking tensions between different races and cultures' which characterise the special needs of *elderly* people living in urban areas. This must be seen against the background of an emerging national age pattern which does nothing to encourage the belief that more support for the very elderly can easily come from their own immediate families. 'Trends in age structure indicate that, amongst the retired there is likely to be a small decline in total numbers, but a very marked increase of over half a million, or about 20 per cent, in those aged 75 and over, particularly elderly women . . . One of the problems for those now entering the 75 and over age group is that the family network which may in the past have helped to support them, is changing. Not only will there be fewer, both absolutely and relatively, of the young elderly, but the children of the very old will have been born during the inter-war years when birthrates were low, and families were small'.[1]

12.4   Particular needs exist among the increasing numbers of elderly members of minority ethnic groups. Social services departments in particular need to have a positive commitment to understanding the specific social services needs of people from these groups. Members of such groups have rightly drawn attention to the potentially damaging effect which inappropriate and insensitive attempts to help may have on families whose cultural norms are different.

12.5   Yet a further vulnerable group in need of the support of good services in these circumstances is *children under five years of age*. Poor and inappropriate housing, unhealthy surroundings and lack of play space in UPAs make life for young children less than satisfactory and sometimes hazardous. In urban priority areas they will more often than in other areas be the children of single parents, and may lack stimulation and amenities. They are likely to reach primary school at the age of five already considerably disadvantaged in comparison with their contemporaries. To say this is not to state anything which is not already widely recognised. Over the years document after document[2] has drawn attention to the needs of these children and the enormous benefits to be gained by early experience of creative involvement in a stimulating social group. Not only do adequate resources need to be devoted to this particularly vulnerable section of the population, but there is also a clear need for all agencies in the UPAs – and especially those concerned with health, education, and social services – to together offer a variety of forms of provision to ensure satisfactory physical care and educational opportunity for all under-fives.

12.6 Many voluntary organisations have contributed very constructively to meeting the needs of parents with young children. We have seen examples of family centres, such as those run by the Children's Society, which actively involve parents and residents of the local neighbourhood in their planning and running. We believe this to be a most important contribution.

12.7 Notwithstanding the work of voluntary bodies (many of them Christian-based) in responding to social needs in the UPAs, there remain particular burdens on, and high expectations of, the statutory providers of personal social services.

Social Services Departments

12.8 In 1971, following publication of the Seebohm report[3] unified social services departments were created, bringing together the scattered provision formerly within health, welfare and children's departments. Social services became one of the largest departments of local authorities, with influential committees and therefore political power. The public were offered a simplified organisation. Expectations of services for disadvantaged people were heightened.

12.9 During the 1970s the determination of pressure groups and the sympathetic support of all political parties resulted in further legislation representing high ambitions. Governments of different political persuasions anticipated continuous growth in provision at a rate of up to 10 per cent a year. Local authorities were required to prepare detailed plans with this level of growth in mind, and there was considerable development and change both in statutory services and in voluntary organisations. This has meant that we have entered the present decade, a period of severe economic restraint, with a legacy of very high expectations and wider public concern for handicapped people, and certain categories of disadvantaged people, than ever before.

12.10 It is important to understand the pressures in these circumstances on those seeking to offer professional services. Although social work training was reorganised in the 1970s in an attempt to provide the professional personnel needed, social workers have felt increasingly overwhelmed by the responsibilities placed upon them, and the extent to which they are expected to remedy problems created by social conditions over which they have very little influence. A lack of resources is leading to many agencies being unable to offer an adequate service – or even to meet present statutory obligations. Cuts in resources are leading to anger and depression as departments and workers see precious services, such as domiciliary care, reduced or even withdrawn altogether.

12.11   On top of this, a lack of a clear sense of direction about policy can lead to politicians and senior management constantly trying to reshape the service at the expense of the morale of those who work in it. Some of the most difficult tasks in supporting children and adults in distress fall onto the shoulders of social workers who need considerable skill, judgement and support in carrying them out. We believe that high levels of dedication, competence, and commitment are not lacking among those who work for social services in UPAs, but these human resources cannot continue to be taken for granted if workers are deprived of personal, political and public support.

12.12   The need for the proper resourcing of the social services is especially illustrated in the policy of trying to offer 'care in the community' to groups of people such as the mentally ill or handicapped, who might otherwise remain in residential institutions and hospitals. Without adequate provision of good social service support (in collaboration with health and housing authorities) such a policy, far from enhancing people's dignity and independence, will leave vulnerable groups without adequate help. In the absence of proper professional support, the extra burdens on women who usually have to care for elderly, handicapped, or sick relatives, will be too heavy for many to bear.

12.13   At the time of writing, a Green Paper is expected to be published to promote debate on a strategic and enabling role for social services departments in relation to informal carers, voluntary organisations, and the private provision of welfare services. Although we are unable to anticipate the content of this discussion document, we believe that it is essential that this strategic approach should take account of the following points:

(i)   *reliance on networks of informal carers*: for the reasons we have given above, supported by evidence from dioceses,[4] the natural supporting networks are likely to be less common in urban priority areas. The level of government support to local services must recognise this.

(ii)   *voluntary organisations:*
(a)   will need to be adequately funded (part of the new deal we recommend in Chapter 8) if they are to provide an increasing share of main line provision of services;

(b)   should not be used for 'main line' work to such an extent that their pioneering, innovative value is lost.

(iii)   *private care*: the vastly expanded use of private residential care funded from Social Security provision has already highlighted:

(a)   the difficulty of ensuring that public funds directed to private care are used to help the most disadvantaged people;

(b)   the uneven distribution of the right kind of private facilities which are likely to be less readily available in poorer urban areas;

(c)   the need for monitoring and enforcement of standards of care.

(iv)   *statutory services*: in addition to the 'strategic and enabling role', there will still be a considerable need for social services to undertake statutory responsibilities, and to provide care, protection, and control for those groups of people for whom informal care is not appropriate.

Voluntary Bodies

12.14   The Seebohm report emphasised the importance of social service departments 'giving support, both financial and professional, to vigorous, outward-looking voluntary organisations which can demonstrate good standards of service, provide opportunities for appropriate training for their workers, both professional and voluntary, and show a flair for innovation'.

12.15   That the nature of urban life puts particular strains on people with disadvantages and disabilities has been recognized in changes of policy by a number of national voluntary organisations, who have shifted resources specifically to these areas of high need. We have received evidence of such shifts in resources from Barnardo's, the National Children's Home, and from the Church of England Children's Society. For example, the Children's Society has, among its 100 projects, 27 Community and Family Centre projects in areas suffering from urban decay. Many of these projects have arisen in the past five years as the Society has become increasingly aware of the need to locate itself in areas of high need and to identify itself with those who suffer the effects of bad housing, unemployment, and poor local facilities. This relocation has had a profound effect on the Society's work. They told us that they had 'realised the strength of working in partnership with oppressed people rather than just providing welfare services. This experience is also affecting our work with offenders, young people in residential care and people with handicaps.'

12.16   It is clear from the evidence we have received that voluntary and secular bodies still look to the Church:

(i)   to influence attitudes ('promoting a more caring climate of public opinion towards the problems of the disadvantaged')[5]

(ii)   to influence local policy ('Churches are concerned about the whole person and all age groups and are therefore in a strong position to give a lead in treating people's needs in the round')[6]

(iii)   to help to provide direct services ('In some neighbourhoods the resources of the Church – paid worker, premises and equipment – are the only ones based locally, and therefore are invaluable to those wishing to organise care schemes')[7]

The evidence from the British Association of Social Workers also emphasised the particular opportunities which the Church has of offering support of a preventive kind to families with whom the Church provides an acceptable contact. Examples include advising elderly and handicapped people of their entitlement to social security benefits, providing relief care in order to allow carers some respite from the strain of constant caring, and using contact with families through the christening of babies to ensure that families, and particularly single parents, have not become isolated through the care of small children.

The Church's Social Work
12.17   The Church of England has a long history of contribution to social work. Much of the present work undertaken in a number of dioceses (and social work within the formal structure of the Church of England is always managed on a diocesan basis) has its roots in the days of Moral Welfare. This was predominantly concerned with the needs of young single pregnant women. Residential institutions allowed such women to have their children quietly, away from the pressure of family and community disapproval, and to develop their skills as parents. Adoption agencies provided for their children to be placed in new family settings if that course of action was agreed. This work was often staffed by women trained in the Josephine Butler scheme, which was a form of social work training specifically Anglican in character. (Its qualifications are not, however, recognised by the profession.)

12.18   Considerable changes have however taken place over the last decade. Standards of practice vary, and salary structures are often well below what staff might command for similar reponsibilities in local authority work, or, indeed, in other voluntary agencies. Nevertheless, even in the work directly arising out of the moral welfare past, there are many signs of the development of a contemporary service welcomed and used by the social service department of local authorities. Residential institutions may be providing a specialist service enabling young single parents to develop the skills needed to be successful in their parental commitment. Adoption agencies may be seeking to place children with particular difficulties in good and appropriate homes. Staff will be fully qualified and committed to working within the voluntary sector in a Christian agency.

12.19   In addition, social work in the Church of England has developed in a number of less traditional directions. It is increasingly concerned with working with disadvantaged groups – for example, the housing problems of Bengali families in a particular area of London, and with groups of single homeless people, battered women, and mentally-handicapped people. It is also concerned with working with church members to discover and develop resources for offering a better ministry to particular groups of people. For example, a number of Anglican agencies are running bereavement counselling projects. Some of the best examples of good practice come from agencies working closely with the parishes. Yet much social work within the Church is still on the margin of mainstream Church activity.

12.20   In the light of this situation, we would ask local Churches in the UPAs to consider four interlocking levels of response, in co-operation with Church social workers:

(i)   *A Wide Concern for the Needs of our Society*
The persistence of poverty, together with inadequate provision in social care, makes its own demands on the Church. Some of the most basic explanations of the present situation lie in the area of public values and public policy. If the Church, as a company of people seeking to be loyal servants of the Gospel, is to respond truthfully and helpfully it needs to be an aware and understanding body. Both at the level of its national organisation and at the level of its congregational life, the Church of England needs a deeper and more informed awareness of social need and public policy.

(ii)   *A Close Experience of and Involvement in the Locality*
The presence of the Church in neighbourhoods is an opportunity
both to understand and serve the people who live there. There are
always temptations to pursue church life without any serious
relationship to the neighbourhood. The Church will not be able to
make its contribution to better social care in the locality unless it is
open to and aware of what is happening there. A small but valuable
example of how local churches can get a better picture of the many
sides of the life of their area is the Board for Social Responsibility
booklet: *The Local Church and the Mentally Handicapped.* The audit for
the local Church which we have suggested will we hope be a helpful
aid in developing awareness of local needs.

(iii)   *Pastoral Support*
We are conscious of the low expectations of many members of the
Church of the help they might receive in the life of the local
congregation in developing their Christian understanding. For
example, professional social workers are rarely enabled to share their
experiences with fellow church members, or encouraged to see them
in the perspective of the Gospel. Local Churches are often tempted to
see their members in terms of what they do for the Church rather
than in terms of their vocations in the neighbourhood. Thus the
Church can become a place of escape and illusion. We believe it
should rather be a place of communication, learning and mutual
support.

(iv)   *The Provision of Services*
There is a number of ways in which the Church can be involved in
specific service provision. One is by making premises available for
use by local groups providing particular services: for example, self-
help groups, play schools, and lunch clubs for the elderly. Another is
through the support and training of members of the Church to
provide a service in the area. This may be in relation to meeting the
needs of bereaved people, of handicapped people, of elderly and
housebound people, or responding to problems in housing, local
transport, schooling, or policing and neighbourhood.

12.21   In the organisation of the Church's social work service we
believe three things to be essential.

12.22   First, that it should be professional, and able, therefore, to
identify with the wider world of social work. The Church has too

often appeared to be satisfied with unqualified, poorly-paid, and inadequately-managed work. The Church ought not to be satisfied with lower standards than those expected of the profession elsewhere in our society.

12.23 Second, church-based social work must clearly identify its work with, and affirm its fellowship with, the wider Church. It needs to be staffed and organised in a way which will command the confidence of the Church. Equally, social work agencies need to be properly managed and supported. The Church must own the work done in its name, and ensure adequate accountability and support. In their professional life the Church's social workers are part of the world of social work. In their Christian commitment they must be part of the Church. The proper management of its social work must be a clear responsibility of the Church.

12.24 Finally, we wish to emphasize the importance of proper training. Our visit to some projects run by the Church highlighted concern about untrained staff engaged in taxing and difficult work. Professional training for church workers needs to be placed in the context of general social work education. We believe that social work training bodies need to work increasingly with voluntary agencies to take account of their special needs, and that provision needs to be made for consideration of the philosophical and ethical issues arising out of social work theory and practice. The Church must devote resources to give grant-aid to those in need of professional qualifications. There is also a need for in-service opportunities for workers to be able to reflect theologically and professionally upon their work and to develop new skills.

12.25 Historically the Church of England has taken a leading role in the social care of the disadvantaged. In the context of a growing awareness of the major public policy issues confronting our society, arising from the persistence of poverty and deprivation in our midst, we believe that there must be a reassessment of the deployment of the Church's social work resources (as many other voluntary organisations have done) in the light of the needs of the UPAs. Dioceses and local churches in UPAs must be enabled to better respond to the social care needs of their neighbourhoods.

Conclusion
12.26 We have outlined the particular pressures facing those

concerned with social care in the UPAs, and have considered the role of the Church of England in this context. We make the following *recommendations*:

1. We commend the use of properly-trained social workers, working with local Churches and neighbourhood groups, as an important part of the total ministry of the Church in the urban priority areas.

2. Church social workers should be trained within the mainstream of social work, but with particular attention paid to the character and needs of social work in the church context. The Church should initiate discussion with social work training agencies to this end.

3. The public policy concept of 'care in the community' for people who might otherwise be institutionalised must be supported by adequate resources to allow the provision of proper locally-based support services for people (especially women) caring for vulnerable and handicapped people.

Community Work

12.27 Much of the evidence we have received, not least at meetings during our visits to urban priority areas, has identified quite specific local problems that are not easily solved – or indeed effectively addressed – by central and local government. In response to these problems many activities can be mounted that may be generally grouped together as some form of 'community work'. This phrase covers a wide range of practices based on different ideas and ideologies.[8] Yet, as we shall argue below, much of this work can bring help to the increasingly powerless and alienated residents of UPAs.

12.28 Many submissions made to us referred in one way or another to 'a *disintegrated* society'. We have received evidence from virtually all over the country that a significant number of people in the inner city and outer estates are friendless and desperately lonely. They include single people living alone, single parents, those abandoned by or withdrawn from their families, unemployed people with no workplace contacts, perhaps emotionally damaged by the traumas and humiliations of redundancy, and people suffering from mental or physical illness. A related theme in the evidence submitted – a symptom as well as in turn a cause of a break-up of 'community' – is the constant shift in many UPA (particularly inner city) populations. There is often a high level of

281

mobility. Yet another factor repeatedly referred to in the evidence was that large numbers of people in urban priority areas are deprived of 'community' by being excluded by *poverty or unemployment* from fulfilling relationships in their neighbourhood.

12.29   Poor people can be forced into isolated and lonely lives. This is perhaps particularly true in some outer housing estates or tower blocks, where social networks have not developed to meet human needs for interaction. We do not wish to indulge in nostalgia for 'communities' of a past era, which were no doubt for some people restricting, and imposed on others by deprivation. It also goes without saying that some people are, by nature or by choice, more 'private' than others. An increasing number of families prefer to adopt a more domestic lifestyle and find their satisfactions in the home rather than in outside associations. This may represent a turning away from one's neighbours which carries its own implications; but it is not the issue with which the submissions to us were primarily directed. The concern was rather with a 'privatisation' which is inflicted upon people by circumstances – the failure of local facilities or a lack of meeting places, the clearance or decay of housing in an area, and the closure of work places.

12.30   Those suffering from poverty and unemployment are likely to find that not only are they no longer members of the wider associations based on the workplace, but also that they cannot afford to travel outside their neighbourhood to take part in town-wide associations, the networks of belonging across a city which for better-off people provide so many of the satisfactions of urban living. The result is an acute form of urban deprivation: deprivation of relatedness, of esteem.

12.31   Women in urban priority areas often have to cope with enormous difficulties. There may be problems with bringing up children, budgeting on a low income, housekeeping in a house which may be damp, cold and in poor repair, and handling the debt trap without much support. Women in UPAs are often confined to the home and sometimes subject to depression and ill-health. Yet it will also be a woman who is expected to care for the sick and the old 'in the community', and most very elderly people are women who sometimes have to suffer the frailties, confusions and indignities of extreme old age. 'In all these priority areas', noted one submission, 'you will find women being forced by public policy, private business and interpersonal relations to a subservient and second-class role'.[9]

12.32   It has been pressed upon us that rigid and restricted views of the family can be particularly unhelpful in relation to domestic violence by men against women. The identification of Christian perspectives with male dominance and female subservience can only serve to reinforce attitudes which encourage the abuse of women in the family, while an emphasis on the need to put up with suffering, however terrible, makes women in these circumstances feel guilty if they seek to leave home. As a result, pastoral advice is often directed towards exhorting the woman to keep the family together, regardless of the risk to herself. Clergy have little to offer women in this predicament.[10] The need to disentangle what is essentially Christian in our understanding of marriages and the family from that which is culturally conditioned is critical.

12.33 Particular problems are also faced by ethnic minorities. Although not all UPAs contain ethnic minorities, the majority of the nation's black people, including those of Asian origin, are located in them. They experience the common problems of the areas. They also often contribute notably to the regeneration of run-down localities. Yet, as we have noted, we have received evidence that they suffer racial harassment and physical violence. Racist graffiti proclaim the ethos which is allowed to prevail in many neighbourhoods, unless determined action by the authorities tackles this issue seriously. In addition, minority groups often need some support to build up the facilities needed for a viable corporate and cultural life for their communities.

What Is Community Work?
12.34 Community work does not rest on the assumption that the problems of an area reside solely within individuals and families, as some patterns of social case work might suggest. Rather, it takes as its starting point that many of the factors combining to bring about the difficulties and injustices experienced in local communities must be located within and between the policies and practices of institutions, authorities or commercial bodies. To these corporate issues a corporate response is required.

12.35 The development of community organisations can not only help to bring widely-felt private concerns to become public issues, but can also help people who experience individual powerlessness to participate in sustained and combined attempts to influence policies and decisions which affect their lives and their neighbourhood. Well-organised or powerful institutions may be active in ways which many local people may dislike, but residents may have no voice or leverage to act in their own interests. Or there may be opportunities to improve some aspect of the life of the neighbourhood, but no group exists to take action; or again, a category of people (for example elderly or young or handicapped people) may be neglected or suffering in some way, but neither they nor anyone else is doing much about it.

12.36   In contrast with social work, therefore, community work is not about delivering services to people. Community work seeks to involve those concerned in purposeful action to change their situation; community work intervention is *with* rather than *for* people. Its process involves local people being enabled to raise awareness of issues, ensuring that the objectives are defined by the participants in a situation, attempting to understand the forces at work, discerning what can and should be done and by whom, and supporting those who have become committed to these tasks.

12.37   Considerable numbers of 'ordinary' people are involved in voluntary action to achieve some sort of change in their neighbourhoods. One can refer to 'activists' in the very positive sense of those who are prepared to give unpaid time and energy to their commitment through an organisation; and it has to be accepted that they will always be a comparatively small minority. Experience suggests that in areas of relative deprivation, community groups are likely to be more effectively sustained if the support of a professional community worker is available. By 1983 there were in the United Kingdom over 5,300 paid staff whose main task was community work and a further 5,000 youth and community workers, with many others in allied voluntary or public sector jobs, often including the word 'community' in their job titles.[11]

12.38   Community work is not value-free. It is seen by many of those involved to be biased towards the interests of the poor and against racist and sexist discrimination. All approaches will, of course, have an implicit or explicit ideology, and those most closely involved are likely to be committed to beliefs which motivate them strongly. Yet local groups are inevitably open to manipulation by those with broader political objectives. This danger must be guarded against. The assumptions behind alternative approaches to an issue need to be spelled out and worked through with an openness which is very different from attempts to impose a tightly-packaged ideology or to manipulate a situation for purposes which lie outside it.

12.39   Yet a proper emphasis of community work in our view is upon increasing opportunities for direct participation to supplement the necessary but sometimes inadequate systems of representative democracy. Unrealistic hopes have sometimes been placed on the idea of participation. Not everyone wants to, or can, be involved in every decision affecting their urban environment. Some power has to be given over to representatives. But there is often some scepticism as to how representative the elected ones are. In plural situations whose interests should they advocate? How is the voice of minorities to be heard? In this context, community work can open up, and make people aware of, channels through which answers can be demanded and implementation monitored. A genuinely participatory style demands a determined political will, for it costs energy and money. There is a sharp distinction to be drawn between a style of urban political decision-making which is as open, participatory and accessible as possible, and a style in which vital decisions are made in private on the basis of restricted information by a small, exclusive group.

12.40   In its essence, community work is concerned with the collective esteem of a locality and its people. Local neighbourhoods, particularly those which are most deprived, cannot achieve their potential without considerable inputs from the wider society; and in any case they are at its mercy in many key areas of life. But the locality has an essential contribution – the skills and energies of its own people. External changes may be inflicted on a neighbourhood, but only the people themselves can achieve any profound transformation.

12.41   The achievements of community work so far are modest rather than sensational. It has no monopoly of insights such as 'working with rather than for people'; these can be and sometimes are effectively applied in other areas of public life. Community work practitioners do not always live up to the standard of their own rhetoric. Situations may sometimes be manipulated or short cuts taken. We must be realistic about the possibilities and limitations of community work. Nevertheless, we believe that it has an important part to play in addressing the issues raised with us by so many submissions: the importance of neighbourhood, the need for relatedness in effective local networks, and the quality of local attitudes and relationships. In other words, we affirm that community work must be an integral element in any serious strategy to regenerate urban priority areas, and we believe that without the sustained involvement of people affected by the problems of such areas at the grassroots, the major issues of powerlessness, esteem and human development cannot effectively be tackled.

285

12.42   In the following paragraphs we offer some practical examples of types of community work response to specific issues in local areas.

(i)   Poverty
12.43   As we have seen in Chapter 9, the main levers of power affecting people's incomes lie outside the neighbourhood; but some things can be done within neighbourhoods which can affect both poverty and powerlessness. Such initiatives include welfare benefits take-up and information campaigns, action to reduce the cost of local facilities for unwaged people or to organise bulk-buying co-operatives, credit unions, or a debt counselling service. These and other initiatives can affect people's incomes. Not everyone, however, puts money at the top of their list of priorities, essential though of course it is. If the hurt of poverty lies in exclusion from community, perhaps the local community may be able to give something of great value to those on low incomes: to take them seriously. As one person said to a member of the Commission: 'The pain of poverty is in being despised, not in having only two shirts. You have dignity when you can stand up and speak *and be listened to.*'

(ii)   Women in the Community
12.44   Initiatives can be taken locally to respond to the particular needs of women. Some examples are 'well women' clinics and centres, women's refuges, also the encouraging of adult studies for women, and ensuring that youth clubs create space in which girls can develop their own activities and programmes. Women are already making a distinctive contribution to local organisations where they are given the opportunity: sharing authority, encouraging participation and minimising hierarchy.

(iii)   Minority Ethnic Communities
12.45   Decisive policies and programmes are required at borough or city level to eliminate racism, both personal and institutional, and to establish a society in which the presence of ethnic minorities is affirmed. Such policies and programmes have to be made effective within neighbourhoods. We therefore believe that there is need for many more community organisations to address the problems of racism in their areas, becoming more alert not only to what is being done, but also to what is left undone. A statement of anti-racist intent may be the starting point to ensure that important questions are not overlooked. Are local ethnic minorities kept informed or are they missing out on events and facilities? Do the leaders of groups keep in touch and discuss needs and

priorities? Do the mainly white organisations discriminate, consciously or unconsciously, against minorities? Or do they stand solidly alongside them when they are oppressed? Are there positive anti-racist attitudes in local youth clubs and community centres? Are the names of black people put forward for local committees, or as magistrates, political candidates or for other positions of public responsibility?

12.46 The local Church should be involved not only in these community activities but also in asking itself some hard questions about the Church as an equal opportunities employer and about the engagement of the congregation in challenging racism. A serious inter-faith dialogue may well start on the basis of local friendship and common action in the community.

(iv) 'Second Chance' Education
12.47 As a final example, we would lay particular stress on the provision of greater access for people in urban priority areas to participate in sustained learning experiences. We refer in the next Chapter to the role that Community Schools can play here. More institutions are opening their doors to mature students, and this is to be welcomed. But there remain two largely unmet needs. First, there is a need for access courses to enable those with potential and commitment to progress by means of these stepping stones along the paths known as experiential learning or 'education for capability'.[12] Second, there is a need for courses for others who may already have the educational basis but who are looking for learning opportunities which are more related to action, and geared to the needs and pace of the learner than conventional education (and offered in less daunting surroundings). No expense is spared in providing further education and training for the new technology, and this is to be welcomed. We would also emphasise the complementary need for learning opportunities to develop *leadership and community skills* in the UPAs. Inevitably such schemes carry the danger of destroying a volunteer without creating a professional, but as experience grows from experimental schemes for community work apprentices in such places as Sheffield, there will be rich rewards in terms of fulfilment.

Resources
12.48 If a genuine attempt is to be made to involve the people living in urban priority areas with the regeneration of their neighbourhoods, a sustained programme of community work is needed within each borough. To meet these needs, adequate resources are required to fund

community work over the long term, and to pay for at least some of the changes arising from such activities. We believe that a primary responsibility lies with the borough or district councils in whose areas the urban priority areas lie to develop cross-party support for a serious commitment to community work and to resource such programmes adequately. We so *recommend.*

The Church and Community Work

12.49   We have made our recommendations about the pattern of Church life which we believe should emerge within urban priority areas, and have emphasised the need for a commitment to neighbourhood and community. We see community work as a legitimate lay ministry. It is an important expression of concern for one's neighbour-in-community, which is as essential to discipleship as the worship to which it is integrally related.

12.50   The principal point at which a local Church's commitment to community work bites on real situations is where lay people are active in local organisations. In our visits to UPAs we have met members of local Churches who have been active in tenants' organisations, community councils, action groups, and in a variety of welfare-oriented groups for elderly and younger people. Many such people have found their faith and fellowship an inspiration for their community work; others have experienced some frustration and tension between the needs of the community and the priorities of the congregation. In the face of so many difficulties in the world around us, it is tempting to relapse into what has been called 'quiet cynicism'. Christians may often need support and encouragement in their commitment to community work, with its sometimes strange alliances, hard decisions and necessary compromises. We hope that our suggested audit for the local Church will be a helpful aid for Churches in discerning the potential for community work involvement in their neighbourhoods.

12.51   In some situations it will be right for a professional community worker to be employed by a parish, a group of parishes, within a deanery or an ecumenical area. A long-term commitment to a sustained policy, evolved in collaboration with other agencies within the neighbourhood, and with other Churches, backed up by effective and well-informed management and support, is crucial. It is also essential to establish clear objectives. The aim should be to enable the community to find its voice, exercise its leverage and develop its people along the lines we have indicated above. The Church should not be motivated in a partisan way to advance its image and influence, nor to take advantage of situations in order to impose its beliefs. Rather it should be explicit about the values Christians try to bring to bear, in that they are about fulfilling the fully human and not the successfully ecclesiastical.

12.52   The evidence we have received suggests that the crucial point at which support for Church involvement in community work should be found is the *diocese*. It is probably at this level that sustained resources can be mobilised and the necessary back-up in training, consultation and personal support can be given. Courses for clergy and others, and seminars to promote awareness of good practice, are likely to be significant features of such support. There is already important work being done in a number of dioceses and by national agencies in local areas, such as the Mothers' Union.

12.53   The main role at diocesan level is to help local people respond to the needs of their situation, not to impose solutions from above. We see the role of the diocese, through its Board for Social Responsibility, as being to provide support by sharing information on relevant social issues, and on such matters as funding and the use of church buildings, linking initiatives with each other, strengthening networks of communications, providing finance and acting as an advocate for community work within the diocese and with other agencies. We *recommend* that dioceses which include urban priority areas should develop and support community work along these lines.

12.54   The Church of England has never been corporately committed to a *national* strategy for community work, although of course some important work has been done. There has been some collaboration with the Community Work Resource Unit of the British Council of Churches. If serious progress is to be made in this field, resources are needed to provide more support for diocesan, and equivalent ecumenical, initiatives. Sustained contact, a supply of well-directed information, literature and video material, the organisation of appropriate regional or national events, or training programmes, will all call for a commitment by the Church of England to a small but significant national resource in this field. We are not in a position to recommend the precise form this should take. However, we *recommend* that discussions should be held between the General Synod Board for Social Responsibility and the British Council of Churches Community Work Advisory Committee with a view to strengthening the national support networks for community work, and that the Church of England should be prepared to devote central resources to this end.

Conclusion

12.55   Evidence has come to us from urban priority areas across the country that very many people experience powerlessness and a lack of local resources, and are deprived of adequate networks of relationships in their neighbourhoods. We see community work as an important element in any strategy for the regeneration of urban priority areas, as articulating the local voice and influence in decision-making, in developing collective community action and supportive networks, and fostering a quality of shared attitudes and relationships which strengthen that experience of human esteem and belonging which we affirm as essential to human fulfilment. We believe that community work can make a significant contribution at local level towards meeting particular needs arising in urban priority areas from the growth of poverty, changes in the role of women and the presence of minority ethnic groups. We wish to re-emphasise the importance of the neighbourhood, not as the solution to all ills, but as an essential ingredient in any effective response to the urban priority areas.

Main Recommendations

1.   We commend the use of properly-trained social workers working with local Churches and neighbourhood groups as an important part of the total ministry of the Church in the urban priority areas (paragraph 12.26).

2.   Church social workers should be trained within the mainstream of social work, but with particular attention being paid to the character and needs of social work in the church context. The Church should initiate discussion with social work training agencies to this end (paragraph 12.26).

3.   The concept of 'care in the community' for people who might otherwise be institutionalised must be supported by adequate resources to allow the provision of proper locally-based support services for people (especially women) caring for vulnerable and handicapped people (paragraph 12.26).

4.   Local authorities in boroughs and districts which include urban priority areas should, with other agencies, develop policies to establish and sustain community work with adequate resources (paragraph 12.48).

5.   Dioceses should, through their Boards for Social Responsibility,

develop and support community work, and should exercise a strategic role in support of local programmes in their urban priority areas (paragraph 12.53).

6.   Discussions should be held between the General Synod Board for Social Responsibility and the British Council of Churches Community Work Advisory Committee with a view to strengthening the national support networks for community work. The Church of England should be prepared to devote central resources to this end (paragraph 12.54).

References

1   Muriel Nissel *Family Care of the Handicapped Elderly: Who Pays?*, Policy Studies Institute, January 1982.

2   For example, see

Under-fives: a local authority associations study, Association of County Councils and Association of Metropolitan Authorities, 1977.

The Under Fives, Trade Union Congress, 1977.

Children Under Five, British Association of Social Workers, 1978.

Co-ordination of Services for Children Under Five, Department of Education and Science and Department of Health and Social Security, 1978.

3   Report of the Committee on Local Authority and Allied Personal Services, chaired by Sir Frederick (now Lord) Seebohm, 1968.

4   Diocese of Leicester: *Report of Working Party on Urban Priority Areas*, 1984, and evidence from Lichfield Diocese.

5   Evidence from the Association of Metropolitan Authorities.

6   Evidence from the National Council for Voluntary Organisations.

7   Evidence from the British Association of Social Workers.

8   There is a growing contemporary literature on the subject. See, for example:

David N. Thomas, *The Making of Community Work*, George Allen and Unwin, 1983.

Peter Willmott with David Thomas, *Community in Social Policy*, Policy Studies Institute, 1984.

Alan Twelvetrees, *Democracy and the Neighbourhood*, National Federation of Community Organisations, 1985.

and especially:

Involvement in Community, a Christian Contribution – a report by the Community Development Group, William Temple Foundation, in collaboration with the Community Work Advisory Group, British Council of Churches, 1980.

9   Submission by the Association of Community Workers.

10   Practical responses to the problems experienced by battered women must recognise the difficulties wives face in ending violent relationships. To leave may be to take the children from a familiar home and a father whom they love to a life of poverty

and loneliness as a single parent family. To stay at home and to evict the husband may involve complicated legal procedures and a risk of continuing danger for the wife. The following notes may be of use to those who are asked for help by battered wives:

(a) *It is not helpful* to suggest to a battered wife that she should 'go back and try again', 'think of the whole family' or 'try to be a better wife'; she has probably been doing all of these for many years. All the research agrees that for most women their first reaction is to tell no one; if the violence continues they may confide in a friend or in another member of their own family; by the time a parish priest hears about it the violence will probably have been going on for many years. Battered wives need support and practical help, not homilies.

(b) Research about the needs of battered women suggests that *the most helpful agencies and individuals* are those who accept the woman's own definition of her problem, who provide support while she considers what to do, and who give relevant and accurate information. For some women the most valuable piece of information is the knowledge that if she leaves her husband she can claim Supplementary Benefit for herself and her children.

(c) *Women's Aid refuges* offer accommodation, protection, advice and support to battered women and their children. The phone number of the local refuge should be familiar to every vicar, social worker, general practitioner and health visitor. Refuges in England are co-ordinated by the Women's Aid Federation, 52-54 Featherstone Street, London, EC1, 01-837-9316.

(d) *The Housing (Homeless Persons) Act* lays on local authority housing departments the statutory duty to provide accommodation for women with children who have to leave home because of violence, or threat of violence. Some housing departments try to avoid this responsibility, but it is mandatory.

(e) *The Domestic Violence and Matrimonial Proceedings Act* makes it possible for women to get a county court order either restraining the husband from assaulting his wife or excluding him from the home. The court can attach a power of arrest to the order so that if he breaks it he can be arrested immediately. A solicitor will arrange for the order to be made and legal aid is available if necessary.

(f) More generally, many local churches have played a valuable part in helping to establish *new refuges* or in supporting those already in existence. However, the provision of refuge places still falls far below a House of Commons Select Committee recommendation of one place for every 10,000 of the population. Churches in urban priority areas should see support for women's refuges as a constructive way of working for a better quality of life for individuals within families.

(For a more extended discussion see Pahl, J. *Private Violence and Public Policy*, London, Routledge and Kegan Paul, 1985.)

11   Willmott with Thomas, *op cit*, p. 13.

12   See, for example, the publications of the Royal Society of Arts programme on Education for Capability; Norman Evans, *The Knowledge Revolution*, Grant McIntyre, 1981. Second chance to learn courses have been pioneered at, for example, the University of Liverpool, Northern College, Barnsley, and at Ruskin College, Oxford.

Chapter 13

EDUCATION AND YOUNG PEOPLE

'Unemployment has dealt us a stunning and crushing blow . . . there is little motivation . . . truancy is high' (Headmaster of a Midlands Comprehensive)

Introduction

13.1   In this Chapter, we first consider education. The Church of England's concern for and involvement in education has a long history. The Church had a considerable influence on the philosophy underlying the 1944 Education Act, which continues to provide the vision and basis upon which schools operate today. As a result of the settlement associated with the Act, a new level of partnership emerged in which the Church of England was given both an institutional presence in the maintained sector and a wealth of opportunity to continue to influence educational thinking.

13.2   The 1944 Act prescribed the development of three progressive educational stages – primary, secondary and further – and declared that 'it shall be the duty of the local education authority for every area, as far as their powers extend, to contribute towards the spiritual, moral, mental and physical development of the community'.

13.3   We start by affirming that a Church which seeks to take seriously its mission to the nation's young people will wish to uphold a system of schooling in which young people are helped to realise their human potential implanted by God, attain maturity and be prepared for life in the wider community.

13.4   Education has a part to play in making human self-centredness less disastrous. The capacity to grasp and experience the redemptive work of Christ is fundamental to the task of the Church. Although the maintained sector of education cannot be in the business of evangelising in the full sense, the Church of England, in partnership, must have commitment to a school system which allows the fullest possible

293

individual development. It must seek to exercise its influence in upholding within the system an organisation, ethos and learning environment which reflects the reality of the presence of the living God in all. The Church must also speak out when it believes that what it holds to be precious is under threat.

13.5   In our various visits to the UPAs we have talked with headteachers, parents, teachers and pupils. We have seen evidence of great commitment by teachers often working in adverse and stressful circumstances. Yet we have been faced with the reality of alienation, poverty, powerlessness, a sense of failure and injustice, and a deepening polarization between the educational experiences of young people in urban priority areas compared with those growing up in 'comfortable Britain'. We are aware that schooling, including church schooling, has offered opportunity for worldly advancement to many children. We are also aware that education is more readily and effectively offered to children with advantageous backgrounds and thus serves to perpetuate social inequality. The UPAs display this inequality in the typically poor academic attainment and unsatisfactory transition to work of their white working class and minority ethnic children.

13.6   The extent of poverty, the quality and nature of housing stock, and degree of social mix are factors in this process. For example, there is a lack of housing mix in many of the catchment areas served by UPA schools. Monochrome catchment areas tend to reinforce low aspiration and low attainment. This underlines the need for housing and education plans to be co-ordinated effectively.

13.7   Schools in all areas have a crucial part to play in encouraging personal attainment and building up self esteem. They do so by creating orderly learning environments in which young people can achieve success, and by accepting that pastoral care implies making academic demands of young people.

13.8   Schools in UPAs face the following problems in achieving these objectives.

Youth Unemployment

13.9   We have referred to youth unemployment in Chapter 9. It has frequently been brought before us as the biggest single problem facing most schools today.

13.10   It has a particularly damaging effect on teacher and pupil morale in certain UPA secondary schools where, for the majority of pupils, the prospect of finding employment is remote. Teachers in UPA schools throughout the country have told us how difficult it is to sustain motivation, especially with their more senior pupils. The pupils we spoke to were friendly and articulate, but in general had little optimism about finding employment. Their apparent acceptance of the situation gave us great cause for concern.

13.11   The 1985 White Paper, *Better Schools*[1] stated that 'It is vital that schools should remember that preparation for working life is one of their principal functions.' We believe that all parents, teachers and young people would agree with this. Yet many pupils in UPAs have reached the view that employment will never be a possibility for them. A recent HMI Curriculum Document[2] in section headed 'The World of Work', suggests that schools ought to take into account that, from a very early age, children are aware of a world of work in which their families are engaged. Yet many pupils in UPA schools today are tragically aware of the world of *un*employment which confronts their families.

13.12   We cannot over-stress the seriousness of this situation. The loss of hope and morale in many UPA schools borders on the catastrophic. It is insufficiently recognised as a matter of major concern.

13.13   The effects of the examination system are relevant here. Even within the comprehensive schools, education continues to be highly selective, competitive and cerebral. The proposed examination reforms may not change this; we understand that the new General Certificate of Secondary Education is designed for only 60 per cent of the year group. This means that in some UPA schools it may be inappropriate for the majority of the year group but will continue to distort the curriculum. The need in such schools is for a curriculum and assessment system which affirms success rather than records failure.

13.14   When school appears to have nothing to give, or when what it gives apparently leads to nothing, there is clearly a problem in finding a way to make its value and authority accepted. Young people who have nothing to gain by their efforts will not try; those who have nothing to lose will not fear punishment.

13.15   Inevitably, a high proportion of young people from UPA schools embark on the Youth Training Scheme (YTS). We have welcomed the scheme, and hope that it will provide a bridge between school and work for all who participate in it. Teachers have, however, told us that they find it difficult to present the YTS to parents and young people in a positive way. Many young people have had bad reports from older brothers or sisters about earlier special schemes. There is much cynicism, and only when the YTS is seen as a genuine source of useful training, which prepares young people to find permanent work, is this overcome.

13.16 Some urban priority area schools are also taking part in the Manpower Services Commission's Technical and Vocational Education Initiative (TVEI) for the 14–18 age range. By 1986 the number of TVEI students will represent 3 per cent of the total age group. The scheme is finding favour in schools, particularly since it makes resources available for curriculum development and the raising of vocational awareness. Unless more employment is available, however, there must again be a fear of raising aspirations which cannot be satisfied. The integrity of education and training depends on the reaction of adequate employment prospects.

Resources
13.17 Education takes a very large share of local rate revenue and of Rate Support Grant. With constraints on both these fronts in recent years, education resources have been seriously reduced, including expenditure on buildings and maintenance, per capita allowances for books, materials and equipment, teaching and non-teaching staff, advisory support services, in-service training, and secondment and induction programmes.

13.18 Despite the efforts of some local authorities, particularly those serving in the areas of greatest educational need, to protect the education service to some degree, there is a sense in the UPAs of a progressively deteriorating environment for teachers and their pupils. The introduction of rate-capping may well put the quality of education in certain urban priority areas at further risk.

13.19 The effect on students in UPAs of public expenditure cuts in higher education also gives us concern. The chances of a young person living in these areas gaining access to university is little different today than it was some 50 years ago. The latest records from the University Central Council for Admissions (UCCA) indicate that the proportion of entrants from families of semi-skilled and unskilled occupations remains disproportionately low.

13.20 The pressure from government to reduce the number of university places is having a clear effect. Figures from UCCA show that in 1984 there were some 15,000 students who failed to obtain a university place whose 'A' Level grades would have guaranteed them a university place before the 1981 spending cuts. A similar pressure on polytechnic places is developing. There is no clear evidence of good correlation between 'A' Level and final degree performances. Students in urban priority areas often have to struggle for good 'A' Level results in circumstances where there is little tradition of extended education and in institutions often poorly resourced. Cuts in expenditure are undoubtedly harming the life opportunities of academically able young people, and our fear is that those in urban priority areas are at particular risk. A recent Green Paper from the Department of Education and Science (*The Development of Higher Education into the 1990s*) gives no grounds for optimism that the next decade will see a widening of access to higher education.

Population Factors

13.21   As a result of a marked decline in the birthrate in urban priority areas, some local education authorities (LEAs) have rationalised educational provision and created 'economically and educationally viable units' by closing and merging schools. The justification has been the need to maintain a sufficiently large school to sustain a broad curriculum. But such mergers can have the effect of destabilising the community by removing secondary schools from the immediate inner city neighbourhoods to some distance away. The consequences can include higher levels of truancy and difficulties in establishing good home-school liaison.

13.22   There are however some LEAs who have maintained small secondary schools in urban priority areas, and a broad curriculum, by adopting a policy of affirmative action through 'curriculum-led staffing' (i.e. having the staffing of the school determined by the curriculum, and not the other way round). The headmaster of one such school told us that on accounting grounds his school of 500 ought to have been closed. But the school was clearly offering rich opportunities and hope to the young people of a very deprived neighbourhood.

13.23   The White Paper *Better Schools* offers advice about size of schools. It suggests that an 11–16 age range comprehensive of five or fewer forms of entry is unlikely to offer a sufficiently broad, balanced, relevant, differentiated and deliverable curriculum without 'disproportionately generous staffing'. The White Paper refers to factors which might necessitate unusually small schools. But it does not mention UPAs nor does it recognise their need for stability, cohesion, and strong school-home-neighbourhood links. We stress the importance of the maintenance of well-staffed primary and secondary schools – which will in some instances mean small schools in the UPAs.

The Pressures on Teachers

13.24   We have recorded our observation of the commitment shown by UPA teachers often working in adverse and stressful circumstances. A local clergyman, in a very poor housing area in the West Midlands, said of the local estate comprehensive, 'The impression I have is of a great deal of caring.' A local parent told us, 'There are a lot of good teachers there . . . they are overworked . . . they lack time.'

13.25   We have to record, however, that we heard some critical comments from parents and others. At the same meeting, in the West Midlands, these views were expressed:

'There are too many teachers there who like to be close to children . . . they don't teach them much there.'

'It's more like a leisure centre than a real school.'

'There's too much freedom . . . the kids don't know where they are.'

13.26   We have heard parents in urban priority areas say that the aspirations of teachers for their children are too low and that their children under-achieve. A black youth leader in Greater Manchester told us that he had sent his seven year-old daughter to a private school, because he felt she would not get a chance in the maintained sector. He told us that at the private school there was more discipline and that it had much smaller classes.

13.27   If there are low aspirations, they are not confined to teachers. At one meeting a parent told us, 'A school is only as good as the area it serves. If there is no emphasis on the importance of education by parents, how can the school hope to cope? The majority of kids in this estate don't want to learn.'

13.28   The pressures upon urban schools are substantial and complex. Teachers often feel trapped between trying to provide an enriching educational experience for all, and going for examination success in a system devised for a minority of their pupils in order to sustain parental confidence. The two are not necessarily mutually exclusive but there is a genuine tension.

13.29   There is a detectable ambivalence amongst teachers in these circumstances. A teacher in a large comprehensive in a large housing estate said to us 'Are we socialising the kids here to accept their situation?' Other teachers in similar situations have expressed genuine anxiety (particularly given the level of youth unemployment) about whether they were raising aspirations and ambitions in the young people which would never be satisfied. Other teachers have expressed concern about under-achievement: 'It is a problem. It is not fashionable to work and study.'

13.30   It can be difficult to recruit good teachers to schools in urban priority areas, especially to secondary schools. These schools need well qualified teachers with high personal qualities, including good communication skills, an enthusiasm for learning, a liking for young people, resilience, good health, a sensitivity to the needs and concerns of disadvantaged children, a sense of humour and a sense of proportion. Some senior staff wonder whether the stress and responsibility is worth shouldering. A high priority needs to be given to the recruitment and retention of good headteachers and staff for urban priority area schools. They must be given opportunities for regular secondment and in-service training, adequate preparation time, additional school/community liaison staff and advisory and ancillary support.

13.31   We have been told that there are relatively few members of the Church of England working as teachers in urban priority area schools. Many teachers are attracted, for a variety of reasons, to suburban, rural or private schools. We would however urge all Christians who are contemplating teaching, or who are already teaching, to consider expressing their vocation in UPAs.

Training
13.32   Teachers have told us of their dissatisfaction with their initial training as a preparation for the complexity of creating a learning environment in urban priority areas.

13.33   The Church of England has had a long tradition of involvement in the initial training of teachers, and we believe it to be important for it to continue to do so. A capacity and willingness to generate new responses to pressing needs must continue to be one of the main justifications for the Church's presence in the publicly-provided sector of higher education.

13.34   The Church colleges do not see their prime role as the preparation of Christian teachers to teach in Church schools. However, there is a clear need for better-equipped teachers of religious education in schools of all kinds, and we believe that the Church colleges still face an important challenge here. They also have a major role to play in the development of resources and teaching strategies to equip teachers to promote the spiritual dimension of the education of young people.

13.35 We would also stress the contribution colleges can make to train teachers to work closely with parents. A survey of initial training of teachers has found that a third of primary and about one half of secondary trained teachers have 'little or no preparation to work with parents'. Teachers attending in-service courses have complained that their initial training did little or nothing to equip them to work with parents and that most of their skills had to be acquired through a painful process of trial and error.

13.36 Not least, Church colleges should be encouraged to play an increasing role in the better preparation of teachers for urban priority area schools. By way of illustration, one positive initiative which we wish to commend is the community-orientated teacher training programme of the Urban Studies Centre in East London.

13.37 The work of this centre was warmly supported by teachers during the Commission's visit to East London. It was originally set up as part of the work of the College of St Mark and St John at Plymouth, and has since been expanded with the assistance of the National Society and the Central Board of Finance. It provides opportunities for undergraduate and graduate teachers in training to spend up to several months living and working in East London. They teach for three days a week in a multi-racial school and for the remainder of the week they engage in school-related social and community work. The majority of students who are placed in the Urban Studies Centre take up their initial appointments with metropolitan authorities.

13.38 The Centre is playing a part in innovatory teacher education. By offering students an opportunity to live and work in urban priority areas it provides a training based on realism. We believe this approach should be developed, and *recommend* that similar centres should be established in other urban priority areas.

Support
13.39 We heard repeated accounts of stress and 'burn out' among teachers. A group of East London headteachers said, 'Teaching in the inner city is stressful and a great deal of support is needed.'

13.40 We were in general greatly encouraged by unsolicited

expressions of warmth towards the Church of England by teachers in UPAs. A group of East London primary school teachers told us that they doubted whether they would have survived the stress and strain of their work had it not been for the support of local Anglican clergy and lay people. A headmaster of a comprehensive school in a most disadvantaged area of the West Midlands wrote to us of the pressures of his role and its effect upon his personal situation saying:

'I am now aware that quiet friendship, prayer and patient support by the Church of those in the "firing line" day by day can be valuable out of all proportion to its appearance. The Church's role in this battle against deprivation is potentially great even in areas where this poverty is not obviously manifested. I have been greatly heartened recently by the public pronouncements of leaders of the Church of England on industrial strife and unemployment. They have contributed significantly to the morale of many Christians and others in the field who can all too easily feel isolated.'

13.41   There is a substantial degree of goodwill towards the Church in these areas: we would encourage local Churches to be sensitive to this and to play an active role in supporting the work of local schools. Sometimes a local Church, acting ecumenically, is in a position to bridge gaps where there is difficulty in promoting closer home-school-community relationships.

13.42   It has been pointed out to us in evidence that the support given to their Church schools, or other local schools, by the clergy and laity is greatly increased if they send their own children to them. Words of support can seem hollow, if by their decisions about their own children they indicate that they think there is a better education to be found somewhere else. We do not suggest that this is the only factor Christian parents in urban priority areas will wish to consider in deciding on the education of their children: obviously there are many factors they will weigh. But we ask them to include this among the factors they consider.

13.43   The evidence we have received reflects a wide variety of different experiences and attitudes to this question by the clergy. They range from expressions of appreciation of the great privilege of living and bringing up their children in a multi-cultural area, to a feeling that the conflict of identity their children face in growing up among children of different backgrounds to their own is putting too great a burden on them. Many different decisions will be made, for many different reasons, in many different circumstances. The clergy questioned in our survey said that the question of their children's education was 'one of the important factors to be considered' in deciding whether to accept a post in an urban priority parish; of those who do work in such parishes, the survey revealed that at primary level 13 per cent of UPA clergy had sent their children to a fee-paying school (the rest being divided between state primary and Church of England primary schools in the maintained sector), a much smaller proportion than that of clergy in non-UPA parishes (23 per cent). At secondary level the proportion of UPA clergy with children who attended a fee-paying school rises to 32 per cent, as we noted in Chapter 6.[3]

Minority Ethnic Groups and Educational Opportunity

13.44   We have found that many schools in multi-racial areas offer a stimulating learning environment with a wealth of opportunities. The children in an inner London comprehensive school told a member of the Commission that it was good to live and go to school in a multi-ethnic area.

13.45   The Commission also visited a happy multi-ethnic primary school in the West Midlands and found it lively, stimulating and friendly. The headteacher of this school told us: 'Problems must be turned into opportunities. We must capitalize on and support the use of the children's mother tongue, so that they use it more fluently, and thereby encourage an improvement in English at the same time . . . the opportunities are all around us . . . the school must take advantage of the fact that many of the children have travelled to and been in countries that teachers have not. There is cultural wealth in the inner city.'

13.46   There is, however, concern about the low educational attainment of many black children. A 1981 DES survey of school-leaver qualifications in six urban LEAs showed that the percentage of those achieving higher grade examination passes was 3 per cent West Indian, 18 per cent Asian, others 16 per cent; the national figure was 22 per cent. Statistics in the Swann report[4] on the education of ethnic minority children show a slight improvement in the examination performance of children of West Indian ethnic origin in these areas subsequently.

13.47   We were made aware of the very strong feeling of some black people who look back upon their own experience of school and speak of a determination that things must be better for their own children. They told us of the stereotyped view that their only possible success could be in sport or dance. One person said to us, 'I felt put down at school. I felt I could not excel at academic subjects . . . my teachers used to tell me not to bother too much with lessons and homework, but to concentrate on sport and athletics.' Many people believe that 'institutional racism' contributes to the poor level of attainment of black young people. A black youth leader and parent remarked, 'There is racism in schools. Teachers do not understand black children and their backgrounds. They do not recognise horse play as horse play.'

13.48   The problem is not confined to those of West Indian origin. Members of the Commission visited Bradford and heard the concern of the Asian population there. At least 30 schools in inner city Bradford have more than 50 per cent Asian children and at least 6 have more than 90 per cent. Of white school-leavers in Bradford, 38 per cent find jobs, compared with only 8 per cent of Asian children. One-half of Asian children leave school with no qualifications in mathematics, 45 per cent with no qualifications in English, and 33 per cent with no qualifications at all.

13.49   There are serious grievances amongst Asians about religious assemblies, dress, physical education and school meals. There is a growing demand by some Muslim parents for separate voluntary-aided schools. Currently there are believed to be 11 Muslim schools in the independent sector. We are challenged to find ways in which Muslim parents can feel that their children are receiving an education that is sensitive to their traditions and their faith, while being aware of the danger of a new division of schools along ethnic lines which could exacerbate tensions in a plural society.

13.50   Concern was expressed to us in this context about the absence of black teachers in schools. We visited a large West Midlands comprehensive with a 35 per cent Asian population. In this school there was a positive multi-cultural approach: yet there was one Asian teacher in a staff of 70. The school had looked actively for other Asian teachers but had been unsuccessful. Outside of London there is only one black secondary headteacher. This Bradford head states: 'I know black people who are discouraging their youngsters from going into the teaching profession because of the lack of promotion and the racism.' It has been suggested to us that racism appears to be a problem more among secondary than primary school teachers.

13.51   The problems and opportunities of a multi-cultural society have many implications for our schools. These include:

(a)   the need to avoid 'ghetto' schools, with the implications of this for admissions policies in the case of Church schools;

(b)   the need for schools to be sensitive to, and to reflect and affirm, the cultures of the pupils, once admitted, and the implications for the curriculum of a multi-cultural school;

(c)   the consequences for religious education;

(d)   the need for the Church – clergy and laity – not to lag behind teachers in understanding and affirming other cultures;

(e)   the need for resources to support multi-ethnic education.

13.52   First, the need to avoid 'ghetto' schools is especially important where hostility exists between different sections of the population, whether it is between Catholic and Protestant, black and white, Christian and Muslim, middle class and working class. A segregated or sectarian education can increase tensions and misunderstandings. It is particularly important for Church schools to examine their student body, to see if it reflects the diversity present in the area, and ask themselves if not, why not? An admissions policy based on Church of England membership, or even one based on length of time resident in the area, can operate to exclude Muslims, immigrants and other groups. We commend to the Diocesan Boards and parishes the General Synod Board of Education discussion document *A Future in Partnership*, especially in relation to its comments on admissions policies.

13.53   We have been made aware on our visits of the concern caused by the existence of only one Church secondary school in a Local Education Authority area. In two cities we have visited, we have been told by teachers that the Church secondary school appeared to be developing as a middle class white school for the children of professional parents. This is not always a problem which can be solved by the unaided efforts of the Church school concerned. It is difficult for one school to devise and operate an admissions policy which turns away academically-able children who are churchgoers, in the interests of a balanced and comprehensive intake. It is easier to achieve balance and avoid the more popular schools 'creaming off' abler children if the local authority has a system to which the Church school must adhere. In the Inner London Education Authority (ILEA), for example, children at eleven are 'banded' by a mixture of tests and teachers' assessments, so that each comprehensive school can be required to include in its intake a fair proportion of children from the above-average achievers, as well as the below-average achievers. This helps to deal with the problems faced by neighbourhood schools with catchment areas where there is no social mix. Church secondary schools are also able to exist side-by-side with the maintained secondary schools, without accusations of 'creaming off'.

13.54   Second, we believe schools must be sensitive to, and affirm, the cultures of the pupils, once admitted, and need to address the implications for the curriculum of a multi-cultural school. We have received evidence from ILEA on this point. That Authority has produced a series of guidance papers on race and multi-ethnic education. A team of multi-ethnic advisers has been formed within each administrative division and the catering branch has been given a specific responsibility for ethnic food and cooking methods. In the Spitalfields/ Brick Lane area of Tower Hamlets, where there is a high proportion of Bengali children who are not fluent in English, a project has been established to increase opportunities for these children, and their families. It helps them to learn English language skills and develop mother-tongue teaching; it involves parents in their children's teaching; and it provides opportunities for young people and adults to learn English as a second language.

13.55   Third, the multi-cultural and multi-faith nature of many UPA school populations raises questions for religious and spiritual education in schools. But the challenge from a different direction is probably stronger still: although 70 per cent of the population say they believe in God, and the majority of people questioned in surveys favour the retention of Religious Education, this does not mean that the majority of pupils in school are open or receptive to the traditional forms of Religious Education, or regard them as important or useful. It is in this context that UPA schools face the further challenge of the presence of children of other faiths (often much more numerous and who are usually much better taught about their faith) than children with any active Church connections.

13.56   How far is it right to teach the Christian faith as *the* religion to be desired and believed? How are the festivals and rituals of the Christian faith to be celebrated when the majority of children are Muslim?

13.57   An Inter-Faith group in Wolverhampton told members of the Commission of the anxiety of Asian parents that religious education in schools should not be exclusively from a Christian viewpoint. They were concerned that in multi-ethnic schools there should be a celebration of our common humanity as well as diverse cultural roots. They were anxious for the Commission to affirm the view that 'no education is complete without a religious perspective'. It must be said, however, that in today's pluralistic society there would be no consensus on this amongst teachers, educationalists and administrators.

13.58　There is no doubt that the present teaching of religious education is unstatisfactory. In some schools it is wholly subsumed into a programme of personal and social development. Many urban priority area schools have told us of their difficulty in recruiting suitable religious education teachers. Some LEAs have no specific religious education adviser. A report by the Religious Education Council has stated that more than half the Religious Education lessons are taught by teachers who have no qualifications in the subject. A research project in 1984 into the status of religious education in inner city schools found that the status of the subject was low, there were few well-qualified teachers of religious education and the subject tended to be unpopular with staff and pupils alike. It also showed that the teachers of Religious Education believed that theirs was a tough job with low status and poor resource support.

13.59　We wish to reaffirm the importance of religious education and a religious and spiritual perspective in the education of young people in UPA schools. One of the major prescriptions of the 1944 Education Act was that schools should contribute to the spiritual development of the community. A recent HMI curriculum document[5] speaks of the importance of the spiritual as one of nine essential areas of learning and experience. Spiritual education is difficult to define but has to do with those feelings and convictions about what it means to be fully human in a created world. This includes awareness of, and response to, a dimension which includes reverence for life and personal commitment. (This is in sharp contrast to a view of education as being narrowly mechanistic and utilitarian.) It is something towards which all teachers, and the curriculum as a whole, have an opportunity to contribute. It is not just the preserve of teachers of religious education. It has been said to us that this aspect of learning is particularly at risk in UPAs. A growing lack of hope about the future, and a deteriorating environment in which their lives are set, makes it difficult for young people to realise their divinely-implanted potential. The opportunity for young people to develop their potential as human beings is, therefore, at serious risk. For this reason we ask the General Synod's Board of Education to consider practical ways (such as in-service training programmes) in which schools and teachers might be helped to develop fresh approaches to spiritual education across the curriculum.

13.60　Fourth, there is a need for the Church – clergy and laity – not to lag behind the teachers in understanding and affirming other cultures. Many teachers have said to us in evidence that they appreciate the help given to them by the local clergy in contacting the leaders of other faiths. Many others have said however that they find it adds to their difficulties in trying to make a constructive approach to what can be a tense multi-racial situation, when some clergy insist on a narrow view of the school as a place for Christian instruction, regardless of the wishes of those being instructed. This attitude can only lend strength to the wish by members of the Muslim community to have their own separate schools.

13.61   There is a possible clash between the aims of Church schools and the need for racial harmony and justice. Some Church schools may not have the motivation and resources to develop the linguistic and multi-faith skills necessary to nurture children of other faiths because of their view, which we understand, that their highest priority is to teach the Christian faith.

13.62   It is not always easy for white people in urban priority areas to see things through the eyes of minority ethnic groups. They may rather see the Christian faith as symbolising their whiteness, and national identity. These religious differences can sometimes pass over into racial conflict and deepen tensions, often placing a great strain upon teachers.

13.63   Two important documents have recently been issued by the Church of England and by the Roman Catholic Church. We commend them both for wide discussion by the Church.

13.64   In 1984 the Board of Education of the General Synod published a discussion booklet, *Schools and Multi-Cultural Education*, which set out in a full and detailed way the challenges, for schools, of pluralism, and their need to create a learning environment which helps young people prepare for a place in a multi-cultural society, without denying their cultural roots.

13.65   The issue also has to be faced in the predominantly white urban areas. A Roman Catholic working party on 'Catholic Education in a Multi-Racial and Multi-Cultural Society' also reported in 1984 and it noted, 'Perhaps the issue which concerned us most was the overwhelming perception on the part of most headteachers and their staff that multi-cultural education is only relevant to black children, and almost universal lack of awareness of the need to educate white children from this perspective.'

13.66   Those who live and are educated in multi-cultural areas have the opportunity of facing (even though sometimes with pain or anger) a great moral challenge of our age; and yet it is equally important that those who are educated in areas that still have a single class or culture should also face this challenge. They are, after all, citizens of a multi-racial world, even though this may not yet be visible within their own neighbourhoods.

13.67   Fifth, there is a need for adequate resources to support multi-ethnic education. Members of the Commission saw at first hand the work of the Minority Group Support Service established by the Coventry LEA in 1977 which seeks to address itself to the needs of children from minority ethnic backgrounds. The service is funded by the LEA and also supported by Home Office grants (under Section 11 of the 1966 Local Government Act). The grants cover three-quarters of the cost of salaries for teacher, welfare and clerical staff; the service works across the age range from pre-school to upper secondary and involves language work, welfare and curriculum development. The schools which we visited paid high testimony to the cost-effectiveness of the service. In one of the primary schools we visited there was a sense of richness, purpose and happiness. It had a teaching staff of twelve, three of whom were 'Section 11 staff'. It was pressed upon us that if these three teachers were removed for any reason, huge problems would be created by a return to a more mechanical and impersonal teaching.

Affirmative Action

13.68   For a variety of reasons, therefore, the education system is under pressure in the UPAs. We have noted some of the problems under the headings above, and in some cases suggested possible ways forward.

13.69   It has been strongly put to us, however, that action needs to be taken on a number of other fronts, under the heading of 'affirmative action'.

(1)   *Pre-school Intervention*

13.70   We have already referred to the needs of the under-5s in Chapter 12. The case for pre-school intervention as an important means of overcoming disadvantage in UPAs has frequently been emphasised to us in evidence. And yet it is a part of the education system which is particularly vulnerable to cuts. A.H. Halsey has written of affirmative action programmes at the pre-school stage: 'A pre-school programme, properly devised, can be a most economical instrument for a government wishing to save money in our schools. And for a government determined to reduce the handicap of those who come from poor families, a pre-school programme discriminating in their favour seems to be one of the crucial weapons in their armoury. In that way education can compensate for society.'[6]

13.71   This view is supported by recent research in the USA, which has followed up a pre-school project initiated over 20 years ago. The cost benefit analysis suggests that in terms of reduced claims for welfare benefits and costs of criminal proceedings the pre-school programme more than paid for itself. The case for pre-school intervention does not however rest solely on economic grounds. We believe with others that it has clear benefits in social and educational terms in helping to alleviate disadvantage.

(2)   The Education of Girls

13.72   The issue of gender has been raised on all of our visits to urban priority areas. There is general concern about the low participation by girls in certain subjects in the school curriculum – particularly computer studies, physics, and craft design technology. It has to be conceded that there is similar concern about the under-representation of boys in subjects such as dance, business studies and modern languages.

13.73   The overcoming of sex stereotyping will be long-term. ILEA and some other LEAs have taken a positive lead in this area. ILEA has adopted a policy on the elimination of sexism in schools and the promotion of equal opportunities for girls and women. In addition they have set up a small Inspectorate for girls education, and to produce non-sexist learning materials.

13.74   One urban comprehensive school in an inner city area in north west England has appointed an equal opportunities teacher with whom we talked at some length. The school has recently held events for junior and senior girls, as a means of challenging stereotyping and building up the confidence of girls. For senior girls this included discussions between the girls and voluntary groups about rape, women's health, relationships, contraception and women's aid. For junior girls it included sessions on computing, trampolining, science, keep fit, hair-braiding and steel and African drumming.

(3)   Community Schools in Urban Priority Areas

13.75   Community schools are another manifestation of a policy of affirmative action. The term 'community school' is capable of many definitions. It implies more than a dual use of school buildings. At its best, it views education as a life-long process to which all have access. Schools represent a considerable investment in terms of buildings, accommodation, equipment and human expertise: these are resources capable of being developed in the interests of the whole community. Community schools in UPAs can play a significant part in developing 'second chance' or 'return to learn' classes for people who find themselves unemployed or redundant, and need to retrain or add to their qualifications – or indeed those who want to pursue learning for its own sake.

13.76 We gladly acknowledge the progress that has been made so far by community schools. But there is a long road ahead. Community schools still tend to attract a greater proportion of higher socio-economic groups in both their educational and recreational programmes: in many cases only few members of manual and unskilled occupational groups are involved. Committee structures may be formalised, and the procedures of some community associations may be a barrier to greater participation by people from manual and unskilled groups. It is apparent that these schools will need to develop new means of reaching the most disadvantaged, and take a fresh look at the style and type of activities offered. They can, in particular, enhance young people's education by developing a community-related curriculum. There is an urgent need for teacher training programmes to be developed in this area.

13.77 Whenever possible we would wish to see Church schools in urban priority areas developing along community school lines. We were privileged to visit such a Church school in Salford serving in an area of very high unemployment. In this school of 290 (aged 3–11) there was a teaching staff of 14, with 2 community teachers and one nursery nurse. The community teachers spent half their time in the school and the other half in the community. The school had developed an excellent home reading scheme involving more than 50 per cent of parents. The parents listen to the children read at home for about 5 minutes, fill in a card and make a comment. The headteacher noted: 'We have to say to parents: do not be threatening, do not punish children for mistakes, reading at home should be cuddles time.'

(4)   *The Management of Schools and Local Participation*
13.78   Many LEAs have made great efforts to widen representation in the government of schools, in some cases involving non-teaching

staff and school students. Some schools have student councils which play a part in decision-making. We have also encountered schools which allow pupils to observe and participate in staff meetings and staff discussions.

13.79   It is especially important that UPA schools open up decision-making, become more aware of the need for proper accountability, and encourage local participation. Professionals often unwittingly take away responsibility. The real agents of hope and change in the UPAs are the local people. Many of the children growing up in these areas are going to live all of their lives in them. Schools have a role to play in resisting the temptation to do things for people, and take the more arduous but productive road which respects people's ability to think and act for themselves.

13.80   An example of an attempt to do this is at a centre based at a Community School in Wolverhampton which provides a range of youth and adult activities throughout the week in an area of severe disadvantage. Its uniqueness lies not in its activities but in its management scheme, which has been approved by the local authority and registered with the Charity Commission. It puts a substantial amount of power, control and initiative into the hands of local people and allows considerable scope for them to develop local courses. Positive discrimination is exercised in favour of the local residents in that those who live outside the area pay more and are placed at the end of a waiting list. The management structure is such that local residents form a majority, the professionals are outnumbered by about three to one and the headteacher does not have a veto. The headmaster of the school writes, 'What is required is that the local people are able to (1) make their own decisions (2) manage resources of their own to the maximum benefit of the whole community. Such a philosophy must command support from all points of the political spectrum (except the totalitarian), for it combines the twin elements of individual responsibility and community enterprise, based on self-esteem and generating mutual care.'

Further Education
13.81   Only a minority of young people move from UPAs to Higher Education, in which the Church of England is well represented in terms of chaplaincies. The majority of young people from UPAs who remain in full-time education on leaving school move into Further Education. In 1983 the General Synod Board of Education asked diocesan Directors

of Education to examine how their Diocesan Boards and Councils might more closely relate to the work of Further Education Colleges. It is already apparent that a variety of support work by the Church of England, sometimes acting ecumenically, is underway. This ranges from the appointment of full- and/or part-time chaplains to colleges of Further Education, the creation of support groups for colleges, and the appointment of Further Education officers to improve the liaison between the Church and the Further Education world. Some dioceses have been active in this field for a number of years.

13.82   For example in the Diocese of Manchester in the early 1970s a Further Education officer was appointed, and the establishment of chaplaincies in the colleges under the auspices of the Greater Manchester Ecumenical Council was pursued. A subsequent report by this Council (*Church and College in Further Education*) outlined the four principal areas of work in the colleges:– (a) focusing a Christian presence in the college; (b) counselling; (c) teaching; and (d) providing a theological insight into the day-to-day life of the insitutions. The report concluded with the view that the Churches working together should invest at least as much money and manpower in the vast field of Further Education as they do in the more specialised and much smaller area of Higher Education. We agree that the imbalance between the two does need to be redressed.

Opportunities for the Church of England
13.83   We must first record that some members of the Church of England are already 'being the Church' in the maintained sector of education as teachers, advisers, administrators, governors of schools and members of local education committees. Some of them are working at great personal cost in the areas of greatest disadvantage. In partnership with others they have an opportunity to influence the ethos, organisation and curriculum of maintained schools; and it is in these maintained schools that the vast majority – 94 per cent – of the children of our country are being educated.

13.84   In this Chapter we have not made a hard and fast distinction between the maintained schools and the Church's voluntary schools; there is in fact no hard and fast distinction – some Church schools are very like their neighbours; Christians can be involved in the management and teaching in both kinds of school. The subjects we have been dealing with have been applicable to both kinds of school: in both youth unemployment has its effect, shortages of resources are beginning to bite, teachers need relevant training and support, minority ethnic groups and children of other faiths are present, and all pupils need an education for a multi-cultural future; both kinds of schools have a legal responsibility laid on them to give religious education, and face largely similar problems in doing so, and the various kinds of affirmative action are needed in both kinds of school.

13.85   But there are questions which have been put to us in evidence which we must put to those employed by the Church. Some have come up under other headings already. Here we must address specifically the clergy's involvement in the management and chaplaining of schools. We welcome the opportunities offered to clergy by invitation, and not by right, to be Governors of maintained schools. The clergy's visits to maintained schools – to teach, take assemblies, speak on speech days, or support the staff – also rest upon the goodwill of those concerned, and are to be welcomed.

13.86   But it has been said to us, on more than one occasion, that far from reflecting a bias to the poor, the Church's involvement in education might reveal a bias towards the 6 per cent of young people who attend private schools. Many private schools employ chaplains. Many schools in the private sector invite bishops to their prize days and Confirmations, and clergy to preach, conduct retreats and take part in festive occasions, or to be involved in the management of the schools.

13.87   All involvement in such an important field as education must be a priority for bishops, clergy and lay people; but it has been put to us in evidence that many of them, especially bishops, spend a disproportionate amount of their time at the schools attended by 6 per cent of the population of the country, and rarely visit the schools which educate the other 94 per cent. We ask bishops, clergy and lay Christians therefore to examine themselves on the use of their time in this respect. It has been suggested to us that bishops tend to go where they are invited, and that the need may be for them to take the initiative in allotting their time.

13.88   The Bishop's diary may symbolise a deeper and wider problem. The evidence from many sides is that private schools in Britain have been divisive of the nation to an extent far beyond their apparently small numerical importance. We readily recognize the long tradition of Christian education and the ethic of service to others which is part of the history of independent schools. Moreover, some of us have great loyalty and respect for private schools. But few of us would deny that their separate life exacts a heavy toll from the maintained schools in three ways. Political energy is drained off from support for state education by parents who are better-off and better educated than the average. Able teachers are drawn away by higher salaries and better conditions of work. Motivated children are removed and thereby take away what can be, especially in an urban priority area school, a crucial minority in support of all-round standards.

13.89   Nor can it be denied that the Church of England has been implicated in this process of division and inequality in the upbringing of children. There is no direct financial Church support involved, but the private sector is much more richly endowed with chaplaincies and with church connections (over one-third of all clergy have attended private schools). As we have already noted, a number of UPA and non-UPA priests take advantage of the opportunities available to send their own children to school in the private sector. Under present circumstances they may have good grounds for choosing this option; but we cannot help regretting that, in Britain in 1985, this option still seems so much more attractive than the other. We believe that it is a high priority to work for closer partnership and greater comparability in standards and facilities between the two sectors.

13.90   Diocesan Boards and Councils of Education are in a position to reflect the Church of England's commitment to partnership in the maintained sector and to reflect a bias to the disadvantaged and powerless. Some are taking important initiatives on wider educational issues of contemporary concern. For example, the Newcastle Board of Education, through its Education Review Committee, is promoting initiatives in the area of school–employer links and dialogue on the effect of youth unemployment on the motivation of young people in school. The Diocese of Southwark has created a new principal committee, the Education Policy Committee, to handle all issues of a major educational nature which require in-depth consideration and policy formation. Other dioceses have embarked upon similar developments.

13.91   Yet all the public policy issues outlined in this Chapter are the proper concern of Diocesan Boards, and of those within the Church of England at national level responsible for education. We make the following further *recommendations*:

(i)   all Diocesan Boards and Councils of Education should give special priority to the educational needs of the urban priority schools for which they are responsible;

(ii)   the governors and managers of Church schools should consider whether the composition of their foundation governors adequately reflects the ethnic constituency of the catchment area.

(iii)   consideration should be given to a further exploration of the ecumenical dimension at secondary level, including the possibility of establishing Church of England/Roman Catholic schools in urban priority areas, which would offer a significant proportion of places to children of other faiths.

(iv)   a review of the Diocesan Education Committee measures should be undertaken, to allow the formulation of diocesan policies for Church schools on admissions criteria and other issues such as religious education and worship, equal opportunities and community education. We do not believe that this would lead to a damaging erosion of the freedom of the individual Church school.

Youth Work

13.92   One of the Commission's most difficult tasks has been to make direct and personal contact with young people, other than in schools. However, our visits to the UPAs, consultation with youth leaders, and the written evidence submitted to us, have given us some confidence in our assessments.

13.93   Again, the variety within and between UPAs needs to be emphasised first of all. The young people we met in a Bengali community in Tower Hamlets were very different from the young Asians we met in Bradford and in the West Midlands – who are, yet again, very different from the young white people we met in Newcastle.

13.94   Yet the overall impression is clear. It is that there are sizeable groups of young people who are trapped in UPAs, who only gain attention when they become a threat, who are denied equality of opportunity and life chances, and with whom the Churches have little or no contact.

13.95   It is difficult to exaggerate how *alienated* these young people are: from adult ideas of how young people should behave; from their peers of different social classes; from agencies they think of as acting on adults' behalf and not usually in the interests of young people, e.g. from the police; from school; and from the Church.

13.96   This alienation is closely related to unemployment; 'the most significant issue adolescents worry about – those experiencing it, as well as those not ready to enter the labour market'.[7] The figures for youth unemployment and our comments about the YTS in Chapter 9 underline this point.

13.97   The increase in youth unemployment has disrupted the normal progression of development from home to school to job; and the time during which a young person is dependent on home and family has been extended. The prolonging of financial dependency creates problems both for parents and for their children, who live in a youth culture which relies on an adequate income. But above all it has removed one of the main ways a young person has of valuing himself or herself. Many young people are extremely resilient and seem able to transcend their environment with hope in their hearts. Others have spoken to us of the hurt of watching young people grow through childhood to adolescence and beyond, and as they do so experiencing a transformation from the normal expectancy and hope of the young, through apparent resignation to the inner pain and anger of a life seemingly without hope.

13.98   There are of course other factors. Elsewhere in our Report we examine the symptoms and causes of the apparent breakdown of order in the UPAs – such as the changing patterns of family life, the anonymity of the large city, the design of local authority housing estates, the conflict between the pressures of advertising and the reality of having little cash in your pocket. Alienation – the making of people, not least young people, to feel themselves to be 'outsiders' – is from a particular *order* that is felt to be unresponsive and uncaring.

13.99   We have heard first hand of the fear of the destructive potential of young people. We have sensed the latent violence as we have walked along the streets; we have seen groups of young people with nothing to do, nowhere to go, and with nothing to lose:

> 'I wouldn't go out without a pair of scissors to defend me.'

> 'If someone steps on your toe every day, and if they keep on doing it, you might do something drastic.'

13.100   Young people often gravitate to the city centres, for a variety of reasons. Those who can afford the pubs and clubs go there. For those who cannot, the city centre may be a meeting place where they can congregate, perhaps in a particular arcade or cafe. 'Going down town', 'hanging around', 'doing nothing' is a common experience, as are reports of 'contact' with police and security guards.

13.101 Contact with young people in these locations across the country is usually the work of detached youth workers. We affirm their importance in this situation: the ideal is for such workers to be part of a team (including centre-based workers) and with a proper support system. We recognize the short-comings of this most demanding of youth work practice, however, and that effective monitoring and assessment has not always been well done.

13.102 Work with young people in city centres is not solely confined to detached work. Other initiatives that youth work agencies have developed in some of Britain's city centres include information kiosks, drop-in centres, and homelessness projects. The fact remains however that initiatives of this sort have a precarious existence.

13.103 We have heard of the increasing need for short-term crisis accommodation for young people in UPAs. This needs to be flexible, small-scale, available at a neighbourhood level, informal rather than institutionally-based. We commend those projects which provide extended family facilities in single households for under 3 nights. This helps to diffuse family friction and reduce the incidence of sleeping rough and of petty crime.

13.104 Young people need premises they can make their own. Extended school-based provision – if you don't like school – can be inappropriate. Yet if youth work premises are unattractive, young people will go for the pubs and the commercial discos, as even many 13 and 14 year-olds are now doing. The commercial exploitation of younger teenagers, and their early introduction to a 'bar culture', challenges the standard and quality of the provision of facilities through both the statutory and voluntary sectors of the youth service.

13.105 It is not only in the inner city areas but the surrounding estates – as the National Youth Bureau have noted – that the needs of young people call for a response. For example in the London Borough of Lambeth there are 157 estates of varying sizes with over 50,000 dwellings, many high-rise. Very few of these estates have adequate community facilities; some are very run-down and all have major environmental problems. To a large extent it is young people, many black and unemployed, from the 157 estates who frequent the centre of Brixton. The major clamp-down on street crime in the centre has resulted in an increased incidence of mugging, violence and vandalism on the estates. Now local residents are demanding a more estate-based youth service response. But the youth service in the London Borough of

Lambeth does not have the resources to respond. We consider this to be serious. Work with young people at risk can reduce the need for custodial care later, with a significant saving in public expenditure. It is far more cost-effective for the youth service to undertake successful preventive work, than for the pieces to be picked up later.

13.106   It is important that we should note here that 43 per cent of the total sample of those involved in the survey *Young people in the '80s* mentioned involvement with the police as one of their worries and concerns. In the UPAs, the survey found that this worry and concern was considerably heightened; and this has been our experience too. We recognize that the police are often left to deal with the consequences of failure elsewhere in our society – in the failure of schools, families, the labour market, and housing. We welcome the work of the Juvenile Bureau, and commend those strategies – all too rare – in which youth workers, the police, teachers, probation officers and parents work together for the wellbeing of their own young people and their local neighbourhoods. More needs to be done to develop such *preventive* approaches rather than to extend the provision for custodial care.

The Youth Service

13.107   Our judgement about the degree of alienation among young people is confirmed by the conclusions of the Report of the Review Group on the Youth Service in England (the Thompson Report), which was presented to Parliament in October 1982. We have seen little evidence that those in authority in Church or state have as yet been seized, despite the Thompson Report, by the seriousness of the alienation with which most of those who work in the youth service in UPAs are only too familiar.

13.108   The youth service in the UPAs is facing more and more the need to undertake crisis counselling. Youth projects are often having to respond with diminishing resources to the needs of the young homeless and unemployed and truants: and the provision for the less disadvantaged suffers as result. The youth service is having increasingly to act as the 'safety net' to cope with crisis, and to compensate for short-comings in other fields.

13.109   As a result, we have heard, seen and felt first hand something of the depressed morale of those who work with young people in the UPAs. Many feel that they work in spite of, not because of, and certainly not on behalf of, those in power. They have to cope with the violence and frustration as it is projected on to them by young people. They know themselves to be overworked and with little or no recognition, and argue that youth work centres are suffering from inadequate funding.[8]

13.110   The submission to us from one senior employee of the youth service can stand for many:

'Being a discretionary service, the youth service is part of "education" in which the school dominates. There is the feeling that the youth service is the "Cinderella" . . . It suffers from a serious shortage of skilled personnel, especially in the area of good centre-based workers, but also in the skill areas of youth counselling, social education, management and organisation, and group work . . . There is an inescapable personal tension in being employed, yet working with the unemployed . . . The need now is to hold the cuts and even have increased budgets . . . More work is needed to develop appropriate strategies for youth provision in relation to Asian and Afro-Caribbean young people. White culture-based youth work is not appropriate.'

13.111   The Thompson Report argued that the youth service had to 'further the social education of all young people whether employed or unemployed, and whether on a YTS scheme or not . . . and to develop new methods of countering the devastating consequences for individuals of both unemployment and also dead-end employment.' It noted that many youth clubs now open for periods in the daytime, but more had to do so: 'More centres are needed, together with project-based work, to cope not just with the officially unemployed but also with the unseen unemployed – those who are too discouraged even to approach a Job Centre.' The Report stressed that the youth service should be 'funded at a high level . . . resources should be available to counter urban deprivation . . . and racism'.

13.112   In its response to the Thompson Report, the Department of Education and Science has issued a circular (No 1/85), in which the Secretary of State makes clear that he accepts 'the need to ensure sound arrangements for the planning, co-ordination and management of the youth service, in order to secure the best return for young people from existing resources. Arrangements for the future must reinforce the partnership between the voluntary and the local authority sectors, so that the potential of the resources available is fully realized'.

13.113   We welcome in particular the government's response in supporting the establishment of a national advisory council, and of a youth unit in the Department of Education and Science. A review has also been undertaken of the National Youth Bureau (and we hope that the reorganisation following this review will enable the Bureau to better serve youth work in UPAs). The DES is also making grant aid available to voluntary organisations for experimental projects in managerial innovation in the youth service, and making funds available for professional training courses and to voluntary organisations for the training of part-time and volunteer staff.

13.114　However, the financial support offered by government is on a pump-priming basis, with the hope that 'organisations will increasingly be prepared, as many are now, to accept responsibility for a continuing commitment'. We believe that this is inadequate and unrealistic.

13.115　The National Council for Voluntary Youth Services has published research which shows that substantial sums allocated for youth service provision in central government grants to local authorities have been reallocated to other services. The local authorities point out that they have by law to maintain certain services, so that the discretionary necessarily suffer if expenditure has to be curtailed. As a result, the future of particular projects and facilities has been put in jeopardy. The result may be effective trained teams of youth workers being disbanded, and well-qualified and experienced youth workers having to move. Consequently there is a danger of greater reliance being placed on part-time, unqualified, and often untrained volunteers.

13.116　We note too that some local authorities have shifted responsibility for the youth service from the education department to the leisure services department. The understanding of youth work as a means of social education of young people, with its emphasis upon their development needs, should be retained; we are concerned that shifts in reponsibility within local government could put too great an emphasis upon optional spare-time leisure pursuits as the purpose of youth work provision. The prime responsibility should we believe remain with the education department although we readily acknowledge that all local authority departments should take on a concern for young people.

13.117　For several reasons, we have paid special attention to the subject of political education – as did the Thompson review group.

13.118　On the one hand there are extremist groups who work aggressively to take advantage of young people and gain their allegiance; on the other are people who talk as if social and political education are separate, almost opposing, entities. In the middle are the young people themselves, whose attitude to politics is often characterised by remarks such as these we have heard time and again –

'Politics is a waste of time'
'It does nothing'
'They're all in it for themselves'.

Three-quarters of 14-19 year olds acknowledged to the Thompson Review Group that they were 'politically apathetic'.

13.119   In recent years, projects on political education have been undertaken with government funding by the National Association for Voluntary Youth Services, the British Youth Council, and the National Association of Youth Clubs. The resources, methods and approaches developed by these organisations need to be more widely known and used. To help young people to make wise choices about their own individual future, and that of the society to which they belong, will involve those concerned with the youth service in unavoidable political issues. We believe it is wrong for youth workers to use their skills as a platform for political propagandizing (as it is for them to do so for religious indoctrination), but we also believe that to evade and avoid reflection on social, economic, and political change is to fail young people. For this reason we welcome the encouragement that has been given to the youth service by Government Ministers to offer opportunities for political and social education.

13.120   Finally in this section, a word about uniformed organisations. Though their limitations were referred to in the Thompson report, we acknowledge the contribution that uniformed orgainsations can make in the UPAs, particularly for the younger age groups. We have taken note of the 'Scoutreach programme' designed to take the values of scouting into areas of poor amenity, concentrating on places where scouting has until now not been available, and the use of experimental methods to attract young people. In central Birmingham, for instance, 50 new Scout groups have been set up with an increase of 4,000 boys over a 5 year period. We welcome such initiatives.

The Role of the Church
13.121   The prime responsibility for work with young people in the Church of England is at parish level. It is ultimately the parishes who decide what kind of provision is to be offered, and appoint either voluntary or paid staff to work with young people. Many local churches

can be focal points in neighbourhoods, and this can enable immediate responses to be made to local needs.

13.122   It is clear that over the years the Church's role in work with young people has changed. During the 1950s and the early 1960s there were a large number of church-sponsored open youth clubs, funded by a variety of means, offering a facility for *all* young people in the area. Many of these clubs located in inner city areas remain effective in the youth work which they undertake. However, over the years, many local Churches have turned more to providing 'club nights' closed to all but the children and young people of its own members. The task of sustaining open youth clubs has proved just too tough.

13.123   It is now very difficult for clergy or laity, paid or unpaid, to do effective youth work in the UPAs unless they are trained and supported. (This is made abundantly clear in the recently-published book by Pip Wilson, youth worker at the Mayflower Family Centre from 1975 to 1985.)[9] Training courses are available, but sadly few church members take advantage of them. Yet some parishes in UPAs, with either charitable funding or in partnership with local authorities, support detached youth workers or provide drop-in centres.

13.124   Most dioceses exercise their responsibility for the support and development of parish initiatives by the appointment of one or more diocesan youth officers (DYOs). Although the prime task of most of these officers is to support work in parishes, there is an established tradition of their involvement in statutory youth work agencies and as advisors to other voluntary youth organisations – often providing important support for those in the statutory youth service whose morale is often at a very low ebb.

13.125   Much of the Church's youth work is state funded, and we affirm the need for a creative partnership between the Church and the state.

13.126   We also believe that the Church must make it clear that serving in the youth service in our cities is a very important Christian ministry – serving the community *outside* the church. It is too often and too easily assumed that the prime responsibility for work with young people in the Church of England is with the 'Church's children'. We do not wish in any way to denigrate that work. Yet we must underline that the alienation that we have found among young people is not least alienation from the Church.

13.127   We *recommend* that the General Synod's Board of Education, with the full participation of DYOs, in response to this Report, moves towards a national strategy for the Church's work with young people in UPAs, and initiates and supports work specifically within these areas.

13.128   Our work as a Commission has put us in touch with some remarkable Church-sponsored youth work projects. A number of them are linked together and serviced by the Frontier Youth Trust. National organisations such as this can help those concerned with youth work (particularly in parishes) with advice on best practice. We believe that what has been done in some places can, with advice and support from such agencies, be done in others. We would like to record our gratitude for what we have seen, and recall the Church to its pioneering responsibility in the field of youth work.

Main Recommendations

1.   Additional Church-sponsored urban studies centre for teacher training should be established (paragraph 13.38).

2.   All Diocesan Boards and Councils of Education should give special priority to the needs of the UPA schools for which they are responsible (paragraph 13.91).

3.   The governors and managers of Church schools should consider whether composition of foundation governors in the school adequately reflects the ethnic constituency of its catchment area (paragraph 13.91).

4.   Consideration should be given to a further exploration of the ecumenical dimension at secondary level, including the possibility of establishing Church of England/Roman Catholic schools in urban priority areas, which would offer a significant proportion of places to children of other faiths (paragraph 13.91).

5.   A review of the Diocesan Education Committee measures should be undertaken, to allow the formulation of Diocesan policies for Church schools on admission criteria and other issues, such as religious education and worship, equal opportunities and community education (paragraph 13.91).

6.   The General Synod's Board of Education, in consultation with Diocesan Youth Officers, should move towards a national strategy for

the Church's work with young people in UPAs, and initiate and support work specifically within these areas (paragraph 13.127).

References

1   *Better Schools* [Cmnd 9469] HMSO, 1985.

2   *The Curriculum from 5–16* (Curricular Matters 2) HMSO, 1985.

3   The survey results show that, of UPA clergy with children, 32 per cent had at some time sent one or more of them to a fee-paying secondary school, 60 per cent had sent one or more to a maintained school, and 35 per cent had sent one or more to a Church of England aided or maintained school. For non-UPA clergy, the equivalent figures are 38 per cent, 78 per cent and 13 per cent respectively.

4   The Swann Report: *Education for All* Cmnd 9453 HMSO, 1985

5   *The Curriculum from 5–16* op cit

6   In *New Society*, 24 January 1980

7   *Young People in the Eighties: A Survey* HMSO, 1983

8   See *Expenditure on the Youth Service 1978-83*, National Youth Bureau, 1985

9   Pip Wilson: *Gutter Feelings* Marshall Pickering, 1985

Chapter 14
ORDER AND LAW

'Order is not always served by law' (South London Industrial Mission)

Introduction
14.1   Urban Priority Areas raise in a sharp form what is often described as the problem of 'Law and Order'. Although we can assume that crimes are committed, and that criminality may well be increasing, at all levels of society, it is evident (as we shall show) from published statistics, as well as from anecdotal evidence, that there is a particularly high incidence of certain types of crime in the UPAs. This does not mean that inner city areas or large council housing estates are necessarily more 'criminal' than other areas; indeed most of the really serious crimes in this country probably occur elsewhere (cases of fraud, for example, under investigation by the City of London police in 1984 involved a total of over £250 million[1]). Nor does it mean that the incidence of crime is the worst blight affecting UPAs, and that if this could be cured other problems would disappear; indeed we shall argue that the opposite direction of causation is the case – if other problems are tackled we can expect the incidence of crime to decrease. Nevertheless there appears to be a particular concentration of crime in UPAs, sufficient at least to warrant our devoting serious attention to it.

14.2   But it is crime of a particular kind. The offences which are committed proportionately more frequently in the UPAs than elsewhere, and to which their residents are particularly vulnerable, are robbery, burglary, theft, vandalism and theft of or from motor vehicles. These offences are committed for the most part by local people, and their victims are for the most part also local people. The result is a serious deterioration of the environment and of social conditions in many urban priority areas. To the outsider, as to the resident, these areas appear lawless, dangerous and threatening. 'Law and Order', people say, 'is breaking down'. There follows an instinctive public demand for

325

the government of the day to 'strengthen the forces of Law and Order' – by which is meant, not the whole range of sanctions and authorities which restrain citizens from all kinds of criminal behaviour, including tax evasion, fraud, motoring offences or cruelty to children, but specifically those agencies which are engaged in detecting and bringing to trial and punishment the perpetrators of 'petty' or 'mass' crimes, who, like their victims, are for the most part relatively poor and deprived. These agencies are the Police, the Judiciary and the Prisons.

14.3   The assumption behind this demand is of course that by providing a larger and more efficient police force and more penal institutions one can reduce the number of crimes committed. But not merely is there no evidence for this: with regard to the police, we shall quote evidence in support of the view that more intensive policing may be actually counter-productive; and with regard to prisons, there are strong moral as well as practical arguments against increasing the prison population of this country which (at some 48,000) is already proportionately higher than that of any other western European country.

14.4   There are therefore good grounds for regarding 'Law and Order' as a slogan which can too easily be used for rallying public opinion behind a popular but ineffective policy of 'containing' alleged criminality in certain areas by 'strengthening the arm of the Law'. We have deliberately inverted the terms in the title of this chapter. What is amiss in urban priority areas is not (we shall argue) a shortage of the agents of the Law, but a partial breakdown of that order which only society can create and maintain for itself. The remedy for the sense of threat and insecurity under which so many people live in the inner city is not (at least in a free and democratic country) to intensify policing but to make a simultaneous attack on the many factors which are causing the inhabitants of these areas to lose respect for each other's persons and property, and to live together in order and peace.

14.5   In seeking to identify these factors we find ourselves aligned with all the main public and official agencies which are concerned with these problems. The Home Office, the Probation Service, NACRO, and the police authorities themselves are all concentrating attention on the role of the 'community' in maintaining order and preventing crime. The Church has resources which it can contribute to this work, and much of this Chapter will be concerned with the more effective use of some of them. But the problems are by no means always practical and empirical ones. Matters of order, law and punishment raise general questions of morality and public policy which are being vigorously debated in many parts of the world. There is a long tradition of Christian thinking which can make a contribution to this debate. Before we turn to practical issues it may be useful to spell out certain considerations which are of particular importance to Christians and which are brought into sharp focus by recent developments in public policy.

1. How does the Christian gospel invite us to approach the institutions and processes of Law? The motivation it encourages consists of love, sacrificial service and mutual concern. Christians can never be satisfied with law-abidingness as a sufficient criterion for moral conduct, nor will they ever think that better laws, or more vigorous enforcement, will by themselves create a moral society. At the same time, they have inherited from the Old Testament a keen concern for justice, and recognise a radical extension of this concern in Jesus' criticisms of the working and interpretation of the Law in his own time. The whole Bible reminds us that, left to themselves, neither the legislature nor the judiciary can be relied upon to create and maintain conditions in which justice will always prevail, and an objective standard is required against which to measure their procedures. Christians relate their standards of human justice to their understanding of the justice of God; but these standards are for the most part ones which are shared by the majority of their fellow citizens. The distinctive service of the Church is to challenge, in the name of God and his justice, all human institutions and procedures when they appear to be falling short of these standards. For instance, Christians can never cease to ask serious questions of a society whose prisons contain a quite disproportionate number of black people[2] or of members of the 'lowest' social classes, or about the evidence which is still widely available of black people being far more exposed to police questioning and arrest on the streets than whites.

2. The Christian faith encourages us to be realistic about human nature. Its doctrine of sin makes us take seriously the tendencies to evil in each one of us, and makes us expect that even under the most favourable conditions there will always be some who will commit criminal offences and whose attitudes seem virtually impossible to 'reform'. We should not therefore be surprised that the 'rehabilitative' principle of punishment has had so little apparent success (in terms of reducing the number of recidivists) or that it has been open to such weighty theoretical objections that it has now, in this country, been officially abandoned.[3] Yet when we observe a tendency towards a more punitive approach to sentencing (in the form either of longer sentences or of a 'short sharp shock' policy) – despite the absence of

any evidence that this reduces recidivism – we are bound to protest. The Christian faith continues to proclaim the infinite worth of every individual in the sight of God, and the infinite possibilities of God's forgiving love. It is impossible for us to acquiesce in the abandonment of the rehabilitative ideal; and indeed prison staff, probation officers and social workers would probably find it impossible to continue their work in a humane way if they abandoned all expectation of some kind of positive response in at least some of their fellow citizens who are convicted of crime.

3. In the Old Testament the justice of God is 'biased' towards the protection of the poor, the weak and the vulnerable. The Christian tradition, following a clear lead given by Jesus (Matthew 25.31-46), has responded to this by showing a particular concern for 'prisoners and captives'. It is a Christian duty to minister to and sympathise with those who are in prison (Hebr. 10.34), and with all others whose social position renders them weak, vulnerable, and subject to victimisation and abuse. As we have seen, such people exist in large numbers in urban priority areas, and this alone justifies us in paying special attention to the problems of Order and Law in the inner city. But in fact this concern may place Christians at a certain distance from public opinion, which tends to take a harsh view of the penalties appropriate to certain kinds of crime, to prefer convicted criminals to be kept out of sight and mind, and to be slow to recognise that some members of society may have fallen seriously behind the rest in terms of rights before the law. On the other hand, most 'professionals' involved in the treatment and care of offenders share at least a part of this traditional Christian concern.

4. This analysis might suggest that the inner city, with its areas of apparent lawlessness and its high rate of 'mass' or 'petty' crime, provides a physical and social context for the release of criminal tendencies among its residents, and that the work of the Church must be to provide its members with the spiritual resources needed to resist and overcome such a threatening concentration of the forces of evil. To a certain extent this may be true. The protection of anonymity, and the infection of the mindless violence of a crowd, may lead individuals into courses of action and types of behaviour which can only be called evil, and all our spiritual resources are required to combat it and save people from it. At the same time, we cannot associate ourselves with a negative view of the inner city as such. A city is a place of dense population, with immensely varied but relatively scarce resources. It is a place both of constant personal

interaction and of tragic loneliness, of richly rewarding co-operative activity and of intense conflict between individuals, groups and classes. But these are precisely the circumstances in which the Christian faith is lived in its fullness. It is in the healing of an imperfect and fragmented society, and in the resolution of conflict through sacrificial service, that the reality of the Gospel is most keenly experienced. If the inner city has more than its fair share of the manifestations of human weakness and wickedness, it can also celebrate a rich harvest of (mainly unrecognised and unacknowledged) saints.

14.6 With these considerations in mind, we now turn to the task of identifying the symptoms and causes of the apparent breakdown of order in urban priority areas. We then draw attention to types of social action which appear to be tackling the root causes and to ways in which the Churches can make their contribution.

Crime in the UPAs

14.7 It is important, in the first place, to set our observation of the incidence of crime in the UPAs in the context of the crime rate for the United Kingdom as a whole. Statistics show that, over the whole country, the rate of reported crime has been rising in a fairly dramatic manner. The following are the figures for persons found guilty in the UK of criminal offences since 1950:[4]

	'000s
1950	821.2
1960	1241.6
1970	1917.1
1980	2502.3

These show a threefold increase in thirty years.

14.8 Has there been a disproportionately greater increase in UPAs? No figures are available to answer this question directly. Moreover we must be careful, in this as in other matters, not to generalise about situations which may be as different from each other as Merseyside is from Inner London and where policing may be based on different strategies. Nevertheless, having spent over a year listening to people who live in inner cities and large urban housing estates, and having received a great deal of written evidence, we are convinced that, even though most crime that is committed in these areas is 'petty', its impact is particularly serious on people already living in conditions of social disadvantage and deprivation. This impression is confirmed by the following facts which can be extracted from the first British Crime Survey (1981), which was based on interviews in about 16,000 households in England, Wales and Scotland:

(a)   Victims of robbery tend to live in the inner city;

(b)   The risks of burglary in the inner city are double those in other areas of conurbations and five times those elsewhere;

(c)   Council properties are more at risk than owner-occupied houses, though the value of losses from the latter tends to be higher;

(d)   Thefts of and from motor vehicles are concentrated:

(i)   where there is street parking at night;

(ii)   in metropolitan areas, especially inner cities;

(iii)   in areas of council housing.

As a result of these factors, more than 25 per cent of households living in inner cities, whose vehicles are kept on the street, suffer theft of or from their vehicles every year, compared with 5 per cent of households outside the city who garage their cars. A more recent survey tells the same story. *Taking Account of Crime: Key Findings from the 1984 British Crime Survey*, discussing rates of crime and anxieties about crime, concludes: 'the poorest council estates and multi-racial areas showed especially high levels of fear, which were matched by high levels of crime'. There was a burglary *rate* of 2½-3 times the national average in these areas,[5] and the *fear* of burglary was nearly twice the national average. The picture of 'mugging' is very similar.[6]

14.9   Paul Harrison, in *Inside the Inner City* (Pelican 1983) writes:

'In 1981 there were more than 23,000 serious crimes in Hackney – one for every three households in the borough. The equivalent of one person in every hundred was mugged, one dwelling in sixteen was burgled, and one car in every four stolen or stolen from. These figures refer to reported crimes only: the experience of the General Household Survey suggests that the true incidence will be anything from 60 per cent to 100 per cent higher.' (p. 324).

The experience of the people we have spoken to in Hackney amply supports these figures.

14.10   We have already noted that by far the greatest number of crimes committed in UPAs may be called 'petty' or 'mass' crime – burglary, robbery, theft, vandalism and theft of or from motor cars. It is precisely these crimes which show a particularly massive increase in recent years. In Greater Manchester, for example, between 1980 and 1983 recorded burglaries rose from 47,380 to 72,925, robberies from 648 to 1,212 and vandalism from 11,957 to 20,511.[7] It might of course be said that these crimes are less 'serious' than others, and their incidence therefore gives less cause for concern. But this would be to ignore the *cumulative* effects of such crime. On some housing estates and in some inner city areas the vandalising of essential services such as lifts and telephones, spates of burglaries, thefts of and from cars, frequent aggressive behaviour within and around the locality – all these combine to make life a constant struggle for the residents and to create an atmosphere of fear.

14.11   Contrary to a widely held assumption, it is the poor themselves who suffer most from this kind of crime. The evidence we received from NACRO supports our own observations:

'... not only is the risk of victimisation higher for already disadvantaged people, but the likely effects of crime are also greater, as they are less cushioned against financial loss. Furthermore, where the disadvantage is linked to being old, a single-parent family, poor physical and mental health, and so on, the emotional support which aids recovery from misfortune may also be less readily available than in some communities. Moreover, the poor are far less able to consider moving away from a high crime area.'

14.12   If we ask, Who is it that commits these crimes?, our evidence – confirmed both by NACRO and the Police – is that crime within disadvantaged areas is particularly likely to be committed by local people. With burglary, for instance, poor homes are particularly vulnerable to the opportunistic, often young, offender, whereas more affluent areas are more likely to attract the professional offender who has travelled purposively to obtain high rewards.

14.13   But of course it is not only crime, but the *fear* of crime, which affects living conditions in UPAs – fear not only on one's own account but for, say, a teenage daughter. We have encountered such fear again and again. Not only are people afraid to go out; they are afraid to let others come in. Once again, our impressions are confirmed by the British Crime Survey. Though it states that

'fear for personal safety is not a national problem ... overall fear levels are neither high nor excessive,'

it nevertheless admits that this is

'an urban problem and particularly an inner city one.'

For example,

'12 per cent of all inner city residents say they never go out alone at night because of crime';

'More than 60 per cent of all inner city women feel at least somewhat unsafe';

and fully 60 per cent of those over 60 feel 'very unsafe'.[8]

These fears may often be excessive; the published figures for robbery, for example, are notably low, and the statistics show that (contrary to a widely held assumption) women and elderly people are not especially exposed to the risk of personal attack. Yet they are real. They are fed by the highly selective reporting of local newspapers, radio and television; and the amount of information normally available to the general public about the real incidence of crime in a particular area is very small indeed. As long as people believe that there is a high level of crime which constitutes a direct threat to them, they will continue to lead restricted and impoverished lives. We have found this to be unquestionably the case in UPAs in general and among groups such as elderly women in particular. In addition, domestic violence cannot be ignored: in any debate about mugging or violence in the streets, it must be remembered that assault on wives is by far the most common form of violence.

Why this Pattern of Crime in UPAs?

14.14 Statistics and anecdotal evidence combine to present an alarming picture. But we must not imagine that this is anything new. Certain types of crime, particularly 'petty' or 'mass' crime, have always been especially prevalent in urban areas; and ever since the industrial revolution successive generations have deplored the apparent increase in lawlessness and violence and have sought reasons for it. At one period in Victorian England one in four of London's policemen was physically assaulted in the course of duty. The word 'hooligan' entered common use after some acute Bank Holiday rowdiness in 1898. There were violent clashes between the police and unemployed people in 1931. Again and again statesmen and commentators have deplored the apparent weakening or breakdown of family life, the decline in the respect shown by young people for their elders, and the general growth of lawlessness.[9] Blame has been attributed to schools, music halls, films, social conditions, and now violence on television. Anything we say on the subject is likely to have been said many times before. Moreover it is notoriously difficult to identify the precise cause of any particular trend in the incidence of crime; indeed every crime that is committed is likely to have a number of 'causes'. In this respect as in others both the people and the environments in inner city areas vary so widely that generalisations are liable to be misleading and any 'blanket' policy of crime prevention is likely to be ineffective. Yet none of this exempts us from attempting to discern the factors, some of them having emerged particularly in the last few years, which have contributed to what Lord Scarman referred to as 'the complex pattern of conditions which lies at the root of the disorders in Brixton and elsewhere'.[10]

(1) *Unemployment*

14.15   Lord Scarman recognised unemployment as a 'major factor'. A recent study, published by the Home Office,[11] has found no evidence to confirm this, but also none to contradict it. The evidence we have gathered ourselves in the course of visits to areas of high unemployment entirely supports Lord Scarman's judgement. To give only one example: in a northern housing estate, a magistrate, of some years experience, said to us: 'I never thought I'd live to be on the side of the shop-lifter here. Not all of them, of course; but some people now are desperately poor because of unemployment. To shop-lift for those dependent on them seems at the moment the only way.' We need not condone such an attitude (though there is an ancient and reputable tradition of Christian thought which justifies a starving person who appropriates the minimum necessary to sustain life). To be unemployed need not, of course, lead to engaging in criminal activity; but it does mean real poverty for many, and time unoccupied with purposeful work: time available for law-breaking and disorderly conduct and for the pressures of the consumer society to have their effect. It may not be possible to prove the connection between unemployment and crime by statistics. But many of those best qualified to form a judgement in this matter regard it as beyond doubt.[12]

(2) *Environment*

14.16   The Family Welfare Association wrote to us:

'Vandalism may often be a protest against the inhumanity of the environment and an attempt to soften some of its harshness. In some places this aspect of vandalism has been channelled into positive directions through community arts programmes . . . Our experience suggests that where a community is constructed on a scale small enough for human relations to be conducted, and for the environment to be cared for by people who live within it, the destructiveness diminishes.'

People have often said to us when they have shown us the particular estate where they live: 'Who'd want to live here?' Bad design and bad housing management (e.g. the withdrawal of resident caretakers) undoubtedly create both opportunities for crime and the fear of crime. An estate already vandalised, with repairs unattended to, encourages a kind of creeping neglect which makes more and more people give up caring for areas outside the actual perimeter of the home and offers open incitement to further vandalism and petty crime.

(3) *Family Disorder*

14.17 A poor environment may undoubtedly damage family life; but a further factor making for disorder may lie within the family – 'parents don't discipline their children any more' etc. There is of course some truth in this. We quote again from the evidence submitted by the Family Welfare Association:

> 'One of the problems of some urban council estates is that they become filled with individuals and families who are internally disorganised and chaotic. That sense of personal and familial disorder helps to create chaotic social conditions which in turn further disturb individuals and their families. It makes sense in those circumstances for some people to "keep themselves to themselves" and to retire behind their firmly closed front doors, and for others who may be better integrated internally to move away to more stable communities. But this has the effect of leaving the estate even less well organised, and of disrupting even further the ordinary kinds of social containers of potentially destructive forces usually found in well established environments. Moreover, it ensures that there is even less social reinforcement for those struggling to subdue their own internal disorder and sustain a precarious sense of integration.'

Nevertheless, we believe that it is unfair to single out parents in a society where adults generally often do not feel authorised to keep order. Moreover, there are strong social pressures working against the traditional patterns of family life. Many immigrant families, whose culture presupposes strong paternal authority and family solidarity, have found their children unable or unwilling to maintain the traditional pattern in the social climate in which they now live. A Director of Social Services in London told us that he has to recognise that traditional two-parent families account for only a small proportion of those for whom he has responsibility. The rest are living in other forms of 'institutional intimacy'.

14.18   In the evidence submitted to us by the dioceses we have noted references to the often serious social consequences of allocation policies adopted by housing authorities. Many housing estates have a large number of single-parent families living in them. Many people live in estates who would never have chosen to go there, and who cannot easily be persuaded to accept responsibility for their environment. Under certain circumstances even a small concentration of families with multiple problems can have a serious effect on the ability of a community to maintain order and self-respect; and even the proportion of children to adults may be a critical factor if other conditions are such as to promote lawlessness. Any appeal to parental authority, and any attempts to strengthen it, must take account of the social realities of family life today, particularly as they are experienced in urban surroundings.

(4)   *Drug Misuse*
14.19   The number of drug addicts notified in the United Kingdom in 1983 (5,850) was 42 per cent up on 1982. The number of *new* addicts notified in 1984 was 5,730, a 28 per cent increase on the 1983 figure (4,186). In 1983, there were 2,784 admissions of patients with drug related diagnoses to mental illness hospitals in England. This marked an increase of 32 per cent since 1982, and of 76 per cent since 1979.[13] There is no doubt, however, that the number of drug misusers is much greater than the number of admissions to hospital or the number of notifications to the Home Office. Some research carried out in 1981 in two urban areas in England suggested that the number of notified addicts was a five-fold underestimate of the addicts in the local population at that time. We have visited a number of council estates in which drug addiction was rife: offences involving hard drugs have increased there ten-fold in two or three years. It is difficult to determine whether people commit crimes because they are under the influence of drugs or in order to finance an expensive addiction which they could not otherwise afford. What is clear is that in UPAs addicts are likely to be poor and that their addiction can be financed only through crime.

14.20   The seriousness of the situation in certain areas is undeniable. That drug misuse is particularly acute in urban areas is underlined by the number of narcotic drug addicts notified to the Home Office in 1983, by Police Force Areas:

Police Force Area	Notified in 1983[14]		
	New Addicts	Former Addicts	Total
Greater Manchester	204	28	232
Merseyside	378	29	407
Metropolitan Police District (and City of London)	1813	880	2693
Hertfordshire	30	27	57
Kent	43	12	55

To illustrate the problem we concentrate on Greater Manchester. In that area the increase in drug addiction recorded by the Home Office over the period 1976-1980 was 47 per cent (the UK average was 52 per cent). In 1980 notifications made to GPs on the North West Regional Health Authority showed a 10.7 per cent increase; in 1981 notifications had increased by 68 per cent. Arrests made by Greater Manchester Police for drug offences rose from 1073 in 1981 to 1278 in 1983. Three deaths were attributed directly to the misuse of drugs. Two-thirds of the drug offences consisted of using, possessing or dealing in cannabis; the second most common drug was heroin. Increasingly the police are finding that heroin is becoming a first step for many drug users rather than a drug to which to graduate.

14.21 What has caused this type of addiction to invade our cities? Doubtless the sheer availability of drugs and the activity of drug-pushers are a major cause; but we cannot doubt that the social deprivation and level of unemployment particularly among young people which we have seen in UPAs is a crucial factor. Vigilance by customs officers, severe sentences for grave offenders, specialised social and medical care and responsible education on drugs in schools all have a part to play in responding to drug abuse; but we are convinced that the underlying problem must be the condition of the UPAs themselves. We would draw attention to the 'Resource Leaflet for Greater Manchester', published by the Board for Social Responsibility of the Diocese of Manchester, as an example of what the Church can do. It provides general guidance on constructive attitudes to the problem, and information on the professional medical, psychiatric and social help that is available.

(5)   *The Consumer Society and Anonymity*
14.22   All these factors peculiar to certain urban situations today must

be seen against the background of a more general and pervasive influence, well expressed in evidence submitted to us by NACRO:

'The growth in material goods available in modern society has increased the opportunities for theft and damage, particularly when goods are very accessible, like cars on the streets and goods in self-service shops . . . Since our society encourages consumerism and exposes all its members to attractive life-styles through the mass-media, yet severely restricts real opportunities for many, particularly if they are black, female, poor or handicapped, it is not surprising that respect for the law should be weakened.'

The monotonous sameness of many housing estates contributes to an anonymity in which what you get up to doesn't seem to matter. Crime may be an outlet for aggression and frustration, a way of making your mark, or simply fun. In a society where *you* don't seem to matter it is easy to think that other people and other things don't matter – hence 'violence against the person' and vandalism.

The Maintenance of Order

14.23   In the face of all this, many people naturally feel alarmed and speak of 'a breakdown in Law and Order'. Stronger policing seems the obvious remedy, and governments are put under pressure to increase the public funds available for 'Law and Order'. This response yields few results. The findings of the Home Office Research Unit in 1984[15] are that an increase in police manpower has a very limited effect on the incidence of crime – indeed, since more policemen often means more crimes detected or reported, the criminality of an area may seem actually to increase when more police are introduced. Moreover the ability of the police to reduce crime simply by a more massive presence is extremely limited: it was a clear lesson of the events leading up to the Brixton riots that over-policing can be as dangerous as a lack of police.[16] To strengthen the police is to tackle – and tackle ineffectively – merely the symptoms of a deeper disorder; any serious analysis of the apparent increase in crime in the inner cities must look for its causes and for means of attacking it at source.

14.24   There is a growing recognition that crime is not a matter which can be left in the hands of the police, the courts and the prisons and forgotten by the rest of the community. In his report on the 1981 Brixton disorders Lord Scarman said:

'. . . local communities should be more fully involved in the decisions which affect them . . . in planning, in the provision of local services

337

and in the management and financing of specific projects . . . Inner City areas are not human deserts! They possess a wealth of voluntary effort and goodwill. It would be wise to put this human capital to good use . . . In order to secure social stability, there will be a long-term need to provide useful, gainful employment and suitable educational, recreational and leisure opportunities for young people' (para 6.7).

14.25   In a debate in the House of Lords on 24 March 1982 the Lord Chief Justice stated:

'Neither police nor courts nor prisons can solve the problem of the rising crime rate.'

14.26   In his report to the Home Secretary in 1983 Sir Kenneth Newman, Commissioner of Police for the Metropolis, said:

'. . . The police cannot alone make a major impact on crime . . . major resources for crime reduction reside in the community itself, and in other public and voluntary agencies.'

14.27   *Criminal Justice: A Working Paper* produced by the Home Office in May 1984 notes:

'Public confidence can also be improved by demonstrating that crime can be reduced. An effective programme of crime prevention is therefore essential, in which not only the police but the community as a whole play a part.'

14.28   It would seem that a consensus view is developing that crime policy cannot be successfully formulated in isolation from the community and that the community should be involved in a programme which has as one of its aims the prevention of crime. We fully concur with this view; but it is based on the presupposition that 'the community' (however defined) regards the Law as its 'friend'. Is this any longer the case?

14.29   In UPAs we have found a widespread ambivalence towards the agents of 'the Law' (particularly police and magistrates). On the one hand the Law is seen as the guardian of the status quo and the protector of the weaker members of the community against the stronger; but on the other hand the status quo itself is felt to be oppressive, and the agents of the Law often appear to be prejudiced against certain classes of people. Black people, for example, must look to the police for protection, not only against burglars, but also against physical attacks and thuggery carried out by racist or extreme political groups; but they may also have personal experiences (such as the feeling that the police take no notice of calls for help coming from areas where they are known to live), and have heard utterances of police spokesmen, which make them believe that the police are prejudiced against them. We have received so many reports of this kind that we cannot discount them. This loss of confidence in the police, and suspicion of racial or class discrimination in methods of policing and among magistrates, can result in substantial groups in the community ceasing to regard the Law as 'friend'.

14.30   There is also a more general respect for the forces of law and order which arises from the sense that the Law is framed to protect inalienable 'human rights'. So long as all new legislation continues to seem compatible with these principles, respect for the Law may reasonably be expected of all. But if a government imposes laws on the whole population which appear to protect the rights of some more than others, this respect for the Law may be seriously weakened. There is now an increasing number of people, mainly concentrated in the cities, who feel that the Law does nothing to protect their rights to decent housing and fair opportunities for available employment. Many of these people are being reduced to the situation of those who seem to have nothing to gain from the 'order' of society and nothing to lose by flouting it. This results in a dangerous situation, in that 'respect for the Law' will have no appeal to them as a motive to restrain them from any opportunities which present themselves for crime, disorder, rioting and looting. The government of the day carries great responsibility for the maintenance of order by the evident fairness and reasonableness of the legislation it promotes.

14.31   It follows from all this that the maintenance of order depends on a large number of factors. In what follows we shall concentrate on those areas where the community and the Churches bear most responsibility and may be able to take the most fruitful initiatives. We shall conclude with some observations on the police and the prison system.

Community Based Crime Prevention
14.32   In view of our primary conclusion that the promotion of order must be as locally based as possible and that community initiatives must be fostered, it is not surprising that we found much encouragement in the circular on *Crime Prevention* issued jointly by the Home Office, the Department of Education and Science, the Department of the

Environment, the Department of Health and Social Security and the Welsh Office on 30 January 1984 which stated that 'a sound policy towards crime prevention should take into account the following points:

(a)   effective crime prevention needs the active support of the community. The methods used by the police are constantly improving but police effectiveness cannot be greatly increased unless the community can be persuaded to do more for itself;

(b)   crime prevention schemes are more successful where the police and local agencies work together in a co-ordinated way towards particular aims;

(c)   patterns of crime vary greatly from one area to the next. Preventive measures are therefore more likely to be successful when designed to reflect local characteristics and focused on particular types of crime;

(d)   whilst there is a need to address the social factors associated with criminal behaviour, and policies are continually being devised to tackle this aspect of the problem, these are essentially long-term measures. For the short term, the best way forward is to reduce through management or design or changes in the environment the opportunities that exist for crime to occur.'

14.33   The circular goes on to mention the growing number of crime prevention schemes in operation up and down the country, and calls for the formation of closer links between the public and those holding positions of authority and outlines the various local bodies – police authority committees, neighbourhood associations, etc – which have a part to play *together*.

14.34   We have been heartened as we have come across such a 'community approach' in initiatives of the Probation Service and NACRO and of other bodies in many inner city and other urban priority areas. The new importance given to local policing ('the policeman on his beat') is a welcome example of this approach; as is 'The Safe Neighbourhood Unit – Community Based Improvement Programmes on Twelve Inner London Housing Estates' (a NACRO project funded by the GLC and London boroughs).[17] We believe that Churches in every locality should help with such initiatives wherever they are appropriate and necessary.

14.35   Over the last decade there have been several studies – not least through the influence of Oscar Newman's idea of 'defensible space' – of a 'situational' approach to crime; hence the increasing use of private security personnel, of electronic surveillance systems in shops and supermarkets and for blocks of service flats. But in UPAs local authorities have been reluctant to adopt such measures (on grounds of expense or practicality). The people living in UPAs are thus less protected. Often little attention was paid in council housing design to crime prevention. Access lobbies and large publicly accessible areas, stairways, terraces, lifts, underpasses, seem to belong to no one; yet re-design is costly.

14.36 We would make four comments on such community based crime prevention.

(1) We welcome this approach, not least because it reflects the locality-based approach which has seemed so relevant to much of our Report.

(2) No one studying 'The Safe Neighbourhood Unit' can imagine that this approach to crime prevention is without its difficulties. Here is another example where that which works in the suburbs may encounter very considerable problems in the UPAs. But there is no alternative to confronting these problems.

(3) The concern to encourage communities to contribute to their own order must be distinguished from the natural tendency of like minded individuals to take what they judge to be the law into their own hands against those whom they judge to be lawless. The Police, the National Council for Civil Liberties and other bodies have expressed disquiet at the danger of Neighbourhood Watch Schemes developing into some sort of vigilante group. The Police have been outspoken in their condemnation of such a development, and we too have had instances of such divisive developments brought to our notice on the part of groups or individuals.

(4) We have already commended the Joint Circular of the Home Office and other central government departments of 30 January 1984. We found ourselves giving it full approval until its final crucial paragraph – *Resources* – where the circular states:

'The suggestions in this circular do not call for a net increase in expenditure; they concern re-direction of effort of existing resources'.

In the short term we believe that this is a misleading statement. Among changes brought about on the estates of the 'Safe Neighbourhood Unit', for instance, have been:

employment of resident caretakers and increased quotas of cleaners;

fitting of stronger doors and locks, 'phone entry systems, high-level lighting in semi-public areas;

opening youth clubs and play centres.

We believe it to be quite unrealistic to think that even these short-term changes – and others that may be deemed necessary – can always be made without 'a net increase in expenditure'. In the longer term, considerable expenditure and improved design will certainly be necessary before savings in costs related to order and law can be achieved. Yet the social costs of disorder are immense. The relatively small costs of crime prevention initiatives now may save massive expenditure later.

Victim Support in the Inner City

14.37 It is too easy to assume that help is always at hand in the inner city from the elaborate range of statutory and voluntary services that fill the pages of welfare directories. Most people do not know what is available and often do not like to ask for help. Even if they are prepared to ask it is not easy for them to find their way through the maze of agencies which exist.

14.38 This is particularly the case for victims of crime, for whom there is as yet only the beginnings of a support system. The *British Crime Survey* is showing what was often suspected – that there is much more crime and therefore many more victims than police statistics show. People do not report all the crimes of which they are victims, for all sorts of reasons. The importance of this is that for every crime, reported or not, there is a victim, and very often more than one. In nearly every case, the suffering and fear will spread out to a wider circle of immediate relations, friends and neighbours.

14.39 Victim Support Schemes are now beginning to meet some of the needs which victims of crime would otherwise be left to cope with alone. There are now Schemes in 255 places in the United Kingdom and In 1984 5,900 people were dealing with more than 112,000 referrals from the police, an increase of 72 per cent over 1983.[18] All the Schemes are voluntary, and exist only in areas where local people have taken the initiative to set them up. They are staffed for the most part by non-professionals, who can contribute their common sense and practical skills to helping the victims of crime, and can if necessary refer them to professional agencies. Probation Officers, Church members, police and representatives of voluntary agencies have been active in establishing new schemes, and Churches have helped to provide volunteers.

14.40 Not surprisingly, good Victim Support Schemes have been harder to establish in the major cities than they have in areas with less petty crime; yet a number exist already in UPAs. Government support in the region of £100,000 is available to the national office of the National Association of Victim Support Schemes, but this does not provide for the financing of any regional co-ordination or training. Schemes in UPAs have to meet a particularly heavy demand. To cope with it they need full-time paid co-ordinators, for whom at present no finance is available. They also need a larger number of volunteers, and experience considerable difficulty in recruitment. Here is a task in which those who live in the suburbs can perhaps give practical service to those who live in the UPAs.

Reparation, Conciliation and Mediation

14.41 The Home Office Research and Planning Unit Paper 27; *'Reparation, conciliation and mediation; Current projects and plans in England and Wales'* is a crucial and most valuable document. Amongst other things it classifies existing projects – which tend to be centred so far in industrialised urban areas e.g. Newham Conflict and Change Project and the Liverpool Dispute Settlement Service. The Commission has come across other projects which are perhaps too young to have been included in Paper 27.

14.42 A typical example of such a project is a Neighbourhood Mediation Centre. This may be described as 'an informal institution designed for the quick and effective resolution of certain types of "minor" disputes'. It 'offers a means of settling disputes speedily and without recourse to the courts . . . it keeps the conflict at the local immediate level and allows the possibility of permanent resolution whereas a court case may aggravate relationships.' It is 'a means of preventing quarrels and disputes developing into violent confrontation on inner city housing estates.'[19]

14.43 It is too early to comment on the viability of such schemes. Yet clearly this kind of development of local reparation, conciliation and mediation is central to the concerns of our Commission, and we cannot do less than commend it in its various manifestations to the attention of the Church and of society today. Several of the projects we have come across have in fact been initiated by the Church, in partnership with the Social Services.

Law Centres

14.44   There are now 55 Law Centres in the United Kingdom, most of which are located in the poorer neighbourhoods of inner cities. Members of the Commission have visited a number of them.

14.45   In October 1979 the Royal Commission on Legal Services recognised a large gap in the existing provision of legal services. Legal Aid alone has not met the legal needs of the disadvantaged. There are too few solicitors in poor areas, and too few who specialize in areas of concern to the poor. There are too many areas of law where Legal Aid is not available. People are unaware of their rights and do not realize that a legal remedy is open to them. Many are frightened by the thought of going to a solicitor, and have little idea how to proceed.

14.46   To meet this need, Law Centres provide specialist legal services. They all employ solicitors, and may also employ community workers, general legal advisers (in such areas as housing, homelessness, welfare rights, and immigration) and sometimes barristers. Each Law Centre is run by a local representative or elected Management Committee.

14.47   No Law Centre can begin to take on the cases of all the people who come to it. The vast majority of people are referred to private practices who can deal with their problems. A new Law Centre in an area generates more work for private solicitors. People become more aware of their rights and less reluctant to seek advice. A Law Centre can reassure people that they will qualify for legal aid and can recommend a solicitor. One typical Law Centre estimates that it makes over 40 referrals to private practice per week. Law Centres are complementary to the legal aid system, not a substitute.[20]

14.48   Even then, Law Centres cannot fill the gap unaided. A further essential part of a legal service to the poor is a general advice agency, such as the Citizens' Advice Bureaux, or independent advice centres. The Royal Commission stressed that advice agencies can function effectively only if there are sufficient specialist agencies to which they can refer cases. Advice agencies cannot provide a full legal service or act on behalf of their clients before the courts; yet this is often necessary if a legal remedy is to be secured. The complementary relationship between a Law Centre and an advice agency can be summed up in a letter from the organiser of a Manchester Citizens Advice Bureau:

> 'The usefulness of having a specialist agency like a Law Centre adjacent to a generalist neighbourhood-based agency like ourselves

cannot be overemphasised. For our part we are able to shield their few staff from the sheer weight of numbers that would certainly fall on them otherwise. For their part they always manage to find time to pass on valuable knowledge to our hard-pressed interviewing team when requested. This is an important training aspect for us.

14.49   Our own observation leads us to concur entirely with the judgement of the Royal Commission on Legal Services:

'The impact of law centres has been out of all proportion to their size, to the number of lawyers who work in them and to the amount of work it is possible for them to undertake. The volume of work they have attracted has shown how deep is the need they are attempting to meet. It has dispelled the possibility of complacency over the institution of the legal aid scheme, has emphasized the importance of a wider distribution of legal services and has shown the desirability of enabling and encouraging lawyers to take up work elsewhere than in their traditional areas of activity and types of practice. The Lord Chancellor's Advisory Committee on Legal Aid summed up informed opinion thus in its evidence:

"We think that law centres are, and should be, here to stay and that they are making a vital contribution to legal services."'

14.50   We would add to this that Law Centres provide a means by which many younger solicitors and barristers can learn at first hand about the realities of urban priority areas, and in general we place a high value on the work that is done in them. We also believe that there are strong arguments for the Church helping to sponsor such Law Centres. There is already the happy example of the Churches' support for a Community Law Centre in Liverpool 8 after the Toxteth disturbances. Support by the Church may free the workers from constraints usually imposed by the need to curry favour with politicians and local government officers who are in a position to give or withhold grants. It involves the local Church with the well-being of local people who are not necessarily members of the Church and it provides a non-patronising link through money and personnel between the Church in urban priority areas and the Church in other areas.

14.51   However, Law Centres need public funds to operate – to provide offices and equipment and to pay their staff. Funding for Law Centres has not come easily. Many Centres have had to seek funds from a variety of sources: charitable trusts, central government and local government. Since central government has no clear policy about how legal services should be funded, no statutory powers for funding have been given to either government departments or local authorities. At present just over £2.5 million comes from the Department of the Environment, £2 million from local authorities and £0.75 million from the Lord Chancellor's Department (which compares with a figure for total expenditure on legal aid, which is the main means by which the government funds legal services, of some £300 million). With 65 per cent of Law Centres dependent on funding from central government departments, and with no commitment to the future funding of Law Centres, the anxiety of those who work in and manage them concerning their future is understandably very great indeed. 'Lack of clear ministerial responsibility and direction for legal services' the Lord Chancellor's Advisory Committee's 34th Report states 'is a chronic problem. However, actual and proposed changes in Urban Programme policy and local government arrangements have made it an urgent problem.' The Report goes on to discuss the likely effects of rate-capping and the abolition of the Greater London Council and Metropolitan County Councils on Law Centres. 'The most urgent need', it states, 'is that alternative funding arrangements for the services affected should be worked out well in advance of abolition of the Councils. In the short term, it is less important what precise form those arrangements take, as long as they do not allow agencies such as Law Centres and CABs to close by default. However, the proposed abolition of the second tier councils raises again the question of overall responsibility for legal services.'

14.52   Recent events have shown that these fears are justified. The funding of Citizens' Advice Bureaux is still precarious. Not only have six 'embryonic' Law Centres been unable to open, but in such areas as North Lambeth and Stockwell – areas of substantial poverty and proven need – Centres are having to close. The Commission was informed by the Law Centres Federation that 55 Law Centres are members of the Federation. Of these, 7 are financed, primarily by the Lord Chancellor's Department, and 5 of them face cuts in the next 12 months from the likely loss of other grants. Of the remaining 48, all may close or be greatly reduced in the next 3 years because local government can no longer be relied on to contribute funds to them. In a debate in the House of Lords in May 1985 the Government was unable to give any assurance of any further funds being available.

14.53   The value, the role and the current need of the Centres, and their present financial predicament, could not be more clearly set out than in the Lord Chancellor's Advisory Committee's Report. We wish to give the fullest support to the proposals of the Lord Chancellor's Committee and *recommend* that they be implemented immediately.

Policing in Urban Priority Areas
(a) *Responsibility and Training*
14.54 Some of the ills experienced in the urban priority areas are blamed upon the police. The disturbances in St Paul's Bristol, Brixton and Toxteth could be described as a rising of the community, or some sections of it, against the police. Yet that is certainly a partial misreading of the situation. Margaret Simey, chairwoman of the Merseyside Police Authority, had her own running disagreements with the police, but she has written: 'eventually and with some dismay, some at least of us arrived at the conclusion that it was "government" that had failed the people of Toxteth, and not the police'. Lord Scarman in Brixton similarly found that the causes of discontent and violence in Brixton were multiple.

14.55 Yet that is not the whole truth. The police may be in law the final local arm of government, but the fifteen years from 1964 up to 1980 witnessed in practice a steady accretion of power in society to the police, relatively free from accountability to 'government'. No other organisation of similar size could live without making some errors and so it unfortunately was with the police. With their own strong sense of team spirit, and increased prestige and operational freedom it became possible for them to grow away from the communities of which they were in theory members. Stories abound of malpractice, and it is likely that some of them are true. As important, a climate was allowed to develop in which it was possible to believe that many of them were true. In many urban areas the police to a degree lost the trust and support of the public.

14.56 This mattered deeply. There is a long and honourable tradition of policing as a service – often the last and only service between the citizen and acute physical or emotional suffering. The loss, real or imagined, of that service was for many people a deep loss, and for society a tragedy. The riots of 1981 gave expression to the sense of that loss (the loss of trust in the police) as well as the sense of being abandoned by 'government'.

14.57 Since police authorities and forces are to a great degree independent of each other, it is dangerous to generalize, but it seems

347

that 1981 defused a good deal of the sense of grievance which people had against the police (some of which, however, was rekindled by the miners' strike). On the other side, the police seem to have learned important lessons. In the Metropolitan Police, training, not just of recruits but also of all serving ranks, is receiving much greater priority. Greater awareness is being shown of the influence of racial prejudice on police conduct – at least at the higher levels, if not always in local police stations. Generally, across the country, police seem less inclined to believe that in peace-keeping and crime-chasing they can 'go it alone' and seem to accept, by contrast, that they will always be frustrated unless they have the confidence of the community. There is greater awareness of the contribution made by the police to local social work, and in many forces abilities in this field are taken into account for promotion as much as a record for detecting and dealing with crime. Co-operation with social workers has improved. However, the picture is not uniform. Increased training does not enjoy the same priority and budget in all forces. Entry to the local community and knowledge of its byways and its ethos is not universal, and neither is willingness to expose methods of policing to local scrutiny.

14.58   All could be put at risk once again, however, if other problems in the urban priority areas are not tackled. There is smouldering anger and quiet despair, and if these are not displaced by hope overt violence or more self-destructive activities may surge again, as recent events in Handsworth and Brixton have sadly reminded us.

(b)   *Accountability and Consultation*
14.59   Policing in urban areas in 1985 is practised against the background of a vigorous public debate over police accountability, democratic control and public consultation.

14.60   It is not always realised that there are important constitutional differences between the accountability of the Metropolitan Police Force and that of the 42 other police forces in England and Wales. In those forces, high level police policy is made within a tripartite framework of the Home Office, the Chief Constable, and the Police Authority. These police authorities consist of an assembly of which two-thirds of the members are locally elected and one-third are magistrates. They are an essential element in the accountability of a police force. But in London the 'police authority' is the Home Secretary himself – one element in the tripartite framework is missing. This means, in effect, that Londoners have a lesser say in the policing of their city than those living elsewhere. It also brings considerable confusion into the question of accountability and control as exercised by police authorities and chief constables, arising ultimately out of an ambiguity in the 1964 Police Act which set up the Police Authorities. The unproductive and sometimes acrimonious debate which continues on this matter can only lead to a further loss of confidence by the public. We believe that it is urgent that this situation be clarified, if necessary by Act of Parliament.

14.61 The 1984 Police and Criminal Evidence Act gave a statutory base to the setting up of local consultative bodies in the form of Police Liaison Committees. These committees vary in their terms of reference, their constitution and their style of procedure, but are all rooted in and report to the elected representative forum, that is, the Police Authority – with the exception of London, where consultative groups stand alone, there being no police authority for them to relate to.

14.62 In our view some local consultative machinery is a necessary development if the public as a whole is to be involved in decision making on police issues and if it is to discharge its responsibilities for policing itself. We believe that policing, and with it the maintenance of order and law, is too important a function to be left to police officers alone. It is a social responsibility, and one in which the members of our society are still too little involved.

14.63 Police liaison committees have come under criticism in some quarters mainly because they lack power to oblige the police either to release information or to alter policy. They are sometimes cynically regarded as a means of 'drawing the sting' from legitimate criticisms of the police. We recognise that failure by the police to provide regular and relevant information on priorities, boundaries and resources, or to give sufficient professional support to the committees, can make them ineffectual; but we believe that the present legal framework should make it possible for the police to become significantly more accountable to the communities they serve. Police Liaison Committees cannot bring about instant changes; but where they are rooted in an elected forum which has statutory responsibility relating to the policing of a specific area (which is at present only possible outside London) we believe that they can exercise a positive influence so long as they have reasonable resources, continuity of membership and accessibility to the local community. We *recommend* therefore:

(i)   that a Police Advisory Committee should be established for Greater London to provide a forum for Local Police Liaison

Committees in the Metropolis, with powers and responsibilities comparable with those of existing Committees elsewhere and with direct access to the Home Secretary;

(ii) that the Church should support the development of local consultative bodies and where possible offer such skills as may be available;

(iii) that the Home Office should encourage police authorities to employ sufficient staff to ensure the efficient servicing and effective development of local consultative bodies, and should ensure that all such expenditure is exempted from rate support grant penalties;

(iv) that Chief Police Officers, through their Association, should support the full involvement of police forces at every level in local consultative groups and encourage a positive attitude towards the providing of necessary and appropriate information.

(c) *Church and Police*

14.64 It could be said that the Police are a front-line social service as much as a crime-fighting organisation. The range of actions which the public calls for from the police extends far beyond those directly connected with crime itself. People often value highly the presence of the police, even if no crime has occurred or is likely to occur. The police have to discharge a diverse range of roles, and to display a matching array of skills. This has implications for recruitment and training. It also adds to the demands made upon them by the public, and this, given their other responsibilities and their comparative isolation when on duty, may expose them to a level of stress which is arguably greater than that applying in other social agencies.

14.65 In some places, and from time to time, the Churches have recognised this vulnerability of police officers, and have set up police chaplaincies. This has usually been a local initiative, stemming perhaps from the gifts and enthusiasm of particular clergy. To date, however, police chaplaincy has not become a regular part of the expectations of either the police or the Churches. An enquiry addressed to Chief Constables by the chaplain at Bramshill Police College showed in 1984 that not more than half the county forces had any kind of chaplaincy. It would be useful to find out what level and type of service existing police chaplaincies offer, what the nature of police demand on chaplaincy service might be, and what policy the Church officially might adopt. As in the case of other pioneering ministries of the Church, the time will come for local initiatives and experiments to be put on a firmer and more permanent basis.

14.66 However, existing Church experience of policing is very varied, and support for the police overall is not unequivocal. Churches sometimes report very adverse reactions in their local communities to particular examples of policing. There was some open Church opposition to the 1984 Police and Criminal Evidence Act and its extension to county areas of stop and search powers such as are used in metropolitan areas. There would probably not be easy agreement within the Churches over chaplaincy arrangements if these appeared likely to inhibit the voicing of community disquiet over police powers and methods, and in some places chaplaincies have actually been withdrawn by the Church. The situation is far more complicated, both ethically and contractually, than in the case, for example, of prison chaplains. Meanwhile there is already a debate within the Churches about policing and police chaplaincy, and this is to be encouraged. Informal contacts between police and clergy can have a great value; and given the difficult ethical decisions which often face quite junior police officers there is much to be said for the formation of 'police ethics groups' at a local level similar to those which already exist between clergy and doctors.

(d) *Racial Prejudice*

14.67 We have heard numerous complaints from black people of alleged discrimination against them by the police and of personal disadvantage (compared with white people) when they come before criminal courts. Indeed, such incidents have occurred in the experience of at least one member of our Commission. Some of these allegations (for example, of discrimination by the police against Afro-Caribbeans, and of refusal to acknowledge and follow up racial crimes against Asians) are well substantiated. We would not wish to use such evidence (some of it hearsay) to level criticism specifically at the police or the magistracy. Black people continue to receive humiliating and discriminatory treatment from their white fellow citizens in many areas of daily life. Manifestations of racial prejudice are liable to occur in every branch of society and in every institution (including the Church) in Britain today. Such treatment is stoically endured by the great majority of black people.

14.68 Nevertheless we note that since the Scarman Report this matter has been taken seriously by police forces, and that awareness of it has become a stated objective of police training. We have also had our attention drawn to disquieting reports of racial disadvantage in the legal profession and in proceedings before magistrates.[21] When an enquiry has been set up in other areas where racial discrimination has been suspected (such as immigration procedures) the facts have been found to be more serious even than the victims themselves imagined. If the same were found to be true in policing and judicial procedures we would be facing a grave situation that could be fraught with long-term consequences for order and law in our society.

Prisons, Prisoners and their Dependants

14.69 There are some 48,000 men and women in prison in this country. By no means all of these come from UPAs. But given that seven out of ten of all those entering prison are unemployed,[22] and that the vast majority of all prisoners are male, young and working class, there is a strong presumption that most prisoners also come from UPAs and that most of their dependants live there.

14.70 Members of the Commission therefore visited HM Prison Manchester (Strangeways) on 18 May 1984. We selected this prison primarily because it is a local prison in a mainly urban priority area. Predictably, we found the rate of unemployment among prisoners to be considerably higher than the national average of 7 out of 10 of those entering prison.

14.71 On the day of our visit there were over 1,400 male adult and young offender prisoners. The prison was built in 1864 to house 774 men and 335 women. We were informed that the prison sometimes now contains 1,700 prisoners. Many cells are shared by three prisoners. Owing to the scarcity of work and educational facilities more prisoners spend the greater part of their time, and many 23 hours of the day, locked in cells. These conditions are insanitary and degrading, and we were shocked to find that they have become a normal part of a prison sentence.

14.72 We were shown the industrial workshops standing empty. The reasons given were the high rate of unemployment in Manchester itself and the shortage of discipline staff. We are aware that there are also objections made to the principle of compulsory industrial work of a repetitive and monotonous nature; in the words of the judicial adage, 'prisoners are sent to prison not *for* punishment but *as* punishment'. Yet a failure to provide opportunities for work or for vocational training contravenes the European Minimum Rules on the Treatment of Prisoners, which state that 'sufficient work of a useful nature should be provided to keep prisoners actively employed for a normal working day' (Rule 72.3). The equivalent Rule (28.1) for prisons in England and

Wales requires a prisoner 'to do useful work' (with an element of compulsion) but places no sanction on prison management when no work is provided.

14.73   We see the present lack of provision for useful work or vocational training as part of the recent and officially sanctioned retreat from a rehabilitative objective in prison administration. Although we recognise that there is little evidence for the success of attempts to make prison a place of rehabilitation we believe that it is still our Christian duty to continue to attempt to make it so. We agree with the conclusion of the Board for Social Responsibility's Report of 1978 (*Prisons and Prisoners in England Today* p. 71) that 'the principal emphasis in prison regimes should be on widening the opportunities for the prisoner to exercise personal responsibilty. The sentence itself defines the limits of punishment; within those limits the opportunities for the prisoner to exercise choice, to take responsibility, should be maximised.'

14.74   In this connection, we were impressed with the work at Strangeways of the Education Department (with severely restricted resources, and threatened with still further cuts, even in the youth custody Allocation Centre) and of the Chaplaincy. Attendance at Sunday services reached 700 in some weeks.

14.75   On the day of our visit over 400 prisoners were on remand. Official statistics show that the average untried population in custody has increased by 110 per cent in the last decade, and that the average time spent in custody by untried prisoners has doubled in that time to 47 days. During their time in prison, they have no access to educational or recreational facilities. Some 40 per cent of these prisoners will be found not guilty, will not be proceeded against or will be given non-custodial sentences.[23]

14.76   In January 1984 the Home Secretary stated that 'at the moment the most acute difficulty in the prison population is not the growth in the number of sentenced prisoners but the growth in the number of remand prisoners'. We are bound to say, on the contrary, that the number of sentenced prisoners is already too high (we have already noted that proportionately it is the highest in Europe); and we believe that the number of remand prisoners is more than a 'difficulty'. Not only is it a great burden on the taxpayer (£2 million per week, excluding the cost of various welfare benefits to which those on remand are entitled), but it has extremely serious social consequences: the disturbance of family life; the loss or blighting of employment prospects; the danger of damage to physical and mental health; the prejudice to living accommodation; the accumulation of debts. The cherished principle of British law that a person must be presumed innocent until proved guilty forces us to protest constantly against a system which visits these consequences, and a form of imprisonment *less* humane (since it offers fewer social and educational amenities) than that imposed on convicted prisoners, on so many who are subsequently not found guilty.

Conclusion

14.77   In this Chapter we have tried to identify some of the factors which threaten the maintenance of order and law in UPAs. In many respects our analysis simply adds urgency to the measures which are recommended in other parts of this Report, and endorses the view expressed by many other agencies that order and crime prevention are the responsibility of the local community and that more resources must be made available for this task at the local level. But we have also drawn attention to some serious shortcomings in the penal system, and we have been led to make the following specific recommendations:

Main Recommendations

1.   The recommendations of the Lord Chancellor's Committee on the funding of Law Centres should be implemented immediately (paragraph 14.53).

2.   The Church, the Home Office and Chief Police Officers should give full support to the work of Police Advisory Committees, and that a Police Liaison Committee for Greater London should be established (paragraph 14.63).

References

1   Source: 1984 Report of the Commissioner of Police for the City of London

2   Source: Director General of the Prison Department, 1982

3   The interpretation of Rule One of the 1964 Prison Rules adopted by the Prisons Board in 1983 omits any reference to rehabilitation in the definition of 'the purpose of training and treatment of convicted prisoners'.

4   Source: Prison Reform Trust

5   *Taking Account of Crime*, Table 8

6   ibid

7   Source: Greater Manchester Council

8   *Fear of Crime in England and Wales* (1984), pp. 31, 37-8

9   Geoffrey Pearson, *Christian Action Journal*, Summer 1984, pp. 5-8

10   *The Brixton Disorders* (The Scarman Report), HMSO Cmnd. 8427, para. 8.48

11   Roger Tarling, *Unemployment and Crime*, Home Office Research and Planning Unit, 1982

12   e.g. Lord (then William) Whitelaw in a debate in the House of Commons, February 1978: 'let no-one have any doubt about the danger that has been created [by the level of unemployment] in terms of crimes of all sorts,' quoted with approval by Lord Elwyn Jones, *One People Oration*, Westminster Abbey, July 1985

13   *Drug Misuse: Prevalence and Service Provision*. A report on surveys and plans in English National Health Service Regions. DHSS, June 1985

14   ibid, Appendix B

15   No 79: *Crime and Police Effectiveness* by R.V.G. Clark and M. Hough (1984)

16   Scarman Report, para. 4.76

17   *Community Based Improvement Programmes on Twelve Inner London Housing Estates*, a Report by John Bright and Geraldine Petterson

18   Source: National Association of Victim Support Schemes (Annual Report, 1985)

19   Southwark Diocesan Council for Social Aid Prison Advisory Group (written submission)

20   Certain restrictions on the work that Law Centres may do have been agreed with the Law Society

21   Report of Race Relations Committee of the Senate of the Inns of Court and the Bar (*Annual Statement*, 1983-4) p. 35: 'black barristers are in general at a disadvantage compared with their white counterparts'; Research in a South London magistrates' Court reported by Maureen Cain and Susan Sadigh, 'Racism, the Police and Community Policing', *Journal of Law and Society*, Summer 1982: 'a pattern consistent with a racist practice on the part of court administrators'.

22   Evidence from Prison Reform Trust

23   ibid

Part IV

Conclusion
and
Summary of Recommendations

Chapter 15

CONCLUSION

'We have found faith in the city.' (The Commission)

15.1 Chapter after chapter of our Report tells the same story: that a growing number of people are excluded by poverty or powerlessness from sharing in the common life of our nation. A substantial minority – perhaps as many as one person in every four or five across the nation, and a much higher proportion in the UPAs – are forced to live on the margins of poverty or below the threshold of an acceptable standard of living.

15.2 The present acute situation of our nation's Urban Priority Areas demands an urgent response from the Church and from government.

15.3 The Archbishops' Commission on 'Church and State' concluded its report in 1970:

'The Church should concern itself first, and indeed second, with the poor and needy, whether in spirit or in body.'

15.4 We echo these words. The Church cannot supplant the market or the state. It can, as we recommend, mobilize its own resources in a way that accords high priority to the poor. It must by its example and its exertions proclaim the ethic of altruism against egotism, of community against self-seeking, and of charity against greed.

15.5 But we are conscious that we have only scratched the surface of some of the major concerns to have emerged from our work. To draw out the implications of some of these, such as the Church's response to the prospect of persistent long-term unemployment, will require more time and resources than have been available to us. There must also be a major national debate on the future of our cities, in which the Church must play a full part.

15.6 Perhaps the most important wider question concerns the

359

structure of our society. One submission to us put it bluntly: 'The exclusion of the poor is pervasive and not accidental. It is organized and imposed by powerful institutions which represent the rest of us.' The critical issue to be faced is whether there is any serious political will to set in motion a process which will enable those who are at present in poverty and powerless to rejoin the life of the nation.

15.7   Here is a challenge indeed. It will call among other things for a clear resolve on the part of Church and government to have faith in the city. We take courage from three realities which are evident to us.

15.8   The first is that changes on a global scale are already upon us, as the era known as industrial society gives place to something new. The industrial city is one of the focal points of that change. In almost every sphere of life and in a brief span of time the future is being shaped by action or by default. The very assumptions of our culture are now open to debate in new ways. We do not pretend to discern clearly what is to come. We present no comprehensive political or economic analysis. That task goes beyond this Commission. At this time of immense opportunity what we can do is to pledge ourselves as citizens to do our best to engage in the daily moral confrontations of public life and personal relations.

15.9   The second evident reality is the experience of justice, love and hope in human history, focused most clearly for us in our religious tradition. We know that there is a transforming power present in human affairs which can resolve apparently intractable situations and can bring new life into the darkest places. If, as we dare to affirm, the true nature of human life is to be discerned in the life of Jesus Christ, we can take heart and pledge ourselves to a deeper commitment to create a society in which benefits and burdens are shared in a more equitable way. Any attempt to base a society or culture upon other foundations carries with it, we believe, its own nemesis of suffering, bitterness and social disintegration.

15.10   But – and this is our third evident reality – somewhere along the road which we have travelled in the past two years each of us has faced a personal challenge to our lives and life styles: a call to change our thinking and action in such a way as to help us to stand more closely alongside the risen Christ with those who are poor and powerless. We have found faith in the city.

SUMMARY OF MAIN RECOMMENDATIONS

To the Church of England

1 A national system for designating UPA parishes should be developed (paragraph 5.9).

2 Dioceses should devote greater attention to the effective collection and presentation of accurate statistics (paragraph 5.16).

3 The internal distribution of clergy by dioceses should be adjusted where necessary to ensure that UPA parishes receive a fair share, and particular attention should be paid in this respect to parishes on large outer estates (paragraph 5.35).

4 Dioceses should explore the possibilities of fresh stipendiary lay ministries, not necessarily tied to one parish (paragraph 5.35).

5 The 'Audit for the Local Church' which we propose should be further developed, and adopted by local UPA Churches (paragraph 5.37).

6 In urban areas the deanery should have an important support and pastoral planning function (paragraph 5.41).

7 Each parish should review, preferably annually, what progress in co-operation has been made between clergy and laity, between Churches, and ecumenically, with the aim of developing partnership in ministry (paragraph 5.49).

8 Appointments should be made to the Boards and Councils of the General Synod, and a new Commission on Black Anglican Concerns established, to enable the Church to make a more effective response to racial discrimination and disadvantage, and to the alienation experienced by many black people in relation to the Church of England (paragraph 5.62).

9 The General Synod should consider how a more appropriate system of representation which pays due regard to minority interests can be

implemented for the Synod elections of 1990 (paragraph 5.74).

10 The appropriate Church voluntary bodies should consider how schemes for voluntary service in UPAs could be extended to widen the age range of those eligible, and to allow for part-time as well as full-time volunteering (paragraph 5.90).

11 Dioceses with significant concentrations of UPAs should initiate Church Leadership Development Programmes (paragraph 6.11).

12 Our proposals for an extension of Local Non-Stipendiary Ministry, including those relating to selection, training and funding should be tested in dioceses, and monitored over a ten-year period (paragraph 6.55).

13 All dioceses should manifest a commitment to post-ordination training and continued ministerial education in UPAs to the extent at least of regular day-release courses (paragraph 6.74).

14 Urgent attention should be given to appropriate training for teachers and supervisors in all areas of theological education, particularly those concerned with ministry in UPAs, and to the provision of theological and educational resources in urban centres (paragraph 6.77).

15 ACCM should be adequately funded to promote and monitor officially sanctioned experiments in theological education (paragraph 6.80).

16 ACCM should be given power, in certain defined cases, to direct candidates to specific courses of training, and bishops should endorse such direction (paragraph 6.81).

17 The role of non-residential training courses similar to the Aston Scheme should be further developed (paragraph 6.82).

18 Dioceses and deaneries should undertake a reappraisal of their support systems for UPA clergy (paragraph 6.97).

19 The Liturgical Commission should pay close attention to the liturgical needs of Churches in the urban priority areas (paragraph 6.110).

20 A reassessment of the traditional patterns of the Church's work of nurture of young people in UPAs is required at parish, deanery and diocesan level (paragraph 6.121).

21   Sharing agreements with other denominations should be adopted more widely, as should the informal sharing of church buildings (other than the church itself) with those of other faiths (paragraph 7.17).

22   In cases of the sale of redundant churches, there should be earlier and more open consultation with community organisations and bodies such as housing associations when future uses are being considered (paragraph 7.57).

23   The historic resources of the Church should be redistributed between dioceses to equalize the capital and income resources behind each clergyman, deaconess and licensed lay worker in the stipendiary ministry. The redistribution formula should take account of potential giving (paragraphs 7.77-7.80).

24   Within dioceses, the acute financial needs of the urban priority area Churches require a clear response (paragraph 7.81).

25   A Church Urban Fund should be established to strengthen the Church's presence and promote the Christian witness in the urban priority areas (paragraph 7.88).

26   The Church of England should continue to question the morality of economic policies in the light of their effects (paragraph 9.52).

27   Churches should take part in initiatives to engage unemployed people in UPAs in job-creating projects. The use of Church premises for this purpose must be encouraged (paragraph 9.112).

28   The Church should build on good practice in ministry to unemployed people: Industrial Mission has an important role to play here (paragraph 9.115).

29   We commend the use of properly-trained social workers working with local Churches and neighbourhood groups as an important part of the total ministry of the Church in the urban priority areas (paragraph 12.26).

30   Church social workers should be trained within the mainstream of social work, but with particular attention paid to the character and needs of social work in the church context. The Church should initiate discussion with social work training agencies to this end (paragraph 12.26).

31   Dioceses should, through their Boards for Social Responsibility, develop and support community work, and should exercise a strategic

role in support of local programmes in their urban priority areas (paragraph 12.53).

32   Discussions should be held between the General Synod Board for Social Responsibility and the British Council of Churches Community Work Advisory Committee with a view to strengthening the national support networks for community work. The Church of England should be prepared to devote central resources to this end (paragraph 12.54).

33   Additional Church-sponsored urban studies centres for teacher training should be established (paragraph 13.38).

34   All diocesan Boards and Councils of Education should give special priority to the needs of the UPA schools for which they are responsible (paragraph 13.91).

35   The governors and managers of Church schools should consider whether the composition of foundation governors in the school adequately reflects the ethnic constituency of its catchment area (paragraph 13.91).

36   Consideration should be given to a further exploration of the ecumenical dimension at secondary level, including the possibility of establishing Church of England/Roman Catholic schools in urban priority areas, which would offer a significant proportion of places to children of other faiths (paragraph 13.91).

37   A review of the Diocesan Education Committee measures should be undertaken, to allow the formulation of diocesan policies for Church schools on admission criteria and other issues, such as religious education and worship, equal opportunities and community education (paragraph 13.91).

38   The General Synod's Board of Education, in consultation with Diocesan Youth Officers, should move towards a national strategy for the Church's work with young people in UPAs, and initiate and support work specifically within these areas (paragraph 13.127).

To Government and Nation

1   A greater priority for the outer estates is called for within urban policy initiatives (paragraph 8.35).

2   The resources devoted to Rate Support Grant should be increased in real terms, and within the enhanced total a greater bias should be given

to the UPAs. Efficiency audits should be used to tackle wasteful expenditure (paragraph 8.55).

3   The size of the Urban Programme should be increased, and aspects of its operation reviewed (paragraph 8.67).

4   The concept of 'Partnership' in the urban priority areas should be developed by central and local government to promote greater consultation with, and participation by, local people at neighbourhood level (paragraph 8.76).

5   There should be a new deal between government and the voluntary sector, to provide long-term continuity and funding for recognized voluntary bodies working alongside statutory agencies (paragraphs 8.94-95).

6   A new impetus should be given to support for small firms in UPAs, perhaps by the establishment of a Council for Small Firms in Urban Areas (paragraph 9.56).

7   There should be additional job-creating public expenditure in the UPAs on capital and current account (paragraphs 9.62 and 9.64).

8   The Government should promote more open public discussion about the current levels of overtime working (paragraph 9.72).

9   The Community Programme eligibility rules and other constraints, including pay limits, should be relaxed, particularly to encourage greater participation by women and unemployed people with families to support (paragraphs 9.79 and 9.83).

10   The Community Programme should be expanded to provide 500,000 places (paragraph 9.80).

11   The Government should extend to those unemployed for more than a year eligibility for the long-term rate of Supplementary Benefit, or an equivalent enhanced rate of income support under whatever new arrangements may be introduced (paragraph 9.90).

12   The present level of Child Benefit should be increased as an effective means of assisting, without stigma, families in poverty (paragraph 9.91).

13   The present levels of 'earnings disregards' in relation to Unemployment Benefit and Supplementary Benefit should be increased to mitigate the effects of the poverty and unemployment traps (paragraph 9.91).

14   The Government should establish an independent enquiry to undertake a wide ranging review of the inter-relationship between income support, pay and the taxation system (paragraph 9.100).

15   Ethnic records should be kept and monitored by public housing authorities, as a step towards eliminating direct and indirect discrimination in housing allocation (paragraph 10.37).

16   An expanded public housing programme of new building and improvement is needed, particularly in the UPAs, to ensure a substantial supply of good quality rented accommodation for all who need it, including single people. Each local authority's housing stock should include a range of types of accommodation, including direct access emergency accommodation (paragraph 10.77).

17   The Housing (Homeless Persons) Act should be extended to cover all who are homeless. Homeless people should be offered a choice of accommodation (paragraph 10.78).

18   There should be further moves towards the decentralisation of local authority housing services (paragraph 10.85).

19   A major examination of the whole system of housing finance, including mortgage tax relief, is needed. It should have the objective of providing most help to those most in need (paragraph 10.98).

20   The concept of 'care in the community' for people who might otherwise be institutionalised must be supported by adequate resources to allow the provision of proper locally-based support services for people (especially women) caring for vulnerable and handicapped people (paragraph 12.26).

21   Local authorities in boroughs and districts which include urban priority areas should, with other agencies, develop policies to establish and sustain community work with adequate resources (paragraph 12.48).

22   The Recommendations of the Lord Chancellor's Committee on the funding of Law Centres should be implemented immediately (paragraph 14.53).

23   The Church, the Home Office and Chief Police Officers should give full support to the work of Police Advisory Committees, and a Police Liaison Committee for Greater London should be established (paragraph 14.63).

AN AUDIT FOR THE LOCAL CHURCH

Why do It?

1.   The audit should be used to help the local Church to understand itself in its situation, to reflect on its purpose, and then to make plans for becoming a more effective, outward-looking and participating Church.

2.   It should have wider benefits because it will help the deanery and diocese to develop better strategies to support the local Church.

3.   It will be an important part of applications to the proposed Church Urban Fund.

How to do it?

This will vary from parish to parish. However we suggest:

(a)   The PCC should come to a common mind as to whether it is prepared for an audit. If it is, it should ask a small group to organise the audit. The group should:

be as representative of the congregation as possible (by age, sex, length of membership, etc);

include one or two 'outsiders' sympathetic to the Church and representative of the locality;

involve an outside consultant from the deanery or diocese to advise in setting up the audit and discussing the results.

(b)   It should involve the congregation and parish and be done as simply and imaginatively as possible.

(c)   It should be completed within six months to a year.

The Audit

The audit has two parts, the *analysis* of the locality and the Church, and *planning for action*.

Part 1: The Analysis of the Locality and the Church
(A) *The Locality*
The aim of this analysis is to build an accurate picture of the parish.

1   The Map
A large map of the parish should be made showing:

(a)   Its boundary and neighbouring parishes; the church and other church buildings.

(b)   Major roads.

(c)   Bus routes.

(d)   Major meeting places – for example, sub-post offices, supermarkets, shops, schools, social and community centres, pubs, fish and chip shops, off-licences, newsagents (all with appropriate symbols using differently coloured, gummed stars).

(e)   Hospitals, old people's homes, etc

(f)   Housing – with blocks coloured differently for council, private rented, owner-occupied; high rise and demolition areas should also be marked.

(g)   Other churches

2   The People
A separate statistical profile should be prepared to accompany the map.

This profile can be built up from census and other information. Local authorities can be of particular help here. It should include a population estimate and a breakdown of the parish by:

(a)   Age

(b)   Sex

(c)   Employment

(d)   Ethnic groups

(e)   Mobility (how long on average do people live in the parish?)

Suggestions as to how to do this analysis can be found in:

i   *Towards Local Social Analysis.* From Church Action on Poverty, 27 Blackfriars Rd, Salford, M3 7AQ (50p).

ii   *Discovering the Poor: a kit for local groups.* Urban Theology Unit,

210 Abbeyfield Rd, Sheffield S4 7AZ (50p).
iii *Mission Audit*. Board of Mission and Unity, CIO Publishing
(£1.50).

3   What do People feel about the Area?
    (a)   One way to do this is to ask people to write down the ten things
    they dislike about the area, and the ten things they enjoy or value
    about it ('ten for sorrow, ten for joy') in a brainstorming session. It is
    helpful to get the views of different groups – youth club, OAPs,
    young parents, etc; it is also important to get the views of people and
    groups outside the congregation. The results should be analysed.
    (b)   Are there conflicts in the area? (Young/old, newcomers/
    established residents, middle class/working class, etc).
    (c)   Who makes the decisions which affect the area? What changes
    are being made? (Roads, housing development, amenities, etc).

(B)   *The Church*
The aim of this profile is to begin to build an accurate picture of the
local Church. A simple questionnaire, completed by all members over a
period of a month, is the quickest way to get information about the
people. It should be brief enough to be completed after the service
without difficulty; the results need careful analysis.

Suggested Questions:
    (i)   Employment status (waged, unwaged, retired, part-time, full-
    time, etc).
    (ii)   Class. What is or has been your job (or your spouse's)?
    (iii)   Age (or age-group).
    (iv)   Length of church membership.
    (v)   Do you live in or out of the parish (if the latter, are you within
    one mile, or further away)?
    (vi)   Which service(s) do you come to, and how often?
    (vii)   What kind of housing do you live in? (Owner-occupied, council
    rented, private rented, etc.)
    (viii) What are your skills or hobbies?
Those undertaking the Audit should also, as a group, seek answers to the
following questions about the Church:
    (a)   Church membership; numbers, and distribution in relation to
    the map, types of housing, etc.

369

(b)   Usual Sunday attendance, and trends in recent years.

(c)   Who are the key people/leaders, and why?

(d)   What proportion of the congregation is handicapped?

(e)   What activities does the Church run, and why?

(f)   What activities are the Church and its individual members involved in, in the community?

(g)   Premises. What are they, in what condition are they, who uses them and when? Is the Church left open during the week?

(h)   Financial trends (budget five years ago and last year, and the likely budget in the coming year).

(i)   How much does the congregation give to the Church per head per week?

Part 2: Planning for Action

The aim of planning for action is to help the congregation to come to conclusions about the nature of the parish and the congregation, and to see the need for the Church to make certain changes in its life and practice if it is to be properly local and outward looking. This planning needs to be done carefully and over a period of time (certainly several months), maybe using particular groups, but always involving the whole congregation in the final decisions.

It may be helpful to use four stages in this planning:

1.   The Audit group should put together in a simple and imaginative way all the evidence from the analysis of the locality and Church, and present it to the congregation. A visual display is particularly important. Discussion should only aim to clarify and agree the emerging picture of parish and Church.

2.   Questions now need to be asked of the Church to discover how effective it is as a Church in the UPA. These questions could include:

(a)   Are local people and cultures, including members of minority ethnic groups, represented . . .

(i)   in the congregation?

(ii)   in the worship?

(iii)   in Church leadership?

(iv)   among churchwardens, sidespeople, leaders of parish organisations?

(v) on the PCC?

(vi) on deanery synods?

(vii) on diocesan boards, councils and committees, and Synods?

(b) Is the Church seeking to be present in the various neighbourhoods, organisations and institutions in the parish:

in the location of its worship centres?

in social outreach projects – including caring schemes, youth work, unemployment projects, etc?

in house groups?

through chaplaincies?

Are there parts of the parish unrepresented in the Church?

(c) Do the church buildings (church, hall, centre, school, etc) and their use reflect a Church which is properly local and outward-looking? For example:

are they used for and by local people and cultures, including other religions?

are they used as drop-in centres for the unemployed, or as advice centres?

are there obstacles to such aims, and if so how can they be removed?

can church land be used for community purposes?

(d) Is the Church served by a team of ministries including:

clergy (stipendiary, NSM, LNSM, deaconesses, lay workers)?

lay ministries?

senior Church officers (wardens etc)?

and to what extent is ministry shared between clergy and laity?

(e) Is the Church collaborating fully with others?

with other denominations?

with other parishes

with the deanery and diocesan boards and councils?

with other local organisations, local authorities etc?

(f) Is the Church actively involved in training its members for such ministries and mission? What kind of training would be most helpful?

(g) Are there any needs in the area (or of neighbouring parishes) which could be met in whole or part through the skills or hobbies of church members?

(h)   Is there anything that can be done in collaboration with other faiths?

3.   In answering these questions, particular objectives for a Church concerned to be more effective in the UPA will begin to emerge. These provisional objectives should be illuminated by a study of the Christian tradition, especially the Bible. Questions to be asked could include: Have the people of God faced this or similar situations before, and what was their response? Are there contemporary examples of similar situations being faced by other congregations, and what solutions have they tried? Are there any diocesan specialists, or others, who can help us?

4.   This should lead to a congregation deciding on its objectives, and selecting several *priorities* for the first year. These should include concrete projects. Projects and other objectives should not be attempted on every front in the first year. Changes should be accomplished gradually over a period of years with careful monitoring and discussion.

5.   Inevitably deep questions will arise about the nature and purpose of the Church and the meaning of the Christian Gospel. People should be encouraged to face them, even if there is disagreement, as long as the discussion leads to action and is not an evasion of it. A sufficient common mind is needed simply for the next step. 'I do not ask to see the distant scene, one step enough for me.'

Appendix B

Appendix B comprises the following tables and charts:

(i) **Urban Area and Other Dioceses**

TABLE 1	– Comparison of various clergy and population ratios
TABLE 2	– Comparative changes over 30 years
CHART 1	– Population/clergy ratios over 30 years

(ii) **UPA and Other Parishes in 12 Urban Area Dioceses**

TABLE 3	– Analysis of parishes
TABLE 4	– Population analysis
TABLE 5	– Distribution of parochial stipendiary clergy
TABLE 6	– Population per clergy
TABLE 7	– Electoral roll members per clergy
CHART 2	– Population per clergy: variations from diocesan average in UPA and other parishes
CHART 3	– Population per clergy in 'Group A' parishes compared with diocesan average

Appendix B

Urban Area Dioceses: Some Comparisons

TABLE 1

	Population per parochial clergy		Electoral Roll Members per clergy B	Usual Sunday attendance per clergy C	Number of churches per 100 clergy D	Land area (square miles) per clergy E	Population density	
	Numbers A	Ranking					Numbers per square mile F	Ranking
BIRMINGHAM	7,094	1	89	107	100	1.4	4,948	3
LONDON	6,092	2	96	103	94	.5	11,573	1
Sheffield	6,010	3	120	98	120	2.9	2,095	7
SOUTHWARK	5,756	4	122	101	103	.8	6,781	2
Bristol	5,750	5	156	146	153	3.4	1,698	9
MANCHESTER	5,732	6	131	118	109	1.2	4,793	4
LIVERPOOL	5,730	7	136	129	93	1.4	4,198	5
Durham	5,469	8	140	101	113	3.7	1,482	14
Chelmsford	5,440	9	112	102	135	3.3	1,657	12
WAKEFIELD	5,338	10	133	117	130	2.8	1,881	8
Southwell	5,319	11	120	107	174	4.5	1,179	17
COVENTRY	5,264	13	158	133	171	4.8	1,102	19
LICHFIELD	5,170	14	138	105	154	4.4	1,174	18
BRADFORD	5,000	17	129	103	137	7.3	685	27
Chester	4,971	18	194	137	126	3.3	1,515	13
RIPON	4,781	20	173	110	171	8.5	563	29
NEWCASTLE	4,715	21	118	102	151	12.6	373	36
Leicester	4,710	22	127	103	192	4.7	993	21
BLACKBURN	4,639	25	248	145	113	3.3	1,405	15
York	4,400	28	116	108	214	9.0	488	30

TABLE 1 (continued)

20 URBAN AREA DIOCESES	**5,419**		**135**	**112**	**132**	**3.6**	**1,498**
23 OTHER DIOCESES*	**3,867**		**163**	**126**	**201**	**6.6**	**590**
ALL 43 DIOCESES	**4,671**		**148**	**119**	**165**	**5.0**	**928**
of which –							
Rochester	5,295	12	165	148	122	2.5	2,149	6
Portsmouth	5,129	15	146	127	138	3.1	1,659	11
St Albans	5,077	16	185	129	137	3.7	1,367	16
Guildford	4,885	19	210	164	121	2.9	1,684	10
Hereford	2,023	43	173	91	335	12.8	158	43

The 20 Urban Area Dioceses are those containing 'designated authorities' under the Inner Urban Areas Act 1978. Block capitals denote the 12 dioceses analysed in Tables 3–7 of this Appendix.

The ratios are derived from the 1985 edition of 'Church Statistics', data from tables 29 and 30 (for 1983/84) being related to numbers of parochial clergy at December 1984 from table 2 of that booklet. The resultant ratios in columns A and B above are thus consistent with one another but *not*, in most cases, with the ratios shown in Tables 6 and 7 (and Charts 2 and 3) of this Appendix.

Appendix B

Urban Area and other Dioceses: Comparative Changes over 30 Years

TABLE 2

	1953	1963	1973	1983	Change since 1953	1953	1963	1973	1983	Change since 1953
			numbers				number per thousand population			
BAPTISMS										
20 Urban Area Dioceses	264	269	176	133	– 50%	10.0	9.4	6.1	4.7	– 53%
23 Other Dioceses	145	165	128	105	– 28%	12.1	10.6	7.2	5.6	– 54%
CONFIRMATIONS										
20 Urban Area Dioceses	84	100	55	44	– 48%	3.20	3.48	1.89	1.56	– 51%
23 Other Dioceses	70	82	46	39	– 46%	5.89	5.26	2.57	2.01	– 66%
EASTER COMMUNICANTS										
20 Urban Area Dioceses	1,096	1,209	817	800	– 27%	41.7	42.3	28.3	28.3	– 32%
23 Other Dioceses	972	1,138	867	869	– 11%	81.4	73.0	48.7	46.3	– 43%
ELECTORAL ROLLS										
20 Urban Dioceses	1,568	1,451	987	754	– 52%	59.6	50.8	34.3	24.9	– 58%
23 Other Dioceses	1,354	1,342	1,034	741	– 45%	113.3	86.1	58.1	42.1	– 63%
TOTAL VOLUNTARY CONTRIBUTIONS: £ *millions*						£ per thousand population				
20 Urban Area Dioceses	4.76	9.98	14.98	55.29	x 11.6	181	349	520	1,955	x 10.8
23 Other Dioceses	3.96	8.77	14.11	52.41	x 13.2	332	563	793	2,791	x 8.4
PAROCHIAL CLERGY										
	numbers		(1971)				clergy per million population (1971)			
20 Urban Area Dioceses	7,052	6,642	6,417	5,218	– 26%	268	232	222	185	– 31%
23 Other Dioceses	7,594	6,707	6,488	4,856	– 36%	636	430	374	259	– 59%

APPENDIX B CHART 1

Population/Clergy Ratios
Gap between Urban Area Dioceses and Others

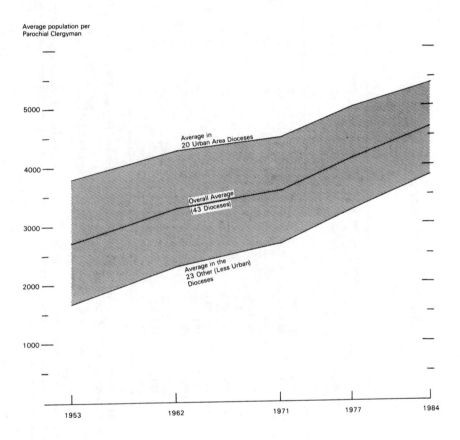

Average population per
Parochial Clergyman

Average in
20 Urban Area Dioceses

Overall Average
(43 Dioceses)

Average in the
23 Other (Less Urban)
Dioceses

5000

4000

3000

2000

1000

1953   1962   1971   1977   1984

377

Appendix B

Analysis of Parishes

TABLE 3

	DIOCESAN TOTAL A	Urban Priority Area Parishes			Neutral Parishes		OTHER PARISHES ('NON-UPA') G
		'Group A' (by DoE criteria) B	'Group B' (diocesan additions) C	TOTAL UPA PARISHES D	City Centre E	Marginal Parishes F	
Birmingham	183	57 (31%)	20	77 (42%)	3	14	89 (49%)
London	435	142 (33%)	4	146 (34%)	56	38	195 (45%)
Southwark	286	92 (33%)	8	100 (35%)	2	23	161 (56%)
Liverpool	209	36 (14%)	19	55 (26%)	1	12	141 (67%)
Manchester	317	71 (22%)	69	140 (44%)	3	9	165 (52%)
Wakefield	202	12 (6%)	13	25 (12%)	5	15	157 (78%)
Lichfield	453	33 (7%)	1	34 (8%)	–	5	414 (91%)
Coventry	202	10 (5%)	5	15 (7%)	2	2	183 (91%)
Blackburn	252	33 (13%)	9	42 (17%)	5	12	193 (77%)
Bradford	133	23 (17%)	3	26 (20%)	–	5	102 (77%)
Newcastle	180	17 (9%)	16	33 (18%)	1	16	140 (78%)
Ripon	196	18 (9%)	7	25 (13%)	3	5	163 (83%)

Diocesan totals: some are built up from latest available diocesan directories; others are as at December 1983 from 'Church Statistics' (with a residual figure in column G). The London total excludes 13 Guild Churches.

UPA designations, and the limitations of the analysis, are described in Chapter 5 (paragraphs 5.5–9)

CAUTIONARY NOTE on Tables 3–7 and Charts 2 & 3

The statistics are built up from a variety of sources – including diocesan directories at various recent dates – and cannot pretend to precise accuracy and consistency. Nevertheless they have been discussed severally with the dioceses concerned, and the general picture emerging is thought to be sufficiently reliable to enable broad provisional inferences to be drawn.

Appendix B

Population Analysis

TABLE 4

| | DIOCESAN TOTAL A | Urban Priority Area Parishes | | | Neutral Parishes | | 'NON-UPA' PARISHES (residual) G |
		'Group A' (by DoE criteria) B	'Group B' (diocesan additions) C	TOTAL UPA PARISHES D	City Centre E	Marginal Parishes F	
Birmingham	1,421,000	450,000	253,000	703,000	2,000	149,000	567,000
London	3,134,000	1,144,000	25,000	1,169,000	101,000	310,000	1,554,000
Southwark	1,950,000	619,000	71,000	691,000	8,000	152,000	1,100,000
Liverpool	1,627,000	317,000	197,000	514,000	9,000	105,000	999,000
Manchester	1,965,000	396,000	440,000	836,000	6,000	67,000	1,056,000
Wakefield	1,044,000	63,000	88,000	151,000	9,000	72,000	812,000
Lichfield	2,066,000	277,000	11,000	288,000	–	83,000	1,695,000
Coventry	744,000	133,000	41,000	174,000	3,000	18,000	549,000
Blackburn	1,221,000	189,000	78,000	267,000	14,000	101,000	839,000
Bradford	616,000	180,000	29,000	209,000	–	45,000	362,000
Newcastle	766,000	103,000	122,000	225,000	1,000	59,000	481,000
Ripon	742,000	156,000	49,000	205,000	6,000	57,000	474,000

Diocesan totals are 1981 Census figures for 'Usually Resident Population'.

Parish population aggregates in columns B–F are based on diocesan published estimates in the case of Birmingham, Lichfield, Blackburn, parts of London, and (after 15% reduction) Bradford. The rest are built up from 1981 Census data with the assistance of local authorities.

UPA designations, and the limitations of the analysis, are described in Chapter 5 (paragraphs 5.5–9)

See also general Cautionary Note at foot of Table 3.

Appendix B

Distribution of Parochial Stipendiary Clergy

TABLE 5

| | DIOCESAN TOTAL A | Urban Priority Area Parishes | | | Neutral Parishes | | OTHER PARISHES ('NON-UPA') G |
		'Group A' (by DoE criteria) B	'Group B' (diocesan additions) C	TOTAL UPA PARISHES D	City Centre E	Marginal Parishes F	
Birmingham	207	66	29	95	4	19	89
London	542	171	4	175	75	43	249
Southwark	333	103	17	120	1	26	186
Liverpool	288	59	29	88	2	18	180
Manchester	361	82	72	154	3	9	195
Wakefield	198	13	15	28	4	13	153
Lichfield	403	45	2	47	–	11	345
Coventry	148	16	5	21	2	1	124
Blackburn	247	32	12	44	6	15	182
Bradford	129	26	4	30	–	8	91
Newcastle	165	21	19	40	1	6	118
Ripon	161	28	9	37	4	10	110

Diocesan totals are mostly as at December 1983 or June 1984; but those for London, Liverpool and Manchester are built up from latest available diocesan directories. The London total excludes Guild Church clergy.

Clergy distributions are based on information (not always clear) from latest available diocesan directories.

UPA designations, and the limitations of the analysis, are described in Chapter 5 (paragraphs 5.5–9).

See also general Cautionary Note at foot of Table 3.

Appendix B

Population per Clergy

TABLE 6

| | DIOCESAN TOTAL A | Urban Priority Area Parishes | | | Neutral Parishes | | OTHER PARISHES (NON-UPA) G | Differences between | | |
		'Group A' (by DoE criteria) B	'Group B' (diocesan additions) C	TOTAL UPA PARISHES D	City Centre E	Marginal Parishes F		Col D and Col G X	Col B and Col G Y	Col B and Col A Z
Birmingham	6,863	6,818	8,723	7,399	400	7,823	6,376	+16%	+7%	− 1%
London	5,783	6,688	(6,428)	6,682	1,348	7,205	6,241	+7%	+7%	+16%
	or 6,495*									or +3%*
Southwark	5,855	6,007	4,194	5,750	7,683	5,854	5,912	− 3%	+ 2%	+ 3%
Liverpool	5,650	5,369	6,814	5,845	4,430	5,823	5,551	+ 5%	− 3%	− 5%
Manchester	5,444	4,826	6,109	5,426	1,953	7,454	5,419	− 0%	− 11%	− 11%
Wakefield	5,274	4,817	5,858	5,375	2,325	5,522	5,311	+ 1%	− 9%	− 9%
Lichfield	5,126	6,154	(5,500)	6,126	–	7,509	4,914	+25%	+25%	+20%
Coventry	5,029	8,318	8,121	8,271	1,722	(17,913)	4,430	+87%	+88%	+65%
Blackburn	4,942	5,919	6,463	6,068	2,259	6,735	4,611	+32%	+28%	+20%
Bradford	4,777	6,940	(7,220)	6,978	–	5,610	3,978	+75%	+74%	+45%
Newcastle	4,642	4,890	6,419	5,620	1,000	9,883	4,074	+35%	+17%.	+ 4%
Ripon	4,606	5,577	5,464	5,550	1,566	5,687	4,301	+29%	+30%	+21%

* London ratio excluding City Centre parishes.

These population/clergy ratios are derived from population figures in Table 4 (before rounding) divided by clergy numbers in Table 5. Bracketed ratios, and all those in Column E except the London figure, are based on very few parishes.

UPA designations, and the limitations of the analysis, are described in Chapter 5 (paragraphs 5.5–9)

See also general Cautionary Note at foot of Table 3.

Appendix B

Electoral Roll Members per Clergy

TABLE 7

| | DIOCESAN TOTAL A | Urban Priority Area Parishes | | | Neutral Parishes | | OTHER PARISHES ('NON-UPA') G |
		'Group A' (by DoE criteria) B	'Group B' (diocesan additions) C	TOTAL UPA PARISHES D	City Centre E	Marginal Parishes F	
Birmingham	119	77	98	83	195	131	152
London	118	77	(55)	76	104	109	153
Southwark	138	84	66	82	114	127	175
Liverpool	139	71	111	89	49	116	166
Manchester	126	85	136	109	162	125	138
Wakefield	161	99	74	86	231	129	175
Lichfield	178	127	(58)	125	–	190	185
Coventry	199	126	113	123	395	(421)	207
Blackburn	285	204	247	215	177	277	307
Bradford	157	110	(107)	109	–	142	174
Newcastle	142	72	110	90	30	187	158
Ripon	204	105	95	102	92	111	250

Electoral rolls at latest available dates have been divided by clergy numbers in Table 5.

Bracketed figures, and all those in Column E except the London figure, are based on very few parishes.

As the dates vary and year-to-year changes can be dramatic – often for reasons unconnected with church adherence – inter-diocesan comparison of numbers within individual columns can be misleading. (This will be evident from a comparison of some of the diocesan averages with those in Table 1.)

APPENDIX B CHART 2
Population per Parochial Clergyman

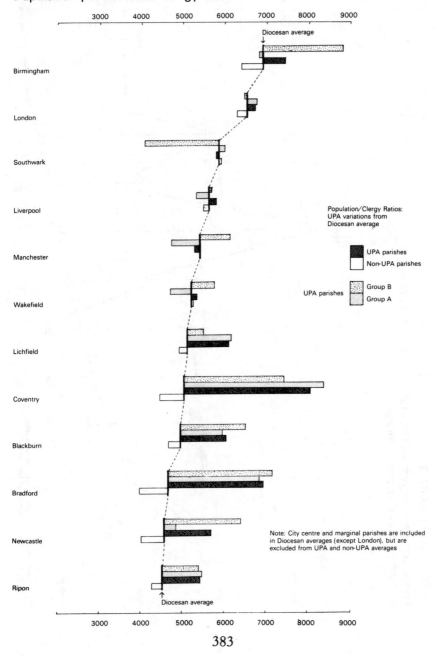

Population/Clergy Ratios:
UPA variations from
Diocesan average

UPA parishes

Non-UPA parishes

UPA parishes — Group B
Group A

Note: City centre and marginal parishes are included
in Diocesan averages (except London), but are
excluded from UPA and non-UPA averages

383

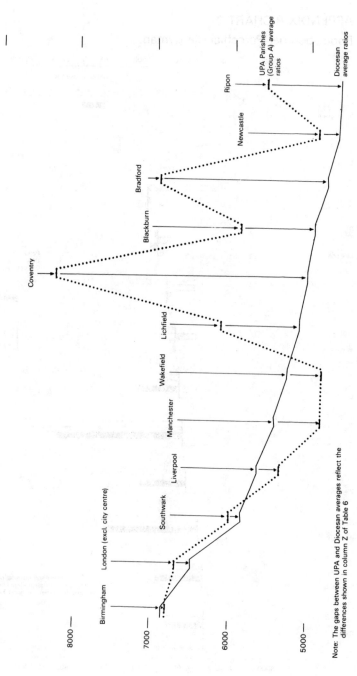

APPENDIX B CHART 3

Population per Clergyman: UPA ratios (Group A parishes) compared with Diocesan average

Note: The gaps between UPA and Diocesan averages reflect the differences shown in column Z of Table 6

384

WORLD COUNCIL OF CHURCHES

6th Assembly – Vancouver 1983

15 per cent of Assembly Delegates

A.   The WCC Rules III, 1.3 (as amended in Dresden) state the following:

'The remaining delegates [to the WCC], not more than 15 per cent, shall be elected by certain member Churches upon nomination of the Central Committee as follows:

1.   If the Moderator or any Vice-Moderators of the Central Committee is not elected [within the provisions of para 2 above] the Central Committee shall nominate such officer to the member Church of which such officer is a member. Paragraphs 5 and 6 below apply to such nominees.

2.   The Central Committee shall determine the categories of additional delegates necessary to achieve balance in respect of:

(a)   the varied sizes of Churches and confessions;

(b)   the historical significance, future potential or geographical location and cultural background of particular Churches, as well as the special importance of united Churches;

(c)   the presence of persons whose special knowledge and experience will be necessary to the Assembly;

(d)   proportions of women, youth, lay persons and local pastors.

3.   The Central Committee shall invite the member Churches to propose the names of persons in the categories so determined whom the Churches would be willing to elect, if nominated by the Central Committee.

4.   The Central Committee shall nominate particular individuals from the list so compiled to the member Church of which each individual is a member.

5. If that member Church elects the said nominee, he or she shall become an additional delegate of that member Church.

6. The member Churches shall not elect alternate delegates for such delegates. Member Churches are encouraged to consult regionally in the election of the delegates described in paragraphs 2 and 3 above, provided that every delegate is elected by the Church of which he or she is a member in accordance with its own procedures.'

B. Central Committee in Dresden agreed that in the appointment of delegates in this category, priority be·given to women, youth, lay persons and local pastors to improve the balance among delegates according to the criteria established by Central Committee in 1980. This will provide for a better balance especially with regard to women, youth, lay persons, local pastors, persons from ethnic and racial minorities and persons with disabilities, than results from the first round of appointment of delegates by the Churches.

Appendix D

Sources of Support for Clergy

Clergy response to Survey: % of clergy in each group citing particular sources as offering 'real support' in their ministry.

CLERGY IN UPA SAMPLE

Main sources of Support	Marital Status		Age group	Churchmanship			Members of Team or Group	Location of Parish		ALL UPA PARISHES	CLERGY IN NON-UPA PARISHES
	Married	Single & widowers	Under 35	High	Middle	Low		Inner City	Council Estate		
	%	%	%	%	%	%	%	%	%	%	%
Wife and family	83	5	51	51	67	72	75	57	73	63	76
Personal friends	50	52	41	46	47	50	50	48	45	49	41
Individuals in parish	49	44	65	49	50	51	46	45	46	49	49
Churchwardens	47	33	32	34	46	52	44	46	37	45	54
PCC/church officers	41	32	19	28	55	37	42	37	46	39	45
Informal group/neighbouring clergy etc	35	45	40	45	31	35	45	33	38	36	24
Diocesan Bishop	26	19	7	21	32	22	32	20	26	26	27
Suffragan Bishop	33	22	25	27	33	30	37	32	28	33	31
Archdeacon	26	16	4	20	27	21	33	22	35	25	31
Rural/Area Dean	33	20	17	27	38	25	32	30	35	29	25
Ecumenical group	27	4	2	16	27	21	26	20	14	21	8
Spiritual director	20	26	29	35	19	9	29	18	28	20	20
Clergy chapter	22	13	13	18	31	12	15	20	15	19	21
Mixed group from parish	19	23	29	22	14	22	15	20	14	22	20
Group/Team Ministry	14	11	12	9	20	12	39	11	20	14	11
Other clergy	12	15	26	15	6	17	4	15	10	14	11

Employment by Industry Group 1954-90

	Share of total employment (%)			Level (thousands)	Net change (thousands)						Growth % p.a.
	1954	1984	1990	1984	1954-75	1975-80	1980-84	1984-90	1984-86 :	1986-88	1984-90
Agriculture	5.2	2.5	2.2	597	-572	-34	-24	-59	-11	-20	-1.7
Mining	3.7	1.3	1.0	304	-515	14	-63	-53	-18	-14	-3.1
Food, drink and tobacco	3.2	2.5	2.3	604	-14	-36	-93	-52	-14	-20	-1.5
Chemicals	1.9	1.7	1.5	399	23	4	-76	-29	-9	-10	-1.2
Metals	2.5	1.1	1.0	265	-78	-101	-137	-24	-3	-12	-1.5
Engineering	13.9	11.0	9.8	2,636	158	-210	-581	-264	-78	-107	-1.7
of which:											
Mechanical engineering	3.9	3.1	2.7	749	63	-72	-154	-104	-20	-47	-2.5
Electrical engineering	2.5	2.9	2.8	686	205	-32	-66	-13	-5	-8	-0.3
Motor vehicles	1.5	1.2	1.0	297	98	-34	-128	-61	-19	-21	-3.7
Textiles and clothing	7.1	2.4	1.9	577	-670	-200	-217	-107	-40	-36	-3.4
Other manufacturing	6.0	4.9	4.7	1,181	84	-112	-209	-54	-24	-12	-0.8
Construction	6.4	6.3	6.4	1,521	191	-35	-130	27	23	5	0.3
Public utilities	1.6	1.3	1.2	322	-31	-1	-30	-24	-9	-9	-1.3
Transport and communication	7.4	6.2	6.1	1,478	-130	11	-145	-0	13	-6	-0.0
Distribution	12.7	14.5	14.5	3,486	265	106	141	9	18	-3	0.0
Professional services	3.8	9.4	10.5	2,265	834	267	272	263	87	82	-1.8
Miscellaneous services	8.9	13.2	15.3	3,156	488	398	188	539	204	146	-2.7
Manufacturing	34.6	23.6	21.3	5,661	-497	-656	-1,313	-529	-167	-196	-1.6
Services	32.8	43.3	46.4	10,385	1,458	782	455	810	322	220	1.3
All industries	84.3	78.4	78.6	18,789	33	70	-1,103	172	139	-14	0.2
Social services	6.6	14.3	14.4	3,429	1,676	159	45	41	-9	22	0.2
Public administration	9.1	7.3	7.0	1,760	-138	-80	-152	-68	-16	-25	-0.7
Whole economy	100.0	100.0	100.0	23,978	1,571	149	-1,210	145	114	-17	0.1

Source: University of Warwick Institute for Employment Research.
Reproduced, with permission, from *Review of the Economy and Employment*, 1985 – Volume 1

WRITTEN EVIDENCE RECEIVED

Action Resource Centre
Age Concern
Armitage, the Rev. Michael (Vicar of St John's, Angell Town)
Ashton Deanery (Ashton-under-Lyne, Hurst, and Stalybridge)
Association of Black Clergy, the
Association of British Chambers of Commerce, the
Association of Chief Officers of Probation, the
Association of Chief Police Officers, the
Association of Community Workers, the
Association of Metropolitan Authorities, the
Attfield, the Rev. D.G. (Team Vicar of Drypool)

Baker, the Rev. Derek (Vicar of St Andrew's United Reformed
    Church, Woolwich and Blackheath)
Baker, the Rev. John (Roehampton Institute for Higher Education)
Ballantyne, the Rev. Roderic (Vicar of St Andrew's, Stoke
    Newington) and other East London clergymen
Baptist Union of Scotland, the
Barker, Mr Edwin (Coventry Diocesan Board for Social
    Responsibility)
Barking and Dagenham Deanery
Barnardo's
Battersea Deanery Synod
Berry, the Rev. Canon Peter (then Bishop of Coventry's Adviser
    for Community Relations)
Birmingham, City of
Birmingham Community Relations Council
Birmingham Diocesan Renewal in the Spirit Fellowship
Birmingham, Diocese of
Black Country Urban Industrial Mission, the
Black Pastors Conference, the
Blackburn, Diocese of
Board for Mission and Unity of the General Synod, the

Commission for Racial Equality, the
Corneck, the Rev. Graham (Vicar of St Nicholas and St Luke,
  Deptford)
Council for the Care of Churches, the
Coventry, Diocese of
Cundy, the Rev. Ian (Warden of Cranmer Hall, Durham)

Damascus Road Association, the
Davies, Mr Randal
Dawes, the Ven. Peter S. (Archdeacon of West Ham) and
  Mr Bernard Nichols
de Waal, Mr John
Deakin, Professor Nicholas
Department of Education and Science, the
Department of the Environment, the
Department of Health and Social Security, the
Department of Trade and Industry, the
Department of Transport, the
Derby, Diocese of
Donnison, Professor David
Driscoll, the Rev. David (Priest-in-charge, Stratford) with Mr Greg
  Smith and others.

Eardley, the Rev. John (Coventry Diocesan Board of Education)
Edmonton, the then Bishop of (the Rt Rev. W. Westwood)
Emms, Pastor John (the Latimer Christian Fellowship, East Ham)
Evangelical Coalition for Urban Mission, the
Evangelical Race Relations Group, the
Evangelical Urban Training Project, the
Eversley, Dr D.E.C.

Family Welfare Association, the
Faull, Mr David
Field, Mr Frank MP
Ford, Mr David F.
Frontier Youth Trust, the
Fuller, the Rev. Canon John, and John Goodall (Directors,
  Southern Dioceses Ministerial Training Scheme)

Garrard, the Rev. Canon Richard (Adviser for In-Service Training,
  Diocese of Southwark)
Gay Christian Movement, the
Gildea, Mr Denis ('Centre 70')
Gill, the Rev. Paul (Vicar of St. Mary's, Pipe Hayes)

391

Gloucester, Diocese of
Goldsmith, Miss Oriole (District Administrator. Coventry Health Authority)
Goodacre, the Rev. N.W.
Gordon, Ms Caroline (the Lord Mayor's Initiative)
Gordon, Mr Ian
Grayson, Mr David (Project North East)
Greater Manchester Police Branch Board of the Police Federation, the
Green, the Rev. Fr Benedict, CR (then Principal, College of the Resurrection, Mirfield)
Green, the Rev. Dr Laurie (Principal, Aston Training Scheme)
Grimshaw, Pastor Jim (the Shaftesbury Christian Centre, Hammersmith)
Guildford, Diocese of

Hackney Deanery Chapter
Halliday, Mr Chris
Halsall, Mr Martin
Hanlon, Fr G. (Chairman, Coventry Council of Churches)
Hausner, Mr Victor
Health Visitors' Association, the
Hereford, the Bishop's Council of the Diocese of
Hewitt, the Rev. David (Leader, Bridge House Fellowship)
Hill, the Rev. Roger (Team Rector of Central Telford)
Hoare, the Rev. Dr Rupert W.N. (Principal, Westcott House Cambridge)
Home Office, the
Houghton, Mr Leslie
Hulme, the Bishop of (the Rt Rev. Colin Scott)
Huyton (parishes of St Michael, St Gabriel and St George, and the clergy of the Catholic and Free Churches of Huyton)

Idle, the Rev. C.M. (Rector of Limehouse) and other East London clergymen
Industrial Mission Association, the
Ingrams, Mary (Manchester Multi-faith Educational Resources Centre)
Inner London Education Authority, the
Inner London Probation Service
Institute of Health Service Administrators, the
Isle of Dogs (parish of Christ and St John with St Luke)

Islington, London Borough of
Ison, the Rev. David (Deptford)

James, Sheila (St Agnes Church of England Primary School,
  Clitheroe, Manchester)
Jarman, Professor Brian (Department of General Practice, St Mary's
  Hospital, Paddington)
Jarrow Deanery
Jennings, Deaconess Anne (St Andrew's, Whitefield, Manchester)
Joan Elizabeth, Sister (Community of St Mary the Virgin, Clapham)
Jobson, the Rev. Paul (Rector of St Peter's, Walworth)
Jubilee Group, the

Kemp, the Rev. Allan (Rural Dean of Barking and Dagenham)
King, Mr J.S.
Kitchener, the Rev. Dr Michael (Principal, North East Ordination
  Course)

Lane, Sir David
Langley, the Rev. Robert (Principal, St Albans Diocese Ministerial
  Training Scheme)
Law Centres Federation
Lay, the Rev. Brian R. (Vicar of St John the Evangelist,
  Sutton-on-Plym)
Leachman, Fr James G., OSB
Leech, the Rev. Kenneth (Race Relations Field Officer, Board for
  Social Responsibility of the General Synod)
Leeds Urban Priority Area Group
Lewis, Marie (Hackney Deanery Community Relations)
Leicester, Diocese of
Lewisham Deanery
Lichfield Diocesan Jubilee Group
Lichfield, Diocese of
Liverpool Diocesan Board of Mission and Social Responsibility
  (Church in Society Committee)
Liverpool Diocesan Working Party on Historic Resources
Liverpool, Diocese of (Board of Education)
London Chamber of Commerce and Industry, the
London Housing Associations
Low Pay Unit, the
Lowe, the Rev. Stephen R. (Team Rector of East Ham)

Macclesfield, Archdeaconry of

Macnair, Mrs Vickie
Macready, Sir Nevil
Manchester Diocesan Council for Education
Manchester, Diocese of
Manpower Service Commission, the
Martin, Mr W. (Coventry Churches Housing Association)
Mason, the Rev. K.S. (Principal, Canterbury School of Ministry)
Mayflower Family Centre, the (Canning Town)
Melinsky, the Rev. Canon M.A.H. (Principal, Northern Ordination
    College)
Merseyside County Council
Metcalf, Mrs Beryl
Methuen, the Rev. John (Rector of the Church of the Ascension,
    Hulme)
Ministry Co-ordinating Group, the
Moreton Comprehensive School, Wolverhampton

NACRO (National Association for the Care and Resettlement of
    Offenders)
Namur, Sisters of Notre Dame of (Glasgow)
National Association of Probation Officers, the
National Consumer Council, the
National Council for Voluntary Organisations, the
National Westminster Bank plc
Newcastle, Diocese of
Newcastle-upon-Tyne, City of
Newcome, the Rev. James (Department of Pastoral Studies, Ridley
    Hall, Cambridge)
Newham Deanery
Nimavet, Bhajwandas Khimdas (Indian Association, Oldham, Lancs)
Noak, Mr Hans
Northolt, the Archdeacon of (the Ven. Dr T.F. Butler)
Northumberland, the Archdeacon of (the Ven. W.J. Thomas)

Ogilvie, the Rev. Gordon (Director of Pastoral Studies, Wycliffe
    Hall, Oxford

Pahl, Jan (Senior Research Fellow, Health Services Research Unit,
    University of Kent at Canterbury)
Palmer, Mr Martin (Centre for the Study of Religion and Education
    in the Inner City, Salford)
Papworth, the Rev. John
Parsons, the Rev. Donald (Coventry Methodist Mission)

St Saviour's Priory, Haggerston
Salam, Mr A. (President of the Cheetham Hill Mosque, Manchester)
Salmon, the Rev. Harry (Westhill College, Selly Oak)
Salvation Army, the
Saxbee, the Rev. Dr John C. (Joint Director, South West Ministry Training Course)
Scharf, the Rev. Julian (Rector of St George-in-the-East, London)
Scott-Samuel, Dr Alex
Scout Association, the
Shaftesbury Project Inner City Group, the
Simey, Mrs M.B. (Merseyside County Council)
Slack, Tim (Sidney Stringer's Community College, Coventry)
Smith, Mr Richard (Administrator, Bow Mission)
Smith, the Rev. Ron
Smithson, the Rev. Canon Alan (Director, Carlisle Diocesan Training Institute)
Smout, the Rev. Michael (Rector of St Michael's, Aughton)
South London Industrial Mission
Southampton Deanery
Southwark Diocesan Council for Social Aid (Community Work Support Group)
Southwark Diocesan Council for Social Aid (Prison Advisory Group)
Southwark Diocesan Council for Wel-Care
Stepney Action Research Team (Audrey Shilling CA)
Stepney, the Bishop of (the Rt Rev. Jim Thompson)
Stockport, Borough of
Stubbs, the Rev. Ian (Industrial Chaplain, Diocese of Manchester)
Summerfield, Birmingham (parish of Christ Church)

Toon, Dr P.D.
Tooting Deanery
Tower Hamlets Deanery Chapter
Trethowan, Ms Christine (Coventry Young Homeless Project)
Turk, Miss Margaret

Underhill, the Rev. Edward (Vicar of St George's, Gateshead)
United Reformed Church, the
UNLEASH (United London Ecumenical Action on Single Homelessness)
Urban Ministry Project

URCHIN (Unit for Research into Changing Institutions)

Wakefield, Diocese of

Wakefield, the Rev. Gordon S. (Principal, The Queen's College, Edgbaston)

Waltham Forest Deanery Pastoral Committee

Wandsworth Deanery

Ward, the Rev. Edward

Webber, Miss Ann

Webster, the Very Rev. Alan (Dean of St Paul's)

Weller, the Rev. John C. (Priest-in-charge, St Matthew's Dudderston)

Weller, the Rev. Paul (Community Relations Officer, Greater Manchester County Ecumenical Council)

Wesson, the Rev. John (Director of Pastoral Studies, Trinity College, Bristol)

West Midlands County Council

Westminster (St Margaret's) Deanery

Wheaton, the Rev. David H. (Principal, Oak Hill College, London)

Williams, the Rev. Canon John H. (Rector of St Saviour's, Forest Gate)

Winchester, Diocese of

Wingate, the Rev. Andrew (The Queen's College, Edgbaston)

Wolverhampton, Diocese of

Woodhouse, the Rev. Patrick and Mr Andrew Jones

Woolhouse, the Rev. K. (Director of Pastoral Studies, Theological College, Chichester)

Worcester, Diocese of

Wright, the Rev. Canon Clifford (Team Rector of Basingstoke)

York, Diocese of

Young, Mrs Jane

Young, Dr Ken

Appendix G

TOWNS AND CITIES VISITED BY
THE COMMISSION

Ashton-under-Lyne
Barnsley
Birkenhead
Birmingham
Blackburn
Bolton
Bradford
Bristol
Bury
Coventry
Dudley
Gateshead
Killingworth
Kirkby
Langley
Leeds
Liverpool
London Borough of Brent
     Camden
     Ealing
     Hackney
     Islington
     Lambeth
     Newham
     Southwark
     Tower Hamlets

Manchester
Newcastle-upon-Tyne
North Shields
Oldham
Plymouth
Rossendale
Salford
Sandwell
Sheffield
Skelmersdale
Solihull
South Shields
Sunderland
Walsall
Wolverhampton